DATE DUE

DEMCO 38-296

Building
Little Italy

Richard N. Juliani

I Building Little taly

Philadelphia's Italians Before Mass Migration

The Pennsylvania State University Press
University Park, Pennsylvania

Library of Congress Cataloging-in-Publication Data

Juliani, Richard N.
    Building Little Italy : Philadelphia's Italians before mass migration /
Richard N. Juliani.
        p.   cm.
    Includes bibliographical references and index.
    ISBN 0-271-01731-7 (alk. paper)
    ISBN 0-271-01732-5 (pbk. : alk. paper)
    1. Little Italy (Philadelphia, Penn.)—History.   2. Philadelphia (Penn.)—
History.   3. Italian Americans—Pennsylvania—Philadelphia—History—
18th century.   4. Italian Americans—Pennsylvania—Philadelphia—History—
19th century.   5. Philadelphia (Penn.)—Ethnic relations.   I. Title.
    F158.68.L58J84   1998
    974.8'1100451—dc21   97-37369
                                                                  CIP

It is the policy of The Pennsylvania State University Press to use acid-free paper
for the first printing of all clothbound books. Publications on uncoated stock
satisfy the minimum requirements of American National Standard for Information
Sciences—Permanence of Paper for Printed Library Materials, ANSI Z39.48–
1992.

Contents

List of Illustrations and Maps

List of Tables

Acknowledgments

This book has had a long history, perhaps too long. The writing began at least ten years ago, but the research on which it is based started more than twenty-five years ago. When I first attempted to write about Italians in Philadelphia, in a doctoral dissertation completed in 1971, I was able to provide only a brief discussion on the earliest Italians to arrive in the city, and concentrated my attention on the mass migration of the late nineteenth and early twentieth centuries. Some time later, when I tried to write a more comprehensive study of Italian life in Philadelphia from its beginnings up to the present time, I discovered that a vast amount of information existed on the initial stage of settlement that had never been examined. I decided to focus, therefore, on the Italian experience before the period of mass migration. I had no idea how long it would take to gather, interpret, and write about this material. During what turned out to be a much longer process than I had anticipated, a number of colleagues offered insight and encouragement. I am not sure that I would have been able to make my own intellectual migration without their support.

Although some of them, unfortunately, are no longer here for the final arrival at our own port of destination, I would be remiss if I did not take this opportunity to identify them. The Reverend Bartholomew Fair, late archivist of the Archdiocese of Philadelphia, first provided me with access to the invaluable records of parishes that served Italians. Edward P. Hutchinson, of the University of Pennsylvania, a great student of the demography and legal aspects of international migration, urged me to limit my focus to the early stage of Italian life in Philadelphia, on the grounds that it had not ever been adequately studied. Robert F. Harney, of the University of Toronto, the most outstanding scholar of his generation on immigration to Canada, emphatically insisted on the importance of what was available in the local setting. And Dennis Clark, the foremost student of Irish life in Philadelphia, if not in the entire country, nourished this project by his unfailing wisdom and good humor, which have touched so many of us. While

I sorely regret that they cannot see the book to which each of them in his own way contributed, I miss them as friends even more.

Philadelphia provides an extraordinarily rich repository of data for the study of local history, but it also offers something even more important to the researcher—the talents of the caretakers of those materials. This study owes an unrepayable debt to several of them: Robert Plowman, Director of the National Archives, Mid-Atlantic Regional Office; Joseph Casino, Director, and Shawn Weldon, Assistant Archivist of the Philadelphia Archdiocesan Historical Research Center; Ward Childs, Chief Archivist, and Lee Stanley, Archivist, of the City Archives of the Philadelphia Department of Records; and Roy Goodman, Research Librarian, of the American Philosophical Society. I am similarly indebted to the Special Collections Department of Baker Library of the Graduate School of Business Administration at Harvard University for its assistance in obtaining access and to the Dun & Bradstreet Company for the use of the R. G. Dun & Company Collection.

At various points, I also received the benefit of the labors of individuals who helped to collect the data on which the study is based. While she was an undergraduate student, Margaret Wenke, now a practicing attorney, diligently pursued and recorded information from various sources in the city. Richard P. Juliani, ever a dutiful son, spent some precious summer weeks reading and transcribing microfilmed articles of city newspapers. Other people contributed by their critical reading and responses at a much later stage. Luciano Iorizzo of the State University College of New York at Oswego, and Spencer M. DiScala of the University of Massachusetts at Boston, read and offered invaluable suggestions for revision of the original manuscript. Professor Robert Melzi of Widener University, lexicographer, Renaissance scholar, and one of the leading authorities on the Italian language, and Philip V. Cannistraro of Queens College of the City University of New York, distinguished professor of Italian American studies, also served by their thoughtful reflection and unflagging support. I want to indicate my gratitude as well to Professor Adele Maiello of the University of Genoa for her advice and assistance, but especially in enabling me to obtain materials from the rare photograph collection of Vito Elio Petrucci.

Several people have put their mark on the research in a uniquely personal manner. If it had been possible to locate the descendants of more individuals and families who have been described in this book, the story I tell would certainly have been different, and probably far richer. But as the reader will soon learn, much of that population has already disappeared. Several exceptions, however, were members of families that occupied important locations not only in the Italian community a century or so ago but also in this account of its history and have had a great impact on my work. Mary A. Snowden, a descendant of one of the most important early figures, graciously contributed information and documentation on the life of Giovanni Battista Sartori and his family. Similarly, the late Inez Cuneo Bieberman, granddaughter of Frank Cuneo and daughter of Frederic Cuneo, provided materials and personal observations that greatly supplemented my account of the later Italian experience. More recently, Louis Arata, a member of both the Arata and the Raggio families, and who most conveniently happens to be an indefatigable student of genealogy and family history, has also become an indispensable source, confidant, and friend. It is appropriate for me to add to my gratitude as an author some sense of my esteem, as a product of later immigration, for these people as members of families that contributed so much to the building of the Italian community in Philadelphia.

A special debt must also be indicated to Peter J. Potter of Penn State Press. This manuscript has been greatly revised from its original draft as a result of the questions and suggestions he offered. But along with an awareness that this attention and support have added greatly to the final product, its author, above all else, wishes to acknowledge his deep appreciation for the confidence that was shown when it was in a far earlier stage.

The identification of people who have made this academic project possible, however, could hardly be complete without including those whose actual lives provide its substance. I must therefore acknowledge my appreciation and respect for all the immigrants themselves, whose courage, sacrifice, and struggle are recorded in the pages of the present work. I have merely sought to describe and understand their lives, but they achieved far more by their efforts. I include here not only the early pioneers of the Italian experience, but also all those who came after them. And with regard to my efforts in documenting their experience, I must mention my own immigrant parents among them. In a sense, this book represents a feeble gift in gratitude to all of them, but especially to my father, whose life was coming to an end at almost the very moment that my writing did.

Finally, there is one other person who has had a great part in this work. Throughout our years together, Sandra Juliani has been my devoted wife, companion, and best friend; throughout the research and writing of this book, she has been my critical reader, thoughtful consultant, and greatest personal resource. Homer said it well in *The Odyssey* when he wrote: "There is nothing nobler or more admirable than when two people who see eye to eye keep house as man and wife, confounding their enemies and delighting their friends, as they themselves know better than anyone." But because of the subject of this book, perhaps its author should find an Italian source to make his point. In that case, we need only turn to our own noble Florentine poet, Dante, because during every step of this long trip together, and only we know how difficult it has been, you, Sandra, have always been "the love . . . that moves the sun in heaven and all the stars."

Introduction

A local newspaper once provided an account of the experiences of one Italian on his arrival in Philadelphia many years earlier. Under a headline that declared that only one other Italian had resided in the city at the time, the article described what the newcomer, Lorenzo Nardi, had found:

> Seventy-five years ago a bewildered immigrant, fresh from the warm shores of his native and beloved Italy, arrived in Philadelphia.
>
> He was timid, abashed, almost afraid of his new surroundings. And his first thoughts, like those of the thousands who have followed him across the Atlantic, were to find some of his countrymen.
>
> He began a painstaking search. Philadelphia, though only an infant compared to its present-day self, was quite a metropolis to the stranger. He searched seven days before he met another Italian.[1]

If this account were accurate, Nardi must have been looking for fellow Italians in the wrong places. At virtually any time during the previous half-century Nardi should have been able to find Italians in Philadelphia. By 1850, when the U.S. Census reported 117 residents of the city as natives of Italy, or two years later, when he actually did arrive, Nardi should have had no difficulty locating them. If Nardi had found his way to the Township of Moyamensing and the Southwark District, just south of the original city limits, he would have noticed the earliest clustering among what would later become a massive Italian colony in South Philadelphia. This community would not only emerge during his own lifetime, but Nardi and others like him would be an important part of the process.

A famous scholar once declared that we really do not know America, unless we know the history of its peoples.[2] He might have added that the history of any American city is the story of each of the groups that has made up its population. So the history of Philadelphia is not the saga of a single people, but of many different groups. Although they often met in a shared mainstream, each also had its own experiences. It is only when we see how these different pathways sometimes intersected and fused, but at other moments diverged and remained distinct, that we begin to understand the complicated labyrinth that is the American city.

He might have also added that a good story must be told from its beginning. It should not start in the middle, or consist only of a conclusion. As one of the oldest American cities, the history of Philadelphia begins in 1682, if not earlier. The history of its ethnic groups similarly begins at an earlier point than for most other cities, and certainly long before the time of the Great Migration that occurred from the 1870s on.

The story of the origins and earliest growth of the Italian community in Philadelphia has not yet been told. The original intention of the present study was to provide a comprehensive history of Italians from the colonial period to the present day, but the focus gradually shifted to the void represented by the almost complete absence of any study of the early stages of the Italian presence in Philadelphia. The neglect of this rich and important chapter once was part of a larger and long-standing failure to compile the history of Philadelphia in general. Since the 1960s, however, this began to change; the city has become the subject of many studies. Yet, the social character of Philadelphia is still too often described from a relatively narrow perspective, and the ethnic dimension of its history remains to be adequately examined.

Although we may be inclined to think of early America as having a population almost exclusively of English origins, it was actually rather diverse, particularly in the Middle Atlantic colonies and states. In the years just before the War of Independence, non-English immigrants already amounted to about one-third of all white settlers in the mainland colonies. The tremendous dearth of scholarly research on immigrants in early American history provides great but still unfulfilled opportunities to explore cultural adjustment, economic and political mobility, and community formation for Philadelphia and the entire society.

It can be argued that Philadelphia was not as important as it had once been as a destination for newcomers, and that it did not have as much ethnic diversity as other American cities, when the United States reached the years of mass migration in the late nineteenth century. Although this point may be valid when Philadelphia is compared with other industrial cities of the Northeast, the city nevertheless did receive a sufficient volume of immigration to produce many ethnic communities in its neighborhoods.

Studies of Italian immigration, and of other immigrant groups that came either to Philadelphia or elsewhere, have often relied on a formula composed of three principal elements: first, the factors in their homeland that disrupted lives and encouraged departure to another place; second, the economic and industrial conditions that attracted individuals and their families to American farms, mines, and cities; and, third, the revolution in transportation technology that increased the speed of sailing vessels and then replaced them altogether with steamships that efficiently connected lands of origin with American destinations. In the case of Italians, two additional elements are frequently included to complete the picture: the conscious recruitment of laborers by the industrial agents and *padrone* bosses; and *chains of migration,* the special bonds that linked *paesani* (individuals who originated in the same villages) with one another, facilitated their migration, and stabilized their adjustment in new locations.

The Italian experience in the United States includes another dimension, which also structured immigration but remains far less known and explored. The conventional perspective, focusing on the era of mass migration that began in the late 1870s, almost entirely ignores the significance of the protocommunities established in earlier years. If migration chains were important, they did not suddenly drop from Mediterranean skies on American shores in the late nineteenth century. And even Italian scholars, whose exhaustive studies of migration from the province of Genoa have plotted a northeastern triangle of destinations, consisting of Boston, New York City, and Chicago, have generally neglected or paid only cursory attention to Philadelphia.[3] Yet the same area, particularly the *circondario di Chiavari,* also generated the first significant chain of migrants to Philadelphia and provided the building blocks for constructing a foundation for one of the largest Italian colonies in the United States. Thus, Philadelphia needs to be added to the geometry of early Genoese settlement in the United States.

One of the first important books on Italian immigration attempts to justify the neglect of the initial stages of this subject: "From the earliest days of the colonization of America up to less than a generation ago, the influx from Italy was barely a trickle, so inconsiderable that a microscope is almost needed to distinguish the Italian resident population in 1850."[4] The authors reported that the next two censuses showed only a slight increase in the number of Italians. While their contentions undeniably had some validity, their view also encouraged the conclusion that the study of Italians in previous periods could yield nothing significant. However, the rapid growth of the Italian population from the 1880s on generally occurred in cities where Italian communities already had been established. The adjustment these Italian immigrants made, and how other Americans saw them, did not appear all of a sudden in the 1880s, nor can it be adequately understood, with this later point as its beginning.

Although the relative scarcity of data in some cities has encouraged scholars to concentrate on the 1880s and later, Philadelphia has preserved an extraordinary record of its earlier history in the repositories of private and public agencies, secular and religious organizations, and city, state, and federal archives, and only a small part of it has been examined. This wealth of information also reveals that Italians had settled in larger numbers and had established a community in Philadelphia at a far earlier time than previously recognized. While some readers may prefer a more impressionistic and anecdotal treatment, the richness of sources for the study of ethnic history in Philadelphia almost dictates that the present work, without any apology or reservation, be based largely on archival materials. This approach neither compromises the integrity of its data nor trivializes its subject matter, but it does recognize, and indeed celebrates, the archival sources that provide the fibers out of which the carpet of social history is woven.

In the past, the few writers who have attempted to examine early Italian migration and settlement have too frequently been "filiopietistic." Like the historians of other ethnic groups, they shared the deficiencies of the initial stages of new intellectual endeavors. Themselves often members of the group they were writing about, they were sometimes more concerned about praising the virtues of their own ethnic community than with constructing an objective analysis of the group's life and institutions. Their orientation produced celebrations of certain heroic accomplishments and individuals to support the claim that the contributions early Italians made to American life had not yet been sufficiently recognized. Although it has become fashionable for revisionist "new historians" to indict such work as hagiographic, these pioneering efforts provided an extensive body of information and identified the founders and early settlers of immigrant colonies. For this reason, the importance of these contributions cannot be dismissed. And recent scholars, who reject the "filio-pietism" of their predecessors, still cannot afford to ignore the earlier stages of ethnic history.

Whatever their number, the Italian experience was not merely a relocation of an aggregate of individuals from one society to another, nor was it the formless movement of a population from one temporal point to the next. As the actions of individuals coagulated into more collective forms of group life, this population transformed itself by establishing institutions and communities. Italians who had previously arrived and settled in Philadelphia and other eastern ports had an important role in regard to subsequent immigration, as well as significance for these cities in general. The choices of destination, the patterns of social and cultural life, and the further development of the ethnic community that occurred in the mass immigration of later years cannot be adequately understood without recognizing the foundations established during this earlier phase of Italian settlement.

The present work answers a series of questions about Italians who settled in an early period in Philadelphia. From where in their homeland did they come? How did they travel here? Why did they come to Philadelphia? What were their lives like in this city? What kind of work did they do? Where did they live? How did they relate to one another? How did they go about building a community of their own? What effects did they have on the civic and cultural life of the city? How were they viewed and received by other residents? And how did the Italian community differ from other communities? Our answers to these questions begin with a series of biographical sketches of the first Italians to leave some traces of their presence in Philadelphia. But as that experience becomes reflected in more collective sources, such as state and church records, the examination shifts to historical demography, until these lives become clear components of an emerging subculture; then, historical sociology provides the narrative and analytic device.

While the social history of Italians in Philadelphia is worth exploring in its own right, the study of any group in a particular city also addresses broader questions about the significance of immigration and ethnic life in shaping the character of urban America. Combining the procedures of the historian and the concepts of the sociologist increases our understanding of complex modern societies, because it reveals that the issues were not unique to the Italian experience in Philadelphia, but shared by other groups and other cities.

This approach rests on several major assumptions about ethnic groups and their community life. First, from the moment of their arrival, most immigrants were no longer what they had previously been; they were already becoming Americans. At the same time, quite paradoxically, the influence of events and conditions in the Old World did not immediately end at their arrival, but continued to affect life in their new society. The transformation of their culture, moreover, was actually a two-way process in which immigrants, as they were becoming American, were also changing America and what it meant to be American. It consisted, furthermore, of an important dimension that existed within the immigrant population that also mediated the relationship between newcomers and other inhabitants of the city. These aspects of intragroup and intergroup life included the images that groups had of one another, the sense of identity immigrants had of themselves, the interactions that immigrants had with one another and with other peoples, and the institutions that immigrants established as they found new patterns of social life. And while to others immigrants may have appeared all quite alike, they were actually a diverse population that continuously redistributed itself within its own community and in its relationships with outsiders. This variation represented a far more complicated process than ordinarily depicted and was a process that cannot be reduced to a familiar "phalanx premise" in which any group is treated as if acculturation and assimilation occurred with all its members in a single row with their arms linking and moving them ahead in lockstep. Instead, an intricate interplay among individuals, events, and conditions reveals the diversity of their lives and provided the parameters within which an immigrant aggregate developed into a community and a more enduring element of the broader urban setting.

During the last thirty years, the study of Italian Americans has reflected some important trends in the study of group life in the United States in general. After a long period in which acculturation and assimilation were presented as virtually inevitable processes, it appeared for a while that the study of immigration and ethnic groups might also be on the verge of extinction. During the past generation, however, the study of ethnicity in the United States has been resumed with renewed vigor. Along with the rediscovery of ethnicity, the study of Italian

Americans has also enjoyed a period of especially strong growth. As a result of the vast amount of new information and analysis that has been accumulated on population size and distribution, income and occupations, political behavior, marriage and family life, educational achievement, religious beliefs and practices, social mobility, recreational patterns, and even folklore, we now know much more than ever about virtually every important aspect of Italian American life.

In the study of human affairs, it is difficult to deny some connection between the substance of research and the more personal motives of the researcher. When Italians arrived in the United States, most expected a society that promised a better way of life than the one they had left behind. But Italians found that America could also be inhospitable as a social and political climate. It abused and exploited them; it caricatured and ridiculed them; it argued that they were genetically and culturally inferior; it sought to transform them. In a few cases, it even executed them for being different. Eventually, it severely limited their legal entry. While they have prevailed and become another component of the kaleidoscope that is modern American society, Italians, like other immigrant groups, paid a substantial price. In only a short period of time, they lost family ties, languages, identities, culture, and collective memories and accepted new ones. They have achieved in education, succeeded in occupation, and climbed in income. They have become as American as anyone else. But it was also an alienating experience: they have forgotten much of their real past.

Being American today certainly does not mean the same thing it did one hundred years ago—or even thirty years ago. If diversity has replaced assimilation as a goal for Americans, then the search for ethnic identity might intensify rather than lessen. In this quest, therefore, it becomes vitally important for all of us to know what happened in earlier generations. Remembering the past, consequently, becomes much more than an empty exercise in nostalgia; it could be an important instrument for living in the present and in facing the future. While this book enables Italian Americans to recover that past, it also may enable other Americans to discover some of the same history as well.

A Note on Names

The reader will see first names or surnames that appear to have been spelled incorrectly, or a name that will sometimes change in spelling, and conclude that we have been careless in these matters. However, the sources used in this research often gave different spellings for these names, which created a problem that is not easily solved. While it is sometimes easy to recognize that an error was made by someone in recording a name, it is not always possible to correct it. In some cases, the "right" form is not even known. It would be a mistake, therefore, to attempt to determine which of two spellings was the correct one; in some cases, either form was correct. Moreover, it is sometimes valuable to know that the individual was being incorrectly or inconsistently identified. The variations represent an important part of the story that is being presented. For example, the experience of someone who started life as Placido Dominico Giuseppe Marabello but whose name passed through several versions as his public identity also gradually evolved until he was known as Joseph Marble is very instructive. Similarly, although one name was consistently given as Ignazio Vincenzo Cavaradossy, the proper spelling was probably Cavaradossi. It is also evident that Giovanno Citti should have been Giovanni Citti. And Power Cochanue's first name was almost certainly Paolo, although his last name remains unclear. An organ-grinder identified as Joseph Repelto was probably Joseph Repetto. Agostino Lagomarsino and Augustus Lagomarsino were the same person, but known by both forms. Such cases occur repeatedly in this study. But rather than attempt to determine what their "real" names actually were, we have usually retained the spellings as they were given in city directories, government documents, church records, and other sources.

Chapter 1

First Arrivals

In the name of God Amen I Placido Dominico Joseph
Marabello, born in the city of Messina in the Island of
Sicily . . . but since my arrival in America am called, and
pass by the name "Joseph Marbell" and Now reside at
No. 93 Passyunk Road in the District of Southwark. . . .

—Joseph Marabello, 1816

Italian immigration has long provided an important
component of the American population. From 1820, when the federal
government began counting new arrivals, to 1986, the entrance of
more than 5.3 million Italians has been recorded. Only Germany has
sent more immigrants to American shores. Later generations have
maintained the size of the Italian American segment of the population.
The federal census of 1990 reported 14,664,550 Americans as partly
or entirely of Italian descent, making them the sixth largest ancestry
group in the nation.[1]

The departure of Italians from their homeland has been a long
diaspora. According to historian Spencer M. DiScala, it began with dissident intellectuals during the Reformation and Counter-Reformation
and became a cataclysmic exodus of artists, musicians, diplomats,
statesmen, and specialized artists that greatly impoverished Italy but
enriched the rest of Europe.[2] When it finally shifted to North America, Italian migration followed a series of distinctly different stages.

The early emigration of Italians was small in volume and the result of conditions in Italy and the United States that were particular to the times. In the late eighteenth and early nineteenth centuries, with political and economic development accelerated on the Italian peninsula, the awakening of stirrings toward independence and unification eventually produced the modern nation of Italy. The same factors also encouraged many individuals to seek their own fortunes and satisfactions elsewhere in foreign lands. These Italians arrived at American cities like Philadelphia first as visitors, then as temporary residents for brief periods, and finally as permanent settlers.[3]

While the situation in Italy might have provided sufficient conditions for departure from their land of birth, the circumstances they later encountered in their destination were more crucial for the decision to remain in Philadelphia. From its origins as the urban center of the colony founded by William Penn, Philadelphia had been a highly favorable destination for travelers, but even as a British colony it was marked by great ethnic diversity. By the time of the American Revolution, it had also emerged as the major center for manufacture and commerce in North America. Its diverse economy enabled Philadelphia to establish extensive trade relations with the major countries of Europe and the Far East.[4]

By the late eighteenth century, despite occasional economic crises as well as recurrent yellow fever epidemics, Philadelphia provided attractive conditions for its inhabitants. As long as one remained healthy, by hard work the ordinary Philadelphian could achieve a decent standard of living for himself and his family. Modest but adequate housing and furnishings, and inexpensive food, were generally available. Except for a concentration of maritime workers and merchants near the docks, the population was well mixed in other residential areas without much regard for class or occupation. Despite slight concentrations of Germans and Quakers, separate religious and ethnic enclaves were almost nonexistent and had no great impact on the city. With political differences of the war largely forgotten, residents freely gathered for activities of daily life on the streets and in taverns. An economy that encouraged highly individual pursuits reinforced the spirit and practice of democracy. One assessment stated: "Pennsylvania and Philadelphia had everything, settlers, natural resources, capital, religious tolerance and comparatively little government."[5] Philadelphia was regarded as the most highly developed coastal city anywhere in North America.[6]

The first Italians were undoubtedly drawn by the same conditions that drew other new arrivals.

Early Perceptions of Italy: A Culture and a People

While disruptive events pushed Italians from their homeland, and more favorable conditions attracted them to America, the attitudes of Philadelphians toward Italy provided another factor in the choice of destination. From its earliest days, residents had held highly favorable perceptions of Italy as a culture. Beginning with William Penn himself as a young man, members of prosperous and prominent families visited Italy in search of intellectual edification, aesthetic cultivation, material gain, and personal adventure. These activities established maritime trade that commercially linked Italian ports and Philadelphia by 1760 and opened a door through which would flow travelers as well as agricultural products, native stone, manufactured goods, technological skills, artistic techniques, scientific knowledge, and philosophical ideas.[7]

These new commercial and cultural bonds rested upon an appreciation of what Italy offered to the rest of the world. The attitude was evident in the curiosity that Benjamin Franklin, probably the most influential American in Europe during his years as ambassador to France, showed in Italian literature, political philosophy, and science. Although he never fulfilled his wish to reach Italy, Franklin frequently indicated his interest in Italian practices and products that might be successfully adopted by American agriculture. On a more prosaic level, Franklin not only revealed an interest in polenta, turnip leaves, and macaroni, but also, as many a later tourist, even admitted: "If I could only find in any Italian travels a recipe for making Parmesan cheese, it would give me more satisfaction than a transcript of any inscription from any old stone whatever."[8]

Through the pillaging of classical antiquities, the copying of art treasures, and the purchasing of artisan products, the scions of leading Philadelphia families introduced the higher art forms and popular crafts of Italy to museums and markets in the city. Although many younger Philadelphians emphatically and indelibly expressed their appreciation of Italian culture, perhaps none surpassed the enthusiasm of the artist Rembrandt Peale. In 1807, after two trips to Europe during which he had not reached the peninsula, Peale poignantly revealed: "Italy, which was my reverie by day, became the torment of my dreams at night." In 1810, when he again failed on his third trip, Peale declared: "The idea that my dreams of Italy were never to be realized, seemed to darken the cloud which hung over the prospect of death itself." Peale finally arrived in Italy in 1828, and at the end of a two-year stay described in the final entry to his diary the role Italy could play in the development of American culture. Since then, no Italophile tourist has expressed his ardent conviction more eloquently than Peale.[9]

From Penn to Peale, Italy provided a powerful attraction for individuals seeking their own personal development as well as the improvement of their community. Motivated by a sense of uncertainty about American culture and a search for self-identity, these "passionate pilgrims" believed that the rich culture and confident character of Italy offered a solution to the problems of American civilization in its formative years. But American visitors were inclined to ignore the political realities of Italy as it entered the early stages of the Risorgimento. Before 1848, they returned home with a view of Italy that was highly focused on the loftier aspects of the arts and humanistic learning.[10]

As with other Americans, the views of Philadelphians toward Italian culture must be distinguished from their attitudes toward Italians. Foreign visitors to Italy often held favorable judgments of its high culture, but not of its people. Rather restricted to higher social classes in their contacts, American visitors interacted only superficially with ordinary Italians they met abroad and did not view them favorably.[11] The attitudes with which they returned to the United States must have been similarly limited, but at the same time complicated, ambiguous, and ambivalent.

Italians who migrated to Philadelphia at this time, however, were not drawn from lower social strata or the peasant villages of Southern Italy, as they would be at the end of the next century, but from other social origins. Their accomplishments in business and their reputations as artists and musicians only reinforced more positive views toward Italian culture. While other groups might stir up occasional trouble, most Italians remained inconspicuous in public affairs, never becoming the subject of anti-immigration tracts or public demonstrations.

Neither the number of Italians nor their behavior seriously disturbed the image held by the privileged class of Philadelphians who had visited Italy, but strengthened the receptive social climate that early immigrants enjoyed in the city.

The initial presence of Italians in Philadelphia is cloudy and difficult to determine; even when the origins of individuals can be identified, their total number remains unknown. As early as 1749, some individuals taking the oath of allegiance to the provincial government of Pennsylvania may have been of Italian origin. In the 1760s, families that brought infants to Old St. Joseph's Church to be baptized also may have been Italian; in 1780 the father of one child is clearly identified as Genoese. Other evidence sometimes confirms that these families were Italian. By the end of the century, the lists of ship arrivals include surnames that appear to be Italian. For the most part, however, not much else is known about these individuals and families (see Appendix).

Musicians and Artists

A common image of Italy and its people, in the past as well as today, emphasizes music and art. The first Italians in Philadelphia during the colonial years were involved in these activities. Although their reasons for coming remain unknown, and they were not a large number compared with other foreign arrivals, nevertheless, these Italians altered the character of everyday life in Philadelphia.

A musician and composer, John Palma (or di Palma), is generally identified as the first Italian to arrive at Philadelphia. In an advertisement in the *Pennsylvania Gazette,* the newspaper published by Benjamin Franklin, Palma announced a concert under his direction at the Assembly Room in Lodge Alley at six o'clock on the evening of January 25, 1757.[12] The notice sternly warned that no one would be admitted without a ticket. The only place where tickets could be obtained was the London Coffee House, the most important tavern and merchants' exchange in Philadelphia and owned by William Bradford, a well-known printer and member of a once Quaker but now Anglican family. An entry in the personal ledger of George Washington, dated March 17, 1757, which listed the purchase of tickets for a concert by

"Mr. Palmas" in Philadelphia, indicates that the future President may have been in the audience for the second concert by Palma.[13]

The disapproval of "musical shows" by the Quakers, who were openly hostile to music in public settings and were the dominant moral voice at the time, may have encouraged Palma to leave for New York City—a more cosmopolitan venue even then.[14] But these condemnations also suggest that the Quakers were willing to allow new arrivals who had different values and practices to settle in Philadelphia. Conflicts within their own community, which led to schism and conversion to Anglicanism, had increased cultural and moral diversity and lessened Quaker control over the character of life in the city. While still unlikely to join Anglicans and Presbyterians at concerts, the Friends were no longer powerful enough to prevent them.

Despite Palma's departure, these conditions also indicated acceptance of secular entertainment. Although previously confined to church services and theatrical performances, Palma's program in January 1757 may have been the first public concert of music alone. If Palma were Italian, his program also probably included works by Italian composers. Unfortunately, his surname is the only available clue to his origins. Although the notice of the concert in the *Pennsylvania Gazette* gave his name simply as John Palma, later writers have made him more Italian by changing it to "di Palma" and even to "Giovanni di Palma."[15] If such claims are valid, then Italians were already involved in the transformation of cultural life in Philadelphia.

In another advertisement in the *Pennsylvania Gazette*, Francis Alberti offered his talent with the violin to the public in 1759, although it is unclear whether he proposed to teach or to perform on the instrument. Alberti may have been the native of Faenza who gave music lessons to the future wife of Thomas Jefferson and became his friend as well. But little else is known about Alberti.[16]

Information about other individuals is similarly limited. After performing as a member of Palma's ensemble, Gaetano Franceschini reportedly composed music and gave concerts on several instruments in Charleston, New York, and Philadelphia from 1774 to 1783. His sonata for two violins, cello, and continuo was recorded in New York as recently as 1951. Even less is known about someone named Trisobio, identified as an Italian who gave vocal and instrumental music concerts in various cities before his death in Philadelphia in 1798.[17]

A newspaper in May 1774 announced the opening of a new academy for the teaching of music, dancing, and the French and Italian languages by three gentlemen who had recently arrived from London: Nicholas Biferi, Pietro Sodi, and Joseph Cozani. While Biferi was described as being a master of music from Naples, the origins of his associates were not given. From their names, the nature of their activities, and their collaboration with the Neapolitan Biferi, it is likely that Sodi and Cozani were also Italian. In June 1774, Sodi announced a "grand concert and ball" at the Assembly Room in Lodge Alley in a notice in the *Pennsylvania Journal* that also described him as having been the "first dancing master of the opera in Paris and London." After a two-act concert by another musician named Vidal, Sodi would perform dances by himself and with Miss Sodi, who may have been his nine-year-old daughter. Sodi also indicated that he intended to open a dancing school and to teach any lady or gentleman at home or elsewhere a variety of dances, including the minuet, the louvre, the allemande, the bretagne, the rigadoon, the cotillion, and English country dances, adding: "Care will be taken to instruct them to walk with propriety." In September 1774, Sodi announced the opening of a "public school, at his room in Chestnut-street, at the back of the Fountain Tavern" for instruction in "all the dances that are danced in the several courts of Europe." While he continued to provide private instruction at the homes of his students or in his own school, Sodi also proposed an evening school "when a sufficient number of scholars shall offer." We know little else about Sodi and his associates.[18]

John Gualdo was arguably the best-known Italian musician in colonial America. After coming from London, he operated a store on Walnut Street between Second and Front Streets, where he sold rum, brandy, Madeira claret, beer, and vinegar in the summer of 1767. In the next year, Gualdo advertised as a brewer of spruce and sassafras beer, and as a music teacher who would give lessons to ladies and gentlemen either from his own home or in the student's home. By 1768, after an argument with a neighbor, Gualdo moved to Front Street, next to the Bank Meeting House, where he sold violins, flutes, guitars, mandolins, spinets, and clavichords. He also offered the services of a German gentleman for lessons on the violin, cello, and French horn, and a servant boy to copy any piece of music for anyone who did not want to purchase the book in which it was contained. In February 1769, indicating his intention to return to Europe on business, Gualdo asked his debtors to pay off their obligations to "enable him to discharge his own debts before he leaves America, for which part of the world every free man, in his right senses, should have an everlasting regard, for reasons before now quoted by gentlemen more learned than the subscriber."[19]

In November 1769, Gualdo led a concert of vocal and instrumental music with "the evening to be ended with a ball, if agreeable to the company." Gualdo's program, including his own flute concerto, symphony, and violin concerto, is regarded by music historians as possibly the first "composer's concert" in America.[20]

Gualdo's personal situation deteriorated soon afterward. In November 1769, he was forced to postpone a trip to Europe. About the same time, he promoted a new series of concerts every other Thursday evening at Davenport's on Third Street. Trying to reverse financial losses, due partly to his own imprudence but even more to what he described as "false friends and malevolents," Gualdo offered an innovative subscription plan of one guinea for nine concerts, paid in installments of half at initial delivery and the balance later, or a ticket for any single performance at the cost of 5 shillings.

Gualdo's concern with the conduct of audiences was reflected in his announcement in the newspapers that "decency, good manners, and silence shall at all times be regarded." Chairs in the best part of the room were provided for the ladies, and benches were available elsewhere for men. Gualdo sternly warned patrons that "the door keepers and other attendants shall have positive orders to give admittance to none but sober and orderly persons."

By 1770, Gualdo sought new ways to attract audiences. His announcement of "a concert of vocal and instrumental music, solos and concertos in various instruments, the favorite mandolin not excepted," indicated an admission of 10 shillings, but "if any lady or gentleman chooses to go away after the concert the porter will return half a crown." This plan allowed patrons to attend the concert without having to remain for the ball that followed. Gualdo may have also been attempting to accommodate a changing local morality regarding behavior in public places; attending concerts was now acceptable, but there was still hesitancy about dancing.

Gualdo's career as a composer, performer, and entrepreneur ended after he became insane, then died at the Pennsylvania Hospital on December 20, 1771. A manuscript of his composition for two mandolins or two violins with a thoroughbass for harpsichord or violoncello is in the Library of Congress, and a printed version of Opus Number Two, six sonatas for two German flutes with a thoroughbass, with the composer given as Giovanni Gualdo da Vandero, is held by the British Museum.[21]

These early cases indicate that Philadelphians, particularly of Anglican background, were receptive to the skills and services that these musicians, composers, and music and dance instructors offered. Thus, a handful of Italians opened a small outpost that later became a compelling magnet for many more. Philadelphians held these Italians in high regard, both for their talents and for their personal character. An Italian, after all, could even publicly offer to teach other Philadelphians how "to walk with propriety," but only if these patrons were willing to remain "sober and orderly persons." Italians had also served Anglicans in their challenge to the more solemn moral and cultural dominance of the colony by the Quakers.

By the late 1770s, if Philadelphia provided a favorable setting for musicians, it also did so for artists as the leading center for painting and sculpture in North America. Philadelphia was in fact "the most scientifically and culturally adventurous city in the colonies."[22] These conditions attracted creative people from different regions of the new nation as well as from foreign countries. In the 1790s, after the French Revolution drove monarchist refugees to Philadelphia, along with Germans who had been settling rural areas for more than fifty years, newer arrivals enabled Pennsylvania to emerge as the most heterogeneous state in the young nation. Although Philadelphia remained predominantly British, it was developing a more cosmopolitan public culture.[23]

Philadelphia's cultural diversity and receptivity to the arts attracted Italian painters and sculptors to the rapidly growing city. As with musicians, however, the record of early artists remains fragmentary. Arriving in 1795, Lewis Pise, one of the first Italian artists to come to Philadelphia, announced in a local newspaper that he intended to stay for six to eight weeks. In 1797, still in Philadelphia, Pise advertised his availability to draw the likeness of any person, but again indicated his intention to remain for only a few months. By the early 1800s, Pise had moved to Baltimore and then to Annapolis, Maryland, where he remained for some years. He is remembered by art historians as a miniaturist, but he may have been surpassed in reputation by his son, Charles Constantine Pise, a Catholic priest and writer in the next century.[24]

Although sometimes dismissed as primarily an art dealer, Pietro Stagi, who had previously worked in Carrara and Leghorn, reached Philadelphia in 1795 and, identified as Peter Stagi, advertised himself as an "Italian carver of statuary to his Majesty the King of Poland." In the next year, Stagi offered for sale "a very large and elegant assortment of Statues, Busts and Chimney pieces, all of the finest marble and the most exquisite workmanship." After announcing his intention to sail for Europe in 1797, as soon as "navigation will permit," he remained in Philadelphia for another two years. Stagi may have been the first of many stonecarvers from the rich marble area along the Tyrrhenian coast to work in the United States.[25]

Even less is known about others involved in art in Philadelphia at this time. The City Directory for 1791 lists "Pratchardo, ———, marble image cutter, No. 145 Walnut Street" as a stonecarver whose first name was not even recorded. He was possibly an Italian who had arrived before Stagi, and he probably was "engaged on the Morris house."[26] Another dealer, who appeared simply as "Provini—from Italy" in a notice in the *Federal Gazette* in 1796, offered chimney pieces and building ornaments along with busts of Washington, Franklin, and Lafayette made of a composition material that looked like marble.[27] Another artist, identified simply as Bartello, was a painter of portraits from which engravings could be made, employed by T. B. Freeman, also in 1796.[28]

Other artists in Philadelphia during these years were more clearly Italian in their origins. After working in Rome and other Italian cities, Jacint Cocchi and Joseph Perovani, two artists from the Republic of Venice, arrived at Philadelphia in July 1795.[29] Perovani was said to be a native of Brescia and about thirty years old when he and Cocchi came. Two months later, they announced the availability of their talents in a newspaper notice: "Having understood the taste for the fine arts is rapidly increasing in these happy states they resolved to quit Italy, and to try to satisfy the respectable citizens of America, by their production."[30]

In addition to historical pieces, portraits, and landscapes in oil or in fresco, Cocchi and Perovani claimed to be able to paint "any theatre, Chambers, Department, with Plafonds in figures, and ornamented in the Italian taste," with a sample of their work available in the home of the Spanish envoy in Philadelphia. Other than a specialty in perspective painting and interior decoration in the Italian manner, little else is known about Cocchi. Perovani, however, remained in the city for a few more years. Later identified as Peruani, a painter and architect, he observed the birthday of George Washington in February 1796 with a statue titled *Temple of Minerva* showing the goddess contemplating a bust of the first President, with emblematic figures representing the individual states. He also probably painted a full-length portrait of Washington in the same year. Later found in the Academia de San Fernando in Madrid, this work was signed "Joseph Perovani Italai in Philadelphia Fecit MDCCXCVI." Perovani executed some works in New York before he moved to Cuba in 1801.[31]

Among Italian sculptors in the United States in the late eighteenth century, the most important, unquestionably, was Giuseppe Ceracchi.[32] Born in 1751, his place of birth has been given as both Rome and Corsica. After probably studying in Rome under Tommaso Righi, Ceracchi went to London then returned to Rome, where he supposedly worked with the neoclassical sculptor Antonio Canova on the decoration of the Pantheon. Ceracchi already had a reputation as an outstanding sculptor when he first arrived in Philadelphia in late 1790 or early 1791. Ceracchi may have been influenced by his friend Francesco Fazzarini, who had completed in Rome a full-length statue of Benjamin Franklin for The Library Company of Philadelphia, the first such work to arrive after the birth of the nation and the first item of monumental art to be installed in the city.

Ceracchi had sought the support of Congress for an ambitious project that would honor George Washington and other leaders in the struggle for independence. He proposed a marble monument showing the Goddess of Liberty riding through the clouds in a horse-drawn chariot and illuminating the universe while calling on the American people to heed her message. Although this dramatic structure was designed to be 100 feet high, it was not to cost more then $30,000. While Congress had no doubt about the fame and skill of the artist, it rejected the project, perhaps because of the expense.

The embittered Ceracchi believed that his failure to obtain the commission was the result of malicious ignorance and intrigue. By the summer of 1792, he had returned to Europe, but his efforts had not been entirely fruitless. In planning the project, Ceracchi had produced busts of more than thirty prominent Americans, including Washington, Franklin, Thomas Jefferson, Alexander Hamilton, John Adams, John Jay, George Clinton, John Paul Jones, and David Rittenhouse. From Europe, Ceracchi attempted to recover some of his financial losses from the ill-fated liberty project by selling these busts to their subjects. While Jefferson and others agreed to the plan, Washington's refusal even to accept his bust as a gift offended Ceracchi. Although whether Ceracchi actually received any money for the busts remains unclear, he attained other rewards. Elected to membership in the American Philosophical Society in 1792, he also gained the friendship and respect of many prominent Americans, with whom he continued to correspond.

After another disappointing trip to the United States, Cerrachi returned to Europe in the spring of 1795, and his life neared its unfortunate and dramatic conclusion. In Paris, he joined the Radical Republicans, with the hope that Napoleon and revolution would eventually bring independence to Italy. Later realizing that this expectation was misguided, he joined a conspiracy to assassinate Napoleon as he sat for the sculpting of a bust. When the plot was discovered, the conspirators were sentenced to be executed. In January 1802, Ceracchi was delivered to the guillotine, according to one version, dressed in the garb of an emperor of ancient Rome and riding in a chariot that he had built for himself. In view of his political values, it may have been more accurate to recognize Ceracchi's choice of costume as that of a Roman senator.

Ceracchi's short time in Philadelphia was significant in several ways. His art had a lingering impact; long after his death, it was still widely admired, praised, and imitated. Moreover, on his first trip, he had joined William Rush and Charles Willson Peale in an effort to establish the Columbianum, a museum and school of art on the model of the Royal Academy in London. While it failed after only one exhibition in 1795, the basic idea of a combined gallery and school was successful ten years later as the Pennsylvania Academy of the Fine Arts, the first such institution in the nation. The presence of Ceracchi, though only temporary, contributed to the development of a level of cosmopolitanism and cultural creativity in Philadelphia that would not be reached by another American city for many years.

Scientists and Scholars

In addition to musicians and artists attracted to Philadelphia by the growing public appetite for their talents, other Italians were motivated by more scientific and intellectual concerns. As early as 1765, Joseph Batacchi described himself in an advertisement in the *Pennsylvania Gazette* as a recently arrived Italian surgeon.[33] He claimed to have been trained in the best hospitals of Italy and to have practiced his arts in Europe with great success. Batacchi declared that his desire to see America had brought him to Philadelphia, where he looked forward to having frequent opportunities to relieve the victims of sickness or accidents. According to the announcement, along with his skill in various forms of surgery, Batacchi's long practice and experience confirmed his medical knowledge. He offered his services in the practice of physic—what today would be called medicine—and dentistry. He could also "remove the Scurvey, and all malignant Humours from the Gums so destructive to the Teeth, and the real cause of the Toothach; and cleans and polishes the most foul, so as to render them white and fair." While prospective patients could find him at his lodgings in Southwark, Batacchi also indicated his willingness to make house calls and to provide free advice to the poor. Batacchi was probably Tuscan, and the same Giuseppe Batacchi whom Filippo Mazzei, as a medical student, had met in Leghorn in 1751, but apart from this notice in the *Pennsylvania Gazette,* little else is known about him.

Twenty years later, in an account of his travels from 1785 to 1787, Luigi Castiglioni, a Milanese botanist, provided the first extensive information on the United States written in Italian.[34] Originally published in Milan in 1790, Castiglioni's *Viaggio* covered a wide range of topics. He described his four-day trip in July 1786 to the Moravian settlements in Bethlehem and Nazareth, Pennsylvania, accompanied by his friend Giuseppe Mussi, a Philadelphia merchant and also a native of Milan. Castiglioni's extensive observations on Philadelphia contained information on William Penn's original plan for the city; the city's early growth, geographical position, weather, physical character, housing, public buildings, religious groups, cultural institutions, marketplace, and class structure; the special influence and behavior of the Quakers and their place in the recent War of Independence; the role of the sciences in the city; and Benjamin Franklin's character and significance. Greatly impressed by Philadelphia, Castiglioni added: "One can consider this city, both for beauty and for size, the metropolis of the United States." In his final chapter, he noted:

> The progress of Philadelphia, settled by Quakers, as compared with other older cities, proves clearly how much influence simplicity of customs has in promoting the welfare of a newly populated country; and the good farmers of Pennsylvania ought to serve as an example to the other Americans.

Before leaving the United States, Castiglioni was proposed for honorary membership in the Philadelphia Society for the Promotion of Agriculture in January 1786. He was elected two months later. In the same year, he was also elected to the American Philosophical Society, the first scholarly association in the United States. These were the highest forms of intellectual recognition the city offered at the time. Because he passed through the region only as a visitor, Castiglioni's impact was probably greater on readers of his book in Italy than on Philadelphia.

Another notable visitor, Giambattista Scandella, a Venetian physician, left a greater mark on the city.[35] Educated at the University of Padua and admitted to medical practice in Venice in 1786, he may have been more interested in research. As a physiocrat who sought to improve human life, he explored the uses of agriculture for society. His treatise on fertilizer, published in Venice in 1790, attracted the attention of scholars. In London, where he served as Secretary of the Venetian Embassy, he became interested in the physical and social character of the New World. After arriving in Quebec about 1796, Scandella traveled widely and soon gained the respect of new acquaintances. Like Castiglioni, the significance of Scandella's accomplishments during his two years in the United States are reflected by the recognition that he received. In a letter written in July 1797, the usually laconic Washington thanked two Englishmen for their introduction of Scandella, whom he found to be "a very sensible and well informed man." In April 1798, Scandella was elected to the American Philosophical Society, and his attendance at a meeting in the next month was recorded in the society's minutes.

Scandella formed a strong friendship with Benjamin Latrobe, the eminent architect and engineer. When Latrobe considered moving from Richmond to Philadelphia, he sought the assistance of Scandella in the spring of 1798, and their correspondence provides some insights into the young Italian's perception of his American experiences. In his letters to Latrobe in 1797–98, Scandella expressed his disappointment at the failure to find genuine hospitality from most Americans, except in the case of Jefferson and a few others at Richmond. In a reply addressed to Scandella at 233 South Front Street in Philadelphia in February 1798, after indicating his inability to leave Virginia, Latrobe added: "It is my interest & my wish; my affection, my vanity, my ambition to point out Philadelphia as the only situation in which I ought to reside,—if I reside in America." Having learned that the Quakers planned to establish a school of literature and mechanical trades, Latrobe asked Scandella to find out if any opportunity for employment existed that would enable him to move to Philadelphia. He also thanked Scandella for his support in an unfortunate romantic involvement. The correspondence suggests Latrobe's belief that his Italian friend was relatively secure in his position in Philadelphia.

Scandella also became personally acquainted with Benjamin Rush, the educational and prison reformer who was probably the most esteemed American physician of his time. In a July 1798 entry in his diary, Rush acknowledged frequent visits from Scandella, "an ingenious native of Venice." Obviously impressed with Scandella, Rush noted: "He was learned and very instructive in his conversation." Scandella's friendships with Latrobe and Rush were soon to have an ironically sad conclusion.

After two years, in June 1798, Scandella attempted to return to London, but his ship was forced back to Philadelphia. He then secured passage on a packet ship bound for Europe from New York City, but the failure of his baggage to arrive from Philadelphia forced him to miss its departure. When the yellow fever epidemic of 1798 broke out, he returned to Philadelphia to care for a family that had been stricken with the disease. Although yellow fever appeared nearly every year, the 1798 epidemic was the worst in five years, and from August on the disease disrupted business and government throughout the city. By October, the flight of so many Philadelphians produced a ghost town of about 7,000 remaining residents. Those who could get far away did, while others created tent cities on the banks of the Schuylkill. In the city, the dead and the dying were carried off in creaking carts. Rush too had remained in Philadelphia to tend to victims of the epidemic.

By early November, 1,292 deaths had been attributed to the disease.[36] After ten days of exposure to the epidemic, Scandella returned to New York, but it was not long before he too became a victim of yellow fever and died within a week.

Along with his grief at the loss of his friend, Latrobe was well aware of the need for an improved waterworks if Philadelphia were to eliminate epidemics. In 1799, after being hired by the city council, Latrobe proposed a radically innovative system that, with modifications by Frederick Graff, became the model for other cities and the centerpiece of Fairmount Park, the most important public monument in the city. By its impact on Latrobe, Scandella's death had influenced the physical development of Philadelphia.

Revolutionists and Philosophers

In Philadelphia, the most significant events of the late eighteenth century were the War of Independence and the fragile new nation's struggle for survival. The war may have been waged primarily over the issues of separation and self-government, perhaps more of a civil war between different factions of Englishmen than a revolution that sought to transform political and social institutions. Consequently, even at this early point, British Americans were fearful of the more radical values and goals that foreign immigration might bring to these shores.[37]

While their role in the political and military events that shaped the nation was rather limited, some Italians were members of the Continental Army. Peter Gully, described in the *Pennsylvania Archives* as "age 20, dark complexion, born in Italy, labourer," enlisted in the service under Major James Moore on October 7, 1783.[38] John Puglia, a private in the First Company, Third Regiment, of the city militia, under the command of Lieutenant Colonel Samuel McClean, was probably the same person as, or the brother of, James Philip Puglia and later a prolific writer on political issues.[39]

A more dramatic part in the cause for American independence was played by the Ceronio family. In July 1777, Joseph Ceronio sent a plaintive letter to Franklin, the American ambassador to France, seeking news of a son Stephen, who had sailed for Philadelphia with letters of introduction to businessmen Thomas Willing and Robert Morris. Having not heard from his son since December 1775, the elder Ceronio appealed to Franklin: "I flatter myself you will extend your bounty towards a distressed Father who is constantly agitated for want of news of his son." Well aware that he had gone to America for a definite purpose, the father referred to his son as "a lover of freedom . . . [who] was resolved to follow its standard even in the deserts of America."[40]

Joseph Ceronio obviously not only knew the significance of the Willing and Morris enterprise but also recognized that his son was involved in activities that were crucial to the American cause. In his letter to Franklin, Ceronio continued:

> They found him useful . . . they have employed him on some affair of trust and of great consequence to the Cause of Liberty in which I am informed he acquitted himself so well that he not only acquired the esteem of his employers, but likewise of the Congress and I believe was sent a second time on another expedition. . . . I shall esteem it as a particular favor you will inform me for should he be a Prisoner in England I shall make proper application to get our Republic to claim him.[41]

In a second letter, written in February 1778, Joseph Ceronio expressed his appreciation to Franklin for enabling the previous mail to reach Stephen Ceronio. The father indicated his son's location as Santo Domingo, where he was "on business for the Congress who's [sic] confidence by his good conduct he had acquired," then repeated his concern about not having more recent news and asked for assistance once more. Franklin was again able to secure the exchange of mail between the father and his son, who was still serving at Santo Domingo.[42]

The exact nature of his "business for the Congress" in Santo Domingo becomes clearer from correspondence between Stephen Ceronio and Robert Morris. In a letter from Cape François in November 1778 that began with a reference to the British occupation of Philadelphia, Ceronio offered his consolation to Morris for the hardships incurred by having to move from place to place. But after noting that Morris had returned to Philadelphia, Ceronio declared that his own situation was worse: "You have no doubt considered the inconveniences, anxiety of mind, insults and threats I have & I am dayly suffering & great many other disagreable things which are the usual concomitants of a person in distressing circumstances."[43]

Although the details were not provided, after alluding to some problems caused by Morris's brother, Ceronio then indicated the specific circumstances of his own situation. He lacked credit; he had no money to pay his bills; and he wanted Morris to send flour as the best commodity to settle his accounts. The letter also revealed Ceronio's awareness of the source of the support for which he asked:

> I must therefore request you for God sake to prevail upon the Secret Committee to send me a cargo of Flour of 1500 bts that I may once pay all the bills and debts to settle with them & extricate me of the disagreable situation in which I am—which situation ruins my credit and fortune. . . . All these things I beg you & they may once take in your consideration, I believe they feel on my account, but what can I do, when pinched to the last extremity, & when treated as a deserter and imposter—you must suppose that amongst the French men there is bad people enough and less obliging than the Europeans—Therefore the West Indies Agents have many times been victims of their caprices and cruelties.[44]

Posing as one who had fled from somewhere else, perhaps from Philadelphia and the cause for American independence, Ceronio had become not merely the representative of Morris in the West Indies but a provisions agent for the Continental Congress as well. In the same letter, Ceronio expressed his concern about the blockade that had already captured more than thirteen French ships and several American ships. After describing the British fleet and warning that American vessels should be careful, Ceronio concluded that trade was either intercepted or dead. In a postscript, Ceronio provided more information on the deployment of British vessels:

> We are informed here or it is reported that Admiral Byron may very soon pay a visit to this Island, if he does succeed in America—if so is the Case we shall be blocked up in Such a manner that no vessel will be able to come in, nor get out. I

beg you Again before all these Things take place to relieve me by sending immediately some flour if I have the misfortune of seeing the publick remittances procrastinated longer than the beginning of next month, I am a ruined man.[45]

Ceronio had indicated more than the prospect of commercial failure, but also expressed the realization that a British presence on the island brought the risk of severe punishment for his political activities. In a letter in a similar vein to Morris one month later, he acknowledged the receipt of "your esteemed favour," which arrived by way of the *Mole*—presumably a ship that had evaded the British blockade and had provided some relief. Ceronio also noted a payment to Captain Briggs of the Continental sloop *Mesopotamia:* "With the usual difficulty advanced him the sum of £8460.19 which I have carried to the Credit of the Secret Committee of Congress account current." But his distress had not been entirely resolved: "I am bleeding every day for the publick but no relief of any kind is sent to me yet." Once more he also provided some naval intelligence:

Since Eight Days we have a Jamaica Fleet consisting of Two Sails of Line. Two Frigates & Two Brigs with one Schooner blocking us up. They have made again some captures but we are in Expectation they will not Lay Long upon our Coasts however the greatest Care & Lookout is required by those vessels that come to this place.[46]

He concluded with instructions to Morris about the shipping of tobacco in case of a renewed embargo.

Ceronio had held a position of strategic importance that often placed him in danger during the war, but, joined by a brother, he continued to engage in controversial activities. In March 1784, John Girard wrote from Cape François to his brother Stephen, who would later become the most important businessman in Philadelphia, and accused the Ceronio brothers and their partner, identified only as Nicoleau, of attempting "for some rascally reason" to ruin a certain Monsieur Henry. Girard added: "If I had the power of attorney, I would have shown what rogues they are."[47]

Three months later Ceronio engaged Jasper Moylan to represent him in Philadelphia in a more personal matter—the disputed estate of William Hicks. Hicks, who had died about twelve months earlier, was the father of Ceronio's wife, Catherine Hicks. Moylan provided John Dickinson, president of the Supreme Executive Council of Pennsylvania, with various documents as evidence—"to finish this business," in the attorney's words. The documents included a note from the Reverend Mathias Hultgreen, rector of the Swedish churches in Pennsylvania, certifying that he had performed the marriage of Stephen Ceronio and Catherine Hicks on May 12, 1784. Two months afterward, Moylan reported that Dickinson had awarded a bond of 75 ounces in gold to Ceronio as the husband of Catherine, as well as a legacy of 300 pounds, left by William Hicks to her, with the accumulated interest of twelve years. Catherine's brothers appear to have been excluded from the award. William, the youngest and his father's namesake, had been apprenticed at the age of fourteen by indenture in 1781 to John Dunlap and David C. Claypoole, the well-known printers. After suffering the death of his father, and indentured and omitted from the will, this misfortune-plagued youth appears to have died in 1784, leaving Ceronio as the principal beneficiary of the Hicks family estate.[48]

Subsequent events continued to cloud Ceronio's personal life. In 1794, in a ceremony at Gloria Dei, the old Swedish church, Catherine Ceronio, identified as a daughter of the late William Hicks, married Jacques Servel, a physician aboard a French frigate docked at Philadelphia. What had become of Ceronio by then, as well as of his marriage to Catherine, is unclear.[49] The angry rival's early characterization of Ceronio's motives as "rascally reasons," and of the person himself as a "rogue," invites speculation about these final years. Presumably a Roman Catholic when he first arrived from Italy, Ceronio had married Catherine Hicks in a Swedish Lutheran ceremony and gained a handsome inheritance through his bride. Yet her brother became indentured only shortly before his own death at a young age. When Ceronio's name later appeared as a donor for the expansion of the chapel and the building of a rectory at Old St. Joseph's, he had resurfaced as a charitable supporter of the Catholic Church.[50] Although Ceronio may well have been, as one writer has claimed, "a secret agent in the employment of the American revolutionaries," the exact nature of his service in the West Indies, as well as other details of his life, remains unclear.[51] The early idealism, first suggested by his father's letters to Franklin, however, may have been replaced by more materialistic ambitions in later years.

As Ceronio disappeared from view, another native of Italy with political interests emerged as a more conspicuous figure in Philadelphia, and in this case better information allows a clearer assessment of his significance.[52] James Philip Puglia was born in Genoa of Swiss and Italian ancestry about 1760. His father, John Dominick Puglia, was a native of Blenio in the jurisdiction of the Swiss cantons of Uri, Switz, and Underwalden, where family tradition held that ancestors had lived for about two hundred years and served in important offices of government. In accord with their father's wishes, James Philip and his brothers traveled extensively in their younger years as a means of learning. About the age of fifteen in 1775, James Philip entered the College of Savona, on the Ligurian coast above Genoa, where he spent seven years as a student.[53]

After completing his education, Puglia achieved some success as a merchant at Cadiz, Spain. By 1787, however, his business efforts had failed and he was jailed. After his release in March 1789, Puglia left Spain. He later blamed the government and the clergy for his misfortunes in Spain. With a brother already in Mexico, Puglia sailed for the United States, and after forty-eight days on the ship *Aurora* he arrived at Philadelphia in July 1790.[54]

Puglia was first employed in Philadelphia as a Spanish teacher and a bookkeeper, advertising his services in a local newspaper. In May 1791, less than a year after his arrival, Puglia became an American citizen by swearing an oath of allegiance before Mayor John Barclay. In August 1792, his fluency in foreign languages enabled him to be appointed as an interpreter for the Board of Health of Pennsylvania, a position that probably also reflected his acceptance into the "official family" of Governor Thomas Mifflin. With former radicals gathering under the leadership of Mifflin, Puglia's political views were moving in a similar direction. Mifflin had played an important part in local affairs during the Revolution, becoming the first governor of the state in the late eighteenth century. Mifflin's Federalist thinking was quite compatible with that of Puglia, who was soon to write a strong defense of the U.S. Constitution. But Puglia's service as a state interpreter lasted only until early 1793, when he resigned, possibly to devote himself to more urgent interests as a political philosopher and writer.[55]

In the years that followed, Puglia wrote a formidable series of articles, pamphlets, plays, and books on a broad range of political and social issues. He had arrived in the United States with intellectual baggage that included "a mind full of French libertarian ideas and a fecund hatred of the Spanish monarchical government and the Spanish Church."[56] For his first major work, a critical examination of the Spanish monarchy and the Inquisition, Puglia sought financial support from the new revolutionary government in France and from Thomas Paine. While he worked on a more complete, Spanish edition, a briefer version appeared as a pamphlet in February 1793. Four months later, Puglia sought assistance from Edmond Genet, when the French ambassador to the United States visited Philadelphia. Although it is not known whether the two men ever actually met, Genet agreed to provide financial support for the book.[57]

In August 1793, the worst epidemic of yellow fever in the history of Philadelphia broke out. With physicians powerless to treat the disease, new cases and deaths rapidly climbed and the population fled the city. Before the epidemic abated in late October, an estimated 5,000 people, nearly one-tenth the population of the city, had died. Among lesser casualties, the epidemic had closed the shop of printer Francis Bailey and halted the publication of Puglia's book on Spain.[58]

In the following year, with the return of normalcy to Philadelphia, Puglia's *El Desengano del Hombre* (*Man Undeceived*) finally appeared. His strength as an author may not have been so much in the originality of thought as in his ability to synthesize existing ideas and his skill at Spanish translation. Although Puglia's attempt to examine universal principles was mainly restricted to the case of Spain, his book "stands as a passionate indictment of the entire Spanish system of government."[59]

While Puglia could not change political institutions so far away, the reaction of the Spanish authorities indicated that he had succeeded in his assault on tyranny. The Council of the Inquisition banned his book in the Spanish Empire. The Spanish envoy in Philadelphia formally registered an objection with the American Secretary of State Edmund Randolph and asked that both its author and the printer be punished, but because such action would violate the Constitution, the American government rejected the request.[60]

Although the State Department had protected Puglia on this occasion, a new incident soon provoked him to make a vigorous criticism of

Secretary Randolph. In the spring of 1794, when he sought a position in the State Department, Puglia was rejected by Randolph himself, possibly as a result of uncertainty about his citizenship. To compound matters, Randolph made an unfortunate choice of words by referring to Puglia as a "stranger." Angered by this questioning of his citizenship, Puglia expressed his reaction in *The Federal Politician,* a defense of the U.S. Constitution against the excesses of popular democracy.[61] The book was printed by Francis and Robert Bailey, one of the partners being Puglia's associate in the controversial previous book on Spain. In the new work, written in the aftermath of the French Revolution, Puglia offered his revised thoughts on the subject of democracy: "I see no material difference between the defects of popular Government and those of despotic." Calm reflection would reveal not only how frequently the concepts of liberty and equality were actually abused at the very moment men appear to give them great reverence, but also that it was even blasphemy to talk about these ideals when in reality the actions of men were prostituting them. He concluded his argument with an eloquent observation:

> I have written in Freedom's cause with as much zeal, at least, as any patriotic writer, but I cannot approve this new kind of liberty. Humanity must shudder at bare recital of such violent measures, which compose a system of Republicanism equally savage, as repugnant to the fundamental principles of true Democracy.[62]

Puglia, who had previously sought financial support for his earlier work from Citizen Genet, had now become an outspoken critic of Radical Republicanism.[63] While political turmoil in postrevolutionary France may have provoked Puglia to reconsider democracy, another stimulus was even closer at hand. The emergence of the two-party system in the United States had been accompanied by substantial vituperation in the press and by mob violence in the streets. As the capital city and political center of the nation, Philadelphia was the principal arena for such struggles. Puglia claimed that the local observer could find enough abuse of the principles of liberty and equality to encourage a reexamination of the philosophical ideals and actual structure of the political system.

Puglia was not merely an academic observer; he had also entered into the public debate as a reformed democrat who had become a defender of Federalist politics. Dedicated to the citizens of his new country, addressed as "Friends & Brethren," whose approval he sought, Puglia indicated a belief, intention, and hope that together provided the foundation of the book: "Federalism signifies Unanimity, and with my best endeavors to promote it, I trust that my claim to the character of one of your warmest votaries will not be deemed a usurpation."[64]

After signing himself "Your affectionate Friend and Brother James Ph. Puglia," the author concluded his dedication, in which he had only hinted at a more personal grievance. While the body of the text mainly provided a detailed exposition of the necessity and virtues of a federal system of government for the United States, it also contained a more explicit response to his personal issue. Puglia had not forgotten Randolph's rejection of his application for employment or his use of the term "stranger," but had taken the remark, which may have been the first recorded slur against an Italian in American society, as a serious challenge to his citizenship. In *The Federal Politician*, Puglia expressed his belief that it was his own manner of language that had prompted the rejection:

> It is certain that he is an Italian born, but neither the American laws nor any person acquainted with them, could at that time look upon him as a Stranger, but as a Citizen and an adopted Son; the said Gentleman, however, took him for such, perhaps on account of the applicant not being naturally conversant with the "British" Dialect.[65]

After providing the details of his arrival in the city, his oath of allegiance before the mayor, and his service as an interpreter for the state, Puglia concluded, obviously annoyed, with a rhetorical question about the date of his rejection: "Can such a man be considered with propriety a 'Stranger' in the month of March 1794?"[66]

Puglia also used *The Federal Politician* to provide further information about himself. In a personal note, Puglia stated that he had been a citizen for four years, had never been married, had no family, had no ambitions to hold any office in the Commonwealth, and had asked his friends not to seek any such position for him. At the end, Puglia included a list of prominent subscribers who had supported the publication of his book, which included William Bingham, merchant, banker, and U.S. Senator; Thomas Fitzsimon, merchant, banker, and former congressman; Stephen Girard, merchant; Alexander Hamilton, former Secretary of the Treasury; Henry Knox, former Secretary of the War Department; James Madison, future President of the United States; Richard Meade, merchant; Robert Morris, merchant, banker, and financier; Nathaniel Miles, congressman from Vermont; Charles Willson Peale, artist and museum founder; William Rawle, U.S. Attorney for the District of Pennsylvania; and Oliver Wolcott, U.S. Secretary of the Treasury. Puglia identified the "patriotic editors" of newspapers that had encouraged his work by publishing some of its proposals in another list, which included not only the staunchly Federalist John Fenno and his *Gazette of the United States,* but also, surprisingly, representatives of the Republican faction, such as Benjamin Franklin Bache, editor of the *Aurora,* and Eleazer Oswald, editor of the *Independent Gazetteer.*[67]

With *The Federal Politician,* Puglia waded into one of the first major controversies in American politics. After the outbreak of war between England and France in 1793, when demonstrations in Charleston and Philadelphia had given Genet an exaggerated sense of support for the French republic, he sought to recruit Americans as active participants in its cause. Genet's efforts initially achieved considerable success; ships sailed from American ports and captured more than eighty British vessels. When President Washington rebuked him, Genet attempted to use the American press to present his case to the people of the United States.[68] While Jefferson and the Republicans supported the French, Hamilton and his followers favored the British. Although Washington responded with a proclamation of neutrality in 1793, which was reinforced by an act of Congress one year later, the debate over American foreign relations continued. After the provocative Jay Treaty with Great Britain in 1794, contending factions renewed their quarrel. These issues not only served as the midwife for the birth of two-party politics in the United States, but also provided a rigorous early test of the newly established system of government. At a time of heightened tension and intense argument by the press, politicians, and the general public, Puglia intended his book to be a calmer and more rational defense of the Federalist system.[69]

In the following year, Puglia resumed the more contentious manner of his earlier writings. With the inauguration of John Adams as the second President of the United States in March 1797, William Cobbett, himself an immigrant and still a British subject, using the pseudonym "Peter Porcupine," emerged as the most vitriolic critic of Republican politics among Philadelphia journalists. From his print shop on North Second Street, across from Christ Church, and using the pages of *Porcupine's Gazette*, Cobbett ardently defended the Federalists, from whom he received financial backing. Against the strongly pro-British and Hamiltonian views of Cobbett, Puglia rejoined the opposition. Although he had previously supported the Federalist position, Puglia vigorously objected to Cobbett's extremist views. Writing as "James Quicksilver" in *The Blue Shop*, published in 1796, and through his humorous commentary on the life and adventures of Peter Porcupine, Puglia argued that political stability could be threatened by excesses in either party. He continued this polemic in *The Political Massacre*, in which "James Quicksilver" again expressed his "observations on the writings of our present scribblers against Peter Porcupine."[70]

In later years, Puglia expanded his interests to other areas. Living in Harrisburg from 1802 to 1805, and in a work that was never published, Puglia wrote an inquiry into the causes, symptoms, and treatment of measles that included two new methods of inoculation against the disease. His interest in public health was further revealed in his appointment by Governor Simon Snyder as Health Officer of Philadelphia in June 1809, a post he held for seven and a half years.

Puglia had also continued his interest in political issues. At the end of the previous year, attempting to remain neutral during the war between Great Britain and France while also protecting American trade, President Jefferson had induced Congress to pass the Embargo Act, a risky and controversial action that halted foreign commerce altogether but provoked much debate. In 1808, Puglia completed *The Embargo,* a three-act comedy play "on that eventual seclusion of American Commerce" and dedicated to Jefferson as a critical gesture against the new law, but it was neither published nor performed.[71]

In the same year, Puglia turned his attention to state politics through another comedy, *The Complete Disappointment; or, A curious touch at modern times,* dedicated to Governor Snyder as an implicit objection to his policies, but it too remained unpublished. In 1810, Puglia completed *The Merry Tragedy,* a three-act play whose subject can only be surmised by its subtitle: "The Father Assassin of his son, through mistake." Three essays published from 1809 to 1811 resulted in a new book, *Capital Punishment,* in which Puglia used "simple morality and incontrovertible logical arguments" along with "the principles of the Christian religion" to condemn state execution as an unjust and unwise policy. In a subsequent, undated work with a theist outlook, *Moral Criticism,* Puglia presented his "periodical discourses on the system of Reason, as anterior to, and independent of Religion in general, calculated to perfect the honest and reform the wicked."[72]

In 1821, the firm of Matthew Carey & Sons published *El Derecho del Hombre,* Puglia's Spanish translation of Paine's *Rights of Man,* followed by *Sistema Politico-Moral,* in its English title *My Politico-Moral System,* which included a translation of Volney's *Natural Law* from French to Spanish. He also compiled his *Notas del Tiempo,* or *Memoirs of the Time,* which contained his correspondence with Edmond C. Genet, Joseph Buonaparte, and John Quincy Adams. Puglia's last work was published in Philadelphia in 1822 under the title *Forgery Defeated,* with the cumbersome extension "or a New Plan for invalidating and detecting all attempts of the kind; for which a patent has been obtained from the United States by James Ph. Puglia, citizen thereof; Professor of Foreign Languages in the City; and Author of several Political, Literary and Moral Works." With this work, which focused on the problem of the counterfeiting of banknotes, Puglia ended his public life in Philadelphia.[73]

Information about Puglia becomes scarce after that point. Newspaper advertisements from January through June 1822 indicate that Puglia operated an agency where he sold lottery tickets, and local directories list him as a "professor of languages" or an "interpreter" in Philadelphia until 1830. Although he remained a bachelor until at least his thirty-sixth year, in a footnote to *Forgery Defeated* he gave instructions to give his unpublished manuscripts, in the case of his death, to his "beloved wife," which suggests not only that he had married but also that he did not expect to live much longer.[74]

Puglia's life came to a tragic end in Charleston, South Carolina, in late August 1831. A coroner's report published in that city described how Jacques Philip Puglia, a native of Genoa, had committed suicide by arranging a musket to fire through his mouth, blowing off his skull. Within the week, accounts of the same event appeared in three Philadelphia newspapers. He was described as "a reduced gentleman, of fine attainments, and, it is said, of a mind, naturally strong, active and penetrating," who had experienced increasing personal problems in his later years, in particular a failure to secure a position with a "literary institution." In letters to several friends, he had described with a remarkable degree of detachment his intention to end his life. His continuing frustrations had driven him not only to suicide but also to a felony that, in the language of one obituary, "subtracts largely from the merits of a life, said otherwise to have been of the most exemplary character." In his will, Puglia left only a single trunk, the contents of which he valued at $2,100, but he instructed that his grave be 8 feet deep with no monument to mark its location, and that his burial take place at midnight. With these bizarre circumstances, Puglia's life came to an end.[75]

Puglia's efforts, though certainly prolific, are difficult to assess. The extensive volume of his works suggests a fertile, creative imagination, and his more polemical works indicate a penchant for critical argument. His attempts as a playwright, however, had limited success, and there is no way to determine how receptive the public was to his writings. While the publication of his writing by Matthew Carey and the prominence of his correspondents suggest some stature for Puglia as a serious thinker, they might also simply reflect the willingness of the printer to accept what could be paid for by an author.

Merchants and Entrepreneurs

While the lives of Ceronio and, even more, Puglia were marked by much frustration and perhaps failure, not all Italians who settled in Philadelphia ended as unfortunately. Not many in number, and not yet with their own community, several Italian merchants achieved some commercial success during the late eighteenth and early nineteenth century. In a few cases, their efforts produced only modest results, or even less, but others, who undeniably prospered, have been all but forgotten. Whether successful or not, they represent the origins of commercial life among Italians in Philadelphia.

One of the first Italian entrepreneurs to test the local economy was Anthony Vitalli. Beginning in prerevolutionary years, Vitalli pursued various business endeavors for a quarter-century. In December 1772, an advertisement in the *Pennsylvania Packet and the General Advertiser* informed the general public what "Anthony Vitalli, Sausage Maker, Late from Italy" offered:

> At his shop in Fourth street, between Walnut and Spruce streets, nearly opposite the house of Edward Shippen, Esq; and at his stall every market-day, opposite the sign of the Indian King, sells all sorts of Sausages, as they are made at Milan, Venice, Bologna and Naples, and over all Italy, fit to eat raw, broiled, fried and boiled, and others to make rich sauces. As he is a stranger in this city, he will be much obliged to the gentlemen and ladies who will please to favor him with their custom, and will use his utmost endeavors to please them, having served his time to this trade, in which he has obtained a sufficient proficiency.[76]

Vitalli's enterprises did not always proceed smoothly. In the summer of 1788, he announced the relocation of his business to Third Street near Walnut Street, where he sold sugars, snuff, and other items from Martinique and hoped that "his former obliging customers will continue their favors as heretofore." Shortly afterward another notice indicated the dissolution of a partnership between tobacconists Antonio Vitalli and Giovanni Dortea, located on Front Street between Chestnut and Walnut. Dortea also declared that he would not pay any debts contracted in their joint names by his former partner. In 1793, when a later partner, Anthony Bazaro, died at Cape François in Haiti, Vitalli was left as sole proprietor of the business. For many years afterward, Vitalli advertised as a manufacturer of bologna sausage, and his name appeared in city directories (although sometimes as Vitally) with shops at 58 South Water Street and at 57 South Front Street in the bustling dock and market area of Lower Delaware Ward, occasionally as a dealer in tobacco, a major commodity in Philadelphia.[77]

Giuseppe Mussi, who first came to Philadelphia about 1784, became even more prominent in city commerce than Vitalli. Two years after his arrival, Mussi took the oath of allegiance to the state of Pennsylvania and became a citizen of his new country.[78] In the same year, on their trip to the Moravian settlements to the north of Philadelphia, Castiglioni described Mussi as "a fellow Milanese of ours, a young man of pleasant manners, who has been established there for some years as a merchant."[79]

By 1795, Mussi was a prosperous member of the business community at 37 North Water Street in the Upper Delaware Ward, only two or three doors away from grocer Stephen Girard, who later became the wealthiest man in the nation. Mussi's own affluence, however, was evident from his generous contribution of 5 pounds and 10 shillings in support of the expansion of the chapel and the building of a residence for priests at Old St. Joseph's Church in Willings Alley.[80]

While his enterprises would develop more in the early part of the next century, Mussi also encountered reversals. In 1819, he was sued by the flamboyant former librettist of Mozart, Lorenzo DaPonte, and DaPonte's wife, over a disputed inheritance of land in New Jersey. Mussi claimed that the land had been sold to him by its former owner, John Grahl, a Dresden merchant and DaPonte's father-in-law, who had died without leaving a will. The court ruled in Mussi's favor that a legal purchase of the land had been made.[81] By 1825, Mussi had moved his business activities to 180 Spruce Street. When he died in 1832 without any immediate heirs, Mussi left his estate to nephews and nieces, the children of his late brother, Frederick, in Milan. At his death, Mussi's principal assets were only slightly more than $1,000, but his estate listed taxes and ground rents on additional property on Old York Road. In its final settlement, his accountant also noted a possible claim against the federal government for supplies Mussi had furnished to French authorities in the West Indies before 1800 for about $15,000.[82]

Other Italians emerged as successful and prominent merchants in Philadelphia during these years. After arriving about 1783, Vincenzo Maria Pelosi had by September of the following year already sworn the oath of allegiance to the state of Pennsylvania.[83] Not long afterward, Pelosi announced the opening of the Pennsylvania Coffee House on January 1, 1785, at 13 Market Street, where he served tea, coffee, chocolate, lemonade, wines, liquors, and cordials to thirsty Philadelphians, as well as beverages that were less known to local tastes but familiar to Italians or the French, such as *orzata* and *capillaire*. The hungry Philadelphian could have an "ordinary," a fixed-price meal at a set time, at two o'clock each weekday afternoon and at one o'clock on Sundays. Pelosi also provided newspapers, journals of the House of Assembly, commercial price lists, city directories, and shipping news, while the bar accepted other messages, advertisements, and notices.[84]

Within a short time, Pelosi's efforts achieved some success. By early March 1785, he "finished very elegantly three lodging rooms for the accommodation of gentlemen who will board and lodge in the Pennsylvania Coffee House." Pelosi also offered an "ordinary" for gentlemen willing to attend their meals in this manner. In the summer months, Philadelphians found ice cream and lemonade among the pleasant refreshments available at the Pennsylvania Coffee House. In August, the advertised specialty was large, dressed turtle on the table at precisely two o'clock in the afternoon.[85]

Public attractions at the Pennsylvania Coffee House went beyond food. At the request of "several gentlemen," Pelosi offered a program of "harmonial music" by an ensemble of clarinets, French horns, bassoons, and flute on Thursday evenings from June through September 1786. A ticket for the entire season cost one guinea; admission for a single performance could be purchased for 5 shillings. In August, patrons could buy tickets for a fireworks display.[86]

By 1786, Pelosi's coffeehouse had become a popular gathering place for local residents. In February, the Adopted Sons of Pennsylvania celebrated the birthday of General Washington with a dinner at the tavern. Throughout the summer and fall, they continued to hold meetings at the Pennsylvania Coffee House. While little else is known about the group, its name suggests foreign birth, but whether Pelosi himself had any role within the organization remains unknown. His business, meanwhile, continued its growth, and in September, Pelosi sought "a professed Woman Cook, who can have a good character for her abilities and honesty."[87]

During the next year, Pelosi changed the location of his establishment. In July 1788, he advertised at Daniel Cooper's Ferry for a tobacco manufacturer before moving across the Delaware River to Camden, New Jersey. In a newspaper notice in December, he expressed his sincere thanks to friends who had patronized his former establishment. Less than a week later, Pelosi announced his intention to open a new coffeehouse at Camden Middle Ferry in New Jersey, where he planned to resume serving wines, liquors, cordials, preserves, tea, coffee, and other items.[88] But the Camden site did not prevail for long, and Pelosi had returned to Philadelphia, where his exchange and coffeehouse at 1 North Water Street on the southern edge of

Upper Delaware Ward, one block west of the docks, again presented entertainment by *al fresco* concerts in 1791.

Pelosi expanded his enterprises by publishing a *Marine List and Price Current*, with news of ship arrivals and departures and commodity market prices—indispensable information for local merchants—for at least nine months from July 1791 to April 1792. Among its subscribers was Thomas Jefferson, the young nation's Secretary of State.[89] Pelosi also speculated in commodities and in real estate and gambled in city lotteries; obtained stock in the Delaware & Schuylkill Canal Company and in the Lancaster Turnpike; acquired a deed to 200 acres in Virginia; spent 1,025 English pounds in a business venture in Madeira; and sold molasses and other goods in local markets. His business acumen enabled him to live comfortably in a house he had purchased from a widow named Bartram on Second Street in Philadelphia.[90]

Pelosi probably lived even better on the Camden side of the river, where he had built a handsome mansion. Although one early local historian referred to Vincent Mari Pilosi (*sic*) as a buyer of building lots around 1780, the time is clearly before Pilosi's arrival in the area. Measuring 66 feet by 22 feet, his three-story house was constructed in an alternating pattern of red and white English bricks, on ground that would later become Cooper Street, and graced by a large garden.[91]

Pelosi suffered formidable setbacks in his investments from time to time. His account books indicate losses in the West Indies and in Madeira that exceeded 1,400 pounds. Toward the end of his life, he lost 1,650 pounds from the sale of property and another 300 pounds from bad debts. When he died, another victim of the yellow fever epidemic of 1793, Pelosi left his widow, Martha, an estate at first valued at more than 1,432 pounds, with other assets that included twelve large Italian paintings, various shares of stocks, lottery prizes on sixty-two tickets worth 69 pounds, and a sum of cash. One year after his death, the inventory of his estate had increased to nearly 1,700 pounds, with claims for unpaid debts filed by Gaetano Perrogalli, Giuseppe Mussi, and John Baptist Sartori.[92]

Pelosi was buried in the garden of his Camden estate. By 1796, Martha Pelosi had remarried. When she died in 1815, Martha was buried in the garden near her first husband. The handsome estate that Pelosi had built would later become a lumberyard, and his remains were removed to the Camden cemetery. The house was reported still standing as late as 1886, being used as a carpenter shop.[93]

Another early Italian pursued a different course but also achieved financial security and a high reputation among his Philadelphia neighbors. Born in Messina, Sicily, on October 5, 1755, the son of Dominico Marabello and Catherine Spada, his name was Placido Dominico Giuseppe Marabello. He came to Philadelphia as a mariner, but both his name and his occupation changed almost immediately after his arrival. Although it is not clear when he actually arrived, Marabello was naturalized by the U.S. Circuit Court in March 1796 and was one of the first Italians to become a citizen by the new procedures of the Constitution. Two years later, in April 1798, Marabello married Elizabeth Weyer, a German-born Lutheran, in a ceremony at Holy Trinity Catholic Church. Although he signed the marriage record as Giuseppe Marabello, the church register listed him as Joseph Marbell. One might say that his Americanization had also begun.[94]

Joseph Marble, as he was known by 1800, lived on South Fifth Street in the District of Southwark, just below the southern boundary of the city, as a respected member of his new community. He prospered enough as a grocer to contribute financially to alterations and improvements of Old St. Mary's Church on several occasions. Marabello later moved to 93 Passyunk Road, a major thoroughfare that cut diagonally through the center of Southwark, where he and his wife, apparently childless during their marriage, remained for the rest of their lives.[95] After a lingering illness, Marabello died at the age of sixty-six in April 1821. In an obituary, he was identified as Joseph B. Marbele and described as being "for many years a respectable citizen of the district of Southwark." He was buried in the cemetery of Holy Trinity parish, where he had been married twenty-three years before.[96] Marabello's will provided a succinct summary of his life:

> In the name of God Amen I Placido Dominico Joseph Marabello, born in the city of Messina in the Island of Sicily, on the fifth day of October anno Domini one thousand seven hundred and fifty five, son of Dominico Marabello and Catharine Spada, but since my arrival in America am called, and pass by the name "Joseph Marbell" and Now reside at No. 93 Passyunk Road in the District of Southwark. . . .[97]

The Sicilian grocer left all his goods and $2,500 to "my beloved Elizabeth." Marabello also assigned $200 to the trustees of St. Mary's to be invested by the pastor and directed that any rent or interest to the church "to be by him applied from time to time in such way and manner as he may deem proper for the good of my soul." Marabello instructed his executors after the death of Elizabeth to sell the house on the eastern side of Passyunk Road between German and Catharine Streets. He further directed that if his brother, Baptiste Marabello, were still alive and had any living children or grandchildren, all property in the estate was to be sold or willed to them. If no heirs were found, Marabello asked that his estate be passed on to "the Roman Catholic Society of St. Joseph for educating and maintaining poor orphan children." If any part of his estate were sold, the remainder was to be assigned to the trustees of St. Mary's, who were to distribute any accruing rents and interest among the poor of the parish at each Christmas, with Marabello's name being announced as the donor on the preceding Sunday. By 1845, twenty-four years after Marabello's death, the pastor of St. Mary's declared that the principal had already been used up and was among the "lost legacies" of the parish.[98]

Several other aspects of Marabello's life that lingered on after his death are worth noting. At his wedding in 1798, Adam and Mary Snyder had served as witnesses. In his will, prepared in 1816, Marabello named Joseph Snyder, a Southwark blacksmith whom he described as one of his good friends, to serve as executor of the estate. His close friendship with the Snyder family indicated a degree of assimilation with his American neighbors in Southwark. For some years, Marabello's widow continued to live at 93 Passyunk Road, but in a later city directory she was identified as Elizabeth Marbelow, a "gentlewoman"—yet another version of a name that was still difficult for other Philadelphians. Shortly afterward, in 1827, Elizabeth Marble, described as the widow of the late Joseph Marble, was married by Bishop Henry Conwell to James Eneu, an old friend who had served as the other executor of Marabello's will and who later became a city alderman. At her own death eleven years later in 1838, however, she was still identified as Elizabeth Marble.[99]

The poignant fragment of Marabello's will presented earlier, along with these other aspects of his life, not only captured important details of his own case but also anticipated the experience of Italians in the years ahead. Marabello was conceivably not only the first Sicilian but perhaps the first native of Italy to settle in the section of the city that would become the hub of Italian settlement. His pattern of friendship with other residents of the area, and his marriage, reflected the assimilation process that would later engulf so many other Italians. His apparent success as a small merchant also prefigured the material well-being that later generations of Italian immigrants would find in Philadelphia. Most significant of all aspects of his life, the change of his identity from Giuseppe Marabello to Joseph Marbell is mute testimony to his transformation from a Sicilian to a Philadelphian, another course followed by so many others in the years to come.

In sharp contrast to previous cases, Paolo Busti achieved a much larger fortune, which endured throughout his lifetime, along with unmatched respect and influence. Despite his formidable accomplishments, Busti is almost entirely forgotten in the early history of Philadelphia. Little is known about his early life. Born in Milan on October 17, 1749, he received a "liberal education." After moving to Amsterdam, he first worked in a countinghouse owned by an uncle, and eventually began an independent career that brought him wealth as well as a strong reputation for his skills and character. In Amsterdam he also acquired a wife, Elizabeth May, daughter of a Dutch captain.[100]

Busti's abilities, and his family ties, not only altered his career but also changed his entire life. His new brother-in-law directed one of the six Dutch banks that had joined together to establish the Holland Land Company. In 1797, Busti accepted a position as the assistant to Theophile Cazenove, the General Director of the Holland Land Company in North America at its office in Philadelphia. Although Cazenove's incompetence disturbed company owners, he could not easily be replaced, because he was deeply involved in resolving the land claims of Native Americans in western New York. Two years later, when Cazenove returned to Europe, Busti was appointed General Agent of the company. Described as "diplomatic, compromising, and urbane," he managed the company from his office in Philadelphia until his death twenty-five years later.[101]

From their residence in the fashionable center of the city at Twelfth and High Streets, Paolo and Elizabeth Busti received new friends and neighbors—among them Robert Morris, the financier, and John Dunlap, the leading newspaper publisher of the city. The Busti home was located on an enclosed block of large trees and high bushes that could have been a public park rather than an exclusive residential area of wealthy Philadelphians.[102]

In July 1804, Busti reached another level of commitment to his adopted city and country when, identified as a native of Lombardy in Italy and a subject of the Batavian Republic, he filed a petition in the District Court to become an American citizen.[103] His citizenship was soon accompanied by an ambitious pursuit of property. After constructing a brick building to replace the earlier frame office of the Holland Land Company, Busti obtained a large plot of land in Blockley Township, where he erected the mansion that served as his summer home. In 1806, he purchased six contiguous tracts of land and meadow ground at a sheriff's sale for $14,500. The original purchase consisted altogether of 112 acres and 25 perches of land, including part of what was known as Mill Creek. Subsequently, Busti purchased Mill Creek Farm, a plantation of another 10 acres and 39 perches, for $600. Busti's plantation, known as the Blockley Retreat, was an elegant estate with a vast panoramic view of the city to the east.[104]

Formed as a result of Dutch financial support for the American Revolution, the Holland Land Company purchased 1.5 million acres in Pennsylvania and 3 million more acres in New York. As General Agent for the company, Busti was responsible for the sale of land to European settlers. In 1799, he authorized Joseph Ellicott, the company surveyor, to find people willing to establish a settlement at the mouth of the Buffalo Creek in western New York. Although acting under Busti's direction, Ellicott became identified as the founder of the settlement, the future city of Buffalo. Busti also directed the founding of other communities, which became smaller cities of the region.[105]

Busti's greater significance for Philadelphia and the nation, however, is in other matters. For instance, he had a role in introducing certain forms of Italian agriculture to American farmers. In September 1806, John Vaughn, the most active and influential figure in the various physiocratic organizations in the city, proposed Busti as a resident member of the Philadelphia Society for the Promotion of Agriculture. In support of Busti's candidacy, Vaughn presented an ear of maize raised by the Italian that ripened only eight weeks after planting, and promised to procure more seed for planting in the next spring. On the strength of this important innovation, Busti was unanimously elected to membership in the following month. At the December meeting, Vaughn presented a letter from Busti and some specimens of the corn, to encourage efforts in cultivating its seed.[106] In later meetings, Busti introduced other techniques and products of Italian agriculture to his new colleagues. In a document dated January 1, 1810, at Blockley Retreat, read to the members a few days later, Busti discussed his efforts to rid fields of "wild garlick" (the weed known today as wild onion), which interfered with crops on the plantation.[107]

After his death in July 1824, Busti's contributions in these matters continued. At its September meeting, the Philadelphia Society for the Promotion of Agriculture listened to a reading of his "Instructions for the cultivation of the Mulberry Tree and of Silk Worms, in order to introduce them into America." In the *Memoirs of the Society,* Joseph Cooper described the desirability of cultivating the Italian mulberry and Lombardy poplar trees. The mulberry would eventually grow abundantly in the Philadelphia area. Shortly before Busti's own essay, Thomas Appleton, the U.S. Consul in Leghorn, had sent to James Mease, vice-president of the Philadelphia Society, seeds of the famed Bologna hemp and Cremona flax, with detailed instructions on their cultivation from a Professor Tozzetti of Florence. Obviously, although a number of individuals had been involved, Busti's role in introducing Italian crops and techniques to American agriculture and the textile industry is noteworthy.[108]

Some candid glimpses into Busti's life are provided in the remarkable Daybook that he kept as proprietor of Blockley Retreat from 1816 to 1823. Along with his bookkeeping accounts in the daily operation of the farm, its pages provide observations on the weather, agricultural practices, actions and attitudes of his workers, and other matters. Some understanding of his success as General Agent of the Holland Land Company is evident in the meticulously detailed ledgers he maintained for his personal estate. After some notes on English standard measures and weights, Busti began his observations in 1816 by commenting that he was no longer able to manage the farm himself and had decided to hire a superintendent. At that point he had two overseers working, but he had chosen to fire Francis Guinette and retain Isaac Taylor. When he later realized that the latter was also dishonest, cheating in many ways in the operations of the farm, Busti decided to dismiss him too, despite the considerable cost entailed.[109]

A more important dimension of his Daybook is the personal character of Busti himself projected by its entries. Written in quite legible script by a person who was not only very fluent in English but elegant in style, the entries reveal Busti's attitudes toward his workers and sometimes include vivid comments on their continued shortcomings and defects. When he described his dissatisfaction with Engelman, who with his family had been hired in 1807, Busti concluded that his worker was more of a gardener than a farmer, and therefore relatively ignorant and unfit to manage the farm. As he explained his reasons for dismissing him, Busti referred to the Dutchman as a "blockhead" in scientific matters.[110]

Busti next hired Matthew Doyle, "a stout healthy robust laborer" who not only lived nearby but also understood farming. But this Irishman, as Busti identified the new man, also was too much of "a politician and a quarrelsome dog" who attended so many meetings, elections, and court sessions that there was soon "an irreparable loss of his time." During harvest time in 1807, Busti declared that every week was marked by battles among the hands hired to do the reaping. When the crop was divided, Doyle had taken more than the share to which Busti thought he was entitled. Busti soon observed the dirtiness of Doyle's house and the filth around it, and objected particularly to the odors of rotten vegetables and onions. Busti also was offended by Doyle's frequent cursing and swearing at his own children and at the other hired hands, and by his wife, who usually returned from town in an intoxicated condition. As might have been expected, Busti soon found it desirable to terminate the employment of Doyle.[111]

Busti's general dissatisfaction with his American workers, as he identified them, can also be noted. In the summer of 1817, Busti concluded that it was impossible to keep the peace among the "rabble of American laborers." He observed: "Quarrel they will; quarrel they must." Busti caustically commented that the slow progress in the work of the farm had a clear cause: "The reason is to be sought in that eternal truth which an experience of many years has proved that American laborers when working for Gentleman do but half of their due." Busti maintained that not only two workers are necessary to do the work of one man, but often a third can be found as an idle observer to these labors. Later in the year, after describing how little work had been accomplished for the entire month, Busti complained: "If ever I had just motive of complaining that American laborers are what a Dutchman would call Dagdissen [idlers] it has been this month."[112]

Italian workers did not escape Busti's criticism. Almost immediately after his complaints about the quarreling rabble of Americans, Busti mentioned Angelo Zocchi, "a Lombard blockhead whom I took for humanity's sake," who left the farm because of disputes with other hands, even though he could not speak a single word with them in the same language. Although Zocchi had worked at Blockley for about five months, Busti asserted that his labors were not even worth what he consumed as food. Busti claimed that he paid Zocchi $60 for this period, but the account had been confused by a bill of exchange drawn by Zocchi on behalf of a brother in Milan. About two years later, Busti hired another Italian who remained employed from November 1819 to July of the next year. Although Busti described the hiring as an act of "pure charity," it is unclear whether he meant toward the worker himself or toward the overseer who wanted more help.[113]

Despite Busti's frequent remarks about how little he received from his workers, it is not clear how justified his complaints were. While his strong standards for honest amounts of labor in return for the wages he paid produced high expectations, Busti was so consistently dissatisfied that his comments might be questioned. But, equally hard on himself, Busti also concluded that his enterprise was not a financial success. In an 1816 entry, he emphatically declared:

> It is a truth too evident to every practicing farmer who thinks to have a claim to the expensive title of a Gentleman, that it is utterly impossible for him to work to any advantage a farm in America. Whether he leases it out, or gives it on shares or keeps it in his own hands the Gentleman farmer will always find that the possession of farms affords no revenue.[114]

Nearly four years later, Busti reiterated this view on an even more personal level:

> The foregoing account showing the result of farming with hired hands had forcibly convinced me that for the sake of profit no individual should ever attempt to imitate me. As it is evident that the owner of such farm sinks really his ready cash for no other purpose but that of raising produce the whole of which is consumed by the very hands he pays, and by the live stock he has to keep and feed on the farm.[115]

Despite his own warnings, Busti continued to operate the farm at Blockley Retreat at least until 1823, the year before his death. It is somewhat curious that a man who left such an impressive reputation for his management of the Holland Land Company should have long maintained another enterprise about which he was so strongly critical.

It is possible he exaggerated the losses while minimizing his material worth. Despite his complaints, the ledgers strongly suggest that he was a shrewd and successful manager of the farm. The 1822 tax records for Blockley Township, moreover, assessed the farm at more than $11,000, making him one of the larger landowners of the district.[116] (It also showed a $2 tax for the four dogs, at a rate of 50 cents for each dog Busti kept on the property.) And while he grumbled about how little his hired hands worked and how much it cost to maintain them, Busti's entries also indicate the income he received from them for their boarding and subsistence.

Busti's life in Philadelphia, however, went beyond what he revealed in his journal. He arrived as a Roman Catholic, but that affiliation changed in later years. In July 1809, for his donation of $100, "Paul Bustee" is listed among the contributors for improvements to Old St. Mary's, the Catholic church on South Fourth Street. But in December 1811, Busti disclaimed any further intention to retain his pew on the south aisle of the main level of the church, which was turned over to a new holder. This entry in its Minute Book denoted not only his withdrawal from the parish, but possibly as a communicant of the Roman Catholic faith as well. When he died at about seventy-five years of age, on July 23, 1824, it was neither sudden nor unexpected; he had made out his last will about two weeks before his death. His burial in the graveyard of Christ Church, where his wife had been interred in the previous year, suggests that Busti had become an Episcopalian.[117] Like other upwardly mobile individuals, successful adjustment and prominence had meant a change of religious affiliation. An obituary praised him as being "endowed with an exalted mind, . . . temperate and exemplary in his habits and decorous on every occasion, . . . impressive in his manners, and dignified in language."[118]

Busti's wealth was reflected by his will, which included stocks and shares in the Philadelphia Savings Fund Society, the Holland Land Company, the Library Company, the United States Bank, the North American Bank, and the Bank of North America, more than $50,000 in investments alone; the farm and a house in Hamilton Village; and a long list of personal possessions. By November 1825, further documentation gave a total value of $119,408.82 for the estate. A year later the figure was slightly under $88,000, which included more than $6,000 in cash in banks, $8,975 in unsettled accounts, more than $50,000 in investments, and almost $17,500 in stocks and funds on hand.[119]

In his will, Busti established a trust for the two children of Sophia Delprat, wife of John Charles Delprat, his nephew in Baltimore. He also provided for a yearly distribution of 3,000 Milanese livres to Angelo Busti, who was not otherwise identified, and the same to "his brother" Christopher, but it is unclear whether Angelo and Christopher were brothers to Paolo or only to each other. (The livre was a French unit of currency of the period with an approximate value of one pound of silver.) Busti asked that the rest of his property be given in equal parts to the married children, male and female, as well as to the descendants of those who would later marry, of his sisters Josepha and Theresa. He appointed P. A. Nicolai of Amsterdam executor of the estate, awarding him twice the customary commission, and directed John Jacob Vander Kemp, his successor as General Agent of the corporation, to dispose of all property in the United States and commissions due from the Holland Land Company. (Vander Kemp would later name a daughter Pauline Elizabeth in esteem for his old friends Paolo and Elizabeth Busti.)

The significance of Busti's life is not found simply in an assessment of his personal wealth and property, for he had been a formidable presence in other ways. Through his involvement in the Philadelphia Society for the Promotion of Agriculture, Busti had influenced farming and manufacture in the United States, and as General Agent for the Holland Land Company, he had directed the settlement and development of new communities in the young nation. Yet, despite the wealth and influence he once had, Busti, as most other Italians of the period, has been virtually extinguished from the early history of Philadelphia.[120]

Any attempt to restore Busti's place in local history must also note a limited role within the Italian experience in the city. The pages of his journal reveal some contacts with a few Italians, as well as Busti's attitudes toward them. Similar connections are found in his will, which included a bond and mortgage for Joseph Mussi for a property valued at slightly more than $1,069, and a claim for wages and funeral expenses by Valentine Boggia, an Italian waiter. While he was not entirely separated from other Italians during his lifetime, the information that remains is too scant to provide more than faint outlines of any relationship to them. Although Busti probably accumulated far greater wealth than any other Italian in Philadelphia during the early part of the century, since Busti left no family dynasty, his influence among them ended with his death.

A quite different pattern is represented by the Sartori family, which remained important and prestigious in Philadelphia throughout the nineteenth century, even though the main residence of the family was about 40 miles away in New Jersey, and the family's sphere of influence was somewhat to the north. The American founder of the Sartori family was Giovanni Battista Sartori, born in Rome during the late eighteenth century, son of Carlo Sartori, the papal jeweler and a close associate of Pope Pius VI. After Napoleon's invasion of the Papal States, the elder Sartori was assigned the task of dismantling Vatican treasures to compensate the victorious French in 1796. His son, Giovanni, because of his financial ability, was sent to Milan, Modena, and Genoa to obtain a settlement from the appraisers of the papal jewelry.

While his arrival was once given as 1800, Sartori must have actually reached American shores a few years earlier. For two years before Napoleon invaded Italy, in an announcement in the *Federal Gazette* in 1794, Sartori had declared his intention "to ship to Europe" and offered for sale the remainder of his marble, which consisted of statues, tables, busts, vases, and pedestals, and a number of pictures and prints. Similarly, in July 1800 a local newspaper reported the death at Civitavecchia in the previous March of Mrs. Henrietta Theresa Musgrave Sartori, daughter of Mrs. Ester Musgrave of Philadelphia, and the wife of John Baptiste Sartori, Esq., U.S. Consul at Rome, in the twenty-seventh year of her life. These items indicate that Sartori had previously been in Philadelphia and had married a resident of the city.[121]

Whatever his earlier experiences, Sartori wrote to Robert Morris in 1797 and suggested that America would benefit by appointing a Consul in Rome to represent its trade interests and to assist travelers. After President John Adams proposed Sartori as his choice, the Senate confirmed the nomination, and Sartori became the first of eleven consuls until the fall of the Papal States in 1870. It is unlikely that President Adams would have nominated and the Senate would have confirmed someone who had not previously been in the United States.[122]

With his marriage to Mary M. Henriette L'official de Woofooin (*sic*), a native of Hispaniola, in a ceremony performed at Lamberton in

1804 by Father Philip Stafford, a priest from St. Augustine's Church in Philadelphia, Sartori settled into a new phase of life.[123] At their estate on the Delaware River known as Rosy Hill, in an area now part of Trenton, New Jersey, the Sartoris shared the companionship of prominent European refugees who had sought asylum in the United States.[124] It was here also that their children were born and grew up. Of fourteen children born to the family, eleven lived to adulthood. Priests from St. Augustine's Church performed baptisms and said Masses at Rosy Hill between 1805 and 1814. At least one daughter was baptized by Father Michael Egan, the Franciscan priest who became the first Roman Catholic Bishop of Philadelphia in 1810.[125]

By various enterprises, Sartori contributed to the economic growth of the area. It is sometimes claimed that he established the first spaghetti factory in the United States. He also supposedly introduced the manufacture of calico into New Jersey with a factory opened at the foot of Federal Street on the Delaware River in Trenton in 1817.[126] But perhaps Sartori's most lasting contribution involved the founding of the first Catholic church in Trenton. In 1814, on behalf of about thirty families of French, German, and Irish Catholics, Sartori and John Hargous, a French refugee and close friend, purchased a lot for the construction of St. John's Church. For about sixteen years, the new church was served by visiting priests from Philadelphia, until the installation of a resident pastor about 1830.[127]

While aiding the development of industry and religion in Trenton, the Sartori family maintained ties with the small Italian population of Philadelphia. In October 1808, John and Henriette Sartori served as baptismal sponsors for a son of the Fagioli family at a ceremony performed at St. Joseph's Church by Father Egan, the future bishop. A year later, when Mary Magdalen Sartori was baptized by Father Egan at Lamberton, Peter Bettini of Philadelphia acted as the sponsor. (The latter was also a friend of Joseph Marabello, the Sicilian grocer of Southwark, who had acted as the voucher at the naturalization proceedings of Bettini.) In 1812, when Bettini married Henriette Doan, the Sartoris served as witnesses for them. These occasions drew members of the Sartori family into the social network emerging among Italians in the city at this time.[128]

In 1828, the death of Henriette Sartori at Rosy Hill, while giving birth to twins, neither of whom survived, soon changed the course of family history. Despite Sartori's appointment as Consul General of the

Papal States to the United States, a position he held until 1841, other difficulties, in addition to the loss of his spouse, soon encouraged new plans. In 1832, he departed with three of his daughters for Italy, where he lived in Leghorn until his death at the age of ninety-eight, never returning to the United States. Over a long period this remarkable man had the unique experience of serving both as the American Consul to the Papal States and as the Papal Consul to the United States.[129]

Several other members of the Sartori family, however, retained their strong ties with Philadelphia, including three sons who had remained in the United States after their father's return to Italy. Charles, the eldest, received his early education at St. Augustine's Academy on Crown Street between 1811 and 1815. He eventually became a physician and later lived at Bloomfield Cottage on Ellisburg Road, about three miles outside of Camden. At one point an ambitious plan was announced for 40 acres of promenades and roads in a public garden on his property. He died about 1874.[130]

Victor, born in Trenton in 1814, moved to Philadelphia about 1833, imported marble from Italy, and became the most important member of the family on the local scene. For about fifty years, Victor remained a prosperous businessman and influential figure in civic affairs, his office located first at 86 South Front Street and later at 103 Walnut Street, and his residence at 305 South Seventh Street. He was an early member of the Union League, a leader in charitable activities, and the Sardinian Consul in the city.[131]

His younger brother, Louis Constant Sartori, distinguished himself as an officer in the U.S. Navy, rising to the rank of commodore. The sons of Victor Sartori—John Baptist, Victor A. Jr., and Frank—and their cousin Peter Jauretche also became successful members of the business community and continued the social prominence of the family until well into the twentieth century.

An Early Assessment

Although the number of Italians remained small as they entered the first stage of their history in Philadelphia, we can make an assessment of their economic, political, and cultural position. In their commercial

PIER FRANCESCO per la Misericordia di Dio Vescovo di Albano
CARDINALE GALLEFFI, della S. R. C. Camerlengo

Essendo debito del nostro ministero di provvedere che nei porti esteri sieno destinate persone idonee incaricate di vegliare agl' interessi e alla protezione del commercio, della navigazione e dei sudditi pontificj; ed essendo noi certificati dell' abilità e probità che vi adorna, con oracolo della SANTITA' DI NOSTRO SIGNORE PAPA LEONE XII., e per l'autorità del nostro ufficio di Camerlengato, siamo venuti nella determinazione di *nominare* voi Sig. *Giovanni Battista Sartori* ___ in Console generale dei Porti ___ colle ordinarie facoltà di esercitare la giurisdizione consolare, e di godere di tutti gli onori, i privilegj e gli emolumenti, che sono congiunti a questo impiego a somiglianza di quello, che si pratica per i rispettivi rappresentanti delle altre nazioni, e a norma delle nostre istruzioni circolari datate alli 28 settembre 1825., e delle altre leggi, che si pubblicassero in appresso.

Vi diamo inoltre la facoltà di scegliere e destinare dietro nostra approvazione secondo che richiederanno i bisogni e i vantaggi del commercio e della navigazione pontificia vice-consoli e agenti consolari secondo la maggiore o minore importanza de' porti ne' luoghi soggetti alla vostra giurisdizione consolare.

Noi preghiamo tutte le Autorità, a cui possa spettare, di riconoscere e trattare il Sig. *Giovanni Battista Sartori* nella qualità alla quale lo abbiamo eletto di Console generale, e di fare che sia riconosciuto e trattato come tale da tutti e singoli i loro subordinati, e le assicuriamo che in contracambio saranno egualmente riconosciuti e trattati quelli, che saranno deputati da loro allo stesso impiego nello Stato pontificio.

Dato a Roma in Camera Apostolica lì *16 Dicembre* 1828

After serving as the American Consul to Rome for several years, Giovanni Battista Sartori was also appointed Consul of the Papal States to the United States in 1828. The appointment document is shown here. Sartori's simultaneous service is unique in American diplomatic history. (Courtesy of Mary A. Snowden) endeavors, while merchants such as Vitalli, Pelosi, Mussi, and Mara-bello achieved only modest success, Busti and Sartori accomplished even more in their careers and reached greater levels of material wealth and social prominence during the late eighteenth and early nineteenth centuries. However, economic accomplishment for a greater number of Italians did not come until later in the nineteenth century.

In the closing years of the eighteenth century, Italians had made even slower incursions into the political life of their new community. Although the Ceronio brothers and Puglia became involved with the turbulent politics in the city during these years, their significance should not be exaggerated. The activities of the Ceronio brothers deserve a long overdue footnote as a contribution to the War of Independence. While the influence of Puglia is difficult to assess, his writings also belong more to the early nineteenth century. Compared with their modest participation in its commercial life, Italians played an even smaller role in the political affairs of the city.

The number of naturalizations provides some indication of the po-litical assimilation of newcomers, but by this measure the penetration of early Italians into the life of Philadelphia was also quite meager. From 1727 to 1775, because of English fears of the consequences of many German and Swiss arrivals, the foreign-born were required to take an oath of allegiance to the Crown of Great Britain and to the Province of Pennsylvania. No Italians at all took the oath during this early period. After the beginning of the War of Independence, foreigners had only to pledge their allegiance to Pennsylvania, but only a few Italians did so from 1777 to 1790. Some men were identified at the time of the oath as being of Italian origins; others can be determined from subsequent information to have been Italian. For example, in September 1784, Vincenzo Maria Pelosi, after one year in his new country, took the oath of allegiance to the state of Pennsylvania. In May 1785, Goetan Perrogalli, whose name appears to be Italian (and probably was Gaetano Perrogalli, the claimant to debt in the estate of Pelosi), took an oath of allegiance in the city of Philadelphia. In 1786, Joseph Mussi, who had arrived two years earlier, swore his new allegiance. In December 1789, Joseph Bartin, a twenty-eight-year-old mariner from Leghorn, in the Duchy of Tuscany, and Francis Bartin, also a mariner and a Tuscan, together took the oath of allegiance. In March 1790, Michael Terman, age fifty, and Antonio Terman, both mariners and natives of a place listed as Catta in the Republic of Venice, took the oath of allegiance.[132]

After ratification of the Constitution gave Congress the power to act, the first naturalization legislation, passed in 1790, restricted citizenship to free whites and required two years of residence by petitioners. However, the suitable procedures for the foreign-born to become citizens remained a controversial issue for a long time. From 1790 to 1854, fifteen naturalization laws were passed as the nation sought to clarify the concept of citizenship.[133]

Even after passage of the federal naturalization law, aliens continued to attain citizenship through the older procedure of the oath to the state. In May 1793, Defondina Rubardo, a mariner and ship master born in Port Maurice (probably Portomaurizio) in Genoa, swore allegiance to Pennsylvania. And after coming from New Orleans to Philadelphia two years earlier, Stephen Greffen, a merchant from Venice, pledged his allegiance to the Commonwealth in November 1793. In August of the next year, Vincent Ghirardini, a fruit seller born in Mantua, followed the same procedure to become a citizen. Although he had first arrived from Orleans, France, at the Port of New York in July 1784, Ghirardini had lived in Philadelphia for three years before his naturalization.[134]

From the first federal act in 1790 through 1800, only seven more Italians were naturalized by the newer procedures. Together with the few individuals who had taken the oath of allegiance to the colony, only about sixteen Italians became citizens in Philadelphia before 1800. In the final decade of the eighteenth century, petitioners who can be clearly identified as having Italian origins included Stephen Greffen, Placido Dominicus Joseph Marabello, Francis Magi, Joseph Ricardo, Lewis Pise, Joseph Provini, and Nicholas Richardson. In June 1795, only two years after taking the oath of allegiance to the Commonwealth, Greffen appeared for the second time as a candidate for citizenship. Identifying himself as a native of Venice, and forsaking his allegiance to the Republic of Venice, he filed a petition for naturalization in the Court of Common Pleas. Although he signed the document "Etienne Greffen," suggesting a French origin, his references to Venice on both occasions make it reasonable to regard him as an Italian. Although this determination is not by inferences made from surnames but from information in naturalization records about places of origin and previous allegiances, the total number of Italians was not very large. If the fears of the Federalists that the Jeffersonian Republicans were recruiting large numbers of the foreign-born ever had any validity, Italians were clearly not involved in any significant degree. Moreover, the handful of naturalizations among them in the late 1700s cannot be linked to any further participation in the politics of the city or the nation during this time.[135]

In regard to the cultural dimension, there is less doubt about individuals who, together, clearly played a part in the history of Italians in Philadelphia. Musicians and composers like diPalma, Gualdo, and others had considerable significance for the cultural life of the city and for the colonies as a whole. Similarly, Italian artists, with sculptor Cerrachi perhaps the most important of the period, spent some time in Philadelphia and left their mark on American art as well. Castiglioni and Scandella, two distinguished scholarly visitors who stayed only a relatively short time, arguably had some influence, while Busti, who for many years lived as a permanent resident, had a more evident intellectual and scientific impact on Philadelphia.

In sum, by the end of the eighteenth century a small wave of Italians had reached Philadelphia. While early records contain other names that may have been Italian in origin, the difficulty in documenting these cases with any degree of certainty leaves questions. The total number was far too small for any kind of ethnic community to emerge or for any major institutions of their own to form, as might be the case in a later period. These Italians had their origins in such diverse places as Venice, Milan, Rome, and Messina at a time when Italy was divided by regional loyalties that produced quite different identities for individuals.

In addition, the few permanent residents who can be unequivocally identified as Italians were also scattered in different locations throughout the city. Their accomplishments were more a matter of individual success than of collective influence. Although they sometimes associated with and assisted one another, as the appearance of their names on such documents as wills, estate settlements, and sacramental records indicated, the few Italians in Philadelphia also mingled with members of the larger community. Despite their regional identities—or ironically because of it—these early Italians may have been far more cosmopolitan than their counterparts in later decades.

From the limited materials documenting the period, it is not possible to determine how these Italians, as a group, were perceived or accepted by the rest of the population. Because they were small in number, the issue is not as important as it would be in the next century. The dominant English population was probably far more concerned with the possible threat to its material control and cultural hegemony in the city from the larger groups of newcomers, especially Germans, to be too concerned about a few Italians. The Italian presence in late-eighteenth-century Philadelphia is only a series of discrete pieces reflected by the lives of these few men who quietly pursued their lives in their new country's most important urban center.

Chapter 2

The Seeding of Community

All of them had recently left their homeland for a new world and could be found in Philadelphia in the early years of the nineteenth century. The innkeeper offered a rare bird called an "ostrich" that had never been seen before in the city. The musician claimed to play five different instruments at the same time in his performance. The importer presented for sale the finest marble art objects from Carrara. The language instructor had written the librettos for Mozart's most successful operas. The fresco painter, perhaps the first in the United States, had the talent to transform an ice cream parlor into a palace. The bogus priest fueled the first major crisis within American Catholicism. The impresario provided a pleasure garden where families could watch theatrical performances and find refreshments and amusements. The "lemonade men" peddled a drink that dampened thirsts but revived throats. They left Italy when it was only a "geographic expression"; they found Philadelphia when it was the most important city in North America.

The small contingent of Italians were components of a colorful kaleidoscope of characters and activities in the rapidly changing context provided by Philadelphia. While a few had left Italy together, many met for the first time in Philadelphia. By their work and occupations, they tested the growing economy of the city. By their naturalization as citizens, they expressed their commitment to a new life as Americans. By their parish activities, they modestly participated in local organizations without forming other voluntary associations. In their social life, they found cordial friendship and cooperation, but also acrimony and conflict. And as they were being transformed by their new experiences, they were also active participants in the process of change. For in addition to the impact that they as individuals had on local life, still only loosely connected to one another, they were planting the first seeds of their own new community.

From Seaport to Industrial City

The emergence of an Italian community in Philadelphia occurred during a period of great growth and change for the entire city. In 1800, with more than 41,000 people within the original town limits and nearly 40,000 more in the rest of the county, Philadelphia had the largest population of any American city. Despite steady growth in the next decade, Philadelphia slipped behind New York by the 1810 census. But it also entered the early stages of change from a bustling seaport town to the first industrial city in the nation.[1]

At the opening of the century, Philadelphia flourished with foreign trade, with a volume of 103,663 tons handled in 1800, but its enormous role in shipping and shipbuilding soon crested. In 1805, a typical year for the period, first-rate ships out of the port carried on regular trade with Marseilles, Leghorn, and Bordeaux, and many staunch second-class vessels called at Bordeaux, Genoa, and Messina. Brigs and schooners from Philadelphia, also engaged in foreign trade, further contributed to the volume of the port. While 547 ships arrived from foreign ports, 617 departed for foreign destinations. Another 1,169 coastal vessels arrived, while 1,231 left for domestic ports. The total volume of cargo for the year reached about 110,000 tons. International politics, however, soon altered this situation.

When President Jefferson's embargo on foreign commerce halted shipping and maritime construction in 1808, Philadelphia began a decline as a port from which it never recovered. After the War of 1812, New York had passed Philadelphia not only in population but also as the principal American port, particularly for trade with Europe. As its shipping shifted to the South Atlantic and the Mexican Gulf,

Philadelphia had fallen behind two or three other American ports in overall marine commerce by 1824.

The decline in maritime activity was tempered, however, by a growing participation in technological changes on land. The location of the city between two rivers, which had previously made it an important trade center, now provided energy for the first large mills and a strategic advantage for early industrialization. But if the great natural resources of the state, such as iron and coal, were to be extracted and delivered to the factories of the city, a new system of transportation had to be developed.

With the major rivers of the state flowing from north to south and separated by mountain ranges, Philadelphia had to be reached by different means. The construction of an elaborate system of bridges, turnpikes, canals, steamboats, and railroads provided the solution. In 1825, the same year as the Erie Canal in New York State, the Schuylkill Canal was opened in Pennsylvania, connecting 108 miles from Port Carbon near Pottsville with the Fairmount section of Philadelphia. Within a few years, the Union Canal, originating just above Reading, and the Lehigh Canal, beginning near Mauch Chunk, were also used to bring coal to Philadelphia. Although considerably shorter than the Erie Canal, which was built over rather level terrain, the canals of eastern Pennsylvania represented a far more complicated achievement. With these and other technological innovations, Philadelphia began its transformation, in the words of one historian, from "a community of merchants, mariners, and mechanics" to "a manufacturing city looking inland and living by mine and mill."[2]

While its population grew in the early nineteenth century, Philadelphia remained relatively unchanged in its diversity. The lull in immigration to the United States, which had declined during the Napoleonic Wars and stopped almost entirely with the outbreak of the War of 1812, provided time and opportunity for previous immigrants to become more acculturated as Americans. Following the pattern of earlier groups, newer immigrants, mainly Germans and Dutch, were abandoning traditional languages, religions, and customs for more American forms of culture and social institutions. By 1815, Philadelphia no longer had even one German-language newspaper.

While Federalist opposition to immigration disappeared with the demise of the party itself, Republican fears of the threat to national unity posed by foreign groups in the United States became greater. By

1815, the manpower needs of a growing society had encouraged a relatively liberal policy toward further immigration, but without offering any particular inducements or privileges to prospective newcomers. In the 1820s, when the federal government began counting new arrivals, the figures climbed slowly, but they remained below the unprecedented levels reached in later decades. Consequently, the ethnic composition of Philadelphia, as well as for most of the nation, changed little in the first thirty years of the nineteenth century.

In the void created by the low volume of foreign arrivals, Philadelphia and the rest of the nation could generally hold a rather favorable view of prospective immigrants. In 1826, Matthew Carey, the well-known publisher, presented "the description of persons to whom emigration to this country would be advantageous, but also a beacon to those to whom it would be unadvisable to remove hither."[3] While he warned that men who had been comfortable in Europe but were lured by golden dreams to come here had already found their fortunes wrecked by the change of hemisphere, Carey added: "There is probably no country where the same degree of comfort and enjoyment can be procured by the working classes, with the same degree of exertion." Although he doubted the need for more farmers, Carey noted that good land only 20 to 30 miles from Philadelphia could be purchased inexpensively, and even more cheaply farther away. He also discouraged the migration of clerks, shopkeepers, teachers, and the members of learned professions—with some exceptions, such as Roman Catholic and Presbyterian clergy. For others, Carey extended a strong welcome. For miners, he wrote: "There is probably no country richer in mines and minerals; and a very small proportion of these boundless treasures has been explored." For laborers, he provided an even more detailed picture of opportunity:

> There is scarcely any limit to the number of labourers, who are now and probably will be for twenty years to come, wanted in this country. The spirit of internal improvement, in canals, rail-roads, and turnpikes, is wide awake in every part of the union; and creates a great demand for that class, of which the number of native citizens bears no proportion to the demand.[4]

Carey displayed a remarkably accurate anticipation of what the future held for the American economy. Although manufacturers and mechanics were not needed because they were created fast enough here, there were many opportunities for carpenters, masons, smiths, and plasterers. Carey pointed out that if the government would ever adequately understand the interests of agriculture and take decisive measures to establish a domestic market of raw materials and provisions for American farmers, "there will be abundant room in the United States for all the manufacturers and farmers that Europe can spare." While he sensed the prosperity that would soon enough be available in the expanding economy, Carey believed that Philadelphia and New York had already reached the point that every person beyond the situation of a pauper could afford to eat meat at least once a day. It was a rather sanguine appraisal of conditions and opportunities for people who planned to immigrate to Philadelphia.

Coming to America

During the period 1800–1820, however, while the maritime fortunes of the city were declining, not more than forty ocean crossings were made by ships from Italian ports that reached the docks of Philadelphia. For most years, only two or three ships made the voyage, but the annual number increased to four or five after the War of 1812. Although sailing mostly from Leghorn and Genoa, a handful originated in Palermo and Naples. They ordinarily carried only a few passengers, who tended to be Americans returning to their native country but sometimes included Italians. When it arrived in late September 1818, the *John Burgwin,* for example, had four Italian passengers in first class and ten other Italians, who were actually a group of priests and students on their way to establish a mission in the West, in second class.

Altogether perhaps only about thirty passengers on these ships can be identified with some confidence as natives of Italy in the first two decades of the nineteenth century. But their cargoes of minerals, marble blocks and tile, alabaster ornaments and candlesticks, watches and jewelry, straw and fur hats, linen rags, quicksilver, Naples brandy, licorice paste, sweetmeats, saffron, fireworks, sundries (intended for J. B. Sartori of Trenton), ice cream molds (for L. Astolfi), and other items (for merchants John Strawbridge and Stephen Girard) indicated

Manifest of the *Water Witch*, which sailed from Genoa in 1817 with cargo for Philadelphia merchants, including John Strawbridge and Stephen Girard. It also carried fireworks, ice cream molds, and sweetmeats consigned to Lawrence Astolfi, the Italian pleasure garden proprietor. The few Italian passengers who traveled to the New World during this period would also be listed on such ship logs. (Courtesy of National Immigration Archives, The Balch Institute, Philadelphia) that the commercial impact of Italy in the American market was much greater than its immigration, at least for the moment.[5]

In addition to those who sailed directly to Philadelphia, some Italians first migrated to other cities before making it their final destination. In subsequent years, when they sought to stabilize their situation by marriage or citizenship, their previous origins, allegiances, and aspects of departure often became clearer. Candidates for naturalization usually gave Italy as their native country, but they sometimes identified more precise origins. About one-quarter of the petitioners gave the city or province of Genoa as their place of origin, while others cited Como, Bergamo, Leghorn, Padua, Volterra, Turin, Milan, Rome, Lecce, or Sicily. Paolo Busti gave his place of birth as "Lombardy in Italy" but identified himself as a subject of the Batavian Republic, one of the buffer states established by Napoleon to protect France. Marriage records at St. Joseph's Church also included individuals who gave Batavia as their place of birth. A petitioner in the Mayor's Court in 1805 named the King of Etruria, described as western Tuscany and Umbria, as his previous allegiance. Other than the Genoese, however, no more than one or two individuals had origins in the same location.

When the brig *Tuyphena* reached Philadelphia in late September 1800, six Italians—identified in vessel records only as Bapt. Loro, J. W. Longenatto, Anto. Poggi, Mich. Lagni, Lucca Massa, and B. Mulinari—were among the passengers.[6] While they obviously shared their moment of arrival in Philadelphia, it is not known whether these men maintained friendships afterward in their new community. They may have been the vanguard of a rather large chain of migration from towns and villages in the area around Chiavari that continued to develop throughout the nineteenth century. The family names of Poggi, Mulinari, and Massa reappeared in the sacramental records of St. Mary Magdalen de Pazzi in the late 1850s and early 1860s, when many Italians gave Chiavari as their place of origin.

Some Genoese applicants for citizenship in the early nineteenth century more specifically identified their native town as Santa Maria di Prato. First given as Santa Maria di Prato in Genoa by Jacob Mereti in November 1815, it was probably also the origin of some petitioners who merely gave Genoa as their native place.[7] Today there is no place with this name in the province of Genoa or in the entire region of Liguria or anywhere else in Italy, but the adjacent villages of Prato and Sopra la Croce, with the parish church of Santa Maria, can be

Map of Italy showing the region of Liguria. Many of the early Italian immigrants to Philadelphia came from the hill towns above Chiavari.

Scenes from Ligurian hill towns. *Top:* The annual fair in September in Cabanne d'Aveto, a town from which emigrants would become successful merchants in Philadelphia. *Bottom:* Genoese housewives find diversion from their daily chores by passing time in the game of *il Cerchietto*. In their lives as immigrants to Philadelphia, their work and play forced them to make many adjustments, leaving such moments as this one far behind them. (Courtesy of Vito Elio Petrucci, Genoa)

289

United States, } *ct.*
District of Pennsylvania. }

Be it remembered, That on this *First*

Day of *November* in the Year of our Lord one thousand eight hundred
and *Fifteen*

Jacob Mereti

a free white Person of the Age of twenty-one Years and upwards, being an Alien,
who has arrived in the United States after the passing of the Act of Congress,
entitled " An Act to establish an uniform Rule of Naturalization and to repeal
the Acts heretofore passed on that Subject," passed on the 14th Day of April
A.D. 1802, and who is desirous to be naturalized, did Report himself to the
Clerk of the District Court of the United States in and for the District of Pennsylvania, in Manner following, that is to say: That he the said

Jacob Mereti

was born in *Santa Maria di Prato*

in *Genoa*

on or about the *First* Day of *May*

in the Year of our Lord one thousand seven hundred and *Eighty*

and is now about the Age of *Thirty Five* Years, that he was born

a Member of the *Genoese*

and owed Allegiance to the *King of Sardinia*

that he migrated from *Tonningen*

to the United States, and arrived at the Port of *Boston*

on or about the *First*

Day of *September* A.D. 1895 and that it is his Intention to settle in

Philadelphia — *Jacob Mereti*

Recorded the Day and Year }
first above-written, by me }

N. Caldwell — Clk. Dist. Ct.

The naturalization petition of Jacob Mereti, a native of Santa Maria di Prato
and an important link in what may be the earliest chain of migration between an
Italian town and Philadelphia. (National Archives, Mid-Atlantic Region)

found in the *circondario di Chiavari*. These petitioners had apparently designated their town "Santa Maria di Prato"—an early example of *campanilismo*, the idea that the range of sound from the church bells of the *paese* (the hometown) defined the safe limits of one's world. In this picturesque area, where the mountains recede in a wide semicircle toward the Gulf of Rapallo, a traveler could begin in the coastal city of Chiavari the ascent inland toward the 5,690-foot Monte Penna on a route that passes through Borzonasca before it arrives at the towns of Prato and Sopra la Croce.[8]

In a later period, after an Italian colony had been established in Philadelphia, its very existence furnished some incentive for prospective immigrants to make Philadelphia their destination. Relatives and friends who had already immigrated offered personal motivation and material assistance for others. But the first links of these chains of migration present a different question. Although the motives of the earliest Ligurians to settle in Philadelphia remain unclear, their occupations may provide some answer. Another possible explanation lies in the political situation of Italy at this time. Required to identify the political state or the ruler to whom they previously owed allegiance, applicants for American citizenship named the Republic of Genoa; the Emperor of France; the King of Italy; Napoleon I; the Emperor of Austria; the King of Sardinia; the Sardinian nation; the King of Naples; the Grand Duke of Tuscany; or His Holiness the Pope. Perhaps each response had its own validity, but the range of the answers also reflected the political situation in Italy at the time.

Some answers indicated these turbulent and chaotic conditions even more vividly. Three early petitioners specified their former allegiance to the Republic of Genoa. When Antonio Poggi and Francis Travelli left at the turn of the century, it was still a republic, but not when Stephano Pichetti left Genoa in the autumn of 1808 or 1809. And there was no longer a republic when any of them petitioned for naturalization, beginning with Poggi in 1807. Napoleon's victory at Austerlitz in 1805, when France annexed Piedmont, Genoa, Tuscany, Rome, and some provinces of the Papal States, brought reforms to the regions, but it also made Italians subject to conscription into the French army. Genoa remained under French control until the Congress of Vienna ceded it to Piedmont in 1814. The anachronistic reference to a republic by these petitioners suggested a symbolic expression of defiance at the loss of self-government, and also a migration prompted by Napoleon's conquest of their region. Similarly, in the Declaration of Intention by Jean Baptiste Spargella in 1817, whose name itself expressed the cultural and political collision of France and Italy, his renunciation of allegiance to the King of Sardinia and the Sardinian nation augured a glimpse of the future for the Italian peninsula.

While the motives for departure from Italy remain clouded, the specific points of embarkation provide another clue. Among Italians who sought naturalization during the first forty years of the nineteenth century, of twenty-nine petitioners who named the ports from which they began their journey to the United States, only eight men left directly from Italian ports, with one each from Santa Maria in Sicily, Naples, and Civitavecchia and the other five from Leghorn. Twenty-one others left from ports outside of Italy, sometimes more unusual ones, which included Amsterdam (3 cases), Nantes (1), Bordeaux (1), Havre de Grace (Le Havre) (1), Liverpool (5), England, unspecified (1), Lisbon (2), Cadiz (1), Tönningen (2), St. Petersburg (1), Gothenburg (1), Copenhagen (1), and Santo Domingo (1). Despite the number of Genoese, the port of Genoa was not cited even once. The range of ports of departure clearly indicates that these early travelers, whether primarily for political or for economic reasons, were already taking unconventional pathways in their lives.

Coming Together in a New World

Despite the meager volume of their migration at the beginning of the nineteenth century, Italians could be discerned on the local scene, but in a quite different manner of personal adjustment and relationship to one another than in later years. Separated in place and in enterprise, the accomplishments of the few Italians in Philadelphia in the early 1800s were largely the result of individuals acting on their own, rather than as members of a more cohesively organized ethnic group. But some traces of ethnic group life were already visible.

The existence of enduring social networks among Italians can be found in their participation in religious ceremonies. Unlike the previous century, with cases that are only arguably Italian in origin, church records from 1800 and later list names that can be linked to other sources of information, such as naturalization records that provide evidence of Italian origins. A more tenuous link is provided by the presence of witnesses or sponsors in religious ceremonies whose origins can be determined by similar means, thus suggesting Italian identity for the principal participants. In sacramental ledgers for the major Catholic churches in the early 1800s, family names clearly show not only the presence of Italians in the city but also that they knew and interacted with one another.

The records of Old St. Joseph's, the first Catholic church in Philadelphia, founded in 1732, contain numerous listings of Italians. In the early nineteenth century, baptisms included the Franchi, Sartori, Fagioli, and Carlino (or Carbino) families of Philadelphia and nearby points in New Jersey. The marriages at St. Joseph's from 1812 to 1830 include the names Bellini (or Bettini), Genari, Trabalice, Ambrosi, DeAngeli, Viti, Battesta, Logno (or Togno), diPisola, Oliveri, and Pizzini, either as spouses or as witnesses. On January 30, 1828, Bishop Henry Conwell presided over the marriage of Vincent Caravadossy (*sic*) deThoel to Mary Antoinette D'Aurainville. Among the many titles of the groom, he was also identified in parish records as the Senior Knight and Royal Consul General of Sardinia to the United States. Among witnesses to the ceremony, N. Garibaldi, identified as the Vice-Consul and Chancellor of Sardinia, was probably Angelo Garibaldi, who later served as the Sardinian Consul in Philadelphia until his death in 1855.[9]

Although Holy Trinity Church was established in 1789 to serve the spiritual needs of the rapidly increasing number of German Catholics in Philadelphia, it also embraced refugees from France and Santo Domingo in the 1790s. By the 1820s, there were nearly as many French parishioners as Germans. Because of French ties to Corsica and Northern Italy in the Napoleonic era, Holy Trinity also drew Italians to its congregation. The baptism of Joseph Marchi included as sponsors Joseph Bosio and Catherine Reiser in January 1800. Joseph Bosio was probably Secondo Bosio, who became a colorful part of the Italian scene in the city. The baptism of Angela Mary Molinari, daughter of Francis and Martha Molinari, listed Anna Bossio (*sic*) as a sponsor in August 1799. The baptism of Catherine Francis Molinari, another daughter of Francis and Martha Molinari, was sponsored by Felix Imbert and Anna Bosio (wife of Secondo Bosio) in June 1802.

Parish records also showed the life cycle and friendship circle of families. John Thomasetti married Catherine Cooker at Holy Trinity, with George Barman and Mary Anna Fielding acting as witnesses in March 1801. Ten days later, the next wedding at Holy Trinity united George Berman and Mary Ann Fielding with John Thomasetti as a witness. In a later entry, Joseph Dominic, infant son of John Dominic Thomasetti and his wife, Catherine, was baptized on May 30, 1802. The sponsors of the Thomasetti child included Mary Bauman, probably the same person as the Mary Anna Fielding who married George Berman (or Barman) one year before. The other sponsor was Joseph Marbello, who was surely Joseph Marabello, the Southwark grocer. Two days later, on June 1, 1802, Rebecca Haughin was baptized, with Secundus and Anna Bosio as godparents. A few days later the baptism of John Jacob Laurent, without any familiar names as sponsors, noted a stipend offering of three gourdins with the word "Italian" following, referring either to the family or to the currency of payment. In November 1803, another Thomasetti son, Edward, was baptized at Holy Trinity, with the sponsors being the Reverend William Elling and Edward and Margaret Bombar. While they had friendships and married people of various backgrounds, Italians such as Molinari, Bosio, and Marabello were also well acquainted with one another and probably close friends.

Italians also participated in the parish life of St. Augustine's Church, founded in 1796 by the Augustinian friars. Such Italian families as Sartori, Fagioli, Zepero, Balordo, Foli, Lametti, Filippi, Luciani, Pittaluga, DeAngeli, Rebolla, Diaccheri, and Peichetti married and baptized their members there from 1804 on. Unlike other churches, however, Italian priests occasionally served at St. Augustine's. From 1806 to 1807, Father Balthassar Torelli, a secular priest rather than an Augustinian, was stationed there; in 1819 and 1821 the Reverend P. Rosetti, also a secular priest, served St. Augustine's. An 1838 census of the parish, however, recorded slightly more than 3,000 members, but only eight natives of Italy or Switzerland together, a number that conceivably represented no more than one family.[10]

As with participation in religious ceremonies, the pursuit of naturalization revealed social relationships of Italians in the city at this time. At first, unable to find their own countrymen who could serve as sponsors, Italians turned to other neighbors and friends, and tended to file for naturalization in the state courts of Pennsylvania. From the first case in 1794 through 1807, of 22 petitioners from Italy, 12 were filed in the state court, 3 in the federal court, 4 in the Mayor's Court, and 3 in the 2 other city courts, with Anglo-Saxon names, if any were listed at all, given for the vouchers. Thus, Joseph Ricardo is listed in 1794, with James Miller swearing the oath on behalf of the petitioner, and Joseph Marabello is listed in 1796, with no witness named.

From early in the nineteenth century, however, the pursuit of naturalization revealed more relationships of Italians with one another. Prior arrivals from Italy increasingly served as witnesses in naturalization proceedings to help later immigrants attain citizenship. Twelve years after his own naturalization, for example, Marabello served as a witness on behalf of Peter Bettini in 1808. Some individuals made a regular practice of being witnesses. In 1804, in the first case involving an Italian to appear as an applicant in the Court of Quarter Sessions, the petition of Dominic Morosi was supported by Secondo Bosio as the witness. Acting in that capacity in six separate cases, Bosio was a frequent witness in naturalization proceedings in subsequent years. In fact, Bosio served as a witness in five cases before he himself became a citizen in 1824. But even after other Italians were available, some individuals still found witnesses outside of their own group. Bosio used John Wilson as the voucher for his own naturalization.

Marriages and naturalizations sometimes linked Corsica and Genoa. Declarations of Intention filed in city courts—first by Pascal Luciani in 1817, then by John Luciana (*sic*) in 1823, and finally by Paschal Luciani in 1827, all natives of Corsica—each gave France as the allegiance being recanted. In 1824, Giovanni Luciani married Sara Flanigan, with Giacomo Antonio Ambrosi as a witness. The latter, as James Anthony Ambrosi, had been married four years earlier at St. Joseph's Church with Hyacinth DeAngeli, about whom we shall soon learn more, as a witness. Although natives of Corsica with political allegiance to France, members of the Luciani family maintained friendships with mainland Genoese.

The Luciani family also established itself in the field of public transportation in Philadelphia. In 1837, P. Luciani placed a petition before the City Councils asking permission for a suitable crossing at Eighth and Market Streets for a proposed railroad line to Fairmount. Although deferred at the time, the petition must have been granted eventually, for in the following year an advertisement in the *Public Ledger* described the Franklin Line of Pleasure Cars, from

Market Street to Fairmount, with its superintendent identified as A. R. Luciani.[11]

Another constellation of relationships revolved around Philip Pittaluga. It began with Giacinto DeAngeli (sometimes also identified as Hyacinth DeAngeli), born in Vico on the island of Corsica in 1787. Having migrated from Leghorn, DeAngeli arrived in Philadelphia in October 1816. He was naturalized in the Court of Quarter Sessions on May 6, 1826, with Bosio as his voucher. On the same day, DeAngeli served as voucher for the naturalization of John M. Togno, another Corsican, in the Court of Common Pleas. In 1829, DeAngeli served as the witness for another petitioner, the previously mentioned Philip Pittaluga. Born in the province of Genoa about 1790, Pittaluga had migrated from Bordeaux, France, and arrived at Philadelphia in March 1820, on the ship *Hunter* (listed under the name "Peterluga" in port records). Pittaluga was traveling as the personal secretary of Godfrey Deabette (or Deabatte), who came with his wife and two children as the Sardinian Consul to the United States.[12] Pittaluga married Adelaide Tasca (identified in parish records as Boreale Tasca), with Hyacinth DeAngeli, Lazarus Rebola, Mary DeAngeli, and Anna Rebolla as witnesses at St. Augustine's in May 1825. When Pittaluga was naturalized in 1829, he gave Italy as his native country and the King of Sardinia as his previous allegiance. (Claudio Pittaluga, possibly Philip's brother, had given Marseilles, France, as his place of origin when he became a U.S. citizen in 1827.) Philip Pittaluga, like Bosio, also served repeatedly as a witness for naturalization petitioners in later years.

At this point another piece reaffirmed the significance of an already familiar location. In five cases involving Pittaluga as voucher between 1829 and 1832, petitioners Dominic, James, Joseph, and Augustus Zanone and Gian Battista Boggiano also gave Genoa and Chiavari, but the latter two specifically provided Santa Maria di Prato as their place of origin. (A letter of administration on the estate of an earlier James Zanoni, who had died in 1821, linked him as a recipient of mortgage payments on property that had been previously owned by Jacob Meretti (*sic*), most likely the same native of Santa Maria di Prato who had submitted a declaration of intention in 1815.)[13] Although sometimes even given as "St. Maria depradt [*sic*]" in Sardinia, the persistent web of interpersonal ties that began with what was identified as Santa Maria di Prato confirmed that Prato and Sopra la Croce were the twin sources of the first visible migration chain between Italy and Philadelphia.

Whether in religious ceremonies or secular events, after their arrival in Philadelphia, although sometimes nurtured by common origins, Italians found a new need to come together in sustained interaction and assistance. In previous years, Italian musicians had passed through, but they left the city in search of audiences in other locations, or had come merely as transient visitors intending to return to their homeland, while only a few merchants had taken up residence and integrated themselves into the broader community. When Antonio Poggi and his companions on the *Tuyphena* arrived in 1800, they found only a handful of Italians, although some were well situated within the life of the city. But with the new century, they became part of a different experience. By informal association and cooperation, these Italians took the initial steps toward establishing the immigrant community that later emerged in the city.

From 1800 on, new arrivals found a small but growing network of permanent residents among the Italians already in Philadelphia. Vitalli, Mussi, and Marabello were well along in pursuit of their own economic endeavors. Among others, after arriving about 1793, by the end of the century, Antonio Maggi was a merchant on Third Street near German Street.[14] Francis Molinari was another prosperous resident of the city. At his death about 1802, Molinari's personal possessions included eighteen Windsor chairs, a walnut table, two large pine tables, two small pine tables, sixteen pictures, ironware, brass pieces, pewter, guns, clothing, animals, and liquor. Together with $400 owed him, he left his wife Martha an estate valued at more than $1,125, a substantial sum for the time. His account books also listed amounts paid to other Italians in the city, such as A. Muraglia and Vincent Ghirardini.[15]

Secondo Bosio: Largo al Factotum—and Others

One of the most interesting and colorful individuals of this period was the ubiquitous Secondo Bosio, identified sometimes simply as a carriage keeper of Southwark, but who was actually much more. He represented a certain type, a real-life factotum, as a result of how he served others around him. Bosio had been in Philadelphia since

1795, if not earlier, and during the next thirty years he functioned in various ways at the center of Italian life in his adopted city. At the same time, Bosio moved through a series of occupations and residential locations in a pattern that suggests a measure of instability in the material circumstances of Italians. In 1795, for example, Bosio was an innkeeper in the 100 block of South Third Street, near Lombard. One of his lodgers was Pietro Stagi, the stonecarver and art dealer from Carrara and Leghorn.[16] His presence from 1795 to 1799 raises the possibility that Bosio's inn already served as a boardinghouse for Italians. By 1800, Bosio was keeper of a livery stable at 100 South Street, on the Southwark District side of the street.[17]

The importance of Bosio for other Italians is indicated by his frequent role as a witness or sponsor for religious and secular occasions over the years. In 1800, Bosio served as godfather at the baptism of Joseph Marchi at Holy Trinity Church, and two years later he was administrator of the Molinari estate. As previously noted, he also acted as a witness in naturalization proceedings for at least six of his countrymen: Dominic Morosi (1804), Antonio Poggi (1807), Francis Travelli (1808), Antonio Maggi (1808), Stephano Pichetti (1818), and Giacinto DeAngeli (1826). And despite his role as voucher for his countrymen, it is ironic that when Bosio filed his own Petition for Naturalization he did not use another Italian as a witness for himself, but someone named John Wilson.[18]

In the course of his lifetime, Bosio pursued various economic opportunities ranging from ordinary to exotic ventures. As early as 1800, at 144 Cedar (or South) Street, an establishment identified by the sign of the Two Brother Sailors, Bosio exhibited an 11-foot-high ostrich that had recently been imported by schooner from Africa. Astutely relying upon information by experts in natural history, and using some type of sign, Bosio advertised the bird as the most voracious animal, with the ability to swallow stones, brass, wood, iron, and leather as easily as vegetables, strong enough to carry two men on its back, and capable of a faster running speed than any four-legged creature. Its feathers supposedly not only surpassed any other species of bird in beauty, but also were preferred to all others for use in women's dresses.[19]

About the same time as the ostrich show, Bosio also advertised an "ice cream house" in Germantown that was possibly the first such establishment in the Philadelphia area. Early writers claimed that local residents had no knowledge of ice cream before Bosio introduced it in 1800. (This is probably only partly correct; Pelosi had advertised his "iced creams" at the Pennsylvania Coffee House as early as 1785.) In a public notice in July 1800, Bosio announced the opening of his ice cream house at 59 South Fifth Street, across from the Spread Eagle Tavern. Although the extent of his success as a forerunner of modern advertising remains unclear, Bosio was one of the earliest "Italian confectioners" to provide sweet new treats for the tastes of Philadelphians.[20]

By 1813, Bosio was still a tavern proprietor at 144 Cedar Street, but he was listed later in city directories simply as a gentleman at the same address. Toward the end of his life, he lived in a boardinghouse operated by Margaret Sibbet on the northwest corner of Fifth and Spruce Streets and again engaged in somewhat unusual financial pursuits by his ownership of a perpetual motion machine that he sold for $13.50. Bosio, who owned two musical organs and two parrots as well, may have been the first Italian street musician in Philadelphia, of the sort that became a common sight in American cities in later years. In his final years, the ostrich and parrots may have also been his last companions, because Anna Bosio, who had been with him in earlier times, appears to have been no longer present.[21]

Bosio died at the boardinghouse after a sore throat and "much debility," with no physician tending him in his final moments in the sixty-fifth year of his life, in December 1826. His friends and acquaintances attended his funeral, which began at the boardinghouse and ended at the cemetery of Holy Trinity Church. He left a modest estate of nearly $850, with the largest item being the "Ostrich Burd" valued at $300, but also other assets, including slightly more than $219 received from public exhibition of the ostrich. Unfortunately, two weeks after the burial of Bosio, the grieving bird followed its master in death, and the carcass was sold for only $45.[22]

From the perspective of the present day, Bosio may appear not merely as enterprising, but eccentric. Despite the bizarre circumstances of his later life, however, he deserves recognition for providing the public with novel amusements and confectionery treats. But Bosio was also an individual of some importance and respect among the Italians of the city in the early part of the century. Beyond simply showing his stature among his countrymen, his activities reveal an increasing interconnectedness in the lives of Italians in Philadelphia.

By the time of Bosio's death, other Italians had established themselves in the economy and social life of the city in more conventional
ways. Gaspar Deabbate, recorded as Godfrey Deabette among the passengers of the ship *Hunter* when he arrived in 1820, was prominently
engaged at 219 Spruce Street as the first Sardinian Consul General
to serve in the city. He held that post until late 1825, when he was
succeeded by Ignacio Vincenzo Cavaradossy. Although little other information exists about him, we do know that Deabbate was accorded
membership in the American Philosophical Society in January 1823.[23]
    At a more modest level, several confectioners presaged the occupa-
tional and residential concentration of Italians in later periods. Among
them, Lazarus Rabolla was located at 59 North Third Street and
at 48 High Street, Giacinto DeAngeli was at 264 High Street, and
Andrew Pichetti was at 334 High Street. Nearby, at 398 High Street,
Francis Pisanell provided some portent of the future by working as a
hairdresser. Another confectioner, Zanobi Trabelessi, was located at
Diehl's Court, in the back of 40 Cherry Street. At the same address,
Giovanni Citti worked as a molder of plaster of paris, probably one of
the first of a long line of *figurinai,* statue makers and vendors, among
the Italians of Philadelphia. Jean Baptiste Spargella operated a dry-
goods store at 66 North Second Street. Augustino Carbin (or Carbino)
was proprietor of an oyster house at 267 North Front Street. Farther
from the river, at 206 South Fourth Street, Vito Viti imported Italian
marble, an enterprise that his family would continue for many years to
come. At 44 South Sixth Street, a Corsican, John M. Togno, offered
his services as a teacher of French and Italian. Still farther west of
the rapidly growing city, Angelo Bogia, who had first arrived from the
province of Como in 1804, lived at 144 or 145 South Eighth Street and
worked as a steamboat engineer. These individuals were of course not
simply pursuing a variety of economic choices, but also distributing
themselves by varying degrees of prosperity and success.[24]

Performers: In Streets and Opera Houses

In the early nineteenth century, Italians remained involved in presenting public amusements that continued what diPalma had begun

nearly fifty years earlier. Italians entertained local audiences with levels of skill, ranging from street musician to concert-hall artist, and sometimes employed novel devices. The organ-grinder was often accompanied by "a sickly monkey, the constrained and melancholy antics of which animal were of immense interest to children, who crowded around the organist, and considered him one of the most wonderful men in the world." At other times, he was "accompanied by a woman, who drubbed a tamburine and shook the brasses fixed in its wooden rim until they jingled again, and then passed around the tambourine among the spectators as a fitting article in which to receive their contributions." Female performers sometimes "sang the songs of their native land with husky vigor, making up for the want of melody by excess of force."[25]

Italians also entertained the public in Philadelphia at a loftier level. An Italian singer named Comoglio gave a concert of opera music at the City Hotel in November 1809. Another opera singer, Signor Gaveli, performed at Masonic Hall at about the same time, accompanied by Signor DaCosta. Sometime afterward, the Granellas, a husband-and-wife team, sang and played piano and guitar at the same site. While Signora Granella sang Italian, English, and Spanish pieces, her husband presented a quartet in the form of a dialogue, attempting to separate four voices audibly and distinctly for the audience. Their efforts must have enjoyed some success, for they were later engaged for nightly performances at the Washington Museum.[26]

As Bosio had done with his ostrich, Italian musical performers were also exhibitors of rare and unique objects. In 1812, the panharmonica, designed to make the sounds of an entire orchestra, was exhibited at Masonic Hall by its owner, a certain Mr. Pardi.[27] The attempt to integrate several instruments into one experimental device was a specialty shared by at least one other Italian a few years later. Although the Peale Museum was reputed to depend on its own merit rather than "adventitious novelty," in 1820 it engaged Signor Helene and his "Pandean Band," who performed on five different instruments at the same time. His bizarre arrangement included the Italian viola, Pandean pipes, Chinese bells, Turkish cymbals, and tenor drum, while he also imitated a mockingbird and a canary with his voice. Many years later, a vivid and indeed unforgettable picture described the performance as "a band all by himself":

By straps, hooks and other contrivances, and by eccentric mo-
tions of his mouth, head, arms and legs, he managed to play the
pandean pipes, beat a drum, clash the cymbals, shake the bells,
and strike the triangle. The air was managed by the pipes, and
the accessories were brought in with all the skill of the leader
of an orchestra, who now encourages the violins, represses the
ardor of the wind instruments, coaxes at the right moment the
blasts of the trumpets, and after a series of piano passages come
to the *ensemble* for the grand crash.[28]

While the eclectic manner of the musical presentation was even
matched by ethnic pluralism in his choice of instruments, it was
not enough. The engagement lasted only a few nights. When Helene
returned in the following year, a few performances were enough to
satisfy any further desire that Philadelphians may have had for this
musical oddity.

The Pardi name, however, remained on the musical scene in the city
for some time. In 1818, a harpist and singer, Madame Pardi, described
as "late from Rome," gave concerts at Masonic Hall, assisted by
her husband, J. Pardi, and brother-in-law, A. Pardi. Sung in English,
French, and Italian, the program was represented as an attempt to
introduce classical music through pieces by Mozart, Rossini, and
others. One can surmise that either male performer identified in this
case may have been the earlier proprietor of the panharmonica. Two
decades later, in his celebrated diary, Sidney George Fisher noted
hearing Miss Pardi, the "Italian harpist," whom he described as "a
young & pretty girl [who] sings very sweetly" at parties in the homes
of such prominent families as the Biddles and the Jacksons. Again, we
can only speculate whether Madame Pardi and Miss Pardi were the
same person.[29]

Although names and aspects of the performances suggest origins in
Italy, not enough is known about some others to conclude that they
were Italian. In May 1815, for example, John Scotti and his company presented an extravagant ball at Vauxhall Gardens to celebrate
General Andrew Jackson's victory in the Battle of New Orleans. Decorating the ballroom with 6,000 lamps, the managers tried to create
a festival with the appearance of an Italian *ridotto*. Scotti declared
that his ice creams were "prepared according to the Italian method,"
suggesting the "water ice" that would later be known as "Roman

punch." But because not much more is known about Scotti, his origins remain uncertain.[30]

Similarly, playing a pedal harp as well as singing, and accompanied by a female singer and a full band, Signor Pucci gave at least two concerts in the city. Alleging to have been the "master of the royal family, Lisbon," his debut in Philadelphia was unsuccessful, which Pucci attributed to his being unknown to local audiences. In an advertisement for his next performance, Pucci declared that he had the support of the first families of the city and that he hoped for greater success. Because nothing else is known about Pucci, his origins too are unclear. Moreover, claims such as having been a "master of the royal family, Lisbon" could easily have been exaggerations if not outright deceptions, and they remain dubious. But whatever they really were, these performers believed that the credibility and the reception of their musical talents by the public would be enhanced if they presented themselves as Italians.[31]

As in the previous century, itinerant musicians gave a few performances before going elsewhere, but some others now became permanent residents of Philadelphia. Carusi was among the names of music professors listed as members of the Musical Fund Society, as well as for two French horn players and a clarinetist in concerts at Masonic Hall in 1812. J. Carusi, a clarinetist, accompanied two singers who had only arrived "lately from Italy" in September 1815. While one was identified as Signor Larenzani, the other had a more interesting name, Signor Chiavere, perhaps signifying a place of origin shared with other recent arrivals from Italy. In 1817, Signor G. Carusi was a composer, music store proprietor, and professor of music at 243 Arch Street; two years later he was at 31 North Sixth Street.[32]

Some Italian musicians were more than performers. Filippo Traetta, born in Venice in 1777 the son of well-known composer Tommaso Traetta of Bitonto, near Bari, had an adventurous early life. After studying in Venice and Naples, he reportedly became a soldier in a patriotic cause. Captured and imprisoned for six months, he was said to have escaped, before coming to America in 1799. Two years later, with two partners, Traetta opened a conservatory in Boston, with himself in charge of the voice program. In Boston and New York, he composed vocal exercises, cantatas, and an opera, then managed an acting troupe in Virginia. About 1828, Traetta moved to Philadelphia, founded a new conservatory, and, over the next twenty-five years, composed a vast number of oratorios, cantatas, and instrumental and vocal quartets, trios, and duets. He also wrote songs, several books on singing, and a general introduction to the art and science of music. Traetta remained a voice teacher and an active director of his American Conservatorio until his death at the age of seventy-eight in January 1854. His obituary invited friends and Masonic brethren to attend his funeral and burial at the Odd Fellows Cemetery of the city.[33]

In their native country, as in Traetta's case, some Italian musicians became involved in political matters that led them to migrate to America. In a public announcement in late 1824 that he had "just arrived from Italy," Giacomo Sega offered guitar lessons "on the approved principles of the Carulli, of Italy" at his studio at the southeast corner of Fifth and Lombard Streets. Sega, who taught Italian at 293 Walnut Street in 1833, was also an author and a poet. The title of one work, *Componimenti poetici d'un italiano profugo in America*, published in Philadelphia in 1829, identified its author as a fugitive, or refugee. In 1830, Sega published two other books, *An Essay on Duelling* and *The Punishment of Death,* which reflected his interest in political issues. He also provoked the animosity of the famed and colorful librettist Lorenzo DaPonte, who made a caustic suggestion to Sega regarding a rope: "I should advise this supreme poet to use one at once."[34] Along with DaPonte's comments, the titles of Sega's works indicate that their author deserves more attention from local historians.

Another figure of Italian origin with a similar involvement in political and military events was identified only by his surname: Ramati. In November 1825, during what was characterized as a relatively dull year for music matters, a concert was given at the Musical Fund Hall for the benefit of Signor Ramati, "a meritorious Italian officer who fought under Mina, in Catalonia, in the cause of liberty . . . [and who had] . . . lately fled from the prisons of Spain and landed on our shores destitute." Ramati may have been not only a brave soldier but also a capable musician who played the guitar on this program.[35]

Lorenzo DaPonte, although a frequent visitor who lived only a short time in the city, where his experiences consistently turned into problems, could also be included among the early Italians in Philadelphia. He first arrived in America at the Port of Philadelphia in June 1805, but almost immediately relocated to New York City. During 1811–18, while living in Sunbury, Pennsylvania, DaPonte made frequent trips for business matters to Philadelphia. In his *Memoirs,* he presented a detailed account of his misfortunes with Lawrence Astolfi.[36] After a series of business problems in Sunbury, DaPonte returned to Philadelphia in August 1818 and in the next year was listed in the city directory as a teacher of French living at 27 Powell Street.[37] He intended to settle with his family in Philadelphia and "spread the language and literature of my country, as I had done in New York." After he encountered Luigi Pittori, a young man who had come to Philadelphia with some of "the principal treasures of Italian literature," DaPonte sought the cooperation of literary figures and directors of the public library to buy the collection. Although he claimed to have the support of a prominent merchant and library trustee, DaPonte was informed that there were no funds available for the books. When further efforts failed, DaPonte concluded: "Philadelphia either did not care, or else was not able to appreciate it at its true worth," but he later succeeded in finding a buyer in New York City.[38]

With the failure of the project, DaPonte planned to return to New York City, but before he left Philadelphia he became ensnared in a dispute with the merchant Giuseppe Mussi that would persist over many subsequent years. The case concerned property once owned by John Grahl, DaPonte's father-in-law, in the Black Creek area of the Susquehanna River valley. After a number of talks with Mussi, DaPonte declared that he had not sufficiently fathomed "either his shrewdness, his rascality, or his rapacity."[39] While most of this section of his memoirs has been lost, enough exists to indicate that his experiences in Philadelphia had generally unpleasant results. Although he once wanted to make Philadelphia his permanent home, it proved to be an inhospitable choice, and in 1819, with great relief, DaPonte returned to New York City, where he lived for the rest of his life.[40]

In New York, DaPonte was apparently more successful in implementing his plan to disseminate Italian literature and culture than he had been in Philadelphia. For his writings and his influence on students, DaPonte is regarded as an important early figure in Italian studies. During this phase of his life, he also acquainted Americans with his original culture by promoting Italian opera, which also brought him back to Philadelphia temporarily. At the age of eighty-three, as the troupe's new manager, he engaged the Montresor troupe at the Chestnut Street Theatre for twenty-four performances in January 1833. However, he again became involved in conflicts that led to his departure from the company. By the fall of the same year, DaPonte was manager of the Rivafinoli troupe, which he brought to Philadelphia for fifteen performances, until a shortage of funds again led to his removal as manager.[41]

DaPonte's years in Philadelphia had been limited to a relatively short span in which his often ambitious plans produced more failure and frustration than success. Yet these events, and his caustic relations with Sega, Astolfi, and Mussi, not only reveal some aspects of DaPonte's own character but also provide another glimpse of Italians in the city—in particular, some of the tensions and conflicts that existed at this time that otherwise might have remained unnoticed and unknown.

Impresarios and Pleasure Gardens

In their efforts to entertain the public, Italians did not restrict their endeavors to music, but also provided amusements of another sort. In 1811, Lewis Chiappi operated the Roman Museum on Market Street just above Fourth, which offered wax exhibitions of such historical figures as Washington and Cornwallis, as well as local characters, and even models of animals, such as a whale that had been caught near Trenton, New Jersey. Similarly, in 1818 a certain Mr. Maffei exhibited at Washington Hall what he described as "a Picturesque and Metamorphosis Theatre" that involved figures two feet tall. Although further details are lacking, Maffei's exhibition may have introduced traditional Italian puppet theater to the Philadelphia public.[42]

The achievements of others were relatively minor compared with the career of Lawrence Astolfi, who was a formidable presence on the theater scene of his time, and DaPonte's occasional adversary. A native of Corsica, Astolfi had arrived in the United States perhaps at the end of the previous century. In October 1809, after two years in Pennsylvania, he petitioned for citizenship, with the seemingly omnipresent Secondo Bosio, not surprisingly, as his witness. Astolfi first worked as a confectioner and a distiller at an establishment at 136 Market Street. By 1812, when he served as the voucher for the naturalization of Peter Manfridi (or Manfredi), Astolfi began to assume an influential role among other Italians.[43]

After a modest beginning, Astolfi achieved considerable success in his business ventures. In his memoirs, DaPonte noted that Astolfi "sold liqueurs and candies in the most frequented center of Philadelphia," but this observation must have been made at an early point.[44] While continuing to operate this business, Astolfi also "indulged in excitement and expected profit as proprietor of a place of public resort." In July 1813, he opened the Summer Theatre at the Columbian Garden, on the north side of Market Street between Thirteenth Street and Centre Square, with "The Imaginary Sick Man," a pantomime program performed by the Manfredi Company. With Astolfi's support, the Manfredi Company was intended to be a permanent part of the local scene.[45]

Astolfi developed the Columbian Garden as a place where Philadelphians, after paying 50 cents for admission, descended into a hollow and entered an amusement park. The public enjoyed this popular place of recreation from the spring months until early October, when it closed for the winter. Astolfi maintained his summer garden as a place of resort and refreshment, but without theatrical productions, until 1816, when he decided to compete with the Vauxhall, the leading theater of the city. In June he announced:

> The Columbian Garden, the first established in this city, stands still—a monument of public patronage. Its central situation, and the circumscription of its local arrangements, warrant both the recreation it is capable of affording, and the decency which should reign wherever the people should meet to enjoy the honest and legitimate pleasures of springs and summers.

On the same day these remarks were published, the new Columbian Garden was opened with great illumination provided by 2,500 lamps. What Astolfi meant by his cryptic message was that the Columbian Garden would again have a program of concerts, theater, performers, and other forms of entertainment.[46]

By 1820, Astolfi was no longer manager of the Columbian Garden, which had changed its name to the Tivoli Garden but continued as a place for song and music. Astolfi now turned his interest to the Olympic Theatre, the scene of the most important theatrical productions in the city since its founding in 1812. Astolfi and some prominent Philadelphians had purchased the Olympic in 1818.[47]

While the personal character of most Italians is difficult to discern for this period, Astolfi was an exception, partly because of unpleasant incidents and disagreements with others that left impressions of him. DaPonte had once regarded Astolfi as "the best man in the world" and declared that popular opinion generally regarded him as "the most honest of men, generous, and a charitable Christian"; this description and judgment had obviously changed by the time DaPonte described him as "a hypocrite who cheated me cruelly."[48]

A later writer, who described Astolfi as "quite a character," summarized his life and career: "His confectionery establishment did a good business, and the garden yielded something handsome to his yearly income. He was a man of warm feelings, and he had his enemies." These comments referred to a suit involving Joseph Chiappi, a wax museum proprietor in New York City and possibly related to Lewis Chiappi of the Roman Museum in Philadelphia. Chiappi, who depicted Astolfi by a wax figure of an organ-grinder with hat extended in his hand soliciting money from two other Italians, described the scene thus: "This is a representation of Mr. Lawrence Astolfi, of Philadelphia, following his business as he did when he first came to this country." The offended Astolfi sued Chiappi for libel, won a judgment of $1,900 from a court in New York, then faded from public view, perhaps returning to Italy.[49] This incident, like the Mussi-DaPonte affair of 1821, clearly revealed again that relations among Italians during these years were not marked solely by harmony and cooperation. But the episode also confirms the presence of the organ-grinder among Italians in American cities in the early nineteenth century.

Joseph Diaccheri came to the United States about the beginning of the nineteenth century and became another prominent figure in the field of public entertainment. In Philadelphia he found a wife and started a family. The sacramental records of St. Augustine's recorded the birth of Teresa in January 1810, baptized in April of the same year, as a daughter of Joseph Diaccheri and Anna Hevas. When he became a citizen in 1811, his name was listed in the court records as Joseph Diaker. He probably was a part of the Corsican-Genoese group within the Italian population of the city.[50]

Diaccheri's first commercial venture came when he took over the Philadelphia Garden on the south side of Race Street near Ninth Street, which had been established in April 1813 by Joseph LeTourno as a place for refreshments but not for concerts or entertainment performances. When LeTourno opened the Camden Vauxhall, the Philadelphia Garden was leased to Diaccheri in 1818. While it is not clear how successful he had been in this initial venture, Diaccheri soon opened his own Vauxhall in Philadelphia in April 1825. At this time, the city directory listed Joseph Diackery as a confectioner at 97 North Third Street.[51]

The programs at the Vauxhall clarify what it meant to be a confectioner in Philadelphia in the early nineteenth century. Diaccheri provided refreshments and recreation at the Vauxhall, which he improved by building the Lafayette Retreat, located at the center of the property and surrounded by flowers. Visitors could satisfy their appetites with items that included ice cream, fruit, liquor, and turtle soup. Although he had not originally planned to include amusements, Diaccheri illuminated the gardens once a week and provided orchestra music for the public. On these evenings, Diaccheri at first charged no admission, but their popularity soon forced a change of policy. In June 1825, he announced that because "the Garden was so infested by boys and small girls" on the previous evening of illumination, he had to begin charging 12½ cents, although this charge could be redeemed at the bar and children accompanied by parents were admitted free. This device was probably intended to restrict the admission of children, since they could not redeem the cost of their tickets by purchasing anything at the bar. Either Diaccheri was dealing early with the problem of juvenile rowdiness that would eventually plague American cities, or he believed that adults were more likely to spend the money that would make his establishment profitable. Along with Astolfi, and individuals such as Pelosi in the previous century, Diaccheri exemplified an early version of Italian involvement in the providing of food, amusement, entertainment, and recreation for the public.[52]

Although not quite as grandly as Astolfi and Diaccheri, other Italians followed similar pursuits. In April 1824, Vincent Chirico opened Washington Gardens, on a corner of Hamilton Street near the Fairmount Waterworks, where he offered cakes, fruit, and ice cream.[53] An even more modest food vendor was the "lemonade man," who announced himself with a sharp cry of "limonad" in a decidedly foreign accent. Usually an Italian or a Frenchman, and with a reservoir strapped to his back and a tube curved around to a faucet in front, the "lemonade man" dispensed his beverage into glasses he carried with him.[54]

While even the most successful enterprises eventually disappeared, they left a legacy to Philadelphia. From the humble activities of confectioners, "lemonade men," and food vendors like Chirico, to the grander pleasure gardens of Astolfi and Diaccheri, one product emerged and remained a great favorite with the public. Before the nineteenth century, although some version of it had been available at Pelosi's tavern, ice cream was a rare and unfamiliar commodity for most Philadelphians. In the early 1800s, Bosio, Chirico, and other confectioners responded to the demand for this delightful treat, but the public garden of summer months was the place where ice cream became widely known to the public. Similarly, the Italian restaurant that later became a popular feature on the local scene also had its roots in the confectioners and ice cream parlors of these early years.

Artistic Images and Monuments

The most enduring and visible mark made by Italians as residents of Philadelphia in the early nineteenth century probably came from a group of talented artists. They represented a variety of specialized talents and applications as portrait painters, miniaturists, sculptors, and stone workers, as well as teachers of these skills. While their artistic success and recognition is worth noting, other aspects of their lives, such as their shared regional origins, their concentration in a particular occupational niche, and above all else the manner and extent to which they interacted with one another, also made them significant for later stages of immigrant experience.

Although information for some individuals is scant and in other cases almost entirely lost, something of their lives can be recaptured. John Marras, an Italian miniaturist painter, arrived with copies of fine pictures from Italy and opened a studio at 180 Spruce Street in December 1808, but virtually nothing else is known about him.[55] In 1813, from his shop at 185 South Fourth Street below St. Peter's churchyard, G. Merlini advertised that he could carve "all kinds of statues, ornamental, etc. in any wood that might be preferred" and offered for sale "the original bust of a distinguished American statesman, its striking likeness precluding the necessity of mentioning his name." Although he claimed "the artist's work will speak for itself," nothing more remains of the subject of this carving or of Merlini the artist carver.[56]

Even when a little more is known, the record often remains hazy. Anthony Francis Terriggi, another miniaturist and chalk artist, came to America about 1820 and by 1826 had exhibited at the Pennsylvania Academy. He had a Philadelphia address in 1824, but his residence for other years is unknown. In 1824, he also exhibited a miniature portrait of the Countess Charlotte de Survilliers (Charlotte Bonaparte).[57] After working from 1819 to 1828 in Rome, Giacinto Riboni, a native of Piacenza, surfaced in Philadelphia in 1835. A portrait and figure painter, he petitioned the City Councils to allow him use of Independence Hall free of charge to exhibit a painting emblematic of justice. The catalogs of the Artists' Fund Society listed works by Riboni during the period 1835–38, including a portrait of Dr. Joseph Togno, a leading patron of the arts among Italians. Although Riboni was said to have died in 1838, the Historical Society of Pennsylvania owned a portrait signed and dated in 1839, in addition to other paintings by him.[58]

Italian artists who were unable to find sufficient support for their work sometimes abandoned Philadelphia, but not all would face as unfortunate an end as Cerracchi at the guillotine. After working in New York City, a stipple engraver, Michele Pekenino (as his name was given), came to Philadelphia around 1820 and not long afterward sold a portrait to raise money to allow him to return to Italy.[59] Other artists, who had greater success elsewhere, were residents of Philadelphia only briefly. Anthony Meucci, a portrait, miniature, and figure painter from Rome, arrived in America with his wife, Nina, in 1818 and lived in New Orleans, Charleston, New York City, and Salem, Massachusetts. By 1824, they resided at a boardinghouse at 241 Market Street in Philadelphia. In the winter of 1826–27, Meucci had returned to New Orleans as a scenery painter for the theater.[60]

While some chose secular and political subjects, other artists produced religious works. In 1836, the thirty-one-year-old Joseph Uberti contributed designs for the newly decorated St. Augustine's Church. His skill enabled him to continue his career in the city with some success. By 1850, he lived in Southwark with his English-born wife, Mary, and owned property valued at $3,500. Three years later, Uberti did frescoes on the interior walls and ceiling at St. John the Evangelist Church on Thirteenth Street, probably on the same surfaces that Nicola Monachesi had worked about twenty years earlier.[61]

While many were truly artists in any sense of the term, other individuals are perhaps more accurately identified in other ways. Louis

Stegagnini, or Stegnani, who came to Philadelphia about 1820, was an ornamental sculptor, a marble mason, or a stonecarver, and perhaps more of an artisan than an artist. He made monuments, urns, vases, and mantelpieces during a career that lasted at least until 1840. In earlier years, his workshop was in North Alley, between Fifth and Sixth Streets; later he operated a marbleyard at the southeast corner of Ninth and Sansom Streets.[62]

Much of the record of these lives has been lost, with only fragments of their days in Philadelphia remaining. Little or nothing more is known of Marras, Merlini, Terriggi, Riboni, Pekenino, Meucci, Uberti, and Stegagnini. Because of the paucity of information, the lives of these artists may raise more questions than they answer. For others, not only is more known, but their work endured longer and left a clearer record of their presence. Although these artists had an impact on their new location, the precise pattern varied.

When Enrico Causici arrived in Philadelphia in November 1816, he claimed to have been a student of Antonio Canova, the foremost neoclassical sculptor in Rome, but some were skeptical. As Cerrachi before him, Causici contributed to the further development of public monumental sculpture. He first came in search of financial support for a model of a proposed statue of George Washington on horseback intended for the Academy of Fine Arts. If approved, the statue would be placed in the potter's field, which was soon to be renamed as Washington Square. During the brief time he lived at 52 South Fifth Street, while he waited in vain for subscriptions to finance his plan, Causici prepared alabaster models for the proposed statue. When he realized that support was not coming, he left for New York, where the corporation of that city backed his project. He completed the statue, which was finally unveiled in a New York City park in July 1826.[63]

Causici later became involved with public projects in other American cities. He executed some of the stonecarving for the U.S. Capitol building in Washington, D.C., but his greatest success was probably a full-length statue for the monument to the first President in Baltimore. Consisting of three separate pieces wrought from a single marble block, this work was 16 feet high and weighed 36 tons.[64] But Causici's success was achieved elsewhere, after he failed to win support and recognition in Philadelphia. Painters, sculptors, musicians, and writers often migrated from city to city until they attained artistic success and financial security. Perhaps Causici's case indicates that the public in

Philadelphia had demanding standards, even for talented artists who eventually succeeded in other places. But it also reveals something about what the city lost in such instances.

While Causici had to leave, other artists, such as the Persico brothers, Luigi and Gennaro, reached their goals at least partly and left a stronger imprint on Philadelphia. Born in Naples, Luigi Persico, who came to Philadelphia in 1818 but spent time in Lancaster and Harrisburg as well, found success quickly. In 1824, he completed a bust of Lafayette that, after being shown at the Philadelphia Atheneum, decorated a dinner in honor of Lafayette's visit to the city. When the students of Dr. Nathaniel Chapman, a distinguished local physician and later the first president of the American Medical Association, sought to honor him, they hired Persico to sculpt a bust of their mentor.[65]

Persico's early achievements led to opportunity and recognition elsewhere. In 1825, he was commissioned to produce several marble sculptures, representing "War" and "Peace" for the East Portico of the Capitol building in Washington and to design a Liberty head coin for the U.S. Mint. In later years, Persico became well known for his marble sculptures of local patrons. His work was exhibited at the Boston Atheneum and at the Artists' Fund Society of Philadelphia. He is supposed to have spent his final years in Europe and died in Marseilles in 1860.[66]

Gennaro (or Gennarino) Persico came from Naples about 1820 and first worked in Lancaster, then Reading and Philadelphia. In 1822, he was a drawing master and miniature painter residing at 86 Chestnut Street. After modest success with chalk and crayon drawing, Gennaro married the daughter of a Reading banker in 1823. Two years later, he was living at 46 South Sixth Street, perhaps in the same house as his brother. Respected by his peers and the general public, Persico was the subject of a miniature portrait by George Catlin, the Pennsylvanian who became the first important painter of American Indians. Persico was invited as a guest to a Wistar Party, that exclusive gathering of distinguished Philadelphians, by Chief Justice William Tilghman of the Supreme Court of Pennsylvania in March 1825.[67]

Gennaro Persico's life eventually led him away from Philadelphia. In the 1830s, he directed an "English and French academy for young ladies" in Richmond, Virginia, and he also served as a vestryman of an Episcopal church. After the death of his wife in 1842, Persico continued to operate the school until it failed, and then returned to

Naples. In 1852, Persico went again to Richmond, where he resumed work as an artist for a few more years. It was believed that he died at sea about 1859.[68]

Beyond the intrinsic value of their own work, the greater significance of the Persico brothers, Causici, and others may have been their influence on the increasing number of Americans who were choosing Italy as the place to study sculpture.[69]

Pietro Ancora and Nicola Monachesi

The most successful Italians in the field of art in Philadelphia, however, may have been two painters, Pietro Ancora and Nicola Monachesi, who made important but quite different contributions. Arriving earlier and working longer than any other resident Italian artist of the period, Ancora came from Rome in 1800, when he was about twenty years old. By 1803, he had opened a drawing academy at the northeast corner of Fifth and Walnut Streets, which was relocated several times in later years. Ancora lived at 53 South Fifth Street from 1807 to 1810, when he filed a petition for naturalization. For the next three years he continued his work at 158 Lombard Street, then at 240 or 246 South Seventh Street, a period interrupted by the tragedy of a stillborn child in December 1811. By 1817, Ancora had moved to 79 South Fifth Street.[70]

Ancora's talents as an artist may have been surpassed by his role as an instructor and an importer and dealer of art. His influence is readily reflected by such pupils as John Neagle, who received his first art instruction in Ancora's studio and later became the foremost portrait painter in Philadelphia. By 1819, Ancora and Charles Bell, a local bookseller, were partners and among the first dealers to import and exhibit paintings from Europe before auctioning them at their gallery at 175 Chestnut Street. Six years later, Ancora was listed in the city directory simply as a drawing master again, at 145 Pine Street.[71]

About forty years after his death, it was alleged that Ancora had been content with the "sure patronage of his school for drawing and painting," without ever executing any paintings that appeared in the prestigious annual exhibitions of the Pennsylvania Academy of the

Fine Arts and Artists' Fund Society.[72] But the works under his name in its published catalogs have led art historians to conclude that Ancora exhibited at the academy between 1829 and 1843.[73]

Ancora's influence on the local art scene sometimes took still other forms. In March 1828, a letter to the director of the Pennsylvania Academy of the Fine Arts signed by twenty-seven local artists demanded greater rights and privileges in regard to exhibitions at the famed institution. Asking that an advisory council of artists be formed, the signers criticized the academy for failing to execute its own resolutions, particularly in the presenting of premiums and awards. The signers included such prominent artists as Thomas Birch, Bass Otis, James Peale Jr., and John Haviland, but also Pietro Ancora and Gennaro Persico. In 1837, when he sought a position as instructor at Girard College, the city's institution for orphan boys, Ancora provided a letter with many signatures in support of his reputation as an artist and art instructor.[74]

While little is known of his private life, Ancora was married and had at least one daughter, Mary. Her marriage to Edward S. Ratcliffe produced another personal tragedy late in the artist's life when his eight-month-old grandson, Edward S. Ratcliffe Jr., died at Ancora's home in 1842. Two years later, Pietro Ancora himself died at the age of sixty-four. He was buried in the graveyard of Old St. Mary's Church on South Fourth Street, where a marker at that site remained until recent years.[75]

Nicola Monachesi was even more significant than Ancora as a productive artist during this period, but the details of his early life are unfortunately obscured by contradictions. While some sources give the date of his birth as 1795, his declaration of intention, filed in October 1839, listed him as thirty-five years in age, making his year of birth 1804 or 1805. The federal census of 1850 recorded him as forty-five, thus supporting the later year. Biographers have given Tolentino in the Marches region of Italy as his place of birth. Both his declaration of intention and his petition for naturalization five years later identified him as a native of Rome and a subject of the Pope, perhaps because the Marches were part of the Papal States. Before emigrating, Monachesi supposedly studied in Rome at the Accademia di San Luca and achieved early distinction for his painting. While one source claims that Monachesi came to Philadelphia in 1832, another places him already there in 1831. According to naturalization records,

Monachesi arrived at the Port of New York City in October 1832. In a letter dated February 21, 1832, Father John Hughes described an artist from Rome at work on the sanctuary of St. John's Church in Philadelphia who was later identified as Monachesi. He was reported as residing in 1832 at the same address as F. Monachesi, who was possibly his son. But if the 1850 census was correct in giving his age as forty-five, it was more likely that the other Monachesi was a brother rather than a son of Nicola Monachesi.[76]

Despite these inconsistencies pertaining mainly to his younger years, Monachesi's later accomplishments are much clearer. He obtained commissions from well-known local residents, including Stephen Girard, Joseph Bonaparte, and the widow of Benjamin Rush, and he acquired a formidable reputation for works executed for private residences. In 1834, he completed an especially admired ceiling fresco in the mansion of railroad president Matthew Newkirk, depicting Cornelia, the mother of the Gracchi brothers, displaying her jewels to Capuano. This fresco became better known to the public after Newkirk's former home was converted to St. George's Hall. In his diary the frequently critical Sidney George Fisher declared that the beautiful frescoes by Monachesi on the walls and ceilings made the parlors of George Cadwalader's house the most attractive in the entire city.[77]

Monachesi's more public works, however, received even greater recognition. In his letter, Father Hughes, who had been authorized by Bishop Francis P. Kenrick to build a new church in the city, wrote: "An Italian, a Roman artist, is decorating our sanctuary, for the purpose of showing advantageously the power of his pencil, without any expense to us." With his paintings already displayed in other churches, Monachesi offered his work to the new Church of St. John the Evangelist on South Thirteenth Street, his only compensation being a voluntary contribution from the members of its congregation. He decorated this church, which at the time was the cathedral of the Diocese of Philadelphia, with what may have been the first real frescoes—paintings on wet plaster—in the United States.[78]

Monachesi's public endeavors were not restricted to churches but could also be found in secular sites. In the same year as the work on St. John's, William Strickland, the city's foremost architect, employed Monachesi as the artist for the ceiling of the new Merchants Exchange Building. This commission, however, became a source of difficulty both for the artist and for the architect. In a letter to the building committee for the Exchange in 1834, Monachesi disagreed over his fee for a lantern and ceilings. Citing an agreement with Strickland, Monachesi asked for $1,000 as payment for his work. The committee replied that Strickland lacked the authority to make the arrangement and offered only $750.[79]

With his reputation unharmed by these difficulties, and because his talents for turning prosaic places into elegant settings were widely recognized, Monachesi remained in demand with the public. Over an elegant marble mosaic floor, his "glorious painting" (in the words of one historian) of the marriage of Jupiter and Juno for the ceiling helped make Parkinson's an ice cream parlor with no equal in the city and an establishment that "represented refinement *par excellence.*" With some irony, after earlier Italians had introduced ice cream to the city, another Italian elevated its consumption to a public ritual of cultivated taste.[80]

In the late 1830s, Monachesi continued his religious work by collaborating in the remodeling of Old St. Mary's Church. He set gilt stars on a dark-blue background in a fresco on the arched ceiling of the historic church on South Fourth Street. Soon he shifted to a far less sacred subject, the murder of James McCrae, for a large painting in 1841–42, while living at 156 Pine Street, almost directly across the street from Pietro Ancora. Monachesi resumed more religious themes with his decorations of the interior and exterior of Old St. Joseph's when it was renovated in 1844.[81]

With the reconstruction of St. Augustine's Church in 1848, after it had been destroyed during the nativist rioting four years earlier, Monachesi produced what may be his best work. After five months the removal of the scaffolding revealed ceiling and wall frescoes by Monachesi and his assistants that the *Public Ledger* praised as "extremely beautiful." In a splendidly detailed depiction of the Crucifixion, one writer declared: "The figures in all these paintings are beautifully drawn—the shading is most soft and delicate, and the colors more vivid in their brilliancy than we have ever seen." The ceiling panels were filled by scrollwork ornamented by arabesque figures so excellently done that "it is impossible from the floor to distinguish the deception and tell it from real carving."[82] Fifty years later, Monachesi's frescoes and altarpieces for Old St. Joseph's, St. Augustine's, and St. Philip Neri's were still being admired.[83]

Success provided Monachesi with a comfortable material position as well as the respect of art patrons. By mid-century, he lived in New Market Ward, where he owned at least $4,000 worth of property. With Ellen, his Irish-born wife, thirteen years younger than her husband, were their daughters, Giuseppa, fourteen years old; Marian, twelve; and Helen, nine, and four-year-old twin sons, Cola (probably a diminutive of Nicola) and Herbert, all born in Pennsylvania. Three other women, probably maids and servants, completed the Monachesi household.[84]

When he died in 1851 his estate consisted mainly of twenty-four paintings. Despite the property listed in the recent federal census, Monachesi's net assets were valued at only $189. The principal administrator of his will was a familiar figure among Italians, Giacinto DeAngeli, who lived at 43 North Thirteenth Street just above Market Street, very near to the Cathedral of St. John the Evangelist, which Monachesi had decorated twenty years earlier. In the years since his death, most of Monachesi's work has passed away too. The ceilings and walls he decorated have been destroyed with the demolition of the proud private residences they graced. His church frescoes have been covered by renovations of those interiors. One work that has endured the passage of time was a portrait of Lorenzo DaPonte in extreme old age that belonged to a private collector.[85]

Stonecarvers: The Carrara Connection

While Monachesi enjoyed much personal success in Philadelphia, stonecarvers had more consequence for subsequent immigration. The Merchants Exchange, designed by Strickland, provided the first venue for their work. In addition to the interior paintings by Monachesi, other Italians contributed to its sculptural adornments. But one of them, identified only as Signor Fiorelli, carved the lions in Italy before they came to Philadelphia. Those lions still proudly guard the east end of the building. Two Tuscan brothers, Peter and Philip Bardi, natives of Carrara, which has been known for its marble quarries and stonecarvers since ancient times, left a conspicuous mark by their work on the column capitals at the Merchants Exchange. Peter Bardi had achieved previous recognition for a relief sculpture of the biblical

Portrait of Lorenzo DaPonte by Nicola Monachesi. DaPonte sought to promote Italian literature and culture in Philadelphia and New York. (From *Memoirs of Lorenzo DaPonte*, ed. and ann. Arthur Livingston [Philadelphia, 1929])

Joseph as the interpreter of dreams, displayed at the Accademia di Belle Arti of Carrara. The skillful contribution of the Bardi brothers to the Exchange building was recognized by the granting of permission for them to sign their work. The Latin inscription "Petrus et Philipus Bardi de Carraria Fecerunt 1832" remains legible on the band between the fluting of the columns and the Corinthian-style capitals of the portico on Dock Street. Strickland himself toasted the Bardi brothers at a dinner celebrating the placing of the capstone of the Exchange. While little else is known about Philip, Peter Bardi returned to Carrara, where he maintained his reputation for ornamental art and taught at the Accademia.[86]

The link between Carrara and Philadelphia was complicated by the arrival in 1806 of other artists and artisans, beginning with Giuseppe Franzoni, son of an official at the Art Museum of Carrara. Accompanied by Giovanni Andrei, Franzoni first worked on sculptural decorations on the Capitol building in Washington, D.C., then on other projects in Baltimore until his death in April 1815. In the next year, Carlo Franzoni arrived to take up the work begun by his brother, accompanied by a cousin, Francesco Iardella, who later married Giuseppe Franzoni's widow. But the younger Franzoni died about the age of thirty in Washington in 1819. At Andrei's death in 1824, Francesco Iardella succeeded him as the head of the sculptural work on the Capitol, until his own death in early 1831.[87]

During these years, members of the Iardella (or Jardella) and Franzoni families also made their mark as artists in Philadelphia. When Giuseppe Jardella arrived in 1792, he was first engaged by James Traquair, an immigrant Scot and master stonecutter for Strickland and John Haviland, as a stonecarver for the Robert Morris mansion, but the financial failure of its owner abruptly ended the project. Jardella later carved bas-reliefs on John Taylor's dry-goods store, another building by Traquair, at the northeast corner of Tenth and Market Streets, from designs by Latrobe that showed the nature of the business conducted there. While less is known about his work, John Franzoni attained greater recognition than Jardella. In 1810, Franzoni was elected an associate of the newly formed Society of Artists of the Pennsylvania Academy of the Fine Arts, placing him among more renowned individuals in the city.[88]

Jardella sculpted busts of George Washington, Alexander Hamilton, and William Penn, supposedly the first ever cut from Pennsylvania marble. Traquair presented the bust of Penn, perhaps the first to be done of him, to the Pennsylvania Hospital in 1802. Carved stone masks of Tragedy and Comedy, originally intended for the Morris mansion, were later adapted for the front of the Chestnut Street Theatre by Latrobe, its architect. Throughout the early 1800s, Traquair advertised busts of historical figures cut in Pennsylvania from Carrara marble and often by Jardella. After Traquair died in 1811, Jardella began a partnership with Christopher Hocker. But discouraged by the lack of profit from higher forms of art, from this time on, Jardella devoted himself to his work as a stonecutter in the marbleyard located on the south side of Race Street between Sixth and Seventh, until the firm was dissolved in 1817.[89]

The Jardella presence becomes murky at this point. In 1800, Andrew Vardelle appeared in the city directory as a marble and stone carver on Arch Street. In subsequent years, until 1825, directories included Andrew or Andrew B. Jardella, as an engraver, sculptor, or marble engraver, at various addresses. The sacramental records of St. Augustine's recorded the birth and baptism of Andrew Bartholomew Yardella, son of Andrew Yardella and Catharine Pepper, in 1805. Art historians identify Andrew B. Iardella (or Jardella) as a sculptor in the city from 1803 to 1831. A bust of Alexander Hamilton is reported to have been exhibited at the Pennsylvania Academy of the Fine Arts by him in 1811, but it may have been by Giuseppe Jardella. Perhaps two stonecarvers named Iardella, both natives of Carrara, related to each other and to more celebrated namesakes in Washington, worked in Philadelphia during these years.[90]

The significance of stonecarvers like the Jardellas, however, went far beyond whatever personal achievements they had as individuals. They also represented the beginning of a long line of Italians as skilled workers in the building and construction trades in Philadelphia. By their success, they had established an early presence in an occupational niche in which other Italians would follow in great numbers as stonecarvers, cutters, masons, and quarry workers and gain the respect of other Philadelphians for their abilities.

Religious Controversy and the Bogus Priest

Italian musicians, merchants, confectioners, impresarios, and artists provided a cast of colorful characters for the Philadelphia public in the early nineteenth century. Some of them made moderately memorable contributions to local life, but an occasional episode also produced less favorable results that many people would have preferred to forget, if only they could have done so. One such character, as theatrical as any other, was Angelo A. Inglesi, a priest (or at least he claimed to be) who first presented himself as a possible solution to the most serious crisis in the history of Catholicism in Philadelphia, but eventually aggravated it.

When Henry Conwell was appointed Roman Catholic Bishop of Philadelphia in 1820, he inherited a diocese that had been plagued for thirty years by conflicts over parish governance, in particular the rights of trustees to nominate pastors, first at Holy Trinity Church and later at St. Mary's Church. But the problems that had simmered at St. Mary's were about to enter a new phase. Only two days after his arrival, Conwell heard William Hogan, pastor of St. Mary's, deliver a sermon in which he attacked the former administrator of the diocese. During the following week, in response to the sermon and reports on immoral conduct, Conwell attempted to apply some mild sanctions on Hogan. But in his sermon the next Sunday, Hogan attacked the new bishop. Conwell swiftly suspended Hogan from his priestly functions, further antagonizing trustees who supported the pastor. Despite attempts to resolve their differences, which only grew greater after the church itself was closed "against clergy and people," the intransigent Conwell formally excommunicated Hogan in May 1821. Hogan now defended himself by means of pamphlets in which he assailed Conwell and other clergy with what was regarded as "abusive language." During the next three years, matters became far more complicated as the schism widened with vigorously disputed elections of trustees, bitter polemics and physical violence, and efforts to solve the dispute in the courts and state legislature. And as conditions remained at an impasse, Inglesi arrived in the autumn of 1823 as a potential device to ease, if not settle, the situation.[91]

Despite the claim that respectable men in Philadelphia were well acquainted with Inglesi, little about his previous life was actually known. And if more information had been available, Inglesi might have been ignored or removed even more quickly from the conflict at St. Mary's. Although he was at one time identified as a native of Rome, Inglesi was born in Perugia about 1795. He came to Quebec as a member of the Royal Scots Regiment in 1814. Already a subdeacon to the priesthood, he pursued such other occupations as comic actor and wine merchant, and he married a Catholic woman in a ceremony conducted by a Protestant minister. But after four years, Inglesi fled from Canada in considerable debt and presented himself as a priest to Bishop William DuBourg of New Orleans in 1818. In Louisiana, Inglesi's success, which included reporting on America Catholicism to superiors in Rome, was quickly recognized; Dubourg named Inglesi a vicar and sent him to Europe to solicit support for Catholic missions. Arriving at a timely moment in Lyons, he met with Catholics seeking to establish a permanent program of assistance for foreign missions and presided at the founding of the Society for the Propagation of the Faith, reportedly at his own residence in May 1822, perhaps his greatest achievement at this moment. From this point on, as disquieting information that raised doubts about his character reached Lyons, Inglesi's fortunes suddenly fell. Reports about ignored creditors, an abandoned wife, and other misdoings came from Quebec, Umbria, and the French ambassador in Rome. While Inglesi traveled from Turin to Naples, the Office of Propaganda Fide in Rome asked for an accounting of the funds he was collecting. And with Bishop DuBourg still providing support, Inglesi made his way to Philadelphia, where he also gained the confidence of Gaspar Deabbate, the Consul General of Sardinia, and of the trustees of St. Mary's. At the same time, however, officials at Propaganda Fide were trying to convey less favorable conclusions about Inglesi to DuBourg and Deabbate.[92]

Having secured permission to minister as a priest from Father William V. Harold, the acting Vicar General, Inglesi celebrated Mass at Old St. Joseph's Church. Expressing his regret over the situation at St. Mary's, Inglesi proposed himself to serve as pastor until it was resolved. With the backing of distinguished members of the parish, the trustees accepted Inglesi's offer in August 1823. Although essentially rejected and humiliated by the appointment, Hogan resigned in an attempt to end the dispute, and the trustees informed the Vicar General that they had nominated Inglesi as pastor. But Father Harold, who also wanted the position, opposed the choice of Inglesi. After a meeting in which Harold threatened him with excommunication, the intimidated Inglesi informed the trustees that he could not accept their offer.

Although Inglesi had withdrawn from the situation, Harold remained unsatisfied and sought to discredit him; and while Harold denounced him as an apostate, supporters defended Inglesi's character. But Harold perhaps already knew what others were about to learn of Inglesi's past; similarly, Inglesi himself probably realized that others would soon know what he had concealed about his life. In the meantime, Conwell also inquired of religious authorities in Quebec about:

> ... Rev. Mr. Inglesi who already has made so much noise in the world. He is in Philadelphia uninvited, and the first Sunday after his arrival he presented himself at mass at the interdicted church, the next day he came to excuse himself, declaring his ignorance of the affair.[93]

The reply from Canada confirmed Conwell's suspicions: Inglesi was somewhat of a fraud. After asking about Inglesi's reported marriage in Quebec, Conwell now claimed to have evidence that the renegade priest had defrauded bishops and others in New Orleans and in Europe. But Conwell himself faced another problem. Rumors had reached him that Deabbate, who had supported Inglesi, now planned to sue the Church.

The debate over Inglesi raged within the larger controversy over Hogan and trusteeism. When the trustees persisted in their defense of Inglesi's character, Harold argued against them, in correspondence to Deabbate. Meanwhile, Inglesi removed himself from the parish and left Philadelphia as well, after attempting to vindicate his reputation in a pamphlet.[94] By September 1823, he had vanished as suddenly as he had appeared, and the trustees reinstated Hogan as pastor. But Hogan himself left only two months later, and the basic conflict lasted until October 1826, when Conwell issued a "general amnesty" that removed all "local and personal interdicts." Although the schism had ended for the moment, personal feuds and controversy continued to threaten the peace, until the situation erupted once more and resulted in a five-week interdict, before being finally resolved in 1831.

After his departure, however, what happened to Inglesi is unclear. One account reported that Inglesi was arrested on charges of criminal conduct and held on bail of $3,000, before he died in Philadelphia in July 1824. Another claimed that Inglesi had died of cholera at Port-au-Prince in Santo Domingo in June of that year. In any case, the final chapter of this brief but strange episode had closed, and a church historian later gave an unflattering portrayal of its leading actor:

> This man was a typical specimen of those misguided clerics who, having left their countries for their country's good,

swarmed into the new United States, and either hoped to escape exposure through the precarious and slow communication with the old world, or trusted at least to avert exposure until they could secure some booty and decamp.[95]

Although Inglesi may have provided the equal of any other dramatic or musical performance by an Italian at the time, it had not taken place on a stage or in a theater, and everyone, especially Catholic authorities in Philadelphia, was glad to see its final curtain.

Becoming an American

In contrast to the Inglesi affair, most Italians more quietly adjusted to Philadelphia. While being incorporated into its economy, they made their own contributions to the material and cultural development of the city. At the same time, Italians were being culturally transformed and socially integrated into the general population. On the most formal level, this was reflected by the adopting of American citizenship, but for many years the number of naturalizations actually remained relatively low. In the previous century, no more than a dozen or so Italians had become American citizens. After 1798, no Italian sought naturalization until 1803. For sixty years, from 1801 through 1860, 155 natives of some part of modern Italy applied for citizenship. Although 7 Italians petitioned in 1804, that number was unusually high. In most years, no more than 2 or 3 applicants appeared—until 1840, when 7 Italians sought citizenship. Applications climbed to 37 cases for the period 1854–57, then fell again to a lower level until after the Civil War.[96]

While political assimilation remained relatively low, Americanization did take other paths. Name changes in which Italian forms were replaced by Anglicized ones, as happened with Marabello, became evident in some cases. Giuseppe Diaccheri, proprietor of amusement and entertainment establishments and a resident since 1802, became Joseph Diaccheri at the baptism of his daughter Teresa in 1810. At his naturalization in the following year, he became Joseph Diacker. By 1825, he was listed in the city directory as Joseph Diackery, a name that reflected a compromise between his Italian origins and his eventual Philadelphia identity.[97] But sometimes name changes followed an even more vacillating course. In March 1822, Giuseppe Antonio Olivieri, a young native of Corsica, arrived at the Port of New York and soon afterward reached Philadelphia. By 1825, as Joseph Oliver, he was an innkeeper at 314 South Third Street. Three years later, in March 1828 in a ceremony conducted by Bishop Conwell, Giuseppe Antonio Olivieri di Pisola of Corsica married Mary Gill Clark. In October of the same year, Joseph A. Oliver, an emigrant from Corsica, became a citizen of the United States but signed the petition for naturalization as Joseph Antonio Olivieri. In 1830, Joseph Anthony Olieveri served as a witness for a marriage at Old St. Joseph's. Finally, Joseph Anthony Oliver, born on Corsica in December 17, 1806, died in Philadelphia on January 16, 1840, at thirty-three years of age and was buried in Vault 21 of Section N at St. Mary's Graveyard.[98] This sequence of names reflected the uncertainty of local authorities as well as the ambivalence of the person himself from the time of his arrival in the city until his death, eighteen years later, with regard to how American he was to be. A similar pattern can be found in other cases in the documentary records of the Italian population in Philadelphia.

The assimilation of Italians was not merely an exercise in name-changing, but included marriages to women of other origins who also were often found in another city or country before coming to Philadelphia, a pattern that began in the previous century. When Vincent Ghirardini, born in Mantua, left Orleans, France, and arrived at New York in 1784, he appears to have been unmarried. In 1787, however, a son was born to Vincent Ghirardini and Elizabeth Kearney in New York City. By 1794, they had resettled in Philadelphia, and in the next year the baptism of Margaret, another daughter, was performed at Old St. Joseph's.[99]

By the early nineteenth century, whether they found their mates elsewhere or in Philadelphia, marriages between two individuals who were both of Italian origins were exceedingly rare. While Italian males could be found in Philadelphia, Italian females were far fewer in number, and a visible pattern of intermarriage had emerged by the early 1800s. John Thomasetti married Catherine Cooker in 1801. Baptisms at Holy Trinity, Old St. Joseph's, and St. Augustine's gave as parents the names of Augustine Marchi and Christina Had; John Franchi and Frances Vanchuyer, a non-Catholic (also listed as Frances McAuley);

Francis Fagioli and Mary Magdalen Ellis; Augustine Carlino and Jane Stuart, also a non-Catholic; John Baptist Sartori and Henrietta Woofoin; Joseph Diaccheri and Anna Hevas; and Louis Lemetti (or Lammetta) and Anna McLaughlin. From 1812 to 1825, marriages at Old St. Joseph's and St. Augustine's united Peter Bellini and Henrietta Doan; Andrew Pichetti and Mary Campbell; Reniory Genari and Grace Hickman; James Anthony Ambrosi and Letitia Clodworthy; Vito Viti and Martha Redman; John M. Togno and Sarah Wood; and Giovanni Luciani and Sara Flanigan, with a special dispensation for the latter who had not been baptized as a Catholic.[100] Because the pool of eligible women of Italian origins had not grown, these men had to marry women of other ethnic backgrounds, and often non-Catholics, if they were to marry at all. This provided a demographic basis for the assimilation of their offspring and a potential threat to the future of Italians as a group.

Because so much of the record has been lost, any general picture of material and social conditions among Italians in the city in the early nineteenth century is difficult. The fragments of information, still mainly about individuals, that can be assembled permit a limited assessment. Although their total number remained small, a slowly increasing population of Italians had settled and distributed themselves in their residential locations. While a few, such as Bosio, occasionally followed unusual enterprises, most were engaged in crafts and trades that were typical occupations in the economy of the city.

The degree of success and wealth that they enjoyed ranged widely. At one extreme, some Italians lived and died in meager material circumstances. When Pieter Purkett, also known as Pietro Pachette, died in 1807, he left an estate of not more than $50. Other Italians achieved modest levels of comfort and security, at least for a few years. When Andrew Pichetti died in 1847, his will listed a three-story house, furniture, and personal wealth of $152.50. A letter of administration, later granted at the request of his widow, reported the personal estate of Andrew Pichetti (presumably the same individual) as not more than $150 in 1851. Still others, such as Molinari, Mussi, and Busti, attained a level of affluence that enabled them to live in comfort.[101]

Some Italians pursued lifestyles marked by cultivated tastes. Ancora and Monachesi produced copies of well-known paintings as well as original paintings for local patrons. Either the same person or the son of a language professor, but by the 1850 census a physician, Joseph

Togno amassed a formidable collection of art that included works by Monachesi, Riboni, and Luigi Persico. Perhaps the cultivation of art included an occasional pretension, but when Togno sat for a portrait by Riboni in which he was depicted in the act of translating an inscription on an antique fragment for a fellow traveler, he was following a popular practice.[102] A few Italians had not only accumulated wealth but also achieved recognition and respectability among fellow citizens. When he died in 1868, Giacinto DeAngeli left modest amounts of cash and stock shares, and numbered among the executors of his estate, at least as an acquaintance if not a friend, Eli K. Price, the prominent real-estate lawyer and state senator who had been the leader of city consolidation in the previous decade.[103] And the life and career of marble importer and merchant Vito Viti represented only the beginning of a family that prospered with prestige until nearly the end of the century.

While it remains difficult to reconstruct the patterns of social life among Italians of this period, it is clear that they constituted only a small part of the total population of Philadelphia. They lived in some proximity to each other, but not yet to any degree that could be described as a concentration. The immigrant ghettos of American cities still remained some decades in the future. Italians in Philadelphia also obviously knew one another in many cases and frequently interacted. More formal occasions, such as religious ceremonies and naturalizations, drew them together, but not to the exclusion of people of other ethnic backgrounds, or at every opportunity.

Although it was a time of great activity for the founding of voluntary associations in the city, Italians, despite these patterns of interaction and support, in contrast to other groups, had not yet established any formal organizations during these early years. Numerous national, political, benevolent, and trade associations had been organized, as well as charitable societies for the support of schools and the advancement of education. It was also the era in which many of the famous, or infamous, fire companies were founded. While benevolent and assistance societies were established among other emigrant groups, including the Irish, the French, the Germans, the Welsh, the Scots, and the English, none was started by or for Italians. This failure partly reflected social and political conditions in the land they had left behind. Whether from Corsica or from the mainland of Italy, most of them had departed from territory that was still under foreign rather than Italian dominion. In naturalization proceedings they sometimes renounced their allegiance to the "French nation." After their arrival in Philadelphia, it is even likely that Italians were incorporated as members into other groups. For example, the reorganization of the Resolution Hose Company in 1823 began a steady inclusion of so many natives of France that this fire brigade eventually became known as "the French Company." Among its newer members in this period, the names of J. Castagnet and F. Tete can be found. A few decades later, John Castagneto was relatively conspicuous as a liquor dealer; similarly, the family name of Teti was fairly common. It is quite possible, therefore, that some members of "the French Company" were in fact Italians.[104]

The number of Italians in Philadelphia was probably too small for such efforts at organization, and immigrants from Italy may not have needed or wanted such assistance. Moreover, the self-consciousness of natives of the peninsula was too strongly linked to different principalities and foreign states to have allowed a more nationalistic identity as Italians at this time. Between 1800 and 1825, despite the material success of some, none appears to have participated in these voluntary associations in a significant manner, except possibly a freemason or two. By the opening decades of the nineteenth century, they formed a social network of loose ties, but not yet a more developed community of a concentrated residential population with its own institutions and organizations.

For their part, other Philadelphians had some curiosity about the culture of Italy and the manner of life to be found there. But that curiosity was no longer restricted, as it had been in the previous century, to the scions of first families with the wealth and leisure that afforded them the opportunity to travel to Italy. Instead, Italy was now being presented to all strata of the local population. At one end of the social scale, talented artists and sculptors could be employed to adorn the homes of the rich and powerful with the "softer arts," but such art was now increasingly displayed in more public venues, to which the less privileged classes of Philadelphians also had access. Similarly, in concert halls, theaters, and amusement gardens, Italian singers and instrumental players offered operatic, concert, and popular music to an expanding audience. But even other more ordinary aspects of Italian life were now visible, sometimes in quite unusual forms. In October 1823, an elaborate exhibition at Earle's Gallery on Chestnut Street offered visitors a mechanical panorama of an Italian village. More than

100 mechanical figures, about 15 inches high, put into motion at the same time, showed the inhabitants working and animals moving in the routine of daily life in the village. The exhibition attracted audiences for several months before it closed. The display perhaps presaged in some sense the transformation of neighborhood that would occur in the years ahead as more Italians found their way to Philadelphia.[105] For the moment, however, the actual Italian presence was more of a canvas of colorful characters whose contributions in art, music, hostelry, and the culinary arts made Philadelphia itself a more interesting place. At the same time, by their interaction they had formed *un circolo* of their own. Within that sphere, these *primi emigranti* had planted the seeds that would evolve from an inchoate aggregate into the embryo of community in subsequent decades.

Chapter 3

The City as Incubator

In late July 1843, Philadelphia newspapers reported the stabbing and death of James Grillo. Both Grillo and his assailant, James Berneiro, were identified as Italian boarders for the previous two weeks in the house of Joseph Merito, on Market Street near Twelfth. Merito was also identified as an Italian.[1] This incident marked a new phase in the Italian experience in Philadelphia. During these years, as their numbers grew, Italians also evolved from a mere aggregate of individuals with episodic moments of informal interaction to a system of communal institutions by which their lives were organized. By the end of this period, those early seeds had clearly sprouted into the first stage of an actual community. In order to understand the Italian experience more fully, it is valuable to broaden our perspective again and consider what was happening to Philadelphia in general.

The complex but interrelated changes that transformed Philadelphia during the generation leading up to the American Civil War tested all elements of local tradition. At the core of this process, the city was forced to respond to the Industrial Revolution. The transformation that affected virtually every aspect of urban life could not take place without great turmoil and turbulence. It was not only unprecedented but also never to be seen again. At the end of this time of growth, upheaval, and adaptation, Philadelphia was a new and modern city, almost entirely different from what it had previously been.[2]

Population Growth and Immigration

The growth of population was one obvious aspect of change during these years. In 1830, some 80,458 persons lived within the original limits of the city, which stretched from the Delaware River to the Schuylkill River and from Vine Street to South Street. Another 108,339 individuals resided in the rest of the county of Philadelphia, and 212,922 more inhabitants lived in the surrounding counties. The entire metropolitan area had a total population of 401,719. In another ten years, by the 1840 federal census, the city had a population of 93,665, with 165,372 in the rest of the county, 230,923 in the other counties, and a total of 488,960 for the entire area.[3]

In the next decade, from 1840 to 1850, Philadelphia grew proportionately more in population than at any other time in its history. The number of city-dwellers increased to 121,376 people, 27,711 more than ten years earlier, a gain of nearly 30 percent. The rest of the county grew to 287,386, an increase of 123,014, or more than 75 percent of what it had been in 1840. These figures taken together reflect a gain from 258,037 to 408,762, a total of 150,725 more people and an increase of more than 58 percent for the city and county in ten years. Never before or since has Philadelphia grown so rapidly, relative to its size. In the following decade, although the rate of growth slowed considerably, the population increased to 565,022, slightly more than 38 percent, for the newly consolidated city on the eve of the Civil War. By this point, Philadelphia was not only the second largest city in the United States but also the fourth largest city in the world.[4]

As population increased, so did internal diversity. Somewhat surprisingly, the number of African Americans would not grow appreciably during these years. In 1830, some 14,460 free persons and thirteen slaves made up the entire African American population for Philadelphia and its nearby wards and districts. By 1860, there were 22,185 African Americans in the city and county combined—only 4 percent of the total population but a larger proportion than in any other northern city.[5]

The foreign-born population represented a more complicated picture. European immigration to the United States first became a large movement of population in the years after the Napoleonic Wars.

During the 1820s, nearly 20,000 newcomers, almost 10 percent of all immigrants to America, arrived through the Port of Philadelphia. With two lines of regularly scheduled service from Liverpool to Philadelphia, Irish and English immigrants paid between five and seven British pounds for Atlantic passage in steerage. In 1835, some 1,890 individuals arrived; by 1840 the figure reached 4,079; and in 1845 some 5,767 immigrants debarked at Philadelphia.[6] Despite its earlier importance to the colonies and the young nation, Philadelphia was about to enter a period of permanent decline, especially with the increasing role of New York as a port of entry for the foreign-born.

In the 1840s, the revolution in transportation by which steamships replaced sailing vessels in Atlantic passage had begun, but the unfavorable location of the port kept the volume of arrivals at modest levels. It was 200 miles farther than New York Harbor and required a tedious 110-mile leg up the Delaware River, after passing Cape May, that could take as long as two weeks. To compound their frustration, nearby shorelines always lay in sight of weary travelers. The often frozen fresh water also impeded ships in winter. Despite offers of reduced rates to Philadelphia, New York emerged as the more important port of entry. In subsequent years, however, Philadelphia retained a greater role in maritime commerce than for immigration. In 1851, some 30,000 ships, barks, brigs, schooners, steamers, barges, and other vessels entered the port. But only one line of regularly scheduled first-class steamers and four sailing packet lines operated between Liverpool and Philadelphia, while several intercoastal companies served the port with passengers.[7]

Whether to Philadelphia, New York, or elsewhere, the journey to America was usually long, unpleasant, and dangerous. The ships arriving carried not only immigrants grateful to have ended their voyage, but also somber news of shipboard deaths during the trip. The figures alternated between periods of very high and low mortality. During a brief span from early September to mid-November 1853, among 16,272 passengers for New York, 1,118 deaths at sea occurred. At the end of November, 1,141 deaths were reported among the 13,762 passengers on twenty-eight ships that arrived at New York in that month alone. Ships from Liverpool often suffered severe losses; one from Havre lost 75 passengers. With a death rate as high as 9 percent of arrivals, newspapers referred to these vessels as the "plague ships."[8]

The absence of precautions before departure, the overcrowding of passengers, indifference to their comfort, and neglect of proper measures to ensure cleanliness were believed to contribute to the high mortality figures, with cholera as the primary cause of deaths. The need to take health precautions before ships left European ports, as well as for sanitary regulations, better food, and sufficient medical attention during the voyage, was clear. Observers who demanded an investigation by government authorities argued that if an epidemic on land caused only half the rate of death as the conditions on immigrant ships, the result would have been not only a general panic but also enactment of strong measures to remedy the situation.[9]

By early 1854, possibly as a result of greater awareness by prospective emigrants of these conditions, a noticeable lull had occurred in the volume of emigration. Ships arrived with only one-third of their berths occupied. Some American companies instructed agents to discontinue carrying steerage passengers as long as the cholera continued. It was also the slow time of the year for transatlantic migration.[10]

The problems of immigrants were not confined to conditions that might impair health during the ocean crossing. After reaching American cities, new experiences threatened the well-being of recent arrivals. Fraudulent offers of assistance became increasingly common. In 1853, emigrants who had paid $3 to an agent for fare from New York to Philadelphia discovered they had been victims of fraud. Not only had they paid twice the normal cost of a train ticket for that part of their trip, but the railroad jobs they had been promised by the agent did not exist. Early in the next year, forty-four Swedish immigrants, mostly women and children, learned that tickets for Chicago purchased from an agent in New York City were good only as far as Pittsburgh.[11]

The widespread exploitation of immigrants led to private efforts to provide protection after their arrival. In 1853, the Emigrant Society of New York asked for a $2 tax on each arrival, to support its work. In Philadelphia, the growing awareness of frauds, most often with the Irish as victims, affirmed the need to develop better protection for immigrants. In 1848, after complaints of persons having to make payments of $20 to $60 to an agency that was supposed to reunite families by obtaining passage for wives and children of immigrants already here, the Emigrants' Friend Society was founded with the purpose "of securing emigrants from imposition upon their arrival here, and directing them to suitable places of accommodation, employment or desirable location for settlement." With a new season of emigration about to begin as ships once again began arriving from Liverpool and Londonderry, the society appealed to the public for funds to support its programs, and in particular a housing plan. In 1853, it opened a boardinghouse at Front and Dock Streets as a refuge for destitute arrivals and to prevent them from begging on city streets. Emigrants would be admitted only if they agreed to perform "any services required of them while in the house, and pay the small price charged for board, out of their future earnings."[12]

Despite the risks of the voyage and uncertain conditions after arrival, many immigrants still chose Philadelphia as their destination. From 1830 through 1847, Philadelphia received about 60,000 people at its port. During the next eight years, more than 120,000 immigrants made Philadelphia the fourth largest port for the foreign-born in the nation. From a peak of 19,211 for 1853, however, the number fell to 7,581 for 1855, a decline to about 5 percent of the national total. But the number of immigrants to Philadelphia cannot be measured only by direct arrivals at the port. Similar, if not higher, numbers of immigrants came to Philadelphia after arriving and debarking at New York.[13]

Not all new arrivals or immigrants who already resided in Philadelphia intended to remain there. As vessels reached the city, other ships also left with passengers for the West Coast. The *Public Ledger* described one festive scene:

> The emigrants did not appear to have had their ardor dampened by the thoughts of leaving home and the many friends from whom they parted, but gaily exchanged cheers with the spectators that lined the wharves to witness their departure, or joined in the chorus of the California gold digging song.[14]

By the middle of the century, the foreign-born were a fairly large and distinctive element of the overall population of Philadelphia. In 1850, of the 408,672 people populating the city and the county, 121,699 (29.7 percent) were foreign-born. The bulk of these immigrants were from Ireland (72,312), Germany (22,750), and England (17,500) with Scotland and Wales providing smaller numbers. In another ten years, in 1860, the total population of the newly consolidated city, which included the old county as well, reached 565,529. Of that figure, 169,430 (29.9 percent) were foreign-born, and the majority still were from Ireland (95,548) and Germany (43,643). Despite these numbers, Philadelphia had fewer foreign-born, relative to its size, than any other major city in the northern states.[15]

Industrialization and a New Social Order

The Industrial Revolution had thrust Philadelphia into prominence as a manufacturing city. The opportunities for work and wages offered by local industries provided incentives for migrants from rural areas elsewhere in the United States as well as for immigrants from Europe. By the middle of the nineteenth century, Philadelphia surpassed all other cities in the world in the number of textile factories. In addition to the great volume of cotton and woolen clothing produced, 4,700 looms in homes and factories were engaged in making carpets, hosiery, and other textiles. The city was also a center for the manufacture of iron products, which included heavy machinery, ships, locomotives, cast ornaments, and household fixtures. While its factories produced things as different and unrelated as bricks and umbrellas, Philadelphia was emerging as the leading place for the tool-and-dye-making industry, which cast the machine parts that made all other forms of manufacture possible.[16]

During this period, the smaller shops of craftsmen had been replaced by the larger establishments and greater scale of investment of a more mature industrial economy. In the fiscal year ending June 1, 1850, larger factories represented an investment of $33,737,911 in capital and another $33,515,366 in raw materials and fuel costs. They employed a monthly average of 43,304 males, who earned $1,062,799, and 14,804 females, earning $208,584. The total value of products reached $62,815,011 for the year. Like its increase in population, the city was experiencing a period of unprecedented industrial growth, while at the same time developing the diversity that became a conspicuous characteristic in the years ahead.[17]

Industrialization not only introduced a new technology within large factories but also reorganized the human dimension. As the process unfolded, large-scale production rested on increased specialization and rationalization of work activities. The new discipline within the factory system also contained "the demeaning impersonality of the emerging corporate order."[18] The factories had imposed upon the worker a new system of servitude that had taken away from the actual producers of goods the right to market their own products.

A new economic order that cared little about the human needs of the worker had emerged. With these new conditions, the relationships among groups and levels of workers also changed. In contrast to the traditional system, the special bond between apprentice and craftsman that had promised mobility was eliminated. The younger worker no longer had the opportunity to cultivate skills in the hope of moving from novice to journeyman or master in a line of work. The new system had created a permanent working class. Under the impact of industry as it reorganized work in America, skilled workers, whether native or foreign-born, stood witness to the erosion of their crafts, as well as of their self-esteem and security. Eventually, the gap between the rich and the poor could only become greater. With a certain irony, as Philadelphia rushed through a remarkable period of growth and development, these changes provided the material basis for an increase in social tensions throughout the city.[19]

It was not only the social organization of work and production, but also the social ecology of residence and neighborhood, that evolved in unprecedented directions between the 1830s and the Civil War. Earlier geographical expansion had established new communities just outside the original limits of the city. Although governed by their own municipal authorities, the adjoining districts were generally regarded as parts of the city. In an obvious exercise in "boosterism," a publication of the time graphically captured the excitement generated by expansion:

> The Schuylkill no longer bounds us. Improvement is now in rapid march through the beautiful district of West Philadelphia. And no less marvellous are the changes taking place in Southwark, Moyamensing, etc. Those of our citizens whose business or inclinations keep them from "rambling around," will be astonished and bewildered on visiting what they are apt to term the "outskirts of the city." A worthy gentleman, residing in Chestnut by Delaware Eighth Street, remarked to us the other day, that he lately took a walk out west of Broad Street, "and," said he, "I could not believe my eyes; I thought this could not possibly be Philadelphia. The change, sir, is most wonderful!"[20]

When the 1854 Act of Consolidation absorbed the districts, townships, and municipalities of the county, the pattern of land use and architectural design also changed, and a new city emerged. At its center, shops increasingly replaced residential buildings. As in the colonial period, the center still contained the shops of old trades and small merchants such as milliners, tailors, boot and shoe makers, bookbinders, printers, carpenters, weavers, grocers, liquor dealers, butchers, cigar makers, tobacconists, cordwainers, coopers, brewers, sugar refiners, blacksmiths, and cabinetmakers. Although some manufacturing remained in the downtown district, new factories were built on less-expensive land on the fringes of the city.[21]

These changes represented the beginnings of the ecological patterns of the modern city. While the downtown area was becoming mainly a cluster of shops, construction of buildings exclusively for manufacturing was creating factory districts. For the individual, workplace was being separated from residence. In response to these developments, the workers of the new industrial order had to find affordable housing for themselves and their families. Industrialization not only changed the organization of work but redistributed the population as well.

The separation of work from home introduced a need for efficient means of moving materials, goods, and people that required innovations in the technology and organization of urban transportation. In 1842, when it inaugurated passenger service, the Philadelphia & Reading Railroad Company entered into direct competition with the canal barges that were still the principal means of moving coal from the mines to the city. By 1844, the railroad was already bringing more coal to Philadelphia than the waterways, and after another three years became the leading freight line in the nation. In 1849, the Pennsylvania Railroad Company was established with a passenger line between Harrisburg and Lewistown. In 1854, it opened a line that connected Philadelphia and Pittsburgh, before it reached Chicago four years later. But trade in coal remained central to the economy of Philadelphia. In 1850, nearly 29 million tons of anthracite with a value of more than $16 million were sent to the city.[22]

In January 1858, public transportation within the city entered a similar period of change with the introduction of horse-drawn cars on rails, which quickly replaced the omnibus lines that had run directly on the streets. Despite the proliferation of street railway lines that soon followed, the need for even more improved transportation continued to grow. The revolution in urban transportation brought new noise, congestion, and dangers to the city. While Philadelphia had only recently been a "walking city," by the 1850s it had clearly become a city of commuting workers.[23]

As population increased, the development of transportation pushed residential areas farther from the center. For some observers, this transformation of the city was a symptom of successful development that could only be described in highly positive terms:

> The enterprise of her citizens was never more displayed than at present. Railroads and canals pour into her lap the treasures alike of our own mountains and the great valley of the glorious West. The city is extending with wondrous strides; year by year streets are being laid out, and houses, extending away for squares, arise, as by the hand of magic, on ground that lately "waved in golden harvest."[24]

Not all who sought their future in Philadelphia found favorable conditions. As immigrants arrived in greater numbers, the city faced a serious housing shortage. These newcomers found a short-term answer in rapidly proliferating cheap boardinghouses and tenements. While this solution endured in New York, it achieved nowhere near the same degree of acceptance in Philadelphia, which had no large stock of older housing that could be easily converted into tenements for new residents and their families. City leaders, moreover, still wanted to uphold the original intention of William Penn, the founder of the colony, to make Philadelphia a place where the families of workers could find decent homes of their own. While New York erected buildings with multiple family units, the strategy in Philadelphia remained the construction of housing for single families.

The physical expansion of Philadelphia also manifested itself in what were becoming monotonously characteristic patterns of housing and neighborhoods. The row house on a very narrow lot with a small yard and rear alley was constructed throughout new areas. From 53,078 dwellings in 1840, the housing supply reached 61,278 homes in 1850, about 23,600 more than New York City at the time. In 1852, it was reported that more than 3,500 buildings had been erected in each of the previous three years. By 1860, the total number of houses climbed to 89,979.[25] One conspicuous design, with three floors but only one room on each floor, intended for the families of workers, became known as the "Father, Son, Holy Ghost," or "Trinity," house. A local promoter glibly presented a favorable picture of the housing situation:

> It is the ambition of many an American belle to be mistress of a "Philadelphia three-story brick." To live within his own family free from interruption, contest, or intrusion, to have his house clean and comfortable, his apartment adapted to their several purposes, and in every respect convenient, is our citizen's delight; to effect all these, the builder exerts his utmost skill. . . . Let foreigners talk of their splendid palaces, mansions, and rich dwellings; theirs is but the parade of pomp and vanity, ours is social comfort.[26]

Although a British journalist reached a similar conclusion, that "Philadelphia must contain in comfort the largest number of small householders of any city in the world," the realities of life in the neighborhoods of workers were much less pleasant.[27] The changing nature of industry itself had a profound effect on residential choices. As newer forms of manufacturing developed, some specialization of factory location became evident. While the production of leather, textiles, woolen goods, and machinery was concentrated in northern districts of the city, the garment industry and its sweatshops began to appear in scattered locations in sections to the south. Workers and their families sought housing in less-expensive areas near their employment. Consequently, dense concentrations of new housing emerged near the larger mills and factories of the city.[28]

Despite the great number of new dwellings in the city, residential construction could not meet the needs of the families of workers. Another response to the housing shortage contributed further to the physical deterioration of older neighborhoods. In back alleys, residents erected shacks and shanties, often of only one or two rooms, or attached sheds to row homes in an effort to expand available space. The poor sometimes even attempted to construct their own housing.[29]

Despite these conditions, the material growth of the city still blinded some observers, who only saw more favorable aspects:

Our city is not so thickly populated, for its extent, as some others. The streets are wide, and the inhabitants of every class enjoy more room than usual in large cities. Not only the merchant, wealthy manufacturer, and persons well to do in the world, occupy each an entire dwelling, but tradesmen of the most humble class can have a house to themselves.[30]

Such comments denied or ignored that the transformation of the city was not equally beneficial in its consequences for the entire population. The wages of most workers deprived them of any opportunity to live in material comfort. At an even lower level, poverty had become a permanent feature of life in Philadelphia for many residents in the 1840s. By the next decade, a grand jury investigation concluded that thousands were starving and homeless in one section, from Fifth to Eighth Streets between Lombard and Fitzwater. A newspaper reporter estimated that as many as 5,000 people survived by begging and stealing in the area. The belief that liquor was the basic cause of such lives gave strong impetus to a new temperance movement. Girls lured into prostitution and women working at starvation wages in clothing shops were also a subject of grave concern.[31]

Under the impact of industrialization, the entire city had been transformed. Noise, congestion, and pollution were among the unanticipated and unwelcomed by-products of the new order for all residents. In areas where factory workers lived, the results were especially unfortunate. While the physical condition of streets was bad, grade-level railroad crossings made them even more perilous. The water supply was insufficient and unhealthy. Pigs roamed and fouled the streets. Housing was both inadequate and dangerous. Violence and crime were common. Public health was a recurrent problem. In response to a cholera epidemic in 1849, the Board of Health issued a bleak report on living conditions in slum neighborhoods. In the next year, after a long period of decline, the mortality rate began a disturbing increase. While epidemics of cholera, smallpox, and yellow fever actually occurred infrequently, more endemic diseases such as typhus, dysentery, scarlet fever, tuberculosis, and malaria often ended the lives of local residents.[32]

Despite the widespread poverty, bad housing, crime, and personal degradation, the city was still commended by boosters who presented a euphoric view of life in Philadelphia. With some hyperbole, one enthusiastic writer claimed:

> Philadelphia is, perhaps, the most healthy city in the United States. The air is sweet and clear, the sky serene and seldom overcast. The streets are wide and airy, crossing at right angles; they surpass all others in the world, in their convenience for trade and accommodation for passengers, and are well paved and kept remarkably clean. At night they are well lighted with gas.[33]

There was, however, a great disparity between accounts of how Philadelphia's factory workers and poor actually lived and the way commentators celebrating the "progress" described the city. They seemed to be describing entirely different cities, and in some sense that is exactly what they were.

The transformation of Philadelphia not only involved physical conditions but also embraced social relations and social structure. The development of industry and the market economy created a new system of opportunities and wealth that aggravated rather than leveled the differences separating the rich and the poor. At the same time, a new middle class with households increasingly adorned by material amenities began to emerge. A new entrepreneurial class challenged the older merchant and professional aristocracy for power and control in the market. Political leadership shifted to the new business moguls, who were somewhat indifferent to local needs while preoccupied with national affairs, and then to full-time bosses by the 1850s. The evolution of the class structure was not, however, the only mechanism in the redistribution of power. Whether dominated by the machine boss or the patrician turned democrat, as the disorders of 1844 indicated, local politics were also moving from primarily class-based issues to emergent ethnic conflicts.[34]

Social Disorder in the City of Brothers

Industrialization had been accompanied by unfavorable social conditions that could be found almost anywhere in the city. In some neighborhoods, such as Southwark, Moyamensing, and Passyunk to the south and Northern Liberties and Kensington to the north, these circumstances contributed to an acutely deteriorating situation. With greater numbers of the poor, these areas had higher rates of disease and mortality; they were also places of proximity and contact between blacks and the foreign-born. In the late 1840s, one-third of the black population resided in a small section of Moyamensing, from South to Fitzwater Streets between Fifth and Eighth Streets. By 1860, nearly two-thirds of the black population remained within the old city limits; the rest were in the outer districts. In contrast, slightly less than 38 percent of the foreign-born were within the original city, while the other 62 percent lived in surrounding areas. Among more than 94,000 Irish, the largest immigrant group, 32 percent lived within the old city, 23 percent lived in Southwark and Moyamensing, 21 percent were in Northern Liberties and Kensington, 19 percent in Spring Garden, Penn Township, and Germantown, and another 4 percent in West Philadelphia.[35]

During the entire period of 1830–60, public order was plagued by sporadic street incidents with the potential to ignite riots that could paralyze the entire city. Disorderly crowds and rioting were common events, often occurring around election time. Holiday celebrations, even Christmas, could also be a source of racial disturbances.[36] But group life became an even stronger source of potential disorder. While earlier animosities had never been entirely resolved, newer encounters began to simmer. Tensions remained among the English, the Scotch-Irish, and the Irish, between native-born and immigrants, and between Protestants and Catholics. Native whites, blacks, and immigrants confronted one another in new neighborhoods, but also in other settings. Although similarly exploited and disadvantaged, and perhaps because of such conditions, newly arrived immigrants, especially Irish laborers, found themselves in competition with blacks, whom they had begun to replace as hod carriers and stevedores. Increasing numbers of Catholics, as well as Jews, arrived in a city that already was a center for militant anti-Catholicism. Although blacks had their own well-developed class system and institutions, other groups ignored such distinctions. The racial ghetto was visible, and antipathy toward blacks was widely shared by other groups. The abolitionist movement in a city with strong Southern sympathies provided another dimension that made the situation volatile. Even within the same religion, ethnic differences provided the potential for conflict. German Catholics suspected that Bishop Francis P. Kenrick favored the Irish in many matters. Philadelphia was a powder keg that had to explode at some moment.[37]

Apart from tensions based on ethnic, racial, and religious differences, the city faced other sources of potential violence. The volunteer fire companies, which proliferated during the period, battled with one another in the infamous firemen's riots that had been long accepted in the city. Gangs of young hoodlums with colorful names, such as the Moyamensing Killers, the Deathfetchers, the Hyenas, and especially the notorious Schuylkill Rangers which almost make the city of today seem safe in comparison, routinely preyed upon helpless victims.[38]

From the 1830s on, the city faced a massive, multifaceted, and constant threat to its social order. While racial, ethnic, and religious diversity contributed to the problem, the underlying source remained the stresses, dislocations, and anxieties generated by the emerging industrial system. The political situation was further encumbered by the multiplicity of townships, boroughs, and districts that surrounded the city and the various corporate or quasi-corporate bodies that served the public. The expanding need of public services such as transportation, water, and gas made life in the city difficult. In the case of public safety, the absence of an adequate, professional police force made it exceedingly dangerous.

Collective violence appeared on the streets with a series of riots that lasted from 1834 until 1849. In August 1834, a race riot that started in the city spilled into Moyamensing and lasted three days. In October of the same year, an election riot between Whigs and Democrats left one person dead and perhaps twenty others injured. In the next two years, while peace was sometimes disrupted by violence between dockworkers and strikebreakers, it was also often threatened by the growing debate over slavery. In May 1838, a mob of 3,000 people angered by antislavery meetings set a fire that destroyed Pennsylvania Hall, the main gathering place for abolitionists in the city. After another night of disorder, the episode ended with condemnation of the incident by the local press but ambivalence by local authorities on the race problem. The worst was yet to come.[39]

The basis of group conflict in Philadelphia soon shifted from race to religion and ethnicity. After four years of relative calm, a two-day riot pitted Irish gangs against blacks in the Schuylkill section in August 1842. Then, after weeks of mounting labor unrest, the

"Nannygoat Market" riot brought Irish weavers, who had sought to enforce their strike action on other workers, into a confrontation with the local militia in January 1843. Although serious violence was averted, the Irish had now become a conspicuous object of official attention. A nativist movement with strong antipathies toward the Irish and Catholicism began strengthening itself by the early months of 1844.[40]

In May of that year, the most serious rioting so far in the history of the city took place. After several days of fighting between nativist and Irish mobs, mainly in Kensington and Northern Liberties, order was restored, but not before one young man was killed and one Catholic church, St. Augustine's, was burned down. The rioting made it apparent that city authorities had acted too slowly to protect the Irish and might do the same again in the future. It was equally clear that mobs could take over the streets, at least temporarily, without serious resistance from the city. In July, the scene repeated itself in Southwark when the militia and a mob clashed, with the eventual loss of fourteen lives and the wounding of many others.[41]

By the late 1840s, this type of violence gave Philadelphia an unenviable reputation around the world. In Paris, an aristocrat who amused readers by his observations on American society wrote that the word "Philadelphia" meant "city of brothers" probably because of the frequent murders and riots that occurred there. While his logic was slightly twisted, the reality to which he referred was widely reported.[42]

Although fire company fights and gang violence continued—and another race riot occurred, in which three persons died and many others were injured after the election of October 1849—Philadelphia had grown weary of disorder. The solution involved a comprehensive reorganization of local government. The outlying districts looked to the city for municipal services, especially with regard to law enforcement; the city, in turn, coveted the increased tax base these districts could offer. In February 1854, the Act of Consolidation established the coterminous boundaries of city and county that remain to the present day.

But even the effort to establish, or perhaps impose, a more harmonious public order on an increasing diverse population sometimes encouraged continued conflict. In June, Robert T. Conrad, a nativist Whig, was elected mayor of the newly consolidated city with strong support from the Know-Nothings. Almost immediately after his inauguration, the new mayor, who did not pursue particularly enlightened policies of civic leadership, began an effort to reorganize the police department. In July, the City Councils passed an ordinance that restricted the hiring of police officers to American-born whites. Although not maintained for long, the new policy, which reflected the influence of Know-Nothing principles on the administration, officially endorsed the harassment of Irish and black residents. When Conrad tried to uphold new "blue laws," which prohibited liquor sales and the distribution of newspapers on Sundays, and used the police to enforce his own views of how the Sabbath ought to be observed, his challenge to the customs of immigrants led to further violence between them and the police.[43]

Paupers and Politics

While the number of Italians in the city remained low, the increasing arrivals of other emigrants, especially the Irish, had clearly emerged as a major public issue. On the eve of the riots in 1844, prominent merchant Thomas P. Cope offered his perception of the foreign population in Philadelphia. After remarking on French exiles in the city, he made a searing indictment of more recent arrivals in his diary:

> The Irish and German emigrants to our Cities contrast very disadvantageously with the French. Trained in the sinks of vicious & hardened mendicity [sic] in their own countries, they at once set to begging on their arrival here & often become a heavy charge on our charity, filling our streets with their clamorous appeals & our alms houses with unproductive, haggard pauperism. A Frenchman rarely meddles with our Institutions, an Irishman interferes at once. One of the number, before he stepped from on board ship—being asked by a countryman who had been here before him whether he was a Federalist or a Democrat—said, "I don't know about them there, but anyhow, I'm against the Government." And Pat said truly, for he must have a bubbery wherever he goes &—ignorant as he may be—he is unwilling to believe that anybody knows more than himself.[44]

During the riots, Cope expressed his conviction that the Irish were largely responsible for the disorder, and on May 7 he entered this observation: "In the Kensington riots, the Irish women are said to have been particularly active." Four days later he added: "Blame attaches to both parties for what happened—but I hold the Irish Catholics the most culpable as the original aggressors."[45] On May 22 he examined the religious factor further:

> Catholicism, as practised under the discipline of the Church of Rome, is not consistent with our free Institutions. I would not insinuate that all Catholics are bad citizens—far from it. I know many worthy men among them. It is the system to which I object.[46]

In the autumn of 1844, after violence had finally subsided and with the coming election, Cope stated his view on the possible impact of the foreign-born on politics. He claimed that 13,000 people had been naturalized in local courts over a period of a few days. Cope believed that the influx of foreigners and their quick naturalization would seriously damage the nation—but again he singled out the Irish, noting his belief that 30,000 of them were being imported into the United States each year. He later broadened his indictment by contending that daily robberies, burglaries, and pickpocketing were the work of foreign rogues who abounded in the cities.[47]

While Cope blamed Irish Catholics as the principal source of local problems, his attitude toward Italians may not have been much more favorable. In the only entry in his diary involving an Italian, Cope mentioned a Charles Panosi, who had sought payment from the estate of Stephen Girard for 600 boxes of vermicelli. As executor of the estate, Cope asked the Italian whether he had a receipt from Girard for the order. From his mimicking of Panosi's response, Cope must have been amused by the matter: "Oh, dere is happen to me one grand a misfortune, de ordare is in me pantaloo, de pantaloo is wash & de ordare is wash." Cope wrote that his answer to Panosi was "Well, my friend, the claim is wash too." Although he left a bill, the Italian never returned to pursue the claim further.[48]

Cope was only one person, but as an important member of the business community he was a more influential source of opinion on public issues than less prominent citizens. The incident with Panosi may have been typical of the perception other residents had of Italians, although the manner in which it was presented suggests that Cope found them to be only a minor nuisance. In contrast to the Irish, the Italians were still far too few and relatively uninvolved in local affairs to represent any serious threat to other Philadelphians.

Sidney George Fisher, whose personal diary also provided a valuable commentary on Philadelphia at this time, expressed a similar view of group relations. Writing a few months after the restoration of order in 1844, Fisher maintained that the rise of nativist politics had its origins in the growing power and influence of "the immense foreign population of the lowest class which is pouring into the country, the great majority of whom are Irish." While Fisher argued that nothing was more absurd in principle or more dangerous in consequences than the naturalization laws, he did not offer a sympathetic judgment of the foreign-born. He contended that even allowing a respectable class of foreigners to participate in politics was unwise, because they too were ignorant of American institutions and lacked proper feelings for the nation. Objecting particularly to what he saw as "the refuse population of Europe, the most ignorant and vile," Fisher saw the immigration laws as "a policy fraught with danger." He was convinced that the consequences of the policy had been severe and extensive in election results, in the measures of government, and in the administration of criminal law. Concluding that the Native American Party and the Whigs shared the same values and goals, Fisher expressed the hope that they would merge and succeed in the Congressional elections of 1844. Fisher was certain that the principles of this merger were destined to spread and possibly even to prevail, because they appealed to the people across the nation.[49]

Fisher expanded his earlier concerns about the growing problem of the immigrant in Philadelphia in an 1847 diary entry. Although he continued to emphasize the political threat presented by the foreign-born, Fisher now added the dangers to public health and other social conditions that came with the arrival of disease-carrying impoverished immigrants. He linked his own earlier political fears with the public health issues the City Councils had raised. After noting that another ship had arrived from Europe the previous day, he declared that the shipment of immense amounts of grain to Europe had not solved the problem of famine and disease there, and that typhoid fever was causing a "frightful havoc in Ireland and among the Irish who have fled to England." Adding "The emigration to this country is unparalleled," Fisher then described the diseased masses in rags and wretchedness that crowded the almshouses, hospitals, and poorhouses, where they were dying by the hundreds. Not only the Irish but also Germans came as entire villages in some cases. Then Fisher once again summarized his real concerns:

> And here they come not only to work and eat, or die, but to vote. That is the danger and the evil. The most ignorant and depraved of Europe, wholly ignorant of our government, our laws, our history, entirely unused to political privileges, unable even to comprehend them, without education or property, or interest in the country come here to govern us, to add to the already swollen ranks of radicals and levellers, to increase the already dangerous power of agitation and demagogues, to degrade still more the already degraded and foul condition of our politics and public morals and opinion.[50]

In only two decades, the rather sanguine and receptive attitude of Matthew Carey had been replaced by the hostile and vitriolic diatribes against immigration of Cope and Fisher, but their views were echoed by more official voices in the city. In 1846, in response to growing public concern, the Select Council noted: "The necessity of some provision being made by law to insure proper medical and surgical attention on board of emigrant ships, and to prevent the embarkation of emigrants who may be affected with any infectious disease." The Board of Health was particularly concerned about the poor physical health in which immigrants sometimes arrived as a result of ship conditions. The Select Council then passed a resolution recommending that Congress make some provision "for the safety and comfort of emigrants arriving in our ports, and the preservation of our own citizens, as they may in their wisdom deem proper." The same resolution was passed by the Common Council. Two years later, the Board of Health began appointing sanitary agents to inspect homes and streets for possible hazards. The concern was now obviously spreading from the diseases of arriving immigrants to the more general condition of the city and its population.[51]

A few years later, in 1855, despite its sometimes convoluted language, a report by the Committee on Police raised similar charges in a remarkable document that also provided further insight into the hostility against the foreign-born. Having identified the masses of newly arrived immigrants as "a dangerous source and element of pauperism and crime," the report added that they were often "marked by the prejudices, the ignorance and the vices which are the natural result of the social habits, institutions, and governments under which they have been born and lived." These differences supposedly explained why foreigners had great difficulty understanding the free institutions that could be found in America. The foreign-born also brought "the hereditary and implacable feuds, the national hatreds, which, in their own countries, divide nations—and separate communities into embittered factions."[52]

The police report argued that newcomers would be able to indulge in their most dangerous passions now that they were in contact with one another and had the freedom afforded by their new country, especially by the privilege of voting. It blamed the recent outbreaks of disorder on these passions, especially when foreigners were celebrating their own national festivals. This tendency justified the use of police force to protect the community from the violence that resulted from conflicts between foreign groups and conflicts that threatened peace and order. The report asserted that foreign governments, not reluctant to see our institutions tarnished and even undermined, had poured their paupers and criminals onto our shores "to infest and burden our large cities." The report concluded that the situation required establishing institutions whose task it was "to punish crimes and prevent their commission."[53]

The report supported its conclusions with information on pauperism and crime. From June 1, 1854, to May 1, 1855, the number of commitments to the county prison was three to four times as many for the foreign-born as for native-born people. Similarly, during a seven-month period the police had arrested 5,410 Americans, among them 886 blacks, but 10,476 persons of foreign birth. From such statistics, the large and still-increasing proportion of immigrants had greatly contributed to the evils found in America's cities. The conclusion that the continuation of Old World passions and conflicts had produced public disorder in American cities was an emphatic indictment of immigrant character, but most of all, it defended the use of force by the reorganized police department of Mayor Conrad.

Although different inferences could be drawn from these statistics, Mayor Conrad made a similar judgment about the impact of recent immigration on Philadelphia. In his annual message for 1855, Conrad claimed that police protection had not been necessary before recent immigration had changed the character of American cities, but that it was now needed more than in the capitals of European nations. The mayor argued that the police report proved that "perverted immigration has filled our cities with pauperism—the fruitful parent of disorder and crime." He charged that many individuals arrested for crime were, in his dramatic phrase, "the exiles of European prisons" who brought foreign vices and habits to American cities and made them "the home of disputes of clans and classes, sects and factions, alien to our character and country." These factors were responsible for the increase of beggars and vagrancy, prostitution, and riots in the cities. Conrad insisted that immigration had introduced class conflict, making cities that would otherwise be happy and harmonious the scene of insurrection and civil warfare. Many Philadelphians probably held essentially the same views at this time.[54]

After previously unsuccessful attempts, and with the aid of Irish voters, the patrician Quaker and Democrat Richard Vaux defeated the Whig-nativist opposition in the mayoralty election of 1856. Despite his alliance with the bosses, Vaux was a mayor of conscience and reform whose administration operated without great personal extravagance, as demonstrated by the brief economic crisis of 1857, when he authorized relief and public works on behalf of the unemployed. But during his one term of office, Vaux's most important contribution probably came from his influence over the new police department, which began a new era of efficiency and professionalism. The hiring of Irish applicants not only began their long tradition as members but also removed the police force from its previous role as a device of control over them. The police also had noticeable success against crime and the gang problem, and no additional riots occurred. However, Vaux's brief career was not sufficient to offset the growing strength of machine politics that dominated the city in later years.[55]

Before consolidation, while the Whigs generally succeeded by guarding the interests of the wealthy and privileged classes within the city, the Democrats found strength in areas outside its boundaries. But such issues as the tariff, the war with Mexico, and the question of race and the abolition of slavery sometimes encouraged surprising coalitions and varied the membership of both parties. While the two major parties struggled for local and national power, political movements with narrower intentions arose. In the early 1840s, with a wide-sweeping ideology and agenda, the Native American Party could be antiblack, anti-Catholic, and antiforeign—all at the same time. In another decade, a similarly nativist political outlook marked the Loyal Order of the Star Spangled Banner, popularly known as the Know-Nothing Party.[56]

Philadelphians played an active role in the political events that swept the nation. In 1856, antislavery Republicans held their first convention for nomination of a Presidential candidate at the Musical Fund Society Hall. Perhaps the strategy of the young party was to establish a presence in Philadelphia, where Republicans were still insignificant in number. But in the fall Presidential election, local voters provided strong support for Democrat James Buchanan, a native of Pennsylvania. That support was probably a reflection of the negative attitude of white residents toward blacks and the abolition movement. In the final years before the Civil War, although public order was occasionally threatened by persisting tensions between antislavery and proslavery factions, serious violence never erupted. With the Democrats divided, when Philadelphia voters supported Lincoln in the election of 1860 the local campaign emphasized tariff protection rather than opposition to slavery, and the ticket had to be camouflaged with the label "People's Party" instead of being called the Republican Party.[57]

Despite widespread bonds and sympathies with the South before the war, Philadelphia solidly supported Lincoln and the Union once it began. While the war renewed opportunity for its industries, Philadelphia also became an important center for medical treatment of the wounded from the battlefields. As it lingered on, however, opposition to the war also appeared. New organizations, such as the Union Club (later reorganized as the Union League) and the Central Democratic Club (founded by the Peace Democrats), reflected both sides of the continuing debate over the war.[58]

In the election of 1864, Lincoln again won the support of Philadelphia voters. While the war ended slavery in the United States, in Philadelphia and in the rest of the nation, the issues of race and civil rights for blacks remained a source of major difficulties. On the day Congress abolished slavery with the passage of the Thirteenth Amendment, streetcar companies reported that their riders had voted in a referendum to segregate passengers by race. But the successful politics of the National Unionist Party, particularly in its support of the war, established the basis for a nearly ninety-year span of Republican control of Philadelphia that would follow.[59]

From the 1830s to the end of the Civil War, Philadelphia, along with the rest of the nation, passed through a time of cataclysmic change. With the Industrial Revolution and its social consequences at the center, the city had already experienced a great expansion of population and physical boundaries, with mass immigration as a contributing factor. The class system and the distribution of wealth, prestige, and power were evolving into a newer structure. The debate over slavery, followed by an agonizing Civil War, had torn the political order apart.

Although its problems could not be entirely solved by consolidation and the revamping of municipal services, Philadelphia sought to make other adjustments necessary for the future. With the loss of informal street activity and the cohesion of earlier patterns of urban life, Philadelphians of all economic levels and social backgrounds formed clubs and associations in response to the problem of community. Parishes, fraternal lodges, recreational clubs, political organizations, and benefit societies were founded to fill the gap. Whether for specialized purposes or more general needs, voluntary associations proliferated throughout the city. But more formal aspects of civic life, such as the municipal corporation formed by the Act of Consolidation, the reorganization of the police force, the modernization of public services such as the waterworks, and the development of the public school system, were also evolving. In short, the destruction of earlier forms of social structure was being met by the invention of new institutions.[60]

At the same time, there was continuity with the past. The diversions that had entertained and amused previous generations, such as taverns, theaters, lectures, newspapers, circuses, museums, and concerts, still attracted and distracted the public. Philadelphia had survived these turbulent years, but it had been thoroughly transformed from the British seaport it once was, even in the years after the Revolutionary War, to an emphatically American industrial city in the nineteenth century. The basic customs, patterns, and institutions of modern urban community life had been established.

Patriotism and Protest

For any racial or ethnic group, the events and conditions of these years provided the parameters within which its own particular experience unfolded in Philadelphia. With this context in place, we can narrow our focus and return to the case of the Italians. Although they were only a small component of the total population, Italians shared many issues with the rest of the city, but their adjustment to Philadelphia also derived from political and economic conditions in Italy at this point. The formation of Italians as a community and as an ethnic group in an American city cannot be understood without some reference to the momentous chapter that was unfolding in the country from which they had departed. While they had left their land of birth, Italians could not immediately and entirely leave it behind them. Similarly, many native Philadelphians had serious interest in the political events unfolding in Italy at the time. Even if Metternich's observation that Italy was "merely a geographical expression" were true, in its own manner the Risorgimento touched Philadelphia. During the 1840s and 1850s, the patriotic fervor and courageous actions that eventually brought independence and unification to Italy stirred the sympathies of Philadelphians. What impact, if any, did the struggle in Italy and the support expressed for it in the United States have on Italians in Philadelphia?

As the nineteenth century continued, Italians in Philadelphia began their first significant growth in population. But more important than size alone, the development of a community depended on the establishing of both informal and formal institutions. By forming interpersonal networks of association, friendship, and support in previous years, Italians had already generated an informal social system. In the middle of the century, these patterns of interaction evolved further and moved from a more preliminary stage to become an actual community within the context that Philadelphia provided.

The existence of informal relations within any community often goes unnoticed, especially to the outsiders who make up the larger society. For Italians in Philadelphia, however, the founding of formal institutions that provided more visible evidence of the community took even longer. The earliest official expression of the presence of Italians

as a group in Philadelphia was the establishment of diplomatic representation, with the arrival of Godfrey (or Gaspar) Deabbate as the Sardinian Consul to the United States in March 1820.[61] With his residence
and office at 219 Spruce Street, except for the Inglesi affair in 1823,
Deabatte's tenure as the Sardinian Consul was relatively uneventful,
and neither did it last very long. Toward the second half of 1825, he
was replaced by the Chevalier Ignazio Vincenzo Cavaradossy.[62]

While Italians had shown a great interest in the ideals of the American Revolution, their attraction to the United States had reached a
different stage as the Napoleonic Wars were ending. Thomas Appleton, the American Consul at Leghorn, had written to Thomas Jefferson
in September 1816:

> The number of applicants to go to the United States has become
> incalculable; from professors of the highest services, down to
> the labouring peasant; and had they the means, as they have the
> will, Italy would be half depopulated. You will naturally infer,
> Sir, from thence there is no amelioration in the political state
> of the country; on the contrary, it is progressing to that sort of
> maturity which must terminate in a universal convulsion: this
> is not a partial evil, but extends to the utmost limits of Italy.[63]

In his letter, Appleton indicated that social conditions in Italy, as
well as the attitudes of individuals, were already conducive to emigration. If his observations were correct, it is surprising that mass
immigration to the United States had not already started. The absence
of a large volume of migration from Italy to America perhaps can
be attributed more to the lack of an adequate system of transportation than to anything else. In view of the serious political upheaval
and enormous migration that soon followed, Appleton's letter was
remarkably prophetic.

A similar sense of what the future might hold was apparently shared
by the officials of several Italian states; by 1830 the governments
of Sardinia, the Papal States, and the Kingdom of Sicily had posted
consular agents in Philadelphia.[64] While these appointments did not
necessarily mean that there already was a significant number of their
citizens in the city, or a considerable volume of trade with the United
States, it did indicate that these states had interests to pursue or
protect. In 1832, for example, perhaps already anticipating an increase

in migration and commerce, the Sardinian Consul in Philadelphia proposed establishing a regular shipping line between Genoa and the United States. Despite his efforts, as well as a treaty designed to promote trade between the two countries six years later, the plan was not implemented.[65]

Similarly, although Rome had appointed Giovanni Battista Sartori as its Consul in 1828, there were probably few occasions when citizens of the Papal States in Philadelphia needed assistance, mainly because such individuals rarely came to America. Similarly, the other major function of a consul was almost as unnecessary, because the volume of trade between the Papal States and the United States never became very large. As the American Consul in Rome, Felix Cicognani, wrote to John Quincy Adams in 1824, "In a country like this, governed by clergy, scarcely anything happens concerning politics or commerce." After a free-trade agreement eliminated duties, the situation changed somewhat and some commerce was possible, but ships from the Papal States still rarely arrived at American ports.[66]

American ships were much more likely to sail to papal ports with cargoes of tobacco, timber, alcohol, lard, petroleum, candles, paraffin, and even cheese. American officials sometimes attempted to increase this trade, as when Consul William Stillman sought greater exportation of wood products, agricultural implements, and refrigerant ice in the 1860s. On their return to the United States, these ships often carried works of art, mosaics, and religious articles. Stillman also sought to establish the importation of Italian wines, then not a well-known commodity in the American market. These efforts were not particularly profitable, and the volume of commerce between the Papal States and the United States never reached a great level. The consular posts probably were often not much more than ornamental positions.[67]

On the other hand, trade by ships that had called on other Italian ports had a greater material impact. Although shipping records are fragmentary, at least five American ships reached Philadelphia after leaving Palermo, Leghorn, and Messina in 1835. In the following year, six more ships docked at Philadelphia after departing from Naples, Messina, Palermo, and Leghorn. In 1837, another six ships brought cargoes from Leghorn, Messina, and Genoa. In the next year, one ship arrived from Messina. The record is interrupted at this point, but it resumes with the appearance of three ships from Leghorn and

Genoa in 1841–42. For the most part, these vessels transported goods, but they also carried a few passengers, such as the nineteen adults and five children that disembarked from the ship *Ohio* in September 1841. Along with the passengers, the modest commerce of these ships provided the needs served by the consular officials of the Italian states in Philadelphia. These Atlantic crossings also suggest the trickling flow of Italians who made their way to the United States at this time.[68]

As in the case of his predecessor, Cavaradossy's tenure as the Sardinian Consul in Philadelphia remained relatively calm and uneventful, without even an Inglesi affair to provide some distraction. The high point of Cavaradossy's years in the city may have been provided by his own wedding in January 1828. Among an impressive list of titles, the marriage record at Old St. Joseph's Church identified the groom as a Senior Knight and Royal Consul General of Sardinia. His bride, Mary Antoinette D'Aurainville, was described with a similar list of titles. But buried in this event is another intriguing detail on the Italian scene in Philadelphia at this moment. Among the witnesses appears a name listed only as Garibaldi, Vice-Consul and Chancellor of Sardinia.[69]

This little-known chapter of Italian life in Philadelphia deserves some consideration, although it also warrants some caution. Angelo Garibaldi was born on July 25, 1804, to Domenico and Rosa Raimondi Garibaldi. His father was a native of Chiavari, a city that later played an important part in Italian immigration to Philadelphia. According to some accounts, when Angelo was three years old a second son was born, named Giuseppe, later to become the most famous military figure in the Risorgimento. One biographer, in discussing the family origins of the great Italian patriot, claims that Giuseppe Garibaldi had two sisters and three brothers. Of the firstborn son the writer says: "Angelo emigrated to the United States, became a wealthy business man in New York, and ended as Sardinian Consul in Philadelphia."[70] The distinguished British historian George Macaulay Trevelyan, in his massive and influential study of Giuseppe Garibaldi, did not even mention an older brother.[71]

When Angelo Garibaldi reached adulthood, he sailed to America, then worked as a merchant for a while in New York City. If published accounts are correct, he was only twenty-four years old at the time of the Cavaradossy wedding in 1828. Destined to have not only far less fame than his younger brother but also a much shorter life, Angelo died in Philadelphia in 1835 at age thirty-one. In November of that year, he had prepared a document in which he referred to himself as the Consul of Sardinia in the United States and indicated his intentions with regard to the disposition of his estate. In these instructions, which were prepared at the home of Domenico Morelli, Consul General of the Kingdom of the Two Sicilies, Garibaldi left his entire estate to his parents. He also asked that his relatives arrange for twenty Masses to be celebrated for his soul ("farsi celebrare 20 messe per l'anima mia da miei Parenti"). His estate was first valued at $2,870.94, almost all in cash at the Bank of the United States in Philadelphia, but it would later increase. He was buried in Philadelphia, but his remains were not allowed to rest for long.[72]

Two years after his death, along with others that had been interred on the north side of St. John the Evangelist Church on South Thirteenth Street, Garibaldi's body was moved to a new burial vault, marked with his image in bas-relief and an inscription in Italian placed in honor by fellow countrymen. When Giuseppe Garibaldi led the fight for Italian unification against the Papal States, the profile image of the person reputed to be his brother still covered a grave at a Catholic church in Philadelphia. Subsequently, the body was supposed to have been returned to Italy, and when the church wall was plastered the commemorative stone was removed.[73]

Some parts of Angelo Garibaldi's life may have been apocryphal and invented on the local scene, especially in view of Trevelyan's failure to mention an older brother. To complicate matters further, a more recent biographer of Giuseppe Garibaldi erroneously gives the date of Angelo's death as sometime in 1853, while yet another states that it was in November 1855. The first writer also contends that when Angelo died he left money to his brother, Giuseppe, who purchased one half the island of Caprera, where he spent his final years.[74] The letter of administration filed after Angelo's death clearly named his parents as the beneficiaries of his estate, without mentioning a brother. Even this detail is unusual, because a letter of administration was usually filed when someone died without a will. Yet that particular document also described a disposition of estate prepared by Angelo Garibaldi before his death. These conflicting pieces of information have left a muddled picture of his life and some uncertainty, in particular, about whether he was indeed the older brother of Giuseppe.

Beyond this curious episode, what were the further implications of a consular presence, possibly representing several sovereign states of the Italian peninsula, for the population that had originated there but was becoming a permanent part of Philadelphia in the early nineteenth century? It was certainly more than for purposes of diplomatic and commercial protection, especially if such services were only rarely needed. The opening of the Sardinian consulate also showed that Sardinia expected that its people would have an increasing role in the public life and affairs of Philadelphia. And ornamental functions, such as the Cavaradossy wedding, were more than private ceremonies insofar as they provided public occasions celebrating origins and identity. These moments enabled expatriates far from their homeland to revitalize cultural loyalties even more than political allegiances in the face of experiences that threatened to erase all bonds with the place from which they had come.

The lives of ordinary Italians sometimes contained other clues to their attitudes toward their native land. Born at Bergamo in 1800, Giovanni Battista Vitalba migrated from Leghorn to Philadelphia seventeen years later. In 1825, he petitioned the District Court for naturalization, naming the King of Austria as the sovereign being abandoned but identifying the applicant as a native of Italy and a former citizen of the Italian nation.[75] Although someone else may have invented these responses for the convenience of the court, it was more likely that Vitalba provided the information himself. If so, then Vitalba's responses expressed in an indirect but powerful manner his own yearning for or expectation of a nation that was still a generation away from coming into being. Undoubtedly shared by other Italians, Vitalba's ideals and aspirations showed that experiences in the new setting could not yet be entirely separated from events and conditions in the native land. With the fate of Italy still relevant in their minds, it was also prominent in their lives. These sentiments generated political and psychological choices that immigrants had to face and resolve as they made their adjustment to life in Philadelphia.

Meanwhile, the disruption of life by political events in Italy had implications in American cities, where these political developments would be not only noticed, but also widely supported by local citizens. On becoming emperor, Ferdinand I of Austria offered to commute the sentences of Italian patriots confined in the infamous Spielberg Prison, if they accepted deportation to America. While some chose to remain in prison until the expiration of their sentences, others agreed to the deportation. Beginning in 1836, early *fuorusciti* settled mainly in New York City, among them Pietro Maroncelli, Count Federico

Confalonieri, Pietro Borsieri, Giovanni Albinola, Gaetano Castiglia, Felice Foresti, and Luigi Tinelli. The practice of deporting political prisoners from Lombardy, Tuscany, the Papal States, and the Kingdom of Naples to New York City continued for the next twenty years, almost until the independence of Italy was achieved.[76]

After their arrival, a few of these political refugees found Boston, besides New York City, to be a suitable location, but hardly any appear to have even spent any time in Philadelphia. Giacomo Sega, discussed earlier, was one, but there must have been others, if only for a short time. In an 1837 letter, Confalonieri informed Borsieri, who was teaching in Princeton, New Jersey, "Albinola è ora a Filadelfia in qualità di clerc dell'attorney *mister* Castillia pei noti affari dell'eredità del Mussi."[77] Although he had not been in the United States long and would not remain much longer, Confalonieri had already begun to adopt an early version of the hybrid language that later immigrants developed further. But even more important, the participation of Albinola and Castiglia in the settlement of the estate of Joseph Mussi, the merchant who had died in 1832, suggests that these political figures had some involvement in the business affairs of fellow Italians who had previously settled in the United States.

Confalonieri, who may not have thought that a small rural town in New Jersey was the most appropriate place for his intelligent and capable friend, attempted to convince Borsieri to leave Princeton and move to Philadelphia, where there were supposedly many people yearning to study the Italian language. For his part, however, Borsieri may have preferred to move to the South—if anywhere else, perhaps to Virginia—because of what he had been told about the "chivalrous nature" of the inhabitants of that state. In any case, it soon all became moot, despite the agreement with their former captors that no *fuorusciti* could come back to Austrian-controlled territory, when Borsieri returned to Milan, his native city in 1840.[78]

In Italy by 1840–41, when political thinkers and activists had renewed their efforts for the independence of their nation, Giuseppe Mazzini emerged as the most influential voice at the center of these activities. His principal intention was to convince Italians, whether in Italy or in other countries, of the need to develop a national consciousness and to prepare themselves to join, when the moment arrived, the movement to liberate their homeland. With a prodigious capacity for correspondence, Mazzini wrote letters almost daily to Italian political exiles in foreign cities. In response to Mazzini, but also to other influences in Italy and elsewhere, a revolutionary movement was being organized.[79]

The Italian patriots who had accepted the opportunity to depart from Austrian prisons had not abandoned their political aspirations and machinations on behalf of their homeland. From their new location in New York City, former participants of the Young Italy movement continued their support of Mazzini's hopes for an independent Italian republic. Shortly after organizing in London, a similar central Congregation was established for the United States in 1841, with a plan that called for branches in American cities. Although Giuseppe DeTivoli was designated to organize the Philadelphia chapter, no further evidence indicates that anything more was accomplished. It also remains unclear how many local units were ever formed outside New York City. Perhaps most efforts never went beyond naming an organizer. But in 1843, Foresti, director of the central Congregation for the United States, wrote to his counterpart in Paris that local chapters had been established in New York, Boston, New Orleans, and perhaps Philadelphia.[80]

In Boston and New York, Italians mobilized not only in support of the political cause in their homeland, but also in response to their needs as a growing community in a new country. The model was a free school and protective association in London that Mazzini himself had organized in 1841 for Italian children who had been brought there by exploitative masters to work as organ-grinders. A similar school was begun in Boston by Pietro Bachi, a Sicilian exile, with free classes for instruction in reading, writing, and history three days a week. By the autumn of 1842, such a school opened in New York City for about forty pupils and expectations for an increasing number in the future. An ambitious curriculum offered reading, writing, arithmetic, history, geography, and English. Classes were scheduled for six to ten o'clock each evening, Monday through Friday. A series of lectures on Italian history by Foresti, who was also director of the school, was to be presented on Sundays later in the same year.[81]

Mazzini's objectives, however, may have been received better by Philadelphia's non-Italian residents than by Italians, who remained remote from political and social affairs, whether pertaining to their homeland or to their newer community. Irish Catholics played a conspicuous role in the tragic violence of 1844, but no other immigrant group was a major participant. While Cope and Fisher condemned immigrants with regard to politics or public health, the handful of Italians could not pose a threat in the way that other groups did. To the contrary, most things associated with Italy were presented in a highly positive manner. Italian opera, for example, was received with such enthusiasm that the *Public Ledger* facetiously warned of its influence in diffusing the language of Italy:

> Now that the operatic troupe has arrived, we may expect to be overpowered with Italian phrases by some of our newspaper critics. We have no objection to a slight sprinkling of them through their criticisms, but, gentlemen, please not be quite as liberal as you were during the last operatic season. We ask this in mercy to Anglo-Saxonism, which will be totally abolished unless you restrain your impassioned ardor.[82]

The serious political situation in Italy in the late 1840s, however, could not be ignored in Philadelphia. If anything, it provided residents with even more opportunity to express their favorable and supportive views toward Italians. With the election of Pope Pius IX in 1846, many Philadelphians turned with optimism toward the politics of Italy. From the first days of his papacy, Pius IX had begun a series of administrative changes that gave him an early reputation as a liberal reformer. In November 1847, a number of influential citizens met in New York City to express their approval of the reforms introduced by the Pope. Similar demonstrations soon took place in other American cities. In January 1848, Philadelphians gathered in the Chinese Museum to declare their support for the efforts of Pius IX to achieve constitutional reforms in the Papal States. But the meeting was also intended as a demonstration of the respect and sympathy of the citizens of Philadelphia for the people of Italy in their struggle for independence. The participants included many distinguished and powerful individuals, such as Richard Vaux, Morton McMichael, and Robert T. Conrad. After listening to various speakers, the audience unanimously adopted several resolutions in support of the liberal reform movement under the leadership of Pius IX. At the conclusion of what the *Public Ledger* called a "magnificent demonstration," an attempt was made to transmit the results of the meeting to the Pope through the U.S. Department of State. James Buchanan, then Secretary of State, later informed the leaders of the gathering that, although he had "the warmest admiration for the character of the illustrious Pope," this means of communication would violate State Department procedures. Nonetheless, it had been a large and enthusiastic expression of support for the ostensibly reformist Pope and the independence movement in Italy.[83]

In the days that followed, revolutionary uprisings that sought to establish republican governments swept across western Europe. In Philadelphia and other American cities, residents repeatedly expressed their sympathy with these political ideals through public demonstrations. In early April, Germans met in Northern Liberties to discuss how they could support their country in its political struggle. Similarly, the Friends of Ireland held meetings in the city at the same time to display their loyalty to the cause of Irish independence. Later in the same month, a massive celebration with bands and flags was held at Independence Square, during which the crowd listened to speeches in English, French, and German. While this event focused on the republican movement in France and Germany, even a group of black Philadelphians heard addresses by some of their own leaders. It is curious that, although the Italian *tricolore* was displayed, there does not seem to have been any conspicuous Italian presence or participation at the event. In October of the same year, while 2,000 Germans met at the Chinese Museum to hear Friedrich Hecker, the leader of the movement for a constitutional republic in Germany, Italians in Philadelphia again remained silent on the situation in Italy.[84]

There can be no question that Italians in Philadelphia were aware of what was happening in their native land. The local press covered the politics of Europe and often emphatically joined in the support of these events. In an 1848 editorial, the *Public Ledger* unequivocally declared its sentiments:

> Nor will the influence of France be less salutary over Italy. But there, as in Germany, several kings must be *cleared out*. The Sicilians have very wisely dismissed the Bourbon King of Naples. The best thing that the Neapolitans can do with him is shipping him off to England, for he is a tyrant and a knave whom no treaties can bind. And the King of Sardinia, belonging to a family historically celebrated for perfidy, is already abating in his patriotic fever for the deliverance of Italy, because the

Milanese want republicanism. We hope that his own immediate subjects, the Piedmontese and the Genoese, will give him a dose of republicanism at home. We hope to see the United States of Italy, comprehending the States of Sicily, Naples, Rome, Tuscany, Sardinia, Piedmont, Genoa, Venice, Milan, Modena, Parma, Savoy and San Marino, just *thirteen*, with the Pope for the first President.[85]

In its editorials, the *Public Ledger* continued its support of Italians in their struggle for independence and even exhorted the U.S. government to play an active role in the cause. In June 1849, the *Public Ledger* declared:

> If ever a people deserved sympathy from the humane, the philanthropic of other countries, that people are the Italians. Their cause is holy, and they are struggling for it against the combined wickedness of all the old European monarchies, and to their everlasting shame be it spoken, of the President, ministry and priesthood of *Republican* France. . . . The Romans are struggling not only for the right of self-government, but for that republican government which is *our* pride, *our* boast, the source of *our* happiness. Their cause is not only the cause of all Italy, but of republicanism, of civil and religious freedom, of humanity. And they are assailed, not only by those old enemies of liberty, the kings and political priests, not only by traitors to liberty in Republican France, but by traitors to the same holy cause in the United States.[86]

While the attempt by Italian revolutionaries in 1849 to establish a republic at Rome came to a disastrous conclusion, their brave effort was widely applauded. In Philadelphia, the appeals in support of the republican movement by influential voices, such as the *Public Ledger*, also had modestly dramatic consequences. In the middle of a cholera epidemic in which 232 people had already died between May 30 and July 2, many residents ignored the risk to their health and joined in a rally on Independence Day to express support once more for the republican cause in Italy. While refugees in New York and Boston displayed their patriotic sentiments in demonstrations, and their intention to rejoin their comrades in their homeland, there were still no indications of public support from the small Italian population in Philadelphia at this time.[87]

While other groups, including native Philadelphians, participated in public demonstrations in support of republican forces in Europe and the struggle in Italy, Italians did not. It is ironic that even French residents of the city met in July 1849 to condemn their government for its role in the war in Italy.[88] Where were the Italians? The small size of the Italian population of Philadelphia may not be enough of an answer. It is possible that Italians joined their compatriots in demonstrations in New York, and it is also possible that Italians participated in such events even in Philadelphia but that their presence went unreported. In the final analysis, however, other factors—the absence of communal institutions and the inappropriateness of what already existed—may have been more important. Neither the Sardinian consulate, which was unlikely to support republicanism, nor the occasional boardinghouse, which was too feeble or indifferent to politics, could have played this role. The public expression of political values by Italians was further frustrated by a paradoxical situation. While political conditions might have encouraged them to begin establishing voluntary associations, Italians could not readily participate in public events without such organizations.

Crime and Italians: A Darker Image Begins

While they had not yet reached the stage of communal development of other immigrant groups, Italians did share the meaner conditions of urban life with them. In contrast to such aristocrats as Cavaradossy, or even untitled but prosperous families like the Sartoris, most Italians were in less fortunate circumstances. From time to time, episodes that brought them to the attention of other residents also revealed a darker side of Italian life in Philadelphia emerging in the early 1840s. In July 1841, a newspaper item reported that "John Andriot, an Italian" had been charged and convicted of being drunk and disorderly on Second Street near Carter's Alley. Andriot was fined and directed to pay a $100 bond. The hapless Andriot was then also charged with obstructing dogcatchers and fined another $100. The newspaper account concluded with a question: "Why don't persons desist from intermeddling with the officers of the law?" This relatively trivial episode may represent the beginning of preoccupation with a criminal dimension in the coverage of Italian experience in Philadelphia that would appear on an almost daily basis in the local press in later years.[89]

Two years after the Andriot case, newspapers reported the stabbing death of James Grillo, who with his assailant, James Berneiro, had been boarding for about two weeks in the house of Joseph Merito on Market Street near Twelfth. The newspaper account specifically pointed out that both men were Italian. The provocation for the violence came during supper on the previous Sunday evening, when Grillo began defaming the section of Italy from which Berneiro had come. (The reporter did not identify the regions of origin involved in this incident.) A fight began outside the house, and Merito attempted to stop it. He was concerned that any public disturbance on a Sunday would cause them all to be arrested. But when Berneiro turned to reenter the house, Grillo jumped him from behind and began beating him severely on the head, back, and shoulders. The large, muscular Grillo was able to hold the much smaller Berneiro in this position for some time. At that point, Berneiro drew a knife and, violently slashing backward, wounded Grillo on the abdomen and chest. When another resident of the same house, a young man named Costa, tried to stop the fight, he was stabbed on his thigh. Finally separated, the wounded Grillo was pulled into the house and the door was closed. Berneiro was left on the sidewalk. It was not immediately apparent that Grillo was wounded. When Grillo went into the yard, Merito followed to see how he was. Grillo lowered his head and began to groan; Merito asked what was the matter. Grillo replied, "I am a dead man. That man has got a knife." At that point, Grillo showed his bleeding wounds to the landlord. Quickly summoned, a physician bandaged the wounds and Grillo was taken to a hospital.[90]

Before he died on the next morning, Grillo gave his own view of the incident. He told hospital attendants the name of his attacker, claiming that there had been no provocation. Both men had recently come to Philadelphia from Richmond, Virginia, where each had operated a grocery store not far from the other. While the coroner reported that the abdomen wound severed Grillo's intestines and caused his death, the wound to the chest, which had penetrated the lung, could have produced the same result. The report added that neither man had drunk anything of consequence on the day of the incident. As for Berneiro, he was last seen after the stabbing without hat or coat but wearing an old pair of faded brown trousers and a calico shirt, walking down Market Street. According to the newspaper account, "He is a small, clumsy man, with dark complexion and whiskers."

Another case involved an Italian beggar identified only as Juan Baptiste who lived in Parker's Alley in Moyamensing in September 1848. Along with a number of organ-grinders and their families, Baptiste had entered the yard of a neighborhood woman, Catharine Gunsyer, and began cleaning mud from his boots at her washtub. When she attempted to stop him, Baptiste grabbed her by the throat and bit her arm, inflicting what was described as a serious wound. As a result, Baptiste was arrested and jailed. The newspaper report of the incident concluded: "Mrs. Gunsyer is a very respectable woman, the wife of a baker in Passyunk road, and the inhuman action of her assailant was entirely unprovoked." The manner in which this event was reported in the local press made it clear that the assailant was an Italian and his victim was not. But the account included nuances of brutality, beggar, and inhuman action that contributed to a different depiction of Italian character than Philadelphia had previously seen.[91]

While these incidents and the newspaper accounts that reported them remained rare, new arrivals from Italy were greeted by an ambiguous situation. On one hand, Philadelphians were becoming increasingly alarmed at the intrusion of newcomers and the competition they represented. Some neighborhoods, because of their proximity to landing sites and industries where employment was available to the foreign worker, were more likely locations for immigrants to seek residence. In the spring of 1848, the citizens of Southwark, an area in which Italians would soon be substantial in number, presented a petition asking the commissioners of the district to establish a police force whose principal task would be "to prevent the landing of foreign emigrants." An editorial in the *Public Ledger* responded: "This is the grandest crusade against foreigners that has been conceived of in modern times." Although it was unclear whether the concern of residents in the district was aimed more against merchants from neighboring New Jersey for whom "emigrant" was being used as a facetious metaphor or the actually foreign born, this was another precursor of attitudes and actions yet to come.[92]

By the late 1840s, although the founding of such agencies as the Emigrants' Friend Society showed that there was concern for the general safety and well-being of immigrants and their families, it was evident that the social climate in Philadelphia was at the same time hostile and obstructive toward them as well as sympathetic and supportive. While nativism was mounting, local apprehensions remained focused on the threats posed by rapidly increasing numbers of German and Irish arrivals; on the other hand, the previously favorable perceptions of Italy and of Italians remained protected by several factors. Philadelphians, especially the most prominent and powerful residents, were enthusiastic supporters of the Italians in their movement for independence and a republican form of government. They could not easily endorse the Risorgimento, while rejecting the Italians as a people. Philadelphians also persisted in their appreciation of the art, opera, and even the language that conveyed the high culture of Italy. The legacy of an earlier time that had made Italy the standard of personal refinement and cultivation retained its influence on Philadelphians. Moreover, Italians who had settled in the city included individuals who had been relatively successful as artists, entertainers, impresarios, and entrepreneurs in ways that met the needs and approval of other Philadelphians. With the number of Italians still not very large, public perception of the character of these foreign-born had not yet been neutralized by the arrival of the mass migration from peasant backgrounds of Southern Italy. That change would come at a later time.

As the 1840s ended, Italians remained at a very preliminary stage in their collective experience in Philadelphia. They were still too small in number to establish any significant neighborhood concentrations. While their origins were quite varied, a Genoese and Corsican configuration that had first appeared early in the century still gave a Ligurian cast to their population, with Tuscany as another discernible source, which the next federal census, in 1850, confirmed.

Public incidents like the Andriot arrest, the Grillo stabbing, and the Baptiste assault revealed more about the internal condition of the Italian population and its relationship to the larger city than might be first suspected. But, most important, these events contained some hints of the future. As early as 1843, Italians were beginning to cluster in small but nonetheless important units, such as boardinghouses. These arrangements became crucial for temporary accommodations, and as mechanisms for indoctrination and adjustment. The boardinghouse was a way-station in which previous immigrants of similar backgrounds offered more recent arrivals information and assistance on how to find employment, how to speak some English, and how to avoid trouble with the law. It was also a place where the tensions and frictions of immigrant life could be vented, though sometimes with fatal consequences. The boardinghouse became the first communal institution of a less formal sort—certainly well beyond the consulate, which was preoccupied with official matters and with the needs of more wealthy and powerful individuals—to function as an important instrument for helping the more ordinary immigrants endure everyday life in a strange city.

Italians in Philadelphia, however, were sometimes a nuisance to each other. Cases from previous decades, such as DaPonte's problems with other Italians, are evidence that this aspect was not entirely new, but by this time it had definitely entered a stage of more violent tactics. The ostensible provocation for the Grillo stabbing was an exchange of insults over the difference in origins in Italy between the two men, although the newspaper accounts did not indicate what their backgrounds were. Given what is known about arrivals from Italy at this time, it is likely that one of the men was a Ligurian. It is instructive to realize how such origins could be perceived by other Italians. A Tuscan proverb, known even by English travel writers, held that Genoa was "Mare senza pesce; montagne senza alberi; uomini senza fede; e donne senza vergogna" ("A sea without fish; mountains without trees; men without faith; and women without shame").[93]

Whatever separation and conflict existed, the violent and tragic aspects of the Grillo stabbing should not obscure the contact, communication, and identification with each other that were also elements of these incidents. Similarly, the case of the beggar Baptiste showed that Italians were visible on the streets as a group, and were a source of concern to non-Italian neighbors. It also revealed that some form of conflict between Italians and others in these neighborhoods was occurring. The newspaper account that identified Baptiste and others as organ-grinders also introduced a sense that the occupational callings of the Italians were shifting to much more modest levels than what had been seen in earlier years. Although the material plight of arriving immigrants in general, along with the occasional expressions of nativist hostility and opposition, had encouraged the formation of protective agencies, the success of these efforts remained limited. The future of the Italians, or any other immigrant group, in Philadelphia would depend more upon the establishment of institutions by their own members and the development of a community controlled by immigrants themselves.

Chapter 4

Shaping a New Life: Census, Parish, and Courtroom

The frustrated census enumerator asked once again, "What is your name?" The Italian, still confused by a new language, stared back and replied with his own question, "Oh, che dici?" Unable to realize that he had just been asked "Oh, what are you saying?" the interviewer carefully inscribed the name "O. Kiddice" in his ledger. With this solution to the language barrier that separated them, another Italian had been officially recorded in the population of Philadelphia by the federal census of 1850. We shall never know the real name of the person identified as "O. Kiddice," who probably did not know how he had been permanently entered in these records. But it is certain that his own friends and acquaintances would never know him as "O. Kiddice."

"O. Kiddice" was a man who had lost his identity. He was not clearly recognized for who he was by the census enumerator, the official representative of the new society. "Kiddice" was surely something different to his own people. At this moment of his life, he must even have been thoroughly confused about who he really was. Perhaps his marginality was part of the price any immigrant would have to pay in adjusting to a new society. Although it probably could not provide him with much consolation, "Kiddice" was certainly not alone. In many ways, this incident captured the ambiguous position, in their own minds and in the perceptions of others, of many Philadelphia Italians in the mid-nineteenth century. Like other immigrants, "Kiddice," who had most likely not been in Philadelphia long, was already being transformed by forces over which he had little control. But he was also far from what he would eventually become in the life that awaited him as a Philadelphian and an American.

European Politics and Emigrant Destinations

While recent arrivals such as "Kiddice" might view the United States as a place where they would find new material opportunities and personal identities, others saw it more as a place to find a solution for the grave political crisis in Europe. When the attempt to establish the Roman republic in 1849 was defeated, the American Consul in Rome issued passports to political refugees who sought to escape punishment after French troops regained control of the city. Some Italian nationalists fled to Genoa, where the Kingdom of Sardinia might offer them protection; others sought safety in Switzerland. At the same time that this situation threatened Europe with serious political and military disruption, it also allowed diplomats to redefine the significance of emigration in a manner that involved personal attitudes and public policies on both sides of the Atlantic.[1]

When Italian refugees were ordered by the local government to leave Genoa, they appealed for help to N. M. Moro, the American Vice-Consul in that city, who in turn sought the advice of Nathaniel Niles, the U.S. Chargé d'Affaires to the Kingdom of Sardinia. In his remarkable reply in February 1850, after advising Moro not to interfere in any way on behalf of the refugees with the actions and regulations of local authorities or the Sardinian government, Niles declared that since the refugees may have been deluded into believing that the passports would offer protection:

> it will be proper for you in disabusing them of this error to inform them individually that they are at liberty to disembark anywhere in the United States, if they choose to go there, without any passports whatever being required of them—that

our whole country is open to them, and that by industry and virtuous habits, they can neither fail of success nor to make themselves acceptable in their new abode.[2]

About a week later Niles reported these matters to John M. Clayton, the U.S. Secretary of State. After a tepid opening comment that nothing of special political interest had occurred since his last report, and a perfunctory paragraph describing a loan from the House of Rothschild to the Sardinian government, Niles devoted the rest of his lengthy communication to the situation of the refugees who had gathered in Switzerland, which was obviously important to the European powers and the U.S. State Department. He indicated that while Austria and Prussia had exhibited "a menacing character," France attempted to use "friendly representations and persuasion" toward the Swiss government, and Piedmont emphasized the dangers to European peace if any attempt to expel these emigrants was made by the military occupation of Swiss territory.[3]

Commenting on a letter from the prime minister of Piedmont, Massimo d'Azeglio, which was included in the dispatch to the State Department, Niles presented his emphatic view of the problem and its solution, arguing : "There can be no doubt that the extraordinary dangers and difficulties under which the continental nations of Europe are now exposed grow out, more or less directly, of a superabundant population." According to Niles, despair and desperation were a natural consequence of the complete blocking of all opportunities for success in business, the professions, the arts, agriculture, and manufacturing for thousands of individuals, who might be good subjects in America but were driven to seek improvement in their lives by means of revolution and disorder in Europe. The gathering of these populations had made all the great cities of Europe hotbeds for fomenting a false and impracticable political philosophy that had destroyed the great pillars of society—namely, moral responsibility, authority, a belief in God, and the rights of private property.[4]

The solution was as evident to Niles as his diagnosis of the basic problem had been:

Now relief for this state of things is to be found on a comparatively uncultivated continent, capable of supporting hundreds of millions of inhabitants, situated at the short distance of from twelve to twenty five days steam navigation. There, this dangerous surplus population, in every part of Europe, would find a congenial climate and a welcome reception—there they could found families and establish the independence and happiness of their descendants for centuries to come.[5]

It is not clear, however, whether Niles had developed much of his thinking independently of d'Azeglio's views. In an obvious attempt to reconcile the European powers, d'Azeglio's eloquent and delicately crafted letter had already provided much of the same argument. Writing officially on behalf of King Victor Emmanuel II, but undoubtedly expressing his own wisdom, d'Azeglio argued that expelling the refugees from Switzerland would leave the problem only half resolved. If the intention of the powers was to deliver the Continent from the socialist menace, that would not be accomplished by making its leaders walk across Europe, for they would merely reunite with their followers in another country. But the more important issue for d'Azeglio was the restoration of authority upon the solid base that would make it again respectable, and that solution must reflect impartiality and justice, rather than the imposition of force by a stronger party upon a weaker one in the Swiss situation. Instead, noting that many individuals had turned toward demagoguery more as a result of their unjust but real suffering rather than their evil passions, he urged the European powers to join together and, with the cooperation of the American government as well, organize and finance a program of mass emigration. In d'Azeglio's eyes, "Europe has arrived at the point that it is no longer possible to blind itself to the consequences of the current situation and that it is necessary to take a part."[6]

D'Azeglio had made an ingenious effort to calm what could become a volatile crisis and to restore European stability. What was even more important about his argument, however, was not its relevance to the immediate situation but its implications for the future and for immigration to America. As Niles pointed out, d'Azeglio had intimated that the European powers should first perfect their social systems in order to reduce the number of people arrayed against them in open hostility. But d'Azeglio was only moderately progressive in his political views. While he endorsed a liberal policy toward nationalists, he was alarmed by what he termed radicalism and demagoguery. But what he also feared was actually the possibility that popular democracy might overwhelm aristocratic oligarchy, and what he proposed as a solution was not too different from exactly what American nativists, such as Sidney George Fisher with his own fears of "radicals and levellers," suspected that European governments might want to do.

As we now know, underneath it all, at least with regard to Italy, d'Azeglio himself was an ardent nationalist who accurately anticipated the inevitable confrontation with other nations that the struggle for Italian independence would entail. But d'Azeglio, who may have been more familiar with Southern Italy through his own travels than any other major political leader of the Risorgimento, was well aware of the problems in those regions and would later be concerned about whether they should have been included in the new nation.[7] Although he died in 1866, by endorsing the emigration of dissidents to America in the previous situation d'Azeglio had also prepared a precedent for a policy addressing the "Southern problem" in later years. Modern Italy had not yet been formed, but the seeds had been planted for solving the problems of overpopulation, political conflict, and social instability by extensive expulsion, although many would prefer to call it mass emigration.

The First Portrait of a People

Meanwhile, on another continent, while the violence and rioting of earlier years continued to smolder, Philadelphia had altered its own geographical and governmental structure in a search for civic order. As the city sought to resolve disorder, the nation moved toward the most disruptive period of its history and would soon be torn apart by the secession of the South and a devastating civil war. At the same time, the Industrial Revolution gained greater momentum in the city and the nation. In Europe, as the transformation of technology and economy accelerated, the peoples of various countries increased efforts to establish independence and self-government. In Italy, the frustration and failure of earlier attempts to achieve freedom from foreign rule did not prevent a renewal of the struggle for a new and unified nation. Although the great challenge remained unresolved for the moment, Italians would reach their goal at the end of the decade. Through the agitation of exiles, the campaign for Italy's independence would sometimes find sympathy and support in American cities.

All these events had implications for transplanted Italians in Philadelphia and elsewhere. By the mid-nineteenth century, the Italian population in Philadelphia had grown sufficiently to be visible. Although their total number was not large—being nowhere near the size of the Germans or the Irish—Italians now represented much more than the handful of colorful and engaging individuals who had enriched the life of the city in previous years. The circle of interpersonal relations that connected them with one another, albeit at times with less-than-peaceful and harmonious activities, had begun to take on more-stable institutional forms, which were reflected both in the consulate and in the boardinghouse. The 1850s experienced an even more formidable period of numerical growth, institutional development, and communal stability. As Philadelphia became more acquainted with the new arrivals and provided a place in which their material and spiritual needs would be met, it also sometimes used them as instruments in political schemes.

The federal census of 1850 provides the first real profile of the Italian population, but it also represents a baseline against which later periods can be measured. In the city and two adjoining areas immediately to the south, 117 residents had been born in Italy (Table 1). The few others who may have lived in other areas would not have added appreciably to this total. Italians were still generally dispersed, but with small clusters within Philadelphia as well as outside of it.

In any city ward, Italians constituted no more than a handful of residents, with the largest numbers being the 8 people in New Market Ward, the 9 in Walnut Ward, the 10 in Middle Ward, and 15 in Dock Ward. Although a single large family or household could have provided any of these numbers, that was clearly not the case in New Market Ward, where 8 Italians resided in 7 different units. On the other hand, the 9 Italians in Walnut Ward were actually 7 individuals in one household and 2 more in another. Ten Italians in Middle Ward lived in 4 different households, although one of those households alone had 5 members; 15 Italians in Dock Ward resided in 7 different households. In view of later developments, the proximity of Dock Ward to the Delaware River and to Southwark District suggests that this group of families would sprout forth as one important font for the Italian colony of subsequent years.

The potential source for an immigrant community, however, was even more evident in areas outside the city. Some 27 Italians in the

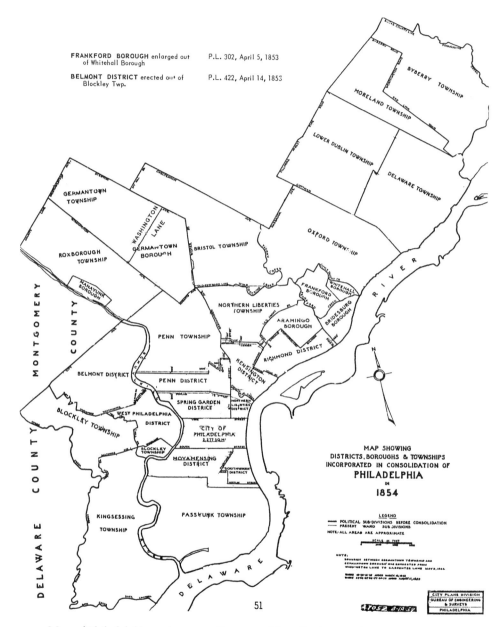

Map of Philadelphia and surrounding townships, districts, and municipalities in 1854, before Consolidation. (Philadelphia City Archives)

Table 1. Italian-born residents by ward, 1850

City of Philadelphia		Township of Moyamensing	
North Mulberry	5	Moyamensing 1st	12
South Mulberry	1	Moyamensing 2nd	12
Upper Delaware	2	Moyamensing 4th	2
North	1	Moyamensing 5th	1
High Street	3	Total	27
Middle	10		
Chestnut	2	Southwark District	
Lower Delaware	4	Southwark 1st	13
South	3	Southwark 3rd	4
Walnut	9	Total	17
Locust	5		
Pine	2		
Lombard	3		
Dock	15		
New Market	8		
Total	73		

Total for city and county: 117

SOURCE: The *Population Schedules* (or census manuscripts), the actual pages of the ledgers of each field-worker who gathered information from door to door for each household, with the questionnaire schedule, provide the data on Italians in Philadelphia at this time. The present analysis relies on these data for all wards of the city, as it was still constituted under its original boundaries, and for the adjacent Township of Moyamensing and Southwark District; see *Population Schedules of the Seventh Census of the United States, 1850* M432, National Archives, Mid-Atlantic Region, Philadelphia.

township of Moyamensing lived in 9 separate units, although 12 of them shared one household in its Second Ward. Similarly, 10 separate units in Southwark had 17 people of Italian origin. This distribution provided a prelude for the part Moyamensing and Southwark would play after the Act of Consolidation of 1854—when they were absorbed into the city as South Philadelphia, an area later densely populated by immigrant Italians.

The social characteristics reported by the 1850 census also revealed that the Italian population of the city was in a very formative phase at this point (see Table 2). Although there were children as well as adults of both sexes, it was mainly composed of young men. Of 89 Italian males, 53 of them, or 58 percent of the total, were between 20 and 49 years of age. Another 14 boys were between 10 and 19 years old.

Table 2. Distribution of Italians by
age and sex, 1850

Age (years)	Males	Females
0–9	1	7
10–19	14	1
20–29	18	5
30–39	19	9
40–49	16	3
50–59	8	2
60–69	8	0
70–79	5	1
Total (117)	89	28

SOURCE: See source note for Table 1.

Males outnumbered females by a roughly 3-to-1 ratio. Of the females, 14, or exactly half, were between 20 and 39 years old, with 8 more, or one-fourth, under age 10. But that result reflects the impact of one or two families on a rather small total number of females.

When we turn to family and household structure, some limitations in the way census-takers reported information make such patterns more difficult to describe than age and sex. Because the census generally failed to specify the nature of relationships within the household unit, the records remain ambiguous and must be used with some caution. It is possible, however, to piece together a sense of families and households from the listings (see Table 3).[8]

Thirty-two men appear to be married and accompanied by their wives, constituting nearly 36 percent of these cases. Nine of the married men had Italian-born wives; 11 more were married to women born in the United States; and 12 men had spouses from other foreign places. The 5 Irish-born wives suggest a tendency that became common among Italian American men in later periods. Of the 37 men who were without wives, some may have been widowers or may have left their wives in Italy.

Of 28 Italian-born women who were in the population in the city in 1850, 13 were married; the remaining 15 were not (see Table 4). Nine were married to men born in Italy; 3 others had husbands born in other foreign countries (France, Hungary, and England); another had an American-born husband; 6 more were unmarried adult women; and 9 were unmarried females under twenty-one years of age.

Table 3. Marital status of Italian males, 1850

Married, wife present		32
Wife born in Italy	9	
Wife born in United States	11	
Wife born elsewhere	12	
Germany	1	
Wales	1	
Nova Scotia	1	
England	4	
Ireland	5	
No wife present		37
Under 21, unmarried		15
Priests, unmarried		3
Unclear cases		2
Total		89

SOURCE: See source note for Table 1.

The nativity of children born to Italian parents provided another dimension of family structure (see Table 5). The population included 23 children under the age of twenty who were born in Italy. The Italian population in Philadelphia, however, consisted not only of individuals born in Italy but others elsewhere. Households in which either a father or a mother or both parents were Italian-born included 81 more children born in the United States, from the newly born to others up to the age of twenty. Almost all were natives of Pennsylvania. Of this group, 17 had both parents born in Italy; 56 others were sons or daughters of an Italian-born father; another 4 were children of Italian-born mothers; and 4 more had a parent of Italian birth in households in which it was unclear where the missing parent was born. From their ward locations, it is evident that many if not most of these individuals and families were living near other households in which all members

Table 4. Marital status of Italian females, 1850

Married		13
Italian-born spouse	9	
Other foreign-born spouse	3	
American-born spouse	1	
Unmarried: 21 or older		6
Unmarried: under 21		9
Total		28

SOURCE: See source note for Table 1.

Table 5. Nativity of children and their parents, 1850

Children born in Italy (under 20)		23
Children born elsewhere (under 24)		81
Both parents born in Italy	17	
Italian-born father only	56	
Italian-born mother only	4	
Either parent Italian; birthplace of other parent unknown	4	
Total		104

SOURCE: See source note for Table 1.

were born in Italy. The coexistence of these generations within the same families also suggests the complexity of household arrangements within the Italian community in Philadelphia.

Occupation provided another important aspect of the immigrant experience in Philadelphia in 1850 (see Table 6). Italians were diversified in their employment. The presence of artists, figure makers, and musicians showed that there were opportunities for work that Italians had pursued for some time. While the artists sometimes represented a higher level of skill and reward in the ornamental fields, the figure

Table 6. Occupations of Italians, 1850

Tradesmen (confectioner/ carpenter/ cabinetmaker/blacksmith/ watchmaker/ capmaker/ shipwright/bottlemaker/ joiner/ barber/ carter)	14
Artist/painter	12
Figure maker/ statue maker/ image maker	12
Businessman/salesman/merchant/shopkeeper/ innkeeper/dealer	10
Musician/professor of music/organist	9
Seaman/sailor	6
Clergyman/priest	3
Laborer	3
Physician	2
Language professor/teacher	2
Servant	1
Retired/pensioner	1
Total	75

SOURCE: See source note for Table 1.

makers were at the more modest end of a familiar spectrum. The two physicians come somewhat as a surprise. Tradesmen and businessmen provided a hint of the incipient community that emerged even more clearly in the years ahead. The range of work in these cases indicated that the small Italian population varied not only in employment but in material rewards and prestige levels as well.

Family, Household, and Identity

While this profile may raise as many questions as it answers, it also provides a general idea of the Italian population as the city reached the end of the first half of the nineteenth century. Some family vignettes provide details that further illuminate components of this picture.

The Treaga household in Walnut Ward consisted of a 40-year-old male born in Italy and employed as a "figure manufacturer." His first name, not easily deciphered from the handwriting of the census enumerator, has been read as Santonio, an unlikely name for an Italian; it probably was Antonio. Other members of the household included Elizabeth, a 37-year-old female; as well as a younger Elizabeth, a 6-year-old female; and Paul, a 4-year-old male. Presumably these individuals were Treaga's wife and two children. Because their birthplaces were not listed in the entry, these other members were probably born in the United States. But the same household included six other men from 17 to 36 years old, all born in Italy and identified as "figure manufacturers." One of them, recorded as Genoza Treaga (again an unlikely first name), may have been the brother of the household head. Three young men—with Lazurane given as their last name—may have been brothers to each other. The first Treaga appears to have headed a small family that included his brother and some friends in an extended household.[9]

Salvadore LeGrasse (*sic*), a 62-year-old cabinetmaker from Sicily, headed a household in Middle Ward. It included Josephine, a 52-year-old Sicilian-born female, probably the wife and mother in this case; Francis, a 30-year-old male; Louis, a 19-year-old male; Adrian, a 17-year-old male—all cabinetmakers born in Sicily and most likely sons of Salvatore and Giuseppina; and two other females, 30-year-old Mary and a 20-year-old whose name is not distinguishable, both born

SCHEDULE I.—Free Inhabitants in _Walnut Ward_ in the County of _Philadelphia_ State of _Pennsylvania_ enumerated by me, on the _27_ day of _August_ 1850, _Jos. Parrish Tuder_ Ass't Marshal.

431

Dwelling-houses numbered in the order of visitation.	Families numbered in the order of visitation.	The Name of every Person whose usual place of abode on the first day of June, 1850, was in this family.	DESCRIPTION.			Profession, Occupation, or Trade of each Male Person over 15 years of age.	Value of Real Estate owned.	Place of Birth, Naming the State, Territory, or Country.	Married within the year.	Attended School within the year.	Persons over 20 y'rs of age who cannot read & write.	Whether deaf and dumb, blind, insane, idiotic, pauper, or convict.
			Age.	Sex.	Color.							
1	**2**	**3**	**4**	**5**	**6**	**7**	**8**	**9**	**10**	**11**	**12**	**13**
		Eliza Mc Laughlin	30	F				Ireland		X	1	
		Robert Ahern	13	M	16			S. Carolina		1		
88	130	Vantonia Treaga	40	M		Figure Manufacturer		Italy				
		Elizabeth "	37	F				"				
		"	6	F				"				
		Paul "	4	M				"				
		Antonia Lapardo	18	M		Figure Manufacturer		"				
		Gonza Treaga	36	M		"		"				
		Louis Damaini	19	M		"		"				
		John Lagerano	21	M		"		"				
		Vantonia "	19	M		"		"				
		Pete "	17	M		"		"				
	131	Adolph Meintzer	28	M		Watch Case Polisher		Switzerland				
		Mary "	26	F				"				
		Albert "	6	M				"		1		
		Mary "	5	F				"				
		Frederick "	3	M				"				

The 1850 census record showing Treaga household. (National Archives, Mid-Atlantic Region)

in Sicily. The household was completed by the 20-year-old Clementina and the one-year-old Domenico. The relationships, however, are not given clearly, so cautious inferences must be made to reconstruct the household.[10]

A household in the First Ward of Southwark was headed by John Patts (or Catts), a 57-year-old Italian-born "figurist." Other members of the household, along with their age, sex, place of birth, and sometimes occupation, included Fortunia (age 37, female, Italy); Orillia (21, male, lithographer, Pennsylvania); John (19, male, Pennsylvania); Theodore (17, male, Pennsylvania); Albania (15, female, Pennsylvania); Lenlia (13, female, Pennsylvania); Adaline (11, female, Pennsylvania); Caroline (9, female, Pennsylvania); Claudia (7, female, Pennsylvania); Charles (4, male, Pennsylvania); Lucretia A. Tiabalary, 70, female, Italy); and Rosanna (35, female, Italy).[11]

As a family made its modest imprint on local life, however, the city often had difficulty recording it. The Patts (or Catts) case reveals the special issue that was inherent in Italian family names as they appeared in other sources. In 1825, Giovanno (*sic*) Citti, a molder in plaster of paris, lived in Diehl's Court, behind 40 Cherry Street. John Citti, an image-maker and portrait painter, lived in Philadelphia from 1850 to 1855, as did Louis Citti, a lithographer born in Pennsylvania about 1827, who worked in the city from 1850 to 1853. In 1850, Louis was also a partner in the firm of Hallman (probably Franklin B. Hallman) & Citti. In 1855, Orelius Citti was a Philadelphia lithographer. John Cutts was a "figurist" born in Italy about 1794 and living in Philadelphia in 1850. His household consisted of Fortunia; Orillio, a lithographer; John, a lithographer; Theodore; and three younger daughters, all born in Italy. In June 1853, Onelio S. Citti married Elizabeth E. Norris. Despite different spellings and variations in information, these individuals were likely all members of the same family.[12]

In other cases, a family left a less ambiguous trail of information in the documents of different agencies and institutions, but still with an inconsistent rendering of its name in the various spellings by which it appeared. E. Venazane, a 52-year-old laborer born in Italy, headed another household in the Third Ward of Southwark District in 1850. Catharine, a 42-year-old female, also born in Italy, was presumably his wife. Other members of the household were Anthony, a 19-year-old cart driver; Mary, 16 years old; John, 14; Emanuel, 12; and Catharine, 7. Except for Anthony, born in Italy, the other children were natives of Pennsylvania. Emmanuale Vernasano, born on April 11, 1839, had been baptized at St. Mary's Church, a parish that Italian families had used before their own could be established, with Nicholas Vernasano and Catharine (Zanona) Vernazano as witnesses for the ceremony on January 19, 1840. The infant, Emmanuele, was obviously the same person as the 12-year-old son who appeared in the 1850 census.[13]

In February 1890, the death of Emanuel Vernazzano was recorded by an Italian parish, although a local newspaper reported the deceased as Emanuel Vernazzo Moore. The newspaper item stated:

> Emanuel Vernazzo Moore died on Thursday at the residence of his son, Charles Moore, 2022 South Eighth street, in the 97th year of his age. He was a native of Italy, but came to this country and settled in Philadelphia sixty-nine years ago. He carried on the fruit trade on Market street until about twenty years ago, when he retired on a competence. About fourteen months ago

he met with an accident to one of his knees, which confined him to his bed for the remainder of his life. Previous to this, his son says, he never had a day's sickness. Several years ago he received his second sight and this, together with his hearing, continued unimpaired up to his death. His wife died twenty years ago. Of their eleven children seven are living, as are also 35 grand children and nine great-grandchildren.[14]

Despite discrepancies among census entry, parish records, and newspaper obituary, the same individual is the subject here. Whether he was actually born in 1793 or 1798, and how his name evolved as Vernasano, Vernazane, Vernazzo, and Vernazzano over forty years as Italian and non-Italian recorders struggled with it, remain relatively minor issues; it is more difficult to understand how it became Moore.

The lives of some individuals can be reconstructed more thoroughly. Joseph Mereto, a native of Genoa, arrived in the United States in 1836 with the stated intention of living in Louisiana. In the following year, at the age of thirty-six, abjuring his allegiance to the King of Sardinia, he declared his intention to become a citizen of the United States. In 1841, Joseph Maretta was listed in the state tax assessor's ledger as a resident of the estate of Casper W. Pennocks, at 370 High Street in Middle Ward. His occupation was listed in an abbreviated and obscured manner, but it appears that he was a confectioner. The same individual was found in other places, but sometimes as Joseph Merito. Another resident at the High Street address is identified as Terence Toner, a cordwainer. In 1842 and 1843, with an address at 424 High Street, Joseph Mereto was a fruiterer. In 1844, Mereto petitioned for naturalization before the court in Philadelphia; Toner acted as the voucher in the proceedings. In 1847, Mereto was still in the city directory as a fruiterer living at 424 High Street. Until this point, Mereto is visible, but only as an individual.[15]

Joseph Mereto reappeared in later censuses with his entire family. Listed in 1850 as a 48-year-old native of Italy, he worked as a shopkeeper and resided in Middle Ward. Within his household were his wife, Mary, a 36-year-old immigrant from Wales, and six children, Mary Ann, 11; William, 9; Jannet, 7; Joseph, six; Thomas, 4; and Amelia, two months. In 1860, Joseph Maredo, a 59-year-old native of Genoa, a storekeeper, resided in the Ninth Ward, with his 46-year-old English-born wife, Mary, and several children, Morgan, 20; William,

18; Joseph, 16; Thomas, 14; Emily, 9; Elizabeth, 7; and Lewis, 5. A 14-year-old girl and a 17-year-old boy, both born in Ireland, and a 54-year-old Italian-born laborer completed the household. Although we may wonder who Morgan was and how he had become a part of the family by 1860, it was undoubtedly an erroneous listing of Mary Ann. The presence of sons William, Joseph, Thomas, and daughter Emily, all at appropriate ages, confirmed the continuity of the family. With the passing of a decade; Amelia had been Americanized to Emily, and Jannet had possibly died. But the family had also increased with the birth of Elizabeth and Lewis. It is odd that the family did not appear in the next census, in 1870. In 1875, Joseph Mereto was a brass-finisher with a residence at 1220 Filbert Street. Louis, a salesman; Thomas H., a partner in the firm of Rogers & Mereto; and William, a clerk, all lived at the same address. In April 1881, the life of Joseph Mereto came to an end. Mary Dickensheets, the oldest daughter of the family and now living at 1220 Filbert Street, was executrix of Mereto's modest estate. Whether he was the same Joseph Mereto who operated the boardinghouse near Twelfth and Market Streets where James Grillo was stabbed in 1843 remains an unanswered question.[16]

The household of Angelo Morozzi, a 56-year-old musician who lived with his family in Pine Ward, provides another interesting case. Among its members, Julia was the wife and mother, 49 years old and born in Pennsylvania. The children included 23-year-old Angelo, also a musician; 19-year-old Virginia; 12-year-old Prunilla; 10-year-old Roma Wildi; and two 5-year-old boys. Many years later, Edna Virginia Morozzi, identified as the daughter of a retail grocer, married Herbert Eugene Wheeler, a prominent Philadelphian. The marriages of daughters to American husbands were another means of assimilation into the mainstream of Philadelphia life. The suitability of a daughter for such a marriage probably signified that the Morozzi family had achieved some measure of material success and respectability in the eyes of a broader population. At the same time, as these choices removed Italian women from their original positions, perhaps to a more elevated social status, they deprived the immigrant community of potential leaders.[17]

The response of census enumerators to the growing immigrant population still complicates any attempt to describe the Italian community of these years. The census manuscripts contain many people identified as Italian in origin but whose names suggest something different.

The 1850 census listed William Walker, Lewis Jennings, Lewis Ninks, George Padelford, Edmund Thornton, Jacob Ambrose, Lewis Baker, Lewis Ryner, Anthony Harmon, John Thomas, Martin Laws, Francis Martelwick, and Joseph Black as Italian-born. American families who were only visitors or temporary residents may have had children during their time in Italy, but the frequency of these names in the census suggests another explanation. While the subjects themselves may have been Americanizing their names, the census-workers were also probably Anglicizing the responses of Italians. Bartley Byberry, a 32-year-old Italian-born musician, lived in the First Ward of Moyamensing Township. Five other people, between the ages of 8 and 25, including two other male musicians with this surname, completed the household. Was the name "Barbieri" altered by the census-worker? Anton Kit, a 45-year-old merchant born in Italy, headed a household in the Second Ward of Moyamensing Township that included Maria Kit, 42, probably his wife, and seven children. Another family that shared the dwelling consisted of Andreas Kunio, a 45-year-old Italian-born innkeeper, and two young girls, Catharina and Theresia (*sic*). Andreas Kunio was almost certainly Andrew Cuneo, an important and influential figure in the Italian community in later years. The most curious case of name-changing was for the 70-year-old Italian resident of Locust Ward that the census reported simply as "O. Kiddice," an unusual name for an Italian. But repeated aloud, with phonetic familiarity of the language, it becomes clear that the subject himself was asking a reasonable question of the census enumerator: "O, che dici?" This poignant episode, however, also exposes the dilemma that some now faced, once others had lost the ability to recognize them and they themselves had begun to lose their own identity as Italians. He might soon have to ask himself another question, "Chi sono io?" ("Who am I?")[18]

The Bedini Affair and a Church for the Italians

A more complex community for Italians in Philadelphia was evolving, and some institutional forms were already in place, but the most significant development in the early 1850s involved religion. The political affairs of Italy were brought to the United States embedded in religious controversy, and the local response to that situation was partly expressed by the founding of the first parish for Italians in the United States.

The failure of the Roman republic in 1849 did not long deter the movement for Italian independence. By 1853, Italians had renewed their efforts, staging uprisings in Milan and other places. Mazzini and his supporters had already called for revolution throughout all of Italy. Writing from Florence, an American reporter described Italy as a slumbering volcano gathering strength for the eruption that would drive foreign despotism and civil papacy from Italian soil:

> The deep, *silent* hatred borne to the Priests and Austrians is rightful. It pervades the very atmosphere, and is drawn in at every breath by all classes but the few sold to their rulers by interest or circumstances. Disguise it as we may, there is a general uneasiness in Europe.[19]

The newspapers of Philadelphia routinely discussed the mistakes made in 1848–49 and what needed to be done for success in the future, while praising the bravery of the Italians and their desire for freedom.[20] As it had done in previous years, the local press continued to encourage and support the movement for independence in Italy. In early 1859, the *Public Ledger* assessed Italian conditions:

> Affairs seem to be approaching something of a crisis in Italy, where Austrian rule has been both insolent and oppressive. . . . The Austrian rule in Italy is both brutal and tyrannical.[21]

Philadelphians' hopes for Italy were also nourished by their favorable perceptions of Sardinia, the only remaining constitutional government in Europe with a free press and a parliament, "the sacred flame of freedom in its last continental refuge."[22] But Philadelphians also recognized the economic implications of Italian sovereignty and anticipated the benefits of a monthly steamship service between Genoa and New York, such as "the riper and more delicate fruits" that could now be shipped to the United States. With the completion of railroads that connected Austria and Bavaria to Italy, an increase in migration from southern Germany was also expected. In the United

States it was confidently believed that this Mediterranean outlet would make it possible for previously sealed-off regions to send thousands of new emigrants and of a better class, journeying on the steamers from Genoa. However, despite an original capital of $6 million, private letters from Genoa soon revealed that the depression of stocks and pressures in the money market in Piedmont had forced the steamship company to abandon the planned line.[23]

But the appreciation of Philadelphians was not restricted to politics and commerce; it included a continuing admiration for other artifacts of Italian culture, such as its more artistic commodities, which could be exported to foreign consumers. The local press enthusiastically noted the first performances of Verdi's new opera, *Rigoletto*, "containing all the known beauties and defects of his style," as it was being presented to full audiences by the Royal Opera House in London.[24] Readers could expect that it was simply a matter of time before a performance would be staged in a local production as a part of the now regular schedule of Italian opera.

In the midst of these positive perceptions, however, a more troublesome situation soon thrust itself onto the North American scene. In June 1853, a few days after plans for a new church for Italian Catholics of the city were announced, the public was informed that Archbishop Gaetano Bedini, the Papal Nuncio, would visit the United States. The Pope had instructed Bedini to investigate problems identified by the bishops at the First Plenary Council of Baltimore during the previous year. Bedini was to meet with priests and bishops in order to gather information related to the trusteeship controversy; the possible formation of new sees; the legal status of church-owned property; the condition of Catholic children in public schools; and the strength of anti-Catholic movements. The prelate was also expected to make a formal call on American government officials in Washington, D.C. While Bedini may have thought that his visit would be confined to administrative matters of the church, it actually had a quite different outcome.[25]

The news of the planned visit by Bedini was almost immediately met by demonstrations against the role of the church in Italian politics. The disturbances were also partly the result of an earlier tour of North America by Alessandro Gavazzi, an exiled former priest who had taken part in the 1848 uprisings in Italy. After his revolutionary ideas and role had forced him to migrate to London, where he joined Italian

Protestants in their condemnation of the Papacy, Gavazzi arrived in New York City in March 1853, only a few weeks before Bedini was expected to reach North America. Three months later, in Montreal, when Gavazzi attempted to condemn the Bedini visit, supporters of the Pope sought to keep the former priest from lecturing on the political situation in Italy.[26]

In the United States, Giovanni Francesco Secchi deCasali, the publisher of *L'Eco d'Italia,* and other Italians came to the defense of Gavazzi. In Philadelphia, while the Gavazzi affair was taking place far away, the local press kept readers well informed of the controversy. The *Public Ledger* defended Gavazzi's freedom of speech and condemned the riots against him in Montreal:

> Gavazzi may be bitter, rancorous and disingenuous in his invective against the Catholic church, but this does not justify any attempt to prevent his speaking to those who wish to hear him. The rights of free speech and assemblage are sacred rights which, in every free country, are protected by the laws.[27]

The Gavazzi affair, confined mainly to the newspapers in Philadelphia, was succeeded by the tumult surrounding the Bedini visit. After arriving in the United States in the previous month, Bedini came to Philadelphia on July 22, 1853. His main purpose was to convince German nationalists at Holy Trinity Church, who had long defied local authority, to submit to episcopal control of parish property and policy. When he went to the church, however, the German members prevented him from entering the building. Bedini aggravated his situation by refusing the hospitality of Bishop Neumann on the grounds that it would compromise his neutrality in any negotiations with the dissenters at Holy Trinity. Claiming to be too busy, Neumann then refused to meet with Bedini. Not only had Bedini now failed in his mission to Philadelphia, but he had also offended its bishop. Only three days after he had arrived, Bedini left Philadelphia to begin his tour of other American dioceses. But his difficulties in Philadelphia were mild compared to what Bedini encountered in other cities.[28]

The opposition to Bedini's presence in the United States reached its peak in late 1853 and early 1854. When he reached Cincinnati in late December 1853, about 500 Germans marched on the house of the archbishop, where Bedini was staying. In the ensuing violence, sixty protesters were arrested, nine individuals were shot, and one person was killed. Less than two weeks later, in anticipation of his visit to Wheeling, West Virginia, a handbill posted throughout the city accused Bedini of aiding the Austrians in the suppression of the 1849 uprising in Bologna. Bedini was thought to be especially responsible for the execution of the patriot Ugo Bassi, who had led the Bolognese in their struggle. The handbill indicated the charges against the prelate:

> FREEMEN, ARISE: Bedini, the butcher of Italian patriots, the tyrant of Italy, is in our midst—he is in this city—aye a guest of the Catholic bishop. He is on a mission through our Union as a kind of papal ambassador, and should nowhere be tolerated by American freemen, as he is not worthy to breathe the free air of this country, yet he is feted everywhere by the Jesuits, to the great annoyance of the free American citizens. Americans! citizens of the greatest and most liberal republic on earth, do not disgrace your reputation by tolerating a monster like this Bedini in your midst. Do not shelter one who has murdered the patriots of Italy. Give us your co-operation, and help us to destroy the secret plans of this Roman missionary; the blood of the martyrs of freedom, the tears of widows and orphans, the poor downtrodden people of Italy cry for revenge! Let them have it—drive this monster back to his bloody master that sends him. Come one and all, and let the cry be heard: Down with Bedini![29]

Refusing to print them, the *Wheeling Gazette* reported that the handbills had been circulated by people who were concerned not with religious issues but with the murder "of their brethren in Italy," without clarifying whether it meant that Bedini's critics were Italians or merely advocates of republicanism. The newspaper also claimed that Protestants were opposed to the message of the handbill and were tearing it down themselves, suggesting that responsible opposition to Bedini had given way to simple nativism. When he arrived at Wheeling, although a mob surrounded the cathedral and broke windows, the occasion passed as only a slight disturbance without injuries. The message contained in the handbill expressed, however, what Bedini might have to risk in other American cities.[30]

When Bedini returned to his lodgings at Fordham University in New York City a few nights later, it was believed that he was preparing to return soon to Europe. A rumor soon circulated that his opponents were planning a grand "farewell procession" to the dock to see Bedini make his departure. Italians and Germans had supposedly prepared a large effigy crowned with a cardinal's hat and dressed in priestly vestments, as well as barricades adorned with death heads and crossbones. It was reported that "in short, nothing that can be done, to inspire terror or create an excitement, has been left unimproved." The mayor and police chief discussed the necessary provisions to preserve public order in case of a disturbance. After Bedini asked for personal protection, the police guarded his residence in New York City. The participants in the planned demonstrations were said to be mainly foreigners and some "Know-Nothing" Americans. In late January 1854, a crowd gathered for his awaited departure from New York, but Bedini did not appear.[31]

While Italians and Germans in New York City made plans for a mass meeting, exiles who had fought in Bologna drafted a statement on Bedini's actual role in the uprising. With Felice Foresti, General Avezzana, and Secchi deCasali among the seventy signers, the document supported Gavazzi's allegations against Bedini. An appendix contained affidavits that substantiated the acts of cruelty and oppression of which Bedini had been accused. Although they had not previously made public remarks about Bedini, the signers of the statement declared that the official honors bestowed on him during his recent visit to Washington made it necessary for them to reveal the real character of their guest to other Americans. When the rally finally occurred, it included a mock trial in which the charges against Bedini were presented again. While it was unclear where Bedini was at the moment, he was believed to have recently returned to New York City. In Boston, an effigy of Bedini was burned. In New York City, handbills announcing another protest meeting, to be held at the Stuyvesant Institute in early February, were being posted. While activities by his opponents were emerging simultaneously in several eastern cities, Bedini uneventfully left Staten Island for Europe on February 4, 1854.[32]

Although it was reported that Bishop John Neumann had once written Bedini that it would be safe to visit Philadelphia, the city now joined into the public protests. On February 11, 1854, a mass meeting at the Chinese Museum responded against members of the

U.S. Senate who had supported Bedini. The program for the event included addresses in English and German. Several anti-Bedini resolutions were unanimously adopted by the audience, which, the local press claimed, included a large proportion of Germans and Italians. The event apparently succeeded in finally galvanizing a part of the Italian population into political activity. As elsewhere, the anti-Bedini activities in Philadelphia had drawn together a wide range of participants that included sincere republicans, "Know-Nothing" nativists, and Italian exiles.[33]

Although it was described as a meeting of Hungarians, Americans were the principal participants at a similar demonstration in July 1859. With only a few Hungarian residents in the city, the proceedings were entirely in English. As in earlier years, while Philadelphians rallied in public expressions of support for republican movements in Italy and Hungary, the number of participants with origins in those countries remained quite small.[34]

In contrast to the federal census only two years earlier, an estimate that their population was possibly as large as 600 in 1852, made by one Catholic source, may help to explain Bishop Neumann's concern about the Italians.[35] As an immigrant from Bohemia, the bishop might have been expected to have an interest in the material and spiritual condition of foreign-born Catholics. In a pastoral letter, the bishop later indicated his views on these matters quite clearly:

> From many parts of Europe our Church received vast accessions for almost a century, every month brought its thousands to our shores, and in a brief period our number has grown beyond every anticipation, . . . and now the poor stranger far from the home of his childhood feels no longer a stranger in a strange land, but he beholds a temple and an altar where he can worship his God and mingle with brethren bound by the same saving bond of holy faith.[36]

Aware of the desire of Italians for their own parish, Neumann soon provided such a place for them. In the early 1850s, Italian children in Moyamensing and Southwark had been given religious instruction on Sunday afternoons in St. Paul's Church on Christian Street by a Father De La Piance. In March 1852, Italian Catholics met in a schoolroom in Old St. Joseph's parish to discuss plans for establishing their own church. In August, Bishop Neumann granted Italians the use of the cathedral chapel for their services. In September, the bishop purchased a small chapel previously used by African American Methodists, a burial ground, and a small house on Marriott Street (now Montrose Street) between Seventh and Eighth Streets, and established the new parish of St. Mary Magdalen de Pazzi, named in honor of a sixteenth-century Florentine noblewoman. It was the first Italian national parish to be established anywhere in the United States, as well as the first of twenty-three parishes for Italians in the Philadelphia area.[37]

The significance of the founding of the new parish of St. Mary Magdalen de Pazzi cannot be overstated. An early study of Italian immigration expressed it well: "A colony must have attained a certain size and stability before it can maintain a priest."[38] Surely this was the case with the Italians in Philadelphia at that particular time. The first pastor of the new church was the Reverend Gaetano Mariani, a native of Florence who had been in the United States since 1851 and had previously taught music at the seminary of St. Charles Borromeo in Philadelphia. In October 1852, the diocesan newspaper noted the opening of the new church, although it erroneously simplified the name of its patron saint:

> "Church for the Italians."—On last Sunday a small chapel, intended for the use of the Italians of this city was blessed by the Rev. Mr. Mariani (by the authority of the Bishop) under the invocation of St. Mary Magdalen. The edifice is situated near Eighth and Christian. It was built and formerly used for Protestant worship, but it has lately been purchased and refitted for its present purpose. It is small, but will, no doubt, answer for some time to come. The congregation formerly worshipped in the Cathedral chapel.[39]

It is possible to see the founding of St. Mary Magdalen de Pazzi simply as the result of the bishop's awareness and concern for the spiritual welfare of the growing number of Italian Catholics in Philadelphia, but it is difficult to ignore the turbulent political circumstances in Italy and the repercussions in North America. Those events may have encouraged the church hierarchy to try to maintain the fidelity of Italians as Catholics by providing them with their own parish.

In June 1853, only a few days after the Gavazzi riot in Montreal, the *Public Ledger,* similarly giving the incorrect name of St. Mary Magdalene, also noted the organization of the new congregation for Italian Catholics in Southwark under the pastoral care of Father Mariani. Plans had been announced for the cornerstone-laying ceremony for the new building, which was designed to accommodate 500 worshipers. Departing somewhat from an older tradition, the new parish would not sell seating in the pews, and would be open to all Catholics. After Bishop Neumann participated in the cornerstone-laying for the new church in May 1854, the actual construction took considerably longer than originally expected. The completed building was not dedicated until October 1857. Father Mariani would serve as the pastor of St. Mary Magdalen de Pazzi until his death on March 8, 1866.[40]

St. Mary Magdalen de Pazzi: The Mirror of a Community

The new church was located within the boundaries of St. Paul's, an older, territorial parish only three blocks away, in Moyamensing District, just below the southern boundary of the city.[41] It was less than a block from the corner of Eighth and Christian Streets. From that location, to the next intersection on the west at Ninth and Christian Streets, a commercial district that would become the hub of the huge Italian colony of South Philadelphia in later years was developing. While the religious needs of Italians warranted the establishment of the new parish, prejudice against them, mainly on the part of the Irish, may also have contributed to its founding. Ironically, parish records indicate that the benefactors and members of the new congregation often included Irish names too.

From its early years, St. Mary Magdalen de Pazzi played an important role as an institution that not only responded to religious needs but also performed important functions in the secular life of Italians. It frequently provided the locus for public celebrations on religious and secular holidays. Religious processions in veneration of saints, and patriotic parades in honor of important Italians or Americans, often began at the church. In these ceremonies, the use of the church served to define the location and the limits of the community.

Early baptismal record from St. Mary Magdalen de Pazzi Parish. The top two entries record the baptisms of Luisa Maria Raggio on February 5, 1854, and Luigi Bartolomeo Repetto on February 27, 1854. The two bottom entries record the baptisms of daughters born to "Irlandesi" parents. Although St. Mary's was founded for the Italian community, the Irish were sometimes a part of parish life. (Philadelphia Archdiocesan Historical Research Center)

During its early years, baptisms provided a profile of both the congregation and the community. From the first baptism in December 1853, to only a handful in the next year, the number of baptisms ranged from eighteen to thirty annually for the next twelve years before the death of Father Mariani in February 1866. The baptisms reveal the modest but steady growth of the Italian population in the area (see Table 7). Although almost all involved Italians, the members of other groups, denoted by terms such as "Irlandesi," were sometimes welcomed into the congregation. The baptismal records for St. Mary Magdalen de Pazzi also show that a more normalized population, consisting of families with children, was beginning to develop among the Italians, but it had a pronounced regional character.

The congregation of St. Mary Magdalen de Pazzi was made up overwhelmingly of families with origins in Northern Italy, but there were others from the central regions and a few even from Sicily and the South. In more than 200 baptisms recorded in the parish, a specific area of origin was given for at least one parent; in other entries, the background of the family was noted simply by the word "Italiani." Most of the population originated in a relatively small area of Northern Italy bordering on the Ligurian Sea. Of 202 cases in which a specific place was indicated, 167 were from a compact area that forms a nearly perfect parallelogram, with a particular city or town anchoring each corner. The port city of Genoa was the place of origin in 12 cases. Tortona, about 55 kilometers north of Genoa, was the place of origin in 5 cases. Bobbio, about 43 kilometers to the east and slightly below Tortona, was the original home of 29 cases. Although Chiavari, about 51 kilometers south of Bobbio, was cited as the place of origin in 113 cases, many families had originated in the villages of the hills above—Prato, Sopra la Croce, Borzonasca, Cabanne, Castagnelo, Fontanarossa, and San Colombano Certenoli. Eight families gave Cicagna, Recco, and Rapallo—three larger towns nearer the coastal area between Chiavari and Genoa—as places of origin. About a dozen families came from Turin, Modena, Poppi, Bergamo, Cuneo, Parma, and Lucca in Northern and Central Italy. Another eight entries more vaguely gave the kingdom or state of Sardinia, which included Liguria at the time, as the place of origin. But even at this early period, Southern Italians were a small part of the congregation. Eight baptisms involved families from Palermo, and five others from Naples. How well they all fitted together in parish

Table 7. Baptisms: St. Mary Magdalen de Pazzi
Parish, December 1853—January 1866

Year	No.	Year	No.
1853	1	1860	30
1854	6	1861	21
1855	26	1862	23
1856	19	1863	23
1857	19	1864	18
1858	19	1865	19
1859	28	1866	1
		Total	253

SOURCE: Baptism Register, St. Mary Magdalen de Pazzi Parish, December 1853—January 1866. These records provide
the basis for the description of the population and community
presented here.

NOTE: The present discussion is limited to the baptismal
entries made by Father Mariani, who usually provided some
information about the families. After the death of Mariani
in early 1866, he was succeeded as pastor by the Reverend
Gaetano Sorrentini, who made his first entry to the baptismal
registers in March of that year. In recording baptisms, Sorrentini limited his entries to ecclesiastical information. The figure
given here for 1866 represents only the final entry by Father
Mariani and none of Father Sorrentini's. An examination of
the actual ledger reveals, however, that there probably were
more baptisms than were listed. Although only thirty cases
can be counted on the pages, a note entered by Mariani at the
end of 1860 gives the number of baptized children of Italian
parents as being thirty-one. In addition, some of the ledger
pages have become stuck together and could not be separated
without damage. The interior of these paired pages appears
to contain more cases.

and community depended largely on the perceptions and relationships
these different components had with one another.

Their different places of origin in Italy did not provide strong
antecedents for harmony and integration for the members of the new
church. The individuals and families with origins near Chiavari, who
made up the core of the parish, were part of the first wave of emigrants
to depart from their native land. About 35 kilometers below Genoa,
where cosmopolitanism had long prevailed, Chiavari, on the Gulf
of Rapallo near the mouth of the Lavagna River, had more than
10,000 inhabitants in the late 1840s. Although abundant vegetation

supported agriculture well in the area, it had long been a center for lace and silk production and ship construction. But it was probably even better known for the light, inexpensive but sturdy chairs made of cherry wood—the *sedie di Chiavari* or *chaises volantes,* as they were called by the French.[42]

Coastal Ligurians and their neighbors were not locked into the feudalistic, land-based system of the rural peasantry and smaller towns of other parts of the Italian peninsula, but had long been linked with the history of Genoa. Since the time of its maritime republic, involvement in trade gave Ligurians a well-deserved reputation as travelers that was well expressed by an old adage "In whatever quarter of the world you open an egg a Genoese will spring from it."[43] While Genoese had long been motivated by economic objectives, the political situation became another factor in their emigration when the Republic of Genoa, after a long period of independence, fell under French control in 1797. After the defeat of Napoleon, and the annexation of Genoa by Sardinia in 1815, the former republic remained as a part of the Kingdom of Piedmont until the establishment of modern Italy. Although many nationalists had fled Italy, political refugees were probably still outnumbered by people who were leaving for economic reasons. Genoa remained the most important port of embarkation from Italy until the end of the nineteenth century, when it finally fell second to Naples. While a much greater number had once sought South American destinations, the volume of immigrants from the port of Genoa to the United States began to increase in the late 1840s.[44]

Whatever the exact conditions and motives of departure, the more personal qualities and character of the Genoese are more complicated to portray, although one early travel writer at the time tried: "The Genoese are laborious, and, on the whole, a robust and well-looking people; but the Ligurian character, both physical and mental, is very peculiar; and they have yet a strong feeling of nationality. Their dialect is almost unintelligible to a stranger."[45]

While it pertained to the residents of the city of Genoa, these comments could have been easily extended to inhabitants of the entire region of Liguria. The same writer, noting that Genoese, or Ligurians in general, from the time of Virgil to Dante and much later, had been unfavorably depicted, cited the blunt words of Dante's *Inferno:*

Ahi Genoesi, uomini diversi
   D'ogni costume, e pieni d'ogni magagna;
   Perchè non siete voi dei mondo spersi?

(Ah Genoesi, of honesty devoid! So base your city, so replete
with guile, Why are ye not at one fell swoop destroyed?)[46]

Other people who had more recently lived among the Genoese could
speak well of them and "the splendid memorials of the charity of past
generations raise at least a strong presumption in their favour." But
modern Tuscans still demeaned the Genoese in proverb, and travel
writers also provided popular images of Ligurians that natives of other
regions could believe. Whether they actually fit the Chiavaresi and
other Ligurians who settled in Philadelphia, popular images and beliefs
did influence the perceptions and behavior of Italians toward one
another. An observation by L. Mossi, the Sardinian Chargé d'Affaires
in Washington in 1852, speaks for itself on the matter: "Almost all
the natives of Chiavari were organ grinders or beggars."[47]

On the other hand, the Genoese could easily recall the persistence
of their republic, until only about fifty years before, while much of
the Italian peninsula had been subdued and subjugated by monarchy
or foreign powers. They could similarly celebrate the receptiveness
of their region to the progressive ideas and ideals of the Italian En-
lightenment while others remained in the darkness of traditionalism.
They could also commend themselves for the cosmopolitanism of
the maritime culture that they had enjoyed while other Italians had
remained locked into feudal localism. Despite what others might think
of them, the Genoese had their own reasons for feeling superior to
the natives of other regions and, as with others of Northern origins,
particularly toward Southern Italians.

The occupations of members of the congregation of St. Mary Magdalen de Pazzi provided a glimpse into another dimension of their lives
in Philadelphia. In the first baptismal entry in parish records that listed
an occupation, the father of the child was identified as a "Palermitano"
and "maestro di musica in Filadelfia, organista nella Chiesa Italiana"
in 1858. Ironically, in this mainly Northern Italian congregation the
initial family for whom an occupation was provided was headed by
a Sicilian musician. In 1859, the records gave no occupations, but
for 1860 there were nineteen cases identified by work, and listed

as "qualità di musicante" (8 cases), "lavorante di terra" (2 cases), "negoziante" (2), "piccolo negoziante" (2), "qualità di geoegliere," "maestro di musica," "qualità di precettore," "qualità di sartori," and "vitrovasi vagantte" (1 each). In 1862, the occupations of four parents were provided as "musicante" (2 cases), "lavorante di terra—cioè contadino," and "piccolo negoziante." In 1863, twenty occupational listings included "musicante" (6), "piccolo negoziante" (5), "lavorante" (2), "piccolo mercante," "negoziante," "maestro di musica," "taverna di Christian St.," "lavorato gioegliere"(sic), "calzolaio," and "uomo di industria." In 1864, 13 listings included "uomo di industria" (6), "lavorante di terra" (2), "piccolo negoziante" (2), "povero musicante"(2), "marinaro," and "impiegato nell'ufficio postale." (It is not clear whether the "povero" applied to the musicians was the pastor's sense of their economic status or his judgment of their musical abilities.) In 1865, four occupational listings included "piccolo negoziante" (2), "figurista," and "uomo di industria." In 1866, the only occupational listed was one "gioegliere."

While "musician" may have sometimes been a euphemism for organ-grinder, the baptisms at St. Mary Magdalen de Pazzi revealed a wide range of employment. If their occupations were typical, families were likely to be headed by musicians and music teachers, small merchants, industrial workers, and a few jewelers. In contrast to the assertion that they were all organ-grinders or beggars, natives of Chiavari and other places found a broader assortment and a somewhat higher level of employment in Philadelphia, which reflected the long tradition of itinerant enterprise among Ligurians.

Contrasting Little Italies: Philadelphia and New York

In order to perceive the distinctive aspects of the Italian experience in Philadelphia, it is useful to compare it with New York City at the time. The first real wave of impoverished Italians reached American cities in the 1850s, when hundreds of them began pouring into the Five Points and the Eighth Ward areas of lower Manhattan. Fruit and flower peddlers, plaster statue vendors, organ-grinders, and bootblacks, including children sent by parents or employers, arrived. Their relative success has sometimes been seen as the decisive factor in the development of the *padrone* system—in which, in its earliest stage, Italian children were imported as street musicians—before it was adapted by American industries as a device for the wholesale recruitment of contract labor in southern and eastern Europe.[48]

Whether economic factors were the motives for coming in the first place, or as conditions of adjustment after arrival, they remained important in the lives of Italians in New York. But other aspects of collective life also played an increasingly significant role. Beginning in 1849, with the founding by G. F. Secchi deCasali of the *Europeo-Americano,* New York had an Italian-language press. Secchi deCasali later established *L'Eco d'Italia,* which continued for the next forty-five years. In 1851, Foresti founded *Il Proscritto,* a weekly newspaper that survived only about two years. Whether short-lived or more enduring, the appearance of an Italian press provided the growing Italian component of the population with a voice.[49]

The Italians of New York made their presence even more visible in their political activities, which manifested their acute awareness and profound response to the struggle for independence in Italy. By the same token, the Italians were demonstrating some degree of solidarity with one another. As early as 1841, Felice Foresti had organized the Congrèga Centrale in sympathy with and support of Mazzini's Young Italy movement. After American militia companies excluded immigrants from membership, Italians formed their own unit in support of the 1848 uprisings in their native land. A decade later, under similar circumstances, Italians formed the Guardia Nazionale Italiana. Italians also raised about $10,000 in a war relief fund for widows and children of the fallen victims of the 1859 battles against the Austrians.[50] In January 1859, the prospect of another revolution in Italy had been hailed by Italian, French, and German exiles in New York City.[51] In May, war news from Europe produced further excitement among exiles in New York City, but especially among the Italians—

> who believe (rather credulously, perhaps,) that the day of re-generation is at last about to dawn upon their unhappy country. Since the first heraldings of the approaching conflict, in January last, numbers of Italians, the Journal of Commerce says, have been preparing to give up their business and leave for their old homes. Many of them have already gone, and many more will

undoubtedly go, to take a hand in settling the ancient grudge which their nation owes to Austria.[52]

Despite occasional public demonstrations, Italians remained a rather peaceful element within the population of New York. In the 1850s, according to the Children's Aid Society, Italians did not quarrel among themselves, rarely became drunk, and apparently did not steal. Although the total number of arrests of Italians reportedly reached 8,000 for 1865 alone, the incidence of actual criminals was insignificant. The majority of arrests appear to have been for vagrancy.[53]

Although in many ways both colonies were similar, politics became an aspect that separated the Philadelphia case from New York. In the early 1850s, Italians in both cities, as well as in America in general, had greatly disappointed Mazzini by their failure to support his political cause through the purchase of bonds.[54] By the end of the decade, however, differences in the reactions to these issues in New York City and Philadelphia had emerged. In contrast to New York, Italians in Philadelphia made little public expression of any concern for the events taking place in Italy at this time. In the autumn of 1858, for example, Italian patriot Alberto Mario and his American wife, Jessie White Mario, arrived in the United States with the mission to implement an elaborate plan prepared by Mazzini to reorganize the republican movement among the Italians in America. The itinerary included New York, Philadelphia, and New Orleans. In March 1859, Jessie White Mario began a series of lectures in Philadelphia. For 25 cents, a ticket to her address titled "Italy and Her Struggle for Freedom" could be purchased at bookstores or at the Sansom Street Hall. The local press described her as "a very eloquent speaker, an enthusiastic lover of liberty, and an able expositor of the causes which have kept Italy in subjection." While these events did not generate the desired financial support anywhere, at least in New York they attracted substantial numbers of Italians for their audiences. In Philadelphia, newspaper accounts do not indicate even a modest number of Italians in the audience to hear Madame Mario. But the American tour of the Marios fell far short of its financial objectives on behalf of the Mazzinian party wherever it went.[55]

A rather selective pattern of immigration may have produced a more politically conscious population of Italians in New York City. Certainly a number of well-known *fuorusciti* were a conspicuous part of the New York scene during these years. The more provocative events, especially those related to international politics, such as the appearance of Bedini, were much more likely to occur in New York than in Philadelphia. But the failure of Italians to take a more prominent role in the occasional public demonstrations in Philadelphia in support of the republican movements in Europe remains puzzling. Perhaps life in Philadelphia was so different that Italians became preoccupied with the exigencies of survival and success. Perhaps also, without the persuasive rhetoric of the more important political refugees, they could ignore the political needs of the Italy that had been left behind.

Organ-Grinders at the Ballot Box and in the Courtroom

While the failure of Italians in Philadelphia to develop a more united political presence denied them protection from abuse and exploitation, they sometimes made themselves vulnerable by their own devices. In 1853, an Italian vagrant named John Baffin, who had been soliciting alms on the streets, was arrested. Baffin carried a printed petition that declared he had once been shipwrecked on the coast of Spain but that now with his large family he was a worthy object of charity. The scheme was apparently a fraud. Brought before a court, he was recognized as the same person committed for begging in the streets four years earlier. The hapless Baffin was sent back to prison for another term.[56]

While individuals such as Baffin could easily encounter these difficulties, and perhaps deserved the outcomes, as long as they remained unorganized Italians remained vulnerable to manipulation by others. The October 1856 election for the office of District Attorney of Philadelphia produced such a situation. Democrat Lewis C. Cassidy, the Irish Catholic ally of Richard Vaux, had defeated William B. Mann, the People's Party candidate. Shortly afterward, twenty citizens contested the election by filing a formal petition for an investigation by the Court of Quarter Sessions of the city. The hearings that began soon after the election lasted well into the spring of the following year. Although alleged abuses were cited for several voting divisions, the proceedings focused on the Ninth Division of the Second Ward, which had only recently been established in South Philadelphia. A series of witnesses testified that a large number of unnaturalized foreigners had voted fraudulently. While the questionable voters were drawn from a wide range of backgrounds, the investigation identified a number of Italians among them. Some citizens had claimed that about fifteen Italians, chiefly "organ-grinders," or at least believed to be so, had been allowed to vote under circumstances that provided strong grounds for concluding that there had been collusion between the inspector and one or more people outside the polling place. In the testimony, the Italians who were identified as the voters who had cast the disputed ballots included B. Fagause, John Cirelli, John Repelto, Joseph Repelto, Augustine Bernero, Louis Angeline, James Ardado, Power Cohanue, Henry Chaiorn, Michael Cannon, Joseph Jacquett, Augustine Ratts, John Chillelia, Seth Morasti, and Michael Cansa. Two other names that appeared in further testimony included John Cademar and Dominick Coronia.[57]

Throughout the hearings, the Mann supporters presented witnesses who described the abuses in their testimony. One of them, John T. Birch, provided a vivid account of what had occurred:

> I was outside of the polls, 9th Division of the 2nd Ward. I was there when the organ grinders were brought up. They were brought up by a man called Harry Monaghan, a policeman. There were five or six of them at one time. I challenged them. Someone in the crowd said: "That son of a bitch is challenging all." Monaghan produced the papers for all. Someone inside asked if he had the papers. He said he did for that day. He pulled the papers out of his pocket, and I did not see more than three in his hand at any one time. Sometimes he would put the papers in his pocket and then pull them out again. He kept the papers himself. When they had voted, he told them to go home. I challenged all generally, but none were sworn, nor the voters themselves. I took them to be foreigners. They could not speak their names. Monaghan said he could repeat the names after he heard it. I did not know the organ grinders as residents of the division. I challenged others, some of whom went away and did not come back again. I withdrew one challenge. Some of them said they knew him, that he was an old resident.[58]

An effort was made to defend the legality of the Italian voters. In the course of the hearings, witnesses testified that the "organ-grinders" were residents of the division. In April 1857, one witness described his own canvass during the previous month, in which he was able to locate several Italians at their addresses in the division. Despite this relatively late and feeble effort to defend them, the final judgment of the court was not favorable. The court referred mainly to the testimony of Chief Inspector Costello, who had described some of the procedures in his division. With voting done by pencil on paper, Costello contended that the ballots were taken so fast by other inspectors that he was unable to determine that the names were actually on the list of taxables.

Although other witnesses disagreed with Costello and alleged that voters were not asked for any evidence of residence or proof of eligibility, the court declared that the votes of the Italians probably were illegal. Several witnesses provided essentially the same testimony as Birch. They identified Henry Monaghan as the police officer alleged to have brought illegal voters into the polling place. According to the witnesses, when these individuals were challenged the police officer pulled their naturalization papers out of his own pocket, although there appeared to be no more than two or three papers for all; those papers were quickly returned to his pocket, and again produced in the same manner for the next group of voters. When asked about these charges, Inspector Costello maintained that he could not determine how many papers there were. When asked more specifically whether the Italians had voted on only two or three papers, Costello declined to answer. But Costello fully agreed with the testimony of the other witnesses about the role of Police Officer Monaghan. The court concluded that the election had been carried on in a reckless manner with the sole object of getting the votes into the ballot box, without concern for their legality.

While the case represented only a small chapter in the political history of Philadelphia, it provided an unprecedented window on the Italian presence at this time. The principal testimony on their behalf was given by one witness, identified in the record of the hearings as Joseph Repelto, himself an Italian, who was one of the "organ-grinders" named in the petition. Despite the consistent identification of the witness as Repelto, his real name was almost certainly Joseph Repetto. His testimony did not succeed in removing the objection to the admission of the disputed votes. Although he could not help his fellow Italians, Repelto's remarks represent the earliest firsthand description of the conditions of life among the Italians of Philadelphia by any contemporary observer. In his testimony, Repelto gave the court a partial summary of some circumstances of his own life, as well as for others. After being sworn in, Repelto said:

> I reside in Marriot's Lane, between 8th and 9th. . . . I reside there still, and have resided there 1½ years. I voted at the October election, 9th Division, 2d Ward, at the corner of 10th and Carpenter. I am a carpenter by trade. I know Augustine Berneo. He resides in Carpenter St., between 8th and 9th. . . . He has resided there 5 or 6 years. I have seen him there steady. I did not see him vote. Berneo keeps —— store, —— a grocery. I know Augustus Ratto. He resides in Carpenter, between 9th and 10th. He has resided there about 1 year. He does not reside there now. He moved about two months ago. I believe he has gone to Chicago. He said he was going there. I don't know if he is going to stay there. I did not see Ratto vote. . . . I know B. Fagause. He lived in Donnelly's Court, No. 2. He lives there now. He has resided there for about 2½ years or so, not in the same house, but in the court. He has resided in that house 7 or 8 months. He plays the organ. I was not present when he voted.
>
> John Cirelli I know. He now resides in Marriot's Lane, between 8th and 9th. He has lived there 5 or 6 years. He repairs musical instruments.
>
> John Chilella I know. He lived in Carpenter St., between 8th and 9th, in October. He moved away some time in November. I don't know where he lives now. I believe he has gone to Italy. He sailed from New York. I was not present when he voted.
>
> John Repelto I know. He resides with B. Fagause, in Donnelly's Court, No. 2. He is my father. He lives there now. He has resided there a year. He is a brush maker. I was present when he voted. My father and I went up to the window together to vote. I can't say who voted first. I know that we started from the house together.
>
> J. S. Ardado I know. His first name is James. He resides in Donnelly's Court, No. 6. He has resided there 8 or 9 months. He lives there now. He plays the harmonic flute in the streets. I was not there when he voted. I saw him at the polls. I saw him around there when I voted.

Power Cochanue. I know him. He resided in Carpenter St. I don't know where he lives now. He resided there last October. I saw him about 20 or 30 days ago at that place. I saw him there. I did not go in the house. He was on the pavement. I did not see him vote. He used to sell fruits and candies. I don't know where he is now.

Nicholas Cansa. He resides in Carpenter, between 9th and 10th. He does not live there now. He lived there in October. He moved about 3 months ago to Charleston. . . . .

Cansa was a brush and ramrod maker for guns. He had lived there 7 or 8 months. I did not see him vote.

John Cademar lives in Donnelly's Court, No. 1. He has lived in that house about a month and a half. Last October he lived in the same court, I think at No. 6. I saw him there in October. I went in his other house, and saw him lying on the settee. He has lived in that court about 2½ or 3 years. I do not know that he is doing anything. He goes out sometimes with an organ.

I did not see my father when he handed his paper in. We both went up together. I handed my paper in. I got it back, and I believe my father got his back. I afterwards saw it in his possession.

I did not see Ardado when he handed the paper in. I did not see it afterwards.[59]

Although focused on the issues raised by the disputed election, Repelto's comments revealed the struggle of recent arrivals to establish their new lives. Some Italians, like Repelto himself, had been able to pursue such trades as carpentry or, as in the case of his father, as brush-making. Others could be found in more expected lines, such as Fagause the organ-grinder or Ardado the flutist in the streets of the city. Some men provided services to one another, such as Cirelli the musical-instrument repairman. A few, such as Cochanue the fruit and candy vendor or Berneo the grocer, had already started small businesses.

The less stable aspects of conditions among the Italians were also clear from Repelto's remarks. Housing arrangements were quite modest. Some men, such as Repelto's father and Fagause, at No. 2 Donnelly's Court, shared accommodations. Several dwellings in Donnelly's Court were occupied by Italians, and Repelto knew them all, although he had not seen several of them in recent days. Some of the men that he was asked to comment on had already moved elsewhere—if he had told the truth—to New York, Charleston, Chicago, or perhaps even back to Italy. Although two men had lived at the same address for five or six years, the remainder lived at any one residence for much shorter periods. It was obviously a small and compact population, but Repelto was unaware of the whereabouts of several other people. The men seemed able to move to new locations without many others being aware of or concerned with it.

When cross-examined in the hearings, Repelto provided further information that amplified his description of the Italians in the area:

> I am a foreigner. Before I lived in Marriot's Lane I lived in Carpenter between 8th and 9th for over 2 years. Before that I lived in Marriot's Lane between 8th and 9th. I have made plaster Paris figures. I have been a moulder, also a farmer before I lived in the city. I have also been a carpenter. I have played the tambourine when I was a boy. I know a person of my name who lived around there, but he has gone. I believe four months ago. It was after the election. His name was Joseph Repelto. He was my cousin. He lived in a little street runs between 8th and 9th, below Prime. I voted in the morning, about 9 or 10 o'clock, as near as I can tell. I handed my paper in when I voted, also my tax receipt. I handed them both in together. I got my naturalization paper in court, I don't know from whom, in 1855. I came in this room to get it. I got my tax receipt from Alderman Eneu in April, 1856. I think it was in April. Both my papers are at home. I last saw them yesterday. I was not told to bring them to court.
>
> Bernero is a foreigner, an Italian. I saw him on election day at this house. I don't recollect seeing him at the polls.
>
> I know two Augustine Rattos. One lives in Carpenter near 9th. The other lived somewhere in Essex Street near Christian. I don't know if that is in another division. I saw one of them election day—the one who lives in Carpenter St. I did not see him vote.
>
> I know only one Fagause, except some boys. Before his present residence, he lived in Essex Street. I have known him about 6 or 7 years. He is an Italian.

John Cirelli is an Italian. I know two of them. Both are named John. One of them lives in Marriott's Lane now. The other lived in Carpenter Street. He gone to Italy.

I was personally acquainted with all these men, and have visited all their houses.

I have known Chillela for 8 or 9 years. I knew two, both of the same first name. The one that lived on Carpenter St. I have known 5½ or 6 years.

I only know John Repelto. He is my father. My father lived in Carpenter St. before he lived with Fagauso. He lived there 3 or 4 years.

I only know one Ardado. Before he lived in Donnelly's Court he resided in Carpenter St. between 8th and 9th in a court. I don't know how long he resided there. I have known him 5 or 6 years. I saw him at the polls election day. I did not see him vote. He is a foreigner.

I know only one Cohanue. I have known him 9 or 10 years. He is a foreigner. Before he lived in Carpenter St., he resided in a street running from Shippen to South, near 5th.

Nicholas Cansa is now in Charleston. I have known him 5 years. When I first knew him he lived in Carpenter St. He is an Italian.

John Cademar I have known for 5 or 6 years. When I first knew him he lived in Essex St. I did not know him in Italy.

I have not been examined before as to these names. I had a list of names given me. I was told to write down the names I knew. Cademar's name in Italian is spelt Cademartier. I have not spoken to Mr. Monaghan about these persons. Sometimes he might say if I had seen them. He asked me if I saw Andrew Bajon and some others. He did not ask me as to any of the persons I have spoken of, or no person else.

Under cross-examination, Repelto described his own occupational odyssey, but soon arrived at the political aspects of greater concern to the court. In his testimony, he presented his knowledge of the other Italians who had been cited in the charges as fraudulent voters; among them were Gaetano Bernero, Augustino Ratto, Biagio Fagausi, John Cirelli, John Repetto, Power (Paolo?) Cohanuo, Nicholas Cansa, Andrew Bajon, James Ardado, and others. The more important issue, however, was not their possible criminal misdoings as individuals, but that they were obviously being exploited by others as instruments of election chicanery.

The presence of a political mechanism that made its own use of these Italians was evident. The manner in which the system operated began well before election day itself and included the process of naturalization. An examination of court records shows that, although the spellings vary, the names of the Italians who had submitted petitions for naturalization from October 1854 to October 1856 were among those later identified by Repelto in his testimony. Dominic Carone (also listed as Caroni), who was unquestionably the Dominick Coronia named in the election case, was among the first applicants of this group, filing his petition on October 6, 1854, in the Court of Common Pleas. Carone had arrived at the Port of New York in 1825, and when he sought citizenship twenty-nine years later, he identified the Emperor of Austria as the sovereign of his former allegiance. On that same day, three other Italians had presented their petitions before the same court. These men identified their prior allegiance in different ways that also suggested an interesting contrast in their perceptions of their homeland. Two of them—identified in the records as John Baptiste Lagamessina, whose name was probably Lagomarsino, and John Smith, whose name was almost certainly something else—gave the King of Sardinia as their soon-to-be abandoned sovereign. The fourth candidate, Joseph Bijon, indicated the Republic of Italy as his original allegiance. The voucher for all four cases was identified as James Signiago, but because he was illiterate and could make only a mark for his name, the court recorder had to transcribe what was probably given orally, leaving his identity somewhat unclear.[60]

Three days later, on October 9, 1854, three more men petitioned the Court of Common Pleas for American citizenship, each identifying the King of Sardinia as his former political allegiance. One of these candidates was listed as Joseph Rippert, but his correct surname was probably Repetto. Although his name is difficult to recognize, Dominic Carone was the voucher for two of these cases, and Joseph Bijon served as witness for the other applicant. In subsequent months, a similar process continued to unfold. On April 25, 1855, four more applicants chose to forsake allegiance to the King of Sardinia in their petition for citizenship. Their surnames included Repetto, Cirelli, and Bigginio, along with an anomalous Lewis Miller. Among the men who became American citizens on this day, Joseph Repetto was undoubtedly the same man who testified as Joseph Repelto during the inquiry of the 1856 election. The voucher in all four cases, despite slight variations in the spelling of his surname, was Dominic Carone.[61]

The same pattern was repeated a few months later. In September 1855, Dominick Cheroni served as voucher for the naturalization of John Repetto and Gaetano Bernero, both identified as natives of Italy and formerly subjects of the Republic of Italy, in the District Court at Philadelphia. About one week later in early October, Dominick Karone was the voucher for Agostino Ratto, Nicholas Cansa, and Power Cohanuo, with the men this time being identified as natives of Italy but formerly subjects of the King of Sardinia. The clerk of the court was having difficulty not only in determining the name of the voucher but also in recognizing the political system of Italy. In another two days, Nicholas Canessa acted as the witness in the petition of Jerome Reppetto. Finally, two days afterward, James Arditto served in a similar capacity for Beagio Fagausi in the District Court again. By now these names were recognizable as the same people identified in the testimony of Joseph Repelto.[62]

Despite the conclusion of the election inquiry to the contrary, the naturalization records also indicate clearly that these particular Italians could have been legal voters in October 1856. At least they were citizens of their new country and qualified to vote if they met other requirements, such as registration laws. Their eligibility to vote, however, would not have precluded the possibility that they had been recruited by supporters of Cassidy. Nor does it take away the question of what interests their votes would serve. If anything, the circumstances surrounding the participation of the Italians as voters, as well as their prior naturalizations, strongly suggest that they had been solicited and mobilized as instruments for the election of the candidate without any particular regard for their own interests as new citizens of Philadelphia. But they were certainly not alone as possible victims of exploitation by a political party and its candidate.

While the report focused on the criminal aspects and political implications, in the final analysis the case has even greater meaning for the broader study of the conditions of immigrant life. The real significance of this case is what it reveals about an aggregate of people who were strangers to a new society in which they had neither secure positions as individuals nor the protection provided by their own communal institutions. Under such circumstances, they remained unprotected from their own inclinations to take advantage of questionable opportunities or to be prey for abuse, exploitation, and manipulation by others. Of course, a more stable personal situation and communal institutions would not guarantee that people had conquered their own weaknesses or would not be exploited by their own leaders. But such institutions, as all normative systems, would have served to protect them both from themselves and from others.

The election fraud case of 1856–57 disclosed one point of articulation between a cluster of Italians and the political system of the city. To be able to make a wider range of connections, it would be valuable to know whether and how Italians were being received by other Philadelphians and absorbed into the life of the city. The federal census and parish records provide a profile of the types of work in which Italians were engaged, but not of the pattern of employment in particular industries at this point. Although there were a handful of exceptions, most Italians may have been self-employed, albeit at modest levels of skill and income.

We can only extrapolate from a handful of isolated fragments what the growing presence of a new group meant to other Philadelphians. Some residents in 1859, for example, were beginning to object to the hand organs played on city streets and sought to have them abolished by law. Such complaints may have reflected an element of ethnic hostility toward the street musicians themselves. At the other end of the cultural spectrum, Philadelphians continued to appreciate the talents of entertainers of Italian origin and background. In the same year as the complaints against the organists, local residents enjoyed the sensational local debut of fifteen-year-old Adelina Patti as Lucia di Lammermoor for what would be her long and celebrated career as an operatic soprano. Such pieces of experience sometimes offer small clues rather than systematic evidence on the material and social position of the Italians at this time. Moreover, these conditions were about to enter a new stage.[63]

As the 1850s drew to a close, the city still faced a period of further growth and change, but also a time of uncertainty. If the people shared this mood, it was not only a result of local conditions but also partly because of a genuine interest in foreign problems as well. By 1859, newspapers made the war in Italy the major international issue in articles and editorials, which focused almost daily on the struggle of Italians for independence. But the population also had great concern for local and national news. Although it appears almost ludicrous today, one persistent debate during the year took up the question of whether passenger railway cars should be allowed to run on the Sabbath. But more easily appreciated issues were also placed before the public. Antislavery meetings became important events in the city. One major convention was held in Philadelphia by the supporters of abolition. In December 1859, the execution of John Brown stirred further controversy in the city and other parts of the nation, as the debate over slavery increased.

Despite mounting tensions, other events taking place at the same time augured well for the future of the city. Although New York had become a more significant port for commerce and immigration, Philadelphia still served as an important destination. On one ordinary Saturday in late June 1859, the volume of marine traffic gave the port what the *Public Ledger* described as "a strikingly business like aspect." Twenty-six vessels of various types arrived, while twenty others were cleared for departure on that day alone. Among the arrivals, the *Wyoming* brought 181 passengers, mainly Irish but also English and Welsh immigrants, in steerage, and a privileged four others in cabin class, along with a large cargo of hardware, iron and dry goods. At almost the same time, the *William M. Moses* was guided into dock, loaded with marble and rags after sailing from Genoa. Similarly, the *Telegrafo*, a brig, arrived from Palermo with 1,030 boxes of oranges and 1,835 boxes of lemons. While most ships discharged passengers who would only pass through Philadelphia on their way to the West on the Pennsylvania Railroad, other vessels were arriving from Italian ports, foreshadowing the shift in immigration patterns that lay ahead.[64]

As their number reached a modest but visible level in Philadelphia and continued to grow in families and extended kinship groups, as well as in boardinghouses, Italians were becoming more concentrated in location. Although composed mainly of Ligurians, their new parish brought people together as Italians. Whether as defendants in the courtroom or as members of their own parish, emerging conditions were reconstructing them as a population. While difficulties with the language of local authorities could sometimes even divest them of proper names and identities, an Italian colony had taken root in Philadelphia. At the very moment that they appeared about to lose their previous sense of self and group solidarity, they were also on the verge of establishing a new identity and community in *la colonia Italiana di Filadelfia.*

Chapter 5

Family, Faith, and Fraternity

Italy is, after France and perhaps in the same degree, the land in which love of country has the deepest roots in the hearts of its inhabitants. The fact is that perhaps nowhere else has nature been so prodigal with its enchantments and seductions. Therefore, although Italy has been, since the fall of the Caesars, the object of European covetousness, the eternal battlefield of powerful neighbors, and the theatre of the fiercest and most prolonged civil wars, her children have always refused to leave her. Save for some commercial colonies hastily thrown upon the shores of Asia by Genoa and Venice, history has not, in fact, recorded in Italy any important outward movement of population.

—Alfred LeGoyt, 1861

Although the observation of Alfred LeGoyt, a French economist and statistician, had some validity at the time it appeared in his study of European migration,[1] his comments soon became obsolete. Italian emigration was about to change in volume, character, and destination. As immigration to the United States grew, an increasing number of Italians soon found their way to American cities. In the 1860s, as it continued its development, Philadelphia provided opportunities and limitations that formed the parameters of individual life and group experience for Italians and other newcomers, whose presence contributed to but also tested the resources and conscience of the city. The contact between immigrant and city eventually involved the modification of images, identities, and group boundaries. But before they could shift entirely to American factors, the events and conditions in foreign lands continued to influence the perceptions and responses of Philadelphians to immigrants.

Foreign Affairs, Local Attitudes

When the decade of the 1860s began, Philadelphians were still absorbed by almost daily newspaper accounts that presented the struggle for Italian independence as the most important foreign issue of the time. The Italian cause had been popular among Philadelphians because it was perceived as an attempt to emulate the earlier American struggle. By their efforts to liberate themselves from foreign domination, Italians were affirming the ideals of Americans and reminding them of their own war for independence. These parallels enabled the events in Italy to capture the imagination of readers in Philadelphia and elsewhere in the United States.

The news from Italy reported the more urgent political events, but also described social conditions and personal character of the people in Turin, Genoa, and Leghorn, that provided impressions of a new nation and its citizens. While respecting the spiritual authority of Pius IX, the *Public Ledger* consistently opposed the Pope's temporal power.[2] When a new war appeared inevitable, the *Public Ledger* endorsed a plan to declare Italy neutral ground and inaccessible to military action, which would balance the precarious relationship of France and Austria, while it greatly enhanced Italian influence in maintaining the stability of Europe. The local press regularly proposed a more active role for Italy in continental politics.[3]

When Garibaldi resumed his military campaign, Philadelphia newspapers provided detailed coverage. Although sympathetic to the Italians, one reporter noted, Americans had not anticipated the eventual success of Garibaldi's expedition. Instead, they saw it as a doomed "dare devil undertaking" and a waste of valuable resources that might have been better utilized elsewhere in the cause of European liberty.[4] But Philadelphians, whose public demonstrations had always been more for republicanism than for nationalism, were unable to respond to the Italian situation with the same enthusiasm as in 1848. By 1860, recognizing Sardinian monarchy at its center, local residents could no longer rally behind republican banners in support of the new nation. With the debate over slavery, and the gathering war clouds at home, Americans also now had more immediate concerns of their own.

Italians in Philadelphia could also follow events in their homeland, in the newspapers in a new language, but their ardor too was subdued. Conspicuous by their absence from earlier demonstrations that had supported the Risorgimento, Italians appeared to have the intention, at least initially, to leave such political concerns behind them. By the late 1860s, however, some of them would not only rediscover but also use Italian politics as a means to organize the immigrant population under their leadership.

In New York City, where Italians tended to be hard-core Mazzinians who shared the political sentiments of republican exiles from other European countries, as had been the case previously, things were quite different. As they anxiously awaited news of Garibaldi's expedition to Sicily, Italians in the cafés of their quarter debated the prospects of a successful campaign, and proprietors promised to post the latest news as soon as arriving steamers brought it from Italy. When word of Garibaldi's landing in Sicily finally reached New York City, Italian, German, and French residents celebrated in the saloons where they had gathered. The *Public Ledger* not only reported but also offered its own interpretation of this situation:

> Nearly all of this class of people are the reddest sort of red republicans, and not a few of them are now exiled from their native land by the government which Garibaldi has gone to help. Their anxiety, therefore, is not surprising under the circumstances. The German and French residents, with whose political opinions the Italians largely sympathize, are scarcely less excited, and should the expedition be successful, the general joy will know no bounds.[5]

With so many Mazzinians among them, Italians in New York may have seen Garibaldi's venture as the last hope for establishing an Italian republic. This difference in political character, rather than the larger size of their population, was probably the source for the reaction in New York, which stood in sharp contrast to the lack of response among Italians in Philadelphia to news from Italy.[6] But while they may have mainly been republicans, Italians in New York were also nationalists who were ready to celebrate any kind of military victory.

Throughout the summer of 1860, as reports of Garibaldi's success reached American readers, the press in Philadelphia became even less certain about his leadership. While recognizing his ability as a military leader, the *Public Ledger* concluded that Garibaldi probably lacked the diplomacy and tact necessary to establish a stable government. An editorial argued: "Notwithstanding all the astonishing successes of this really great man, he is becoming too venturesome for any great confidence to be felt as to the amount of his ultimate success." At this time, however, it was not apparent to Philadelphia journalists or Piedmont politicians that Garibaldi's aspirations were mainly military rather than political. Meanwhile, the high esteem and hope of ultimate success in which he was held by ordinary Philadelphians was whimsically indicated by the popularity of a horse named Garibaldi that scored its own kind of victory in a match race in October 1860.[7]

At the end of 1860, now aware that Garibaldi had no political aspirations for himself, the *Public Ledger* commended him as too democratic for European sovereigns and Italian conservatives, who dreaded republicanism and preferred Victor Emmanuel II as more moderate and sensible, and therefore better suited to be entrusted with the affairs of Italy. The same writer, however, concluded that Garibaldi might have become another George Washington.[8]

Despite the lingering question of unification, the initial success of Italian nationalism was formally celebrated in Philadelphia with the arrival in May 1863 of the *San Giovanni,* an Italian warship from Genoa. Anchored off the Navy Yard, after its twenty-gun salute was greeted by an American ship, the *Princeton,* the officers and crew of the Italian vessel came ashore. Nearly three weeks later the *San Giovanni,* gaily decorated with flags, observed a national holiday by hosting a number of prominent Italian residents of the city. At sunrise, noon, and sunset, its cannon salutes were answered again by the *Princeton.* The

San Giovanni and its crew had made a handsome impression during their brief visit.[9]

The diplomatic visit by another warship, the *Principe Umberto,* pride of the Italian fleet, with its fifty-two guns and crew of 600, attracted much attention in October 1864. As a schoolship for eighty-four midshipmen, the 3,500-ton frigate with a 600-horsepower engine, was compared favorably with the best ships of the American Navy. During its stay, officers sought to recruit skilled shipwrights with the inducement of $5 a day as salary. After sixteen days in the Delaware River, the frigate began its return voyage. The triumph of independence, along with ceremonial contacts by the new nation on such occasions as the visits of naval ships, might bode well for Italians as immigrants, at least for the moment. But much more was to happen, in Italy as well as in Philadelphia, to complicate matters.[10]

The final chapter in the unification of Italy opened with Rome and the Papal States as the remaining prize in 1867. After Garibaldi's capture by French and Papal troops, the *Public Ledger* reported an imaginative attempt to use a previous visit to the United States in an endeavor to rescue him. Claiming that he had become an American citizen in New York during his stay of 1850–51, friends of Garibaldi asked the American Ministry at Florence to obtain his release. While refusing to intervene on that point, the American envoy requested clemency for the prisoner. The *Public Ledger*'s favorable reaction to these efforts was an indication of the continuing sympathy for the Italian cause among Philadelphians.[11]

The news that reached the American public was not always about political and military events, nor was it necessarily a positive portrayal of events in Italy. One item reported an incident in Calabria in which several suspects blamed for the spread of cholera were hacked to death by an enraged and frightened mob in 1867. An editorial in Philadelphia used the case to argue for the importance of civilized institutions to protect the rights of individuals and to ensure social order. In contrast to the sympathy for the political cause, violence of this sort presented American readers with a less favorable view of Italians.[12]

Negative news continued to arrive from Italy. In late 1867, statistics of the Italian Life Assurance Society reported by the Philadelphia press showed an annual mortality rate of 22.5 percent of infants born in Italy, an exceptionally high figure when compared with other countries. Similarly, life expectancy, even in the healthiest districts, was only 33.43 years, a much lower figure than in France or England. The number of births was also less in Italy than in France and England. Whether specific events or general conditions, these aspects of life and death fostered impressions of Italy that were quite different from the romantic reveries of Italophiles of the past.[13]

A New Immigration and a New City

In Philadelphia during this period, another kind of social change was taking place. In the federal census of 1860, Philadelphia, with 565,529 residents, remained the fourth largest city in the Western world, exceeded only by London, Paris, and New York. Both in its size and in its unprecedented diversity, Philadelphia was developing as a modern city in a newer sense than the world had previously known. Within its population, 373,914 individuals were American-born, but another 169,430 people, nearly 30 percent, were of foreign origin. Of the foreign-born, the largest single group, 95,548 people, were of Irish birth, another 43,643 had been born in various German states, 19,278 originated in England, and nearly 11,000 more came from other countries.[14]

With the start of the American Civil War, the volume of immigration to Philadelphia began a temporary decline. In the spring of 1861, when the *Westmoreland,* a packet ship from Liverpool, arrived with a full cargo but no passengers, migration from England and Ireland seemed to be at its end. The *Public Ledger* reported: "At no time for a number of years have there been fewer passengers from Ireland to this port than now." The letters of an Irish clergyman, the Reverend Dr. Cahill, being circulated in Philadelphia but intended for readers in his homeland, advised the people of Ireland not to come to America in its present disturbed state of affairs. Some observers were convinced that Cahill's warnings had already substantially reduced the number of Irish immigrants to Philadelphia. But in another year the volume of arrivals from Great Britain had returned to its previous level. When the *Zered* from Londonderry and the *Saranak* from Liverpool arrived in May 1861, they brought 640 cabin and steerage passengers. Ignoring Cahill's warnings, about 100 of the 295 passengers of the *Zered* were returning to this country after visiting in Ireland. But local authorities acknowledged that the number of arrivals had fallen below the level of the previous year. When the *Zered* reached Philadelphia in November, it carried only six passengers. Eventually the figures increased again, resuming earlier levels, but the *Zered* itself would have less good fortune: it was lost at sea in 1863.[15]

The fluctuating number of new arrivals was not the only concern for Philadelphians. The developing rivalry with New York City as a port of entry made the role of immigration in local affairs itself an important matter. In early 1860, citizens and merchants complained in a petition to the state legislature that taxes on immigrant arrivals were responsible for a decline in foreign commerce that was going instead to New York. A thirty-year-old law, which authorized the Guardians of the Poor to regulate procedures, taxed each immigrant $2.50 as a precaution against the individual becoming a public charge. An additional 50-cent baggage tax on arrivals from foreign ports was used to finance quarantine procedures. The *Public Ledger* agreed with the petitioners that these fees encouraged immigrants to prefer New York as the port of entry. Arguing that few immigrants actually became charges, and that such taxation severely damaged commerce, it proposed that regular service from Liverpool to Philadelphia be established. In the following month, however, a new line connected the Mediterranean ports of Gibraltar, Genoa, Leghorn, Messina, Palermo, and Malaga with New York City.[16]

Although the use of steamships for immigration had been initiated in the early 1850s by the Inman Line between Liverpool and Philadelphia, they did not entirely replace sailing ships in the North Atlantic until the 1860s. That decade marked the beginning of a new era of transoceanic service in which the journey lost almost all the risk that had deterred prospective passengers in the past. In early 1860, the *Hungarian* was reported as only the fourteenth ship to sink since steam navigation between Europe and America had been introduced. In 1863, a group of Philadelphia merchants declared that the most important commercial need of their port was the local ownership and control of steamship lines. A stock subscription of $200,000 was announced for a line serving Philadelphia, California, and Europe, with the Pennsylvania Railroad Company pledging a similar amount for the enterprise.[17]

By 1866, the importance of steamships for transatlantic commerce between Europe and North America was widely recognized. The Inman Line sent two ships each way every week, and the Cunard Line sent one and sometimes two ships weekly. The Montreal, the National, and the British & North American Lines each sent one ship weekly. Several other lines—the North German, Lloyd's, the Hamburg, the American, Guion & Company, the London & New York, the London & Boston, the Liverpool & Philadelphia, the Liverpool & Baltimore, the Anchor, and the Transatlantic—sent one steamer each way every two weeks. The North American, Lloyd's, and the New York & Havre each sent another steamer each way at four-week intervals. These lines together accounted for a total of 1,196 trips across the Atlantic during the year. An average of two steamers left some port on either side on any weekday. Although the increasing demands of commerce had led to the formation of new companies, the construction of new ships, and an increasing number of scheduled trips by older lines, the demand now surpassed the number of available crossings. The fleet of more than 100 steamships, with a total of 250,000 tons, was crowded to excess.[18]

While the American Civil War had slowed immigration to the United States, the return of peace ignited the largest movement of population in world history. As it increased, with large numbers from Great Britain and Germany still arriving, the pattern of immigrant origins did not immediately deviate from the recent past. Of 2,565,644 arrivals for 1855–68, some 1,215,540 came from Great Britain, 909,834 came from Germany and Prussia, 108,531 came from British America, and 331,739 came from elsewhere in the world. Italy sent only 11,691 individuals, less than 1,000 people yearly. When annual immigration increased from slightly more than 90,000 in the early 1860s to more than 300,000 later in the decade, it then shifted in origins. In the spring of 1868, as 600 to 700 persons arrived daily, Denmark, Sweden, Poland, Italy, and France became newer sources of population.[19]

The arrival of immigrants posed new problems and demands for more services at all levels of American government. While Philadelphia struggled unsuccessfully with how to increase the number of arrivals, in New York the problem became almost the opposite—that is, how to deal with the growing volume of immigration. As Philadelphians debated the negative impact of city taxes on newcomers, the emigration commissioners in New York opened a labor exchange building at Castle Garden, where the skilled and unskilled could find employment and where employers could look for workers. As New York became the main port of entry, fewer immigrants settled in Philadelphia; many passed through the Pennsylvania Railroad Company depot to final destinations in the western states. Yet this situation should neither obscure the presence of the foreign-born nor minimize their impact on Philadelphia during the period of the Great Migration.[20]

Philadelphians were certainly aware that newer sources of immigration could encourage a return of the ethnic hostilities of earlier decades. But despite sporadic racial incidents, intergroup relations in the city were calmer now, and avoided any major outbreak of violence. The two largest components of the foreign-born population—the Germans and the Irish—were both geographically dispersed throughout the city and had already experienced considerable social mobility. The availability of steady employment in a strong labor market, and the increased accessibility of decent housing, not only eased social tensions, but also reinforced the perception of Philadelphia as a favorable destination for immigrants. Although not entirely eliminated, the potential for ethnic conflict was greatly reduced by such conditions.[21]

As public discourse in Philadelphia turned to the issue of the character of immigrants now arriving in the United States, the initial conclusions were highly favorable. At first, the newspapers provided the comforting finding that the same groups that had come in the past still dominated the renewed immigration; and they were generally regarded to be people of good personal character. One local observer noted: "The class that come are generally industrious and thrifty, and their labor is worth a great deal to the United States." In this swelling tide of immigration, a New York newspaper warned, the only thing to deplore was that many Danes and Swedes had joined the Mormons, and it was feared that there already were too many of the latter. Even though the 352,569 arrivals for the fiscal year that ended in June 1869 was the largest contingent of immigrants in fifteen years, the interpretation remained favorable: "There was a time when this vast influx of foreign born people was looked upon with apprehension by considerable numbers of our native born population, but that time has happily gone by." As in earlier years, America was believed to be broad enough to absorb immigrants who "have added to our productive strength, and rapidly become assimilated to the rest of the population." This view was strengthened by the migration of more settlers to the farmlands of western states.[22]

Confident that these newcomers would be quickly and thoroughly transformed into Americans, some observers enthusiastically declared: "There is no more decided American than your boy or girl whose parents were emigrants to this country." Although national character was rapidly crystallizing, the influx of foreigners had the least influence in this process, because, "as they always have they always will, whether with set purpose to do so or not, come into our fashions, and 'do in America as Americans.' "[23]

Potential problems, such as how immigrant groups would relate to one another and to native-born Americans, could be easily ignored or dismissed. It was asserted that, instead of being in conflict, they would balance one another in a positive manner. A Philadelphia editorial reproduced the favorable view of a British newspaper:

> The phlegmatic, cautious, economical German will be a healthy counterpoise to the mercurial, reckless and extravagant American, and that the Teutonic element is required to counterbalance the vast influx of Celts. Germans, for the most part, value education, and have certain aesthetic and intellectual tastes which it is desirable to introduce among the utilitarian Yankees.[24]

One wonders, however, whether the British press sought to convince Americans of the benefits from immigration out of fear that the same masses might otherwise redirect their destinations to England.

Reassured that immigrant origins had not fundamentally changed and that the new arrivals were of good personal character, could be easily absorbed, and would even get along with one another, public opinion remained emphatically optimistic. In 1866, a Philadelphia editorial offered a broad theory of immigration and individual character throughout history. After commenting on the rapid growth of the immigrant part of the American population, as well as on the degeneracy of the laboring classes in Europe, the writer declared:

> It is the energetic who emigrate, the timid who stay at home; and by this sort of natural selection in the course of ages, when we come in contact with the older tribes of man, such as the

Chinese in California, we find how much we have gained as a whole upon the ancient stocks, and how God has designed that the world should grow, and that the race of man become better, and not worse, in the lapse of ages.[25]

To the question "Why is it that the tide of emigration is also that of progress?" the answer was that migration selectively infused a new vigor into a race, because the strong moved while the decaying and inert stayed, and the stagnant masses were left behind in their homeland, "with all their old sources of rottenness and feeble life." The argument concluded that as the inferior who remained gained power their civilization would then deteriorate. This interpretation of immigration and its consequences was the opposite of what later nativist ideologies asserted.[26]

Despite these euphoric views, the diversity of the population had already disrupted, if not destroyed, traditional notions of community for such cities as Philadelphia. Rapid demographic growth and social change again threatened public order, but, in contrast to the 1840s, it was now manifested in the inability of city government to meet the needs of residents for the ordinary services of everyday life, such as an adequate supply of potable water or an efficient transportation system or clean and safe streets. The Act of Consolidation in 1854 had been intended to facilitate a more orderly means of organizing and governing the city and to reduce the likelihood of the rioting that had devastated public order in previous years. It had created a strong police system under the authority of the mayor, which may have been the most successful immediate accomplishment of the new municipal system. But other services were assigned to departments of local government or to the City Councils, which were far less efficient in their policies and practices. Yet as one historian termed it, the same chaos also reflected a period of "exuberant growth" that characterized the American city, fraught with the danger, excitement, and challenge that still attract so many people today. It could even be said that "Philadelphia was disorderly and often ugly, yet thoroughly vital."[27]

With an extremely favorable location, Philadelphia had abundant agricultural resources—in rural Pennsylvania counties to the west, as well as across the Delaware River in southern New Jersey—to feed a growing population; and through the Delaware and Lehigh Canals, the city had access to energy sources in the anthracite coal fields of northeastern Pennsylvania. By means of similar routes, city factories could be supplied with raw materials, such as the iron ore from the southeastern part of the state. As the home of the greatest railroad company in the nation, Philadelphia also remained a major center for finance capital and business organization. These conditions provided almost unlimited potential for further development. Despite continuing to lose ground as a seaport to New York, Philadelphia approached an era of unprecedented productivity and prosperity.

With its strong foundation of manufacturing, commerce, and finance, the city easily returned to the levels of productivity and prosperity that it had enjoyed before the Civil War. Unlike such centers of heavy industry as Pittsburgh, Cleveland, and Chicago, Philadelphia predominantly manufactured finished products and consumer goods. This aspect of local industry also meant that employment opportunities were greater for semi-skilled and skilled workers. Similarly, Philadelphia industry was not concentrated in a single area of production, but spread over a wide range of goods that included textiles and clothing, metal products, printing and publishing, leather goods, oil and sugar refining, drugs and chemicals, meatpacking, furniture, locomotives, streetcars, and cigars. The diversity of industrial production in the city made the labor force relatively immune to economic cycles that brought instability and high unemployment to more-specialized cities elsewhere.[28]

The level of industrial production enabled Philadelphia to claim that it was the most important manufacturing city in the United States—and the second in the entire world, behind only London. In 1867, some 96,983 people were employed in 1,266 factories, mills, and foundries, with gross earnings of $135,969,767. In numbers of industrial workers, Philadelphia was said to be 16,000 ahead of New York, despite the latter's larger population. Philadelphia also led New York in the number of industrial establishments, in the number of males and females employed, in the amount of capital invested in the manufacture of fourteen specific products, and in the overall total of invested capital, but not in the annual cost of labor. Throughout this era of "boosterism," the promotion of one city against another, New York City was Philadelphia's rival, but it had also become the measure of urban life. Even so, Philadelphia was a formidable industrial center.[29]

The demographic and spatial growth of the city provided a newly expanded framework for the renewal of older, unresolved issues inherent to urban growth. Without the distractions of war, Philadelphians once again discovered the difficulties of life in a rapidly growing city. The lower classes still lived under conditions far different than more affluent Philadelphians did. Whether native or foreign-born, many dwelled under wretched physical and social conditions. In 1861, after visiting Bedford, Small, Spafford, and other streets in the area, the Board of Health reported that it "had witnessed scenes of the most abject poverty and moral disease, where crime, degradation and misery were seen in bold relief." Streets, alleys, and courts reeked with filth. Cellar tenements were a particularly acute problem. In 1862, residents of Catharine Street complained that the people who cleaned privy wells and slaughterhouses at night used carts that dropped their contents along the streets as they passed. In many neighborhoods, streets remained unpaved and undeveloped. Railroad crossings at grade level made many thoroughfares dangerous. Pigs allowed to roam made streets quite unsavory. Bad water threatened public health. When cholera returned in 1866, the response of the city was reportedly less adequate than that of public agencies in a similar epidemic nearly two decades earlier.[30]

In response to such conditions, the city attempted to provide better housing and living conditions for the population. The typical Philadelphia residence was already an owner-occupied single-family home, and construction of new housing was rapidly advancing. In South Philadelphia, even during the war, improvement of existing structures and construction of new housing proceeded. In 1862, a considerable buildup of new residential construction occurred on Passyunk Road, from Moyamensing Prison to Broad Street, as well as on the streets crossing Passyunk Road, west of Tenth Street. Most new structures were three-story brick dwellings with modern improvements, which would be typical for South Philadelphia in the years ahead. The section below the county prison had grown fast in only a few years and was already thickly settled. In 1864, more elegant homes on the east side of Broad Street just above Wharton, with brick fronts and marble trim were completed—the last of the improvements begun two years before. The character and appearance of the area had been so improved by these handsome, spacious, and comfortable dwellings that this part of South Philadelphia was now a desirable residential location, and more improvements were expected.[31]

The "boosterism" of the period proudly called attention to the physical character of the city. In 1868, a report showed the number of buildings and floors, as well as the materials used in construction (see Table 8).

Table 8. Heights and materials of buildings, 1868

Height	Number	Material	Number
One story	2,023	Brick	80,800
Two story	32,280	Stone	6,885
Three story	63,037	Frame	13,819
Four story	4,516		
Five & over	648		

SOURCE: "The Growth of Philadelphia," *Public Ledger,* January 14, 1868, 3.

NOTE: The discrepancy in the totals for this information appears in the original tabulation; the figures are given here as they were published.

The report asserted that, "beyond the power of conjecture," Philadelphia was unlike other cities in that it afforded a separate house for nearly every family and an environment that elevated "the manners, habits, morals, family ties and domestic harmony" for most of its population. The familiar rival, New York City, again appeared in contrasts "between the average social life of a 'fast' city like New York, and the general healthy tone of family society in Philadelphia." Quite aware that it had fallen well behind New York in influencing the national economy, supporters of Philadelphia compensated by an argument on the "quality of life." Claiming to be the "City of Homes and Churches," the Philadelphia booster insisted that "all the colossal individual fortunes, and all the immense aggregate of wealth of the great commercial metropolis of the United States would not repay us for what we lose, in losing the homes that gave us a thrifty, industrious and virtuous population."[32]

Neither actual improvements nor vigorous assertions about the quality of life, however, kept pace with the housing shortages faced by an even faster-growing population. The need for more housing produced substandard new buildings and unsafe additions to older structures that contributed to the growth of slum districts in Moyamensing and Passyunk. The condition of the streets and the cost of public transportation gave workers little choice but to seek housing nearer to their places of employment in the mills and the factories of the city. The age of the immigrant ghetto had begun.

"Little Italy": Demographic and Social Patterns

At first glance, one of the great anomalies in the history of Italy is that almost at the same moment that national independence was finally achieved, great numbers of Italians began to leave their homeland. As emigration increased, they also shifted in their destinations and began the climb that in later decades made Italians the largest component of the "new immigration" to the United States. With the growth in the number of Italians in Philadelphia, other residents were also more likely to encounter them. But while the perceptions of and attitudes toward Philadelphia Italians might have posed some threat in an earlier time, the future of Italians now depended less on what others thought of them and more on what they would do for themselves. As they began to concentrate in their residential locations and to establish their own communal institutions, Italians in Philadelphia were also taking control of their future.

The growing number of Italians in the city represented the first important dimension of this transition. From 1820, when the U.S. government began counting, until 1860, some 11,202 individuals originating from the Italian mainland, another 2,030 natives of Sardinia, and 560 more from Sicily also came to America. In all, 13,792 people with origins on the Italian peninsula or the islands landed at American ports during these four decades. But in the late 1850s, migration between Italy and the United States increased substantially. In 1854, the number reached 1,263, a much greater figure than for any previous year except 1833, more than twice as large as 1853, and more than three and a half times as 1852. In each of the next six years, the number of Italians hovered just above 1,000, with the exception of 1859, when arrivals fell to slightly below 1,000. In 1861, it dropped to a much lower level—until 1865, when a higher number reappeared.[33]

In 1860, the federal census reported 622 persons born in Italy as residing in Pennsylvania. This number was exceeded in only three other states: California, the most popular place for Italians, with 2,805; New York, with 1,862; and Louisiana, with 1,134. The Census Bureau reported 485 Italian-born residents in Philadelphia, the second largest settlement in the nation, behind the 1,463 Italian-born in New York but ahead of the 249 in Boston in 1860. The manuscript census

records, however, revealed only 417 Italian-born residents in Philadelphia.[34] It had grown by 300–370 people in ten years, an increase
of more than 250 percent, and perhaps as much as 315 percent,
depending on which number is used. But the total for Italians was
still relatively small, compared with the huge numbers of Irish and
Germans, or even the 3,299 Scots and 2,625 French who remained
distinctive elements of the local population.[35]

The growth of the Philadelphia Italian population was accompanied
by an important change in where they lived. In 1850, there were only
slight concentrations in Middle Ward and Dock Ward of the city, in
the First and Second Wards of Moyamensing, and in the First Ward
of Southwark, which in each case did not exceed fifteen people. In
another ten years, Italians displayed a pattern of clustering that was
quite different.

By 1860, the Italian population in Philadelphia reached a level that
made sizeable concentrations also possible (see Table 9). The largest
number, 299 (more than 70 percent of all Italian residents), lived in the
Second, Third, and Fourth Wards, just below South Street, the area
that previously was the Township of Moyamensing and the Southwark
District. The Second Ward, which extended from Wharton Street
northward to Christian Street and from the Delaware River west to
Passyunk, then west along Ellsworth Street to Broad Street, contained
129 individuals born in Italy, the largest single concentration. The
Second Ward was typical of the entire area, with a large number of
native-born Americans and Irish immigrants but also many Germans
and English, a sprinkling of Canadians, French, and Swiss, and pockets
of Italians. Just above it, the Third Ward, which ran from Christian
Street north to Fitzwater Street and from the Delaware River to Broad
Street, held another 99 individuals born in Italy. The Fourth Ward,
which fell between Fitzwater Street and South Street and the Delaware
River and Broad Street, housed 71 natives of Italy. At this time the
area unmistakably held the roots of the Italian neighborhoods that
eventually dominated much of South Philadelphia.

In contrast to what this population would later become, however,
the backgrounds of Italian residents remained skewed toward origins
in Northern Italy in 1860. With the final unification of their nation of
origin still in the future, many immigrants preferred to give regional
states as their places of origin; others identified themselves, or were
identified by census enumerators, as being from Italy. When they

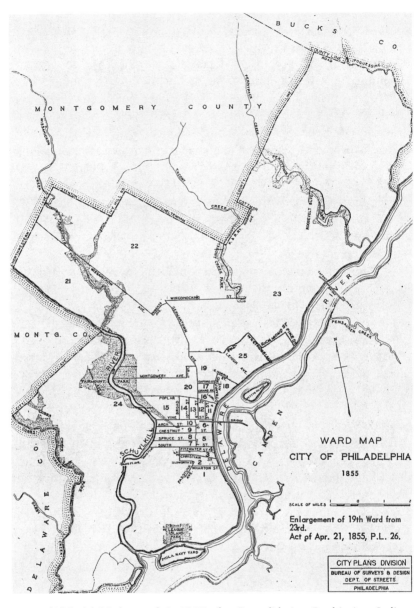

Map of Philadelphia by wards in 1855, after Consolidation. By this time, Italians began to concentrate in the new section of South Philadelphia containing Wards 2–4, formerly the Township of Moyamensing and the Southwark District. (Philadelphia City Archives)

Table 9. Residential locations of Italians, 1860

Ward	Number	Ward	Number
1	3	13	3
2	129	14	2
3	99	15	3
4	71	16	0
5	22	17	1
6	4	18	1
7	5	19	4
8	18	20	13
9	6	21	1
10	13	22	5
11	0	23	0
12	7	24	7

Total: 417

SOURCE: These figures are derived from *Population Schedules of the Eighth Census of the United States, 1860,* M653, National Archives, Mid-Atlantic Region, Philadelphia.

indicated a particular location, 127 Italians gave Genoa as their place of origin, far more than anywhere elsewhere. The only other significant number of Italians with a common background were 26 residents who were natives of Tuscany. Seven others revealed backgrounds that were spread among Sicily, Venice, and Milan. Although the regional origins of those who simply gave Italy as their place of birth is unclear, the Italian population in Philadelphia in 1860 remained heavily dominated by Genoese, with Tuscans second.

The population was augmented by 140 other people born in the United States with at least one Italian-born adult in the household, who appeared to be a parent. Some 80 other American-born children and adults were in households with both an adult male and a female born in Italy, who appeared to be parents, and 38 people lived in households with an adult male born in Italy but a female born elsewhere. Living in households with an Italian-born female and a male born elsewhere were 22 others. In some cases, these individuals may have already become partly Americanized, or may not have been Italian at all, but the majority were also members of households and of a community that had an Italian character.

Although these household units can easily be seen as families, they may have been something else. When a male was listed first, signifying head of household, followed by a female who was near in age, with younger members also included, it seems reasonable to infer that the arrangement was a family. But the failure of the census to indicate the relationship of any others listed to the head of the household makes it unclear who such people actually were and how they were related to one another. Moreover, children working either as *figurinai*—image-makers and sellers of plaster of paris statuettes—or as street musicians were in Philadelphia as early as the 1840s. Although children were sometimes sent into the streets by their parents, they could also be apprenticed and even sold by families in Italy as "slave children" for employment in foreign cities. Their new masters, in turn, protected the system against local authorities by disguising these arrangements as families.[36] While the situation would visibly erupt in Philadelphia with police raids and state legislation to eliminate such practices in 1873–74, whether the household units reported in the 1860 census represented real families or groups of unrelated child workers perhaps remains a moot point.

Although some misrepresentation had probably taken place, the age and sex distribution of the Italian-born population indicates that real families were present in Philadelphia in 1860. The situation of sixty-nine Italian-born children ranging from infancy to fourteen years old provided an important clue to the question (see Table 10). If the census information was accurate, these children of households with both an adult male and an adult female present were arguably not "slave children," but members of families. Unless the people involved were quite effective in disguising the system of slave children, something much more ordinary was generally found among Italians in the city at this time. Furthermore, even though young men form the largest single category, the rather large number of females and the comparable numbers in almost all age categories support this conclusion. Except for the oldest category of individuals, those age sixty and older, the ratio of males to females does not exceed 2 to 1. This distribution suggests a relatively "normalized" community rather than a consciously recruited and specialized population.[37]

The household and family structure of Italians in Philadelphia in 1860 similarly reflects a conventional family system, although there were variations. (With some caution, because the census never identified their actual relationships, we shall assume that individuals with common surnames who lived in any particular household

Table 10. Distribution of Italians by age and sex (1860)

Age (years)	Males	Females	Totals
0–14	41	28	69
15–29	92	63	155
30–44	61	42	103
45–59	38	25	63
60+	19	4	23
Unknown	—	4	4
Totals	251	166	417

SOURCE: *Population Schedules, 1860.*

were members of the same family.) Table 11 shows various living arrangements and the number of cases for each type among the Italians of the city.

About 64 families included parents who both were natives of Italy, with children born in Italy or the United States. In these situations, in addition to parents and their own children, one or two other individuals, whether related or unrelated, might also be present. Frequently these individuals were adults, but they could be children, and they were found in almost all the remaining types of households as well. In 11 other families, both spouses were natives of Italy but there were no children in the household.

In 18 families, in which the father was a native of Italy but the mother and children were born elsewhere, patterns of intermarriage begin to emerge. Most Italian men who married outside their group chose women who were natives of Ireland, but Pennsylvania, England, Germany, France, and Switzerland also provided mates. In 6 families, the wife had been born in Italy and the father and children had been born elsewhere. For these marriages, Germany provided the spouse twice, and England, Scotland, Switzerland, and Hungary once each. For 7 married couples where one of the spouses was born in Italy, there were no children. In these cases, 3 Italians were married to natives of Pennsylvania, and one each to a spouse from France, Corsica, England, or Germany. In considering the pattern of intermarriage, even though the sample was quite small, it is interesting to note the popularity of the choice of Irish wives by Italian men and the total absence of Italian women married to Irish husbands.

In a few cases, one parent was missing from the household. In 5

Table 11. Parental nativity and family structure, 1860

Both spouses born in Italy: children	64
Both spouses born in Italy: childless	11
Husband born in Italy; wife elsewhere: children (Ireland, 8; England, 3; Pennsylvania, 3; Germany, 2; France, 1; Switzerland, 1)	18
Wife born in Italy; husband elsewhere: children (Germany, 2; England, 1; Switzerland, 1; Scotland, 1; Hungary, 1)	6
Either spouse born in Italy; mate elsewhere: childless (Pennsylvania, 3; England, 1; France, 1; Germany, 1; Corsica, 1)	7
Father born in Italy; no wife present: children	5
Mother born in Italy; no husband present: children	8
Both parents born elsewhere; children born in Italy	2
Males, related or unrelated, living in groups	4
Unclear arrangements	4
Compound arrangements	1
Other situations involving Italian-born individuals*	55

SOURCE: *Population Schedules, 1860.* We must be cautious in relying on census manuscripts for a picture of family and living arrangements. Because the census did not clearly identify relationships of people living in the same household, it is difficult to be sure what the arrangements were.

* That is, living alone, in non-Italian households, or with unrelated others; priests; inmates; etc. Unlike the previous categories that indicate the number of cases, this refers to the total number of individuals found in these situations.

families, an Italian-born father was alone with children; in 8 others, an Italian-born mother was alone with children. There were two anomalous cases, in which both parents were natives of other foreign countries but their children were born in Italy. In all probability, these families were either not really Italian but had spent sufficient time in Italy to have had children born there, or reflected errors in recording by the census enumerator.

Households that contained Italians were not always families in the conventional sense. Four groups of Italian-born men, who shared the same type of employment as well as housing arrangements, probably were work gangs. There were also 3 priests in a rectory or seminary; 7 inmates at institutions, such as the almshouse or Eastern Penitentiary; and about 40 lodgers in boardinghouses or hotels—all born in Italy. The latter places served a diverse public, rather than being exclusively Italian lodgings common in later decades. Four groups of Italians had living arrangements that could not be determined.

The number of household units within the same dwelling is also evident for the Italian population in 1860. At 76 sites, the basic household either consisted of spouses who were both born in Italy, whether parents or childless; or were headed by an Italian-born male or by an Italian-born female living with her children but no spouse; or by an all-male group. About 36 of these units appear to have been living in their own dwelling place with no one else, while the remainder shared housing with others in some manner. A shared dwelling usually included two to three distinct households at the same address. The shared dwellings were also more likely to consist exclusively of Italian families in the three wards of their highest concentration. In other wards, however, an Italian family in a multiple-family dwelling was more likely to be sharing it with a family of another ethnic background. At the extreme, a dwelling contained five or six discrete family units. Table 12 shows the configuration in one building in the Second Ward.[38] The Moneil family, as it was recorded, consisting of parents and their three children, all born in Genoa, constituted the primary unit of their dwelling. In another household unit, Francis Copello, a 40-year-old organist born in Genoa, lived with his wife, Angeline, and their three children. Sometime perhaps in 1859, the Copello family welcomed its first American-born child. Charles Cunnion, 28 years of age, another organist from Genoa, also lived here with his wife, Mary, and their daughter. In this household, another male and female, Francis and Mary, both in their early twenties and born in Genoa, were also listed under the surname Cunnion and were possibly siblings of Charles, or a brother and his own wife. Joseph Beech, a 23-year-old artist from Genoa, also lived at this address, with his young wife, born in Pennsylvania, as well as their 3-month-old daughter. In the same dwelling were Anton (probably Anthony) Guana, a 23-year-old organist and his wife, Mary, both born in Genoa. Yet another family, Joquin Artita, a 24-year-old organist, his wife, Rose, both born in Genoa, and their two-year-old daughter and 8-month-old son, both born in Pennsylvania, constituted another unit. Joseph Curria, a 22-year-old organist, also a native of Genoa, lived alone.

This candid but limited sketch enables us to make further inferences about these individuals and their relationships to one another. Their common origin, listed as Genoa, indicate a *paesani* group. They are young families that have committed themselves to life in a new country. They are almost surely street musicians, but as members of families,

Table 12. Households in a building, Second Ward, 1860

Name	Age	Sex	Occupation	Personal Estate	Place of Birth
Moneil, Benditti	58	M	Peddler	$100	Genoa
———, Angelina	50	F			Genoa
———, John	18	M			Genoa
———, Joquin	14	M			Genoa
———, Stephen	7	M			Genoa
Copello, Francis	40	M	Organist	$100	Genoa
———, Angeline	30	F			Genoa
———, John	7	M			Genoa
———, George	4	M			Genoa
———, Angeline	1	F			Pennsylvania
Cunnion, Charles	28	M	Organist		Genoa
———, Mary	30	F			Genoa
———, Jane	3	F			Genoa
———, Francis	21	M	Organist		Genoa
———, Mary	20	F			Genoa
Beech, Joseph	23	M	Artist		Genoa
———, Jane	17	F			Pennsylvania
———, Sebina	3/12	F			Pennsylvania
Guana, Anton	23	M	Organist		Genoa
———, Mary	22	F			Genoa
Curria, Joseph	22	M	Organist		Genoa
Artita, Joquin	24	M	Organist		Genoa
———, Rose	18	F			Genoa
———, Jane	2	F			Pennsylvania
———, George	8/12	M			Pennsylvania

SOURCE: *Population Schedules, 1860.*

rather than as "slave children" under a *padrone* boss. Two families have recently been expanded by children that represent the beginning of an American-born generation. These families also appear to be at a very early stage of the immigrant experience. These fragments from the census, however, also generate questions about their lives that cannot be as easily answered. How did they actually share this dwelling? How did they interact with one another? How well did they fare in their efforts? What became of these families?

An alternative housing arrangement contained only males living in small groups. In the Second Ward, Anthony Raffeto, a 24-year-old bootmaker who headed one such group, must have been somewhat successful in his craft because he possessed the modestly substantial sum of $500. The same unit included Louis Raffeto, 18 years old, an apprentice bootmaker, and probably a brother; John Raffeto, 12 years old and probably another brother; and Joseph Raffeto, 58 years old and identified as an apprentice. The Raffeto circle was completed by another apprentice, Amele DeMenny, a 38-year-old male. All these were Italian-born. In the same dwelling, however, the family of Patrick Moriarity lived. In another dwelling in the Second Ward, a group headed by Andrew Otiani, a 25-year-old harpist, included four other male harpists, all with the same surname, ranging in age from 16 to 22, and all born in Genoa. They looked more like the Italian musicians who were becoming a colorful nuisance on the streets of the city to other Philadelphians.[39]

Not all the males who grouped together in this manner were musicians, nor were they all from Genoa. In the Fifth Ward, one unit was headed by Sebastian Babista, as the census recorded his name, a 55-year-old male plaster cast maker from Tuscany. It contained eight other men, ranging in age from 20 to 50, with five of them from Tuscany and the other three from "Venetia," but all listed as plaster cast makers. These men were in some sense the vanguard of the unattached workers that came in great numbers in search of economic opportunity in America and made the all-male boardinghouse a common feature of the Italian community in later years.[40]

While a precursor of the boardinghouse was even more evident in the complicated situation headed by another maker of plaster statues who was erroneously identified in the 1860 census, it was significant in several ways for the Italian experience.[41] The Hardie (or Nardi) household (see Table 13) contained the only Italians in the Twentieth Ward of North Philadelphia, located above Poplar, west of Broad Street, in 1860. Like the street musicians, this group of Tuscan plaster figure makers was a fairly common type of an early Italian in some American cities. The household was a complex structure that consisted of at least one family and possibly two, but also ten other males as boarders. The Tuscan origins of its adult males illustrate the persisting influence of regional origins in the work and living arrangements of these people. The most important aspect of this case, however, is that its head was actually Lorenzo Nardi, a well-known figure in the Italian community in later years.

Table 13. The Hardie (Nardi) household (1860)

Name	Age	Sex	Occupation	Personal Estate	Place of Birth
Hardie, Lorenzo	42	M	Artist, plaster images	$200	Tuscany
———, Angela	25	F			France
———, Raffaello	32	M	Artist, plaster images		Tuscany
———, Charles	1	M			Pennsylvania
———, Settima	26	F			Tuscany
———, Ferdinand	18	M	Artist, plaster images		Tuscany
———, Lorenzo	26	M	Artist, plaster images		Tuscany
Francis Barsotte	18	M	Artist, plaster images		Tuscany
Frostino Grannelli	33	M	Artist, plaster images		Tuscany
Michale Belli	18	M	Artist, plaster images		Tuscany
Giovanni March	17	M	Artist, plaster images		Tuscany
Lorenzo Pero	23	M	Artist, plaster images		Tuscany
Domenico Belli	22	M	Artist, plaster images		Tuscany
Angelo Methedi	24	M	Artist, plaster images		Tuscany
Amato Belli	23	M	Artist, plaster images		Tuscany

SOURCE: *Population Schedules, 1860.*

The details of the Nardi case force us to reconsider the earlier issue of the groups that disguised themselves as families when they were actually gangs of street musicians and statue vendors involved in child exploitation. In view of the success and influence, and above all the genuine respect of other Italians, that Nardi later achieved, it is all but impossible to see him in such a role in earlier years. While Nardi's case may have provided the most dramatic illustration, other street musicians and statue vendors also adapted their original skills to more conventional occupational niches. And rather than continuing an itinerant pattern that carried them away to other locales, these individuals, like Nardi, began their climb toward more permanent and respectable positions within the emerging Italian community of the city.

The variations in family and household structure also reveal the inventive adjustments that immigrants made in their new environment. The challenges of life in a huge foreign city, difficult enough for its American-born population, was even more complicated for new arrivals who were geographically separated from the familiar culture from which they had emigrated. Their willingness to accept and endure this challenge, even by altering family and living arrangements, was either a measure of their inability to pursue any alternatives or testimony to their determination.

The 1860 census record showing the household of Lorenzo Nardi (erroneously listed as Hardie on line 10) from Decimo, in the province of Lucca. Nardi would emerge as a leader of the immigrant community. At this early point his household included his own family members as well as a group of artists (*figurinai*) who made and sold plaster statues on city streets. (National Archives, Mid-Atlantic Region)

The acceptance of living conditions that were far from ideal was tempered by the opportunities for work and income in Philadelphia. In addition, the wide range of occupations Italians held shows the roles being assigned to them—as well as in some cases introduced by Italians themselves—in the economy of the city. Among Italian-born residents of Philadelphia, 189 were employed in a broad range of occupations (Table 14). The greatest single concentration consisted of sixty individuals who worked in some manner as musicians. Most of them were organ-grinders who plied their trade with their distinctive instrument. They were men and women, young and old, and almost always with origins near Genoa, who sometimes performed on an accompanying instrument, such as the street harp or the tambourine. While undeniably colorful, these musicians were in subsequent years often the subject of debate about the desirability of their presence on the streets of the city. In particular, their image was tarnished by great concern about the problem of the so-called "slave children" sometimes associated with them. Theirs was also not a calling that had great promise of upward mobility for later generations.

Italians who made and peddled plaster statues of historical or religious figures represented another characteristic line of work at this time. But while somewhat itinerant, the twenty-seven *figurinai*, often with origins in the province of Lucca, may have had a better experience

Table 14. Occupations of Italians, 1860

Tradesmen (bootmaker/shoemaker/brushmaker/carpenter/caulker/ confectioner/cordwainer/jeweler/lampmaker/ornamental brass molder/paper box maker/perfumer/printer/rigger/seamstress/ tailor/type founder/related apprentices)	34
Artist/Sculptor	5
Plaster of paris figure maker/image-maker/plaster images	27
Agent/businessman/clerk/dealer/importer/innkeeper/boarding- house/cake and candy stand/candy store/druggist/fruit dealer/ fruiterer/grocer/orange dealer/storekeeper/showman/trader/ related apprentices	24
Musician/organist/organ girl/organ-grinder/organ player/ harpist/tambourine player	60
Mariner/sea captain	2
Priest	3
Laborer	6
Teacher/professor of music	5
Bootblack/coachman/cook/domestic/servant/washerwoman/ waiter	14
Peddler	2
Farmer/farm hand/gardener	5
Rag dealer/rag picker	2
Total	189

SOURCE: *Population Schedules, 1960.*

in Philadelphia than in other cities. As the Nardi family experience illustrated, *figurinai* could reach more permanent and prosperous outcomes in later years.

Thirty-four Italians found employment in trades that placed them in more-conventional positions in the industries of Philadelphia. They worked as boot and shoe makers, carpenters, jewelers, molders, printers, and tailors, and in other occupations. The skill levels required by these occupations ranged from relatively simple demands to the more-complicated techniques of some crafts. Younger Italians were also already apprentices in these trades. Italians were becoming more integrated into the labor force of the city.

Twenty-four other Italians worked as agents, businessmen, and clerks in a broad and mixed range of commercial occupations that is perhaps the most difficult category to describe. They included at one end the wealthy entrepreneur and importer, Vito Viti, owner of real-estate valued at $100,000 and a personal estate of $25,000, and Natale Parelli, a music professor who claimed a personal estate valued at $60,000. At the other end were young apprentice workers and small retail shopkeepers of far more limited personal wealth. But these workers also revealed a diverse participation of Italians in the local economy. In some cases, the shopkeepers served a localized market of immigrants and residents of their own neighborhoods, while others were merchants who provided wares and services for a much broader segment of the public at large.[42]

Music, Marble, and Fruit—Paupers and Crime

Although the total population of Italians was still quite small, and despite concentrations as street musicians or *figurinai*, the distribution of other workers in the city's economy held much promise for the future. The diversity of employment that Philadelphia immediately offered furnished an attractive incentive for new arrivals. The success that such individuals as Viti had already achieved provided a loftier vision of the future for the more ambitious.

The increase in the numbers, along with the greater variety within their population, also complicated how other residents of the city perceived the Italians. Philadelphians continued to appreciate the accomplishments of Italians in the arts, education, and business, as well as the products they delivered to the city. The more-affluent and cultivated residents were avid patrons of Italian opera, since its introduction by the performance of Giocchino Rossini's *Barber of Seville* in 1822. DaPonte reinforced its availability with his efforts in 1833. The Italian Opera Company of Havana, the favorite of audiences in 1847–52, introduced the music of Giuseppe Verdi to the city. Well established by the early 1860s, the appearances of such distinguished performers as Pasquale Brignoli, Alessandro Amodio, and Gaetano Ferri established the Italian opera season as a popular form of entertainment. After her much-celebrated debut as a child prodigy in 1852, Adelina Patti remained a frequent performer and favorite of Philadelphia audiences throughout her long career. In 1861, Carlotta Patti joined her sister as a performer at the Musical Fund Hall and the Academy of Music. Natale Parelli (sometimes given as Perelli) directed vocal concerts at the Musical Fund Hall in 1849 and 1850, when his four-act tragic opera, *Belschazzar,* was first performed. In 1866, Parelli conducted the debut of another opera, *Clarissa Harlowe,* at the Chestnut Street Concert Hall. Parelli was an important figure in local music until his death at age fifty-one in February 1867. At his funeral at St. John's Church, prominent professors and performers joined in choruses and concert pieces in tribute to Parelli. Father John Patrick Dunn, pastor of St. John's, eulogized Parelli as a teacher of humanity and described the elevating and refining effects of his career in music. Philadelphians with a taste for opera were not merely aware of Italian music but also appreciated a certain type of an Italian.[43]

In education as well as opera, the acceptance of Italians by other Philadelphians depended on their competence. In 1853, the Board of Trustees at the Polytechnic College of the State of Pennsylvania elected Dr. Vincenzo deAmarelli, a native of Rossano in Calabria, as a professor of French and Spanish languages and literature. Ten years later, as professor of Italian languages and literature at the University of Pennsylvania, deAmarelli was described as a respected gentleman whose reappointment was the best evidence of his ability to fill that position.[44]

The business enterprises of some individuals provided Philadelphians with another arena for becoming acquainted with Italians. For many years, the firm of Vito Viti & Sons engaged in various commercial ventures, such as the importation of marble from Massa Carrara to Philadelphia. After Vito Viti's death in 1866, his sons operated the business for many more years and played an important role in the affairs of the Italian community. The Vitis were important to the history of the Italian experience in Philadelphia not only by their own success and prominence, but also because they served as conduits for the extension of Italian material culture to the local economy.[45]

Besides marble, other products of Italy reached Philadelphia in the 1860s. Many Philadelphians already appreciated foods from Italy, particularly the massive amount of the citrus fruit and nuts that regularly reached the markets and homes of the city. In February 1861, some 27,600 boxes of oranges and 5,000 boxes of lemons arrived, almost entirely from Palermo and Messina, along with large quantities of walnuts and almonds. In the following months, other ships brought more oranges, lemons, and prunes.[46] At any point during winter and spring, newspaper items announced:

> The lovers of foreign fruit will be gratified to learn of two arrivals from Italian ports, both vessels, the Eolo and Imogene, being loaded with oranges, lemons and other fruit. The whole number of boxes of oranges was 6,734, of lemons 2,000. Shelled almonds and filberts were also brought.[47]

Whether they attended the opera, studied foreign languages, collected imported marble, or simply enjoyed eating fruits and nuts, Philadelphians continued their esteem for cultural and material commodities from Italy. But some residents were now beginning to take a new view of Italians. It was shifting away from the appreciation of musicians, artists, and merchants that had amused, entertained, and fed the public in earlier decades and toward a less positive and sometimes even sinister depiction. Philadelphians were becoming increasingly aware of, and frequently in contact with, a much larger population of Italians of humbler origins and more ordinary pursuits. Moreover, with the rapid growth of the city, residents could easily link its emergent problems to the increasing presence of foreign groups.

The newspapers, which for so long had praised them and their political cause, now nearing its final resolution, introduced a different image of Italians. For instance, the press vividly described the "low life of the city" in areas not far from the center of Italian settlement in South Philadelphia. And if what was happening within the city was not alarming enough, the newspapers provided other issues that fanned the fears of local residents, such as the arrival of an immigrant train from New York that brought an insane and impoverished Italian to Philadelphia. The account even suggested that New York City sought to solve its own problems by sending its paupers to Philadelphia.[48] But crime was the most salient component in a depiction that provided readers, in addition to their own real and imagined experiences, with reasons for a newer sense of Italian character and community life.

While Philadelphia newspapers had previously reported an occasional crime by an Italian, a series of vivid articles in the early 1860s marked a new stage in which such coverage began to appear more regularly. In May 1861, an Italian burglar, when encountered by a twelve-year-old girl, turned on the child, beating her on the head and seriously injuring her. Similar accounts often reported stabbings. In an 1864 case, the coroner investigated the stabbing death of John B. Williams by Joseph Begeo at the tavern of Antonio Chenghino at Eighth and Christian Streets. A few years later Battista Rosenza was accused of stabbing William Dunn at the corner of Front and Washington Streets, after a quarrel while both men were at work. Another Italian was accused of striking Dunn on the head with a sledgehammer. It is not clear whether the ethnic differences provoked such incidents. The accounts of stabbings by Italians, with Italians as well as others as victims, continued in the years to come. Sometimes the Italian himself was the victim of a crime by someone who was probably of a different ethnic origin. When Antoine Smith, who was identified as an Italian, was knocked down and robbed on Baker Street just above Seventh in November 1866, his attacker was probably not an Italian. But the identification of Smith as an Italian may have indirectly reinforced the association of crime with ethnicity.[49]

In other cases, theft without violence was described, or the portrayal did not involve an assignment of guilt, such as the trial of an Italian accused of stealing foreign coins and other property from a fellow countryman in 1861. When the jury rendered a guilty verdict, the *Public Ledger* protested: "No case has ever been tried in Quarter Sessions in which a defense was more clearly established." But whether the accused were innocent or guilty—such as the lodger who had stolen beds, coverlets, blankets, sheets, and pillowcases at a boardinghouse on South Eighth Street, then pawned the goods—the public now read about Italians who preyed upon their own people. Taking advantage of a wartime opportunity and enlisting in the army, he sold the pawnbro-ker's tickets to the wife of another recruit. When the woman tried to claim the property, the tickets were traced to the thief, who was then arrested. In 1864, another Italian, only recently released after four years at Eastern Penitentiary, was arrested and charged with stealing diamond rings valued at $3,000 from a jewelry store on Chestnut Street. A police search of his room discovered jewelry stolen from shops in Washington, Baltimore, and New York, towels from the Continental Hotel, and a subscription book that authorized him to collect money for a local church. A few months later, two Italians were charged with counterfeiting postal currency. While informing the public that Italians were contributing greatly to the crime problem of the city, these reports also generated an image of Italians that evolved into a popular stereotype in subsequent years.[50]

Like other newcomers, however, Italians encountered a broad range of misfortune. Although probably rarer than for other immigrant groups, a suicide attempt by an Italian revealed the difficulties in adjusting to life in a new setting. Drownings, work mishaps, and train accidents also injured or killed Italians. Some relatively harmless crimes reflected the conflict between immigrant cultural values and the more restrictive laws, such as the charges brought against Joseph Malatesta for selling liquor without a license. Ironically, Malatesta later achieved success and wealth as a liquor importer and restaurant owner, before his appointment as first captain of the police patrol service and superintendent of vans some years later. Reports of crimes, however, especially when violent and with a knife as the weapon, often described as a "stiletto" when its wielder was an Italian, were becoming more important in establishing the new image.[51]

The decade of the 1860s also saw growing attention to the problem of importing Italians to be workers in the United States. For Italians in Philadelphia, some version of the "*padrone* system" had already played a role in the importation of children as street musicians. In an 1867 case, two Italian musicians contested each other for the custody of an eight-year-old boy. One man testified that he had brought the boy from Naples through an agreement to pay the boy's mother $20 a year for the service of her son as a street musician, and to return him after a period of four years. Saying that he had been badly treated, the boy had fled from the man and found shelter with a second musician, who claimed to be his cousin. The boy stated that he earned from $1 to

$3 a day by playing his violin on the streets. Both men offered bonds to the court to guarantee the care of the child. While the first musician promised to return the boy to his mother in Naples, the second offered to send the boy to school for a reasonable period. When reported by the press, these cases only confirmed the new perception of Italians by Philadelphians.[52]

From Yankee Soldiers to American Citizens

Although these events disturbed the peace and tarnished perceptions in the city, the outbreak of the Civil War presented a far greater disruption of life throughout the nation. Until the conflict ended, America was not a suitable destination for prospective immigrants, and, as previously noted, the volume of immigration from Italy sharply declined. For the foreign-born already in America, however, the war brought new opportunities. Many Italians served in the Civil War, and perhaps more than 200 became officers on both sides. In the Union army, an Italian Legion that was eventually absorbed by another unit was formed, and at least three Italians reached the rank of general.[53]

With the war, immigration from Italy to Philadelphia diminished, and the growth of the Italian community also paused. Italian residents, however, responded to the call to serve their new country. In August 1861, local newspapers announced that a company of Zouaves had been mustered into service under the command of Captain Granello.[54] The new company was to be attached to the Twenty-third Infantry Regiment, which was seeking recruits. Later in the month, plans were announced for formation of another company, at 23 South Seventh Street, which was to be made up exclusively of Italians and Frenchmen who had prior military experience in Europe, and the War Department was expected to appoint an American officer as its captain. Two lieutenants, A. Zajotts and A. D'Orsoline, already in its ranks and apparently representatives of the two foreign components, had previously served with the three-month volunteer units of the Union army.[55]

In their enthusiastic support of the war, the Irish, the Germans, and African Americans quickly announced similar plans to form military units. In September, the Chasseurs des Alpes, a company composed of foreigners who had served in European wars, was reported as having been established and under three days marching orders from their armory. A few days later the Zouaves d'Afrique announced an exhibition drill at the Academy of Music with a program of French, German, and Italian national songs, obviously intended to induce foreign-born recruits.[56]

Whether as members of special units of the foreign-born or in more regular units, along with other residents of Philadelphia, Italians were called to service during the war. When the draft lists were published, Alonzo Viti, John Barsulia, Anthony Ferigeno, Lewis Namone, Fred Imadore, Victor Chicone, Antonio Delaotz, Frank Gannello, Augustine Magliocio, A. D. Padanna, Gaetano Maizzolo, Joseph Moreto, and Joseph Antonio were among the names for 1863 and 1865.[57] Whether these men actually served or not, the record of others with ties to Italy is certain. With previous allegiance to the King of Italy, Justice Buttinghausen joined the Union army as a volunteer in October 1862 and served in the Third Pennsylvania Heavy Artillery Regiment before his discharge three years later. Samuel Bright, another former subject of the King of Italy, who enlisted as a volunteer in August 1864, was a private in the 198th Pennsylvania Infantry Regiment and remained in the service until June of the following year. John Patroni enlisted in the Fourth Regiment of the Provisional Cavalry in November 1864 and returned to civilian life slightly more than a year later. With a judicious sense of timing, Joseph Barsuglia (probably the Barsulia of the draft lists), enlisted on April 8, 1865, the day before Lee's surrender to Grant and, after service with the 215th Regiment of Pennsylvania Volunteers, was discharged less than four months later. Ignazio Allegretti served as a volunteer line soldier from April to September 1861. Carlo Capelli was a private in D Company, 104th Regiment of Pennsylvania Volunteers from October 1861 to October 1864. Baldo Muzzarelli attained the rank of first sergeant in H Company, 43rd Regiment of Illinois Volunteers, from October 1860 until his discharge in December 1864.[58] Whether entering military service or remaining as civilians, Italians had joined their fellow Philadelphians in support of the Union cause. At the end of the war, when John Wilkes Booth assassinated President Lincoln, Italians also shared in the grief. From his residence at 1435 Walnut Street, Alonzo M. Viti, the marble-importer who later served as Italian Consul, displayed "a splendid Italian flag appropriately draped in mourning" for the dead president.[59]

With the return of peace, Italians manifested their commitment by seeking naturalization as American citizens. The procedure represented a challenge for the immigrant, especially if his knowledge of English was still limited, as it was likely to be, or if his expectations about the outcome were uncertain. A large crowd usually assembled in the courtroom for the hearing of applications by people who wanted to be naturalized. Accompanied by a witness who served as a voucher, each immigrant presented the presiding judge with an application for naturalization. After examining this document, the judge asked the voucher about his acquaintance with the applicant, then asked the applicant questions about his residence in America and his age; about the form of government in the United States; and finally whether he had given careful consideration to the matter of becoming a citizen and renouncing his allegiance to his native country. If the replies were satisfactory, the applicant was formally admitted to citizenship. Whatever assistance he may have had, these procedures tested the resolve of the immigrant to become an American. This process also created an important role for the individual who was already a citizen and had enough knowledge, experience, and influence with the system to serve as a voucher. Some Italians who had themselves arrived only a few years earlier, but had these qualifications, routinely assisted. Such services provided them with a strategic position that led to greater power and prestige in the immigrant community.[60]

The late 1860s saw a substantial increase in the number of naturalizations among Italians in Philadelphia, which had reached an earlier peak during the period 1854–56, when the number of petitions for all groups had risen greatly. Before this point, no more than 7 Italians had become citizens in any single year, and in most years the number had been 3 or less. In 1854, however, 10 naturalizations for Italians were granted, and then 14 in 1855 and 13 in 1856. During the war years—except for 1862, when none at all were recorded for Italians—the yearly figure declined to only 2 or 3 individuals. With the return of peace, the number resumed its climb. In 1866, some 14 Italians gained citizenship; in 1867 another 15 were naturalized; and in 1868 there were 30 who became American citizens. In the entire period before the Civil War, only about 200 Italians had filed either the declaration of intention or the petition for naturalization in city, county, or federal courts of Philadelphia. But between 1866 and 1870 alone, 65 Italians filed documents for citizenship. While this increase in naturalization, which reached even higher levels after this point, sometimes resulted from recruitment of voters by party workers as elections approached, it also denoted the steadily rising presence of Italians in the population, as well as the transformation of their political identity.[61]

Religious Life: "A Period of Trouble . . ."

In the years after the war, other forms of public expression further strengthened the Italian presence in Philadelphia. In particular, the Church of St. Mary Magdalen de Pazzi, after a period of some turbulence, gained an even stronger position as an institution in the immigrant community. In 1865, Father Gaetano Mariani, the church's only pastor since its founding twelve years earlier, was injured in a fall in the church. After several months of failing health, he died at the age of seventy in March 1866. The large number of mourners, including many priests, required that his Funeral Mass be celebrated at St. Paul's, the larger and mainly Irish church nearby—a rather ironic site because of the periodic tensions between Italians and Irish Catholics. During his tenure as pastor, Mariani had not only secured the position of his own parish within the community, but also earned a personal reputation that reached beyond the Italian and even the Catholic population of the city. He was praised for ministering to and curing people who had come to the rectory from all over the city in ill health, and his death was described as "a source of sincere sorrow not only to his congregation but to a large number outside of the Catholic Church."[62]

As pastor, Mariani had also accumulated a modest degree of material wealth. His will left all his real estate, which consisted of the parish buildings, in trust to Bishop Wood, but for the benefit of St. Mary Magdalen de Pazzi. Some of this estate was personal wealth, for Mariani left sums of money totaling more than $1,200 to several Catholic agencies. With his abilities and reputation, Mariani would be a difficult person to replace as the leader of the congregation, but the conditions of his will made it even more complicated, as the events of the next four years proved.[63]

At this point, the parish entered a brief but troubled period. Upon Mariani's death, Father Gaetano Sorrentini became the new pastor. In his first months as pastor, Sorrentini made physical improvements to the church, including a new altar, a fresco behind it, and statues of Mary and Joseph, for which he was praised. But his success was short-lived. After only eleven months, in February 1867, Father Sorrentini's service as pastor came to an unhappy end. Official sources of parish history cryptically reported: "A period of trouble, and Church closed." A much later newspaper account declared that Sorrentini left because of "some misunderstanding between him and the people." Actually, Mariani's earlier bequest of parish property had precipitated a dispute between the bishop and trustees over its ownership. There were also other issues, which Sorrentini had aggravated and was unable to resolve. After the parish was reopened, it was served by Father Charles Cicaterri, a Jesuit; then by Father James Rolando, a Vincentian; and then by Father Joseph Rolando. None of these priests served more than a few months, and the church continued its difficult days until the end of the decade, when the appointment of Father Antonio Isoleri opened a new and significant period in the history of the parish.[64]

The establishment of formal institutions provided the Italian population with the decisive instruments for development as an immigrant community. The parish of St. Mary Magdalen de Pazzi was the oldest and possibly the most important device in this process. It was not merely a center of religious services, but provided for the secular and material well-being of its members. Father Mariani, its first pastor, had even acquired a reputation as a healer of physical illnesses. In the absence of physicians and lawyers who were Italian-born, or at least competent in the language, the role of the priest was undoubtedly much wider than today and embraced the services of these professions at times as well. But the continued evolution of the Italian experience led to the development of other types of institutions, and the late 1860s were an appropriate period for such activities.

Secular Organizations: *La Società*

In Philadelphia, as well as the entire nation, the development of the industrial system in the nineteenth century transformed, and perhaps even destroyed, the personal bonds and social order of many Americans. By 1860, the city's rapid growth had almost completely erased the informal neighborhood street life that had characterized and integrated individuals into somewhat cohesive communities in earlier periods. In the second half of the century, urban dwellers who wanted to restore personal identity and social solidarity found it necessary to create newer institutions. In their response to this situation, Philadelphians of all ethnic backgrounds and class levels formed new clubs and associations in an attempt to restore meaning and stability to their lives. It was, as one historian has succinctly declared, "*par excellence* the era of the urban parish church, the lodge, the benefit association, the social and athletic club, the political club, the fire company, and the gang."[65]

While other racial and ethnic groups had already established formal voluntary associations that reflected their search for common identity and group cohesion, Italians had not. Black Philadelphians in 1861, for example, had formed a society to facilitate migration to Haiti, and the preamble to its constitution declared their view of life in the United States: "In this country, ours is a hard and wearisome journey." In the fall of 1861, a large number of black Pennsylvanians, including some residents of Philadelphia, reportedly left for Haiti. In the same year, Jewish women established the Ladies Hebrew Relief Association of Philadelphia, for the purpose of making garments that could be distributed to the poor of the city. By 1866, Jews in Philadelphia had fourteen institutions and organizations that addressed the problems of health, education, fuel, sewing, relief, widows and orphans, and other matters within their population. During the same years, through spontaneous demonstrations as well as more enduring organizations, the Irish in Philadelphia repeatedly expressed their response to events in their homeland. In 1868, an estimated 5,000 people participated in a public protest in the city against the execution of "Irish martyrs" in England. There also were the French Benevolent Society, the German Society, the Hibernia Society, the St. Andrew's Society, the Scots' Thistle Society, and the Swiss Benevolent Society—all for the relief of distress and for general fraternization, as well as a number of religious groups with ethnic overtones.[66]

Although still a small population, Italians faced problems similar to those of other groups in Philadelphia in the 1860s. Like African Americans, assisting immigration, even though it might be to rather than away from the United States, as well as facing their own "hard and wearisome journey," were certainly problems for Italians, but there was no Italian Emigrant Union in Philadelphia. Similarly, like the Irish case, the local press frequently conveyed the news of abuses against Garibaldi and other Italian patriots to their compatriots here, but there was no Italian Fenian movement in Philadelphia. And like the Jews and other ethnic groups, certainly poverty, housing, health, education, employment, and widowhood were sources of distress among the Italians, but there was no Italian Relief Association in Philadelphia.

Despite their long presence in Philadelphia, Italians did not form their first fraternal or beneficial association until the late 1860s. The size of the Italian immigrant population was one factor, but other circumstances contributed more to the process. How Italians regarded one another, as well as how other Philadelphians perceived and treated them, were important aspects in group life. Although they had been conspicuously absent from public demonstrations throughout the decade, Italians in Philadelphia had quietly celebrated the triumph of nationalism in Italy and reflected on its implications for a new sense of identity and cohesion. Events and circumstances, both in their land of origin and in their new location, contributed to the formation of the first voluntary association of Italians in Philadelphia.

The idea of organizing a mutual aid society for Italians and their families in an American city originated with the efforts of Giuseppe Avezzana, a political refugee in New York who had been a supporter of Mazzini and the Young Italy movement. After serving in the struggle for popular government in Spain and Mexico, and then in the Italian revolution of 1848–49, Avezzana became minister of war in the ill-fated Roman republic. After its defeat, when he rejoined his family in New York City in August 1849, Avezzana was greeted as a hero by Italians but also by the mayor and the Common Council in a reception at the city hall that far exceeded what even Garibaldi received in the next year. In 1857, Avezzana organized the Società di Unione e Fratellanza Italiana in New York not simply as a mutual aid society but also with the hope of promoting his political agenda for Italy. It was soon followed by the formation of La Società Italiana di Mutua Beneficenza in San Francisco in October 1858. Italians in Philadelphia might have made a similar effort shortly afterward, but the outbreak of the American Civil War postponed it for another decade.[67]

Philadelphia's Italians began holding meetings to discuss establishing their own organization in September 1867. The early meetings resulted in a committee chaired by Agostino Lagomarsino; other members included Bartolomeo Alfredo Cavagnaro, Lorenzo Nardi, Frank Cuneo, Stefano Ratto, Giuseppe Mazza, Antonio Raffetto, Paul Cavagnaro, and Stefano Cuneo. The group formally organized the Società di Unione e Fratellanza Italiana; elected temporary officers, with Mazza as president, Lagomarsino as treasurer, and Giovanni Patroni, the Civil War veteran, as secretary; and admitted fifty-eight members at a general meeting at McCullough's Hall on Walnut Street in November 1867. They met again one week afterward to elect permanent officers, but that election was declared void. In January 1868, the members voted Antonio Corvini as president, Ferdinand Allegretti as vice-president, Patroni as secretary, and Lagomarsino as treasurer.

In early February, a charter filed in the Court of Common Pleas incorporated the Philadelphia Società as a public entity. After meeting at temporary sites, the Società purchased the Moyamensing Hose House, former headquarters of an old volunteer fire company at 746 South Eighth Street. With renovations that provided meeting rooms, the building was renamed Columbus Hall at dedication ceremonies in July 1874. Almost from the beginning, the Società placed the celebration of Columbus Day at the center of its activities, with an annual ball taking place on October 12 from 1869 on.[68] But the activities of the new organization embraced a broad range of objectives that enabled members to reconcile political and religious values in Philadelphia while nation and church remained separated in their homeland. The patriotic elements involved both Italy and the United States. In testimony to their continuing devotion to the Italian cause, the members elected Garibaldi as honorary president in December 1867. While parades in honor of the new Kingdom of Italy still expressed the memory of their origins, the members of the Società also held public ceremonies that celebrated events and individuals in American life.[69]

The Società found a more urgent agenda in the material and social needs of Italians. In March 1868, local newspapers reported that the new organization had been founded for the mutual aid and improvement of its members. Its charter even included, among other objectives, the purpose of "establishing schools and libraries for the use of the families of the members of said Society." However, the benevolence of the organization was never entirely restricted to its own members,

HOME OF THE

Societa' di Unione e Fratellanza Italiana
744-746 SOUTH EIGHTH STREET -:- PHILADELPHIA, PENNSYLVANIA

Columbus Hall. For many years, this building on Eighth Street, above Christian, served as the meeting place for the Società di Unione e Fratellanza Italiana and other organizations in the immigrant community. (From *History of the Società di Unione e Fratellanza Italiana*, 1929) but regularly extended to recipients in other parts of the United States and Italy. For example, it contributed $306.50, the proceeds from its Columbus Day Ball of 1869, to the victims of the Great Chicago Fire two years later.[70]

The success of the Società depended on resolving several problems, which included achieving financial solvency, integrating regional differences among members, and finding capable leadership. The organization was sustained primarily through members' dues, but also by contributions of benefactors—such as the Viti brothers, who donated $50 at the start and continued to provide monetary support in later years. Members included a broad range of individuals—from affluent and powerful men, such as Lagomarsino, a partner in a large macaroni factory, to others involved in more modest enterprises, such as Raffetto, a shoemaker, or Ratto, a grocer. Its early leadership, however, was dominated by individuals of Ligurian or Tuscan origin. Their responses to these challenges provided a remarkably successful formula, and unlike other organizations that lasted only briefly, the Società endured for more than sixty years.[71]

While the Società later proclaimed itself as only the second organization of its type in the United States, it was actually the third, after previous efforts in New York and San Francisco. After being established in several American cities, the leadership of these societies became concerned that they had been working too separately from one another. In the summer of 1868, plans were announced for a convention in Philadelphia to bring together all the Italian societies in the United States, and Patroni was chosen to represent the local society at the meeting. Delegates or some form of communication represented Italians in Philadelphia, New York, Boston, Chicago, Cincinnati, Louisville, St. Louis, Washington, and elsewhere. At the opening session, after Patroni introduced the delegates, Ratto was elected temporary president. The participants later elected an Ohio delegate as permanent president and Patroni as vice-president.[72]

The principal objective of this convention of Italian societies was to adopt measures that would bring about a more united effort toward mutual aid and improvement of the condition for Italians in America. After several days, in which articles for the proposed unification were approved under the name Unione Italiana, or the Italian League in the United States, a constitution and bylaws were adopted, and then the convention adjourned. A key provision approved by the delegates enabled anyone who belonged to a local society to secure membership in other cities with a simple application. By making it possible for needy members to find aid anywhere an affiliated society existed, it recognized not only the likelihood of material needs but also the geographical mobility that was common among Italian workers in the United States. While final unification of their homeland had yet to be won, immigrant Italians had achieved fraternal consolidation in their new country.[73]

Communications from societies in other cities, as well as from the Italian Minister in Washington, endorsed the aims of the new confederation and expressed the hope that it would serve Italians everywhere in the United States. The conspicuous roles of the local participants also showed that the Italians in Philadelphia not only had established their own mutual aid society but also were playing an important part on the national scene. In the following year, when the Knights of Pythias announced that they intended to spread their order into Italy, Patroni was given this responsibility, and the Italians of Philadelphia had also acquired a role in fraternal affairs at the international level.[74]

The Società combined a patriotic devotion toward Italy, a concern for the material and social welfare of Italians here, a desire to demonstrate loyalty and citizenship as Americans, and an expression of the Catholicism of its members. Its activities also revealed and strengthened the continued development of the Italian population in Philadelphia. These events signified several different decisive aspects of the Italian presence in the city. First, the location of the meetings and activities of the Società affirmed the physical center of the Italian settlement in Philadelphia as radiating from Christian Street toward Sixth and Ninth Streets. While this location undoubtedly reflected where Italians had already gathered in the pursuit of work and residence, it also served as a powerful magnet to attract even greater numbers of Italians in later years who faced similar choices. Second, the founding of the Società more firmly rooted and expanded the organizational base that served the Italian population. It put another crucial element in place, in both a geographical and an institutional sense, for transforming Italians from what had previously been merely a discernible but structurally underdeveloped component of the population. Third, the program of the Società, with its peculiar blend of politics, temporal welfare, and religious concerns, manifested more fully the Americanization of Italians, both as individuals and as a group. By the end of the 1860s, the Italians in Philadelphia had completed their embryonic phase and had emerged as a small but visible and viable immigrant community. It was also now a permanent community that in time became more American as it left its own imprint on the further development of Philadelphia.

Chapter 6

The 1870 Census: A Community Portrait

In his influential early study of Italian migration, Robert F. Foerster declared that, before 1860, arrivals to American cities were mainly from Northern Italy and included "many Lucchese vendors of plaster statuary and street musicians with monkeys— fantastic vanguard of the brawny army to follow."[1] Although his comments greatly simplified the past, Foerster was essentially correct. But while Italian organ-grinders once held a virtual monopoly as street musicians, the American Civil War provided the first challenge to the colorful and entertaining performances of these wandering minstrels in Philadelphia. As they returned to civilian life, former members of the Union army, many limbless, went into the streets, playing organs as a means of earning a living, and challenged the hold of the Italians in this occupation. Although he might not play very well, even after the introduction of a smaller, lighter instrument, the soldier quickly gained the sympathy of the public. The most relevant aspect of this succession was expressed by a newspaper article that reported: "So long as the maimed soldiers have control of the street music the able-bodied Italians find their occupation gone."[2] In some sense, however, their displacement as street musicians was even more significant as a hint of much greater changes that awaited Italians in the near future.

The return of peace initiated a period of technological and economic development for the city and the nation that fundamentally altered the situation of Italians in Philadelphia. But along with economic and industrial strength, and undoubtedly to a large extent because of it, the demographic and geographical growth of the city also steadily continued. By 1870, its population had reached 674,022. Of this number, 183,624 were foreign-born, representing 27 percent of the total population, a proportion that was a little less than what it had been ten years earlier but still would never be reached again. When their children are included, the total foreign stock population was even higher. Furthermore, because the mass immigration from southern and eastern Europe had not yet begun, although the foreign-born population remained, as it had been for some time, overwhelmingly Irish and German in origins, Philadelphia was still a city with a rich mixture in its population and civic culture. In physical distribution, the population stretched along the Delaware River for about seven miles and, having also crossed the Schuylkill River, extended the city three to four miles toward the west.[3]

A noted labor economist who reported on work and life in 1870 described Philadelphia as being in "an exceptional condition." In contrast to most nations, where it was only "a dream and a delusion," he could argue:

> In the industrial development that distinguishes this city and its surroundings, there have always been features of peculiar interest, marking a large departure, originally from the standards of other manufacturing districts. Starting with greater comparative intelligence, skill and persistence, our people have gone on to create a higher social and civil state, until now it may safely be said that no other community equals—certainly none excels—us in the measure of advancement we have attained above mere helpless, brute, factory labor.[4]

As a result of the opportunities to be found in Philadelphia, skilled workers lived in their own houses, or at least single houses; maintained their families with ease; and had access to education for their children. While some unskilled laborers might have lived in rooms or tenement houses, the city was described as being conspicuous for its many houses of abundant neatness and comfort, owned and occupied by single families who were sustained by employment in manufacturing industries. And in addition to their comfortable housing, these workers were able to provide for other needs by the ample wages paid by local employers. While this depiction might appear to retain a strong trace of the "boosterism" that marked earlier years, in this case the observer was at least also in the nascent stage of modern economic analysis.[5]

Whether it was being exaggerated or not, the continued growth of the city enabled Italians to leave the era of the statue vendor and organ-grinder behind and join other residents in the pursuit of individual opportunity and communal development. By 1870, the Italian population in Philadelphia had completed its first stage of maturation as a community. Because the recent war had sharply reduced immigration and slowed the growth of foreign groups in the city, the number of Italians had only increased to about 500, but they now showed a clear pattern of residential concentration. They had also established communal institutions, such as the parish and the beneficial society, that enabled them to pursue concerted action. Several powerful and prominent individuals who had assumed leadership had emerged among them. With a visible location, a few formal institutions, and some social structure, they could now begin to be seen by themselves and by other Philadelphians as a community. And although the process had begun more than a century earlier, it was only the beginning of far greater immigration and a preliminary phase of community formation. It was a pivotal moment in the history of Italians in Philadelphia.

"Little Italy": Population and Family Patterns

When it conducted its enumeration of the population in 1870, the U.S. Census Bureau recorded the last group portrait of Italians in Philadelphia before the beginning of mass immigration. It provided a detailed profile of the rudimentary foundation for the community that, when augmented by mass immigration, would begin to expand shortly afterward. With a reported count of 516 people, Philadelphia ranked second among American cities in the size of its Italian-born population—after New York with 2,793 Italians, but ahead of Boston with only 263 Italians. After Philadelphia, Allegheny County, with 106 Italians, was the only other place in Pennsylvania with any appreciable number of Italians. With only 784 reported for the entire state, Philadelphia contained about two-thirds of all natives of Italy in Pennsylvania.[6]

The families and households of Italian immigrants in Philadelphia also included their children, born for the most part in the United States, who accounted for 278 additional Italians. While 155 children had both parents born in Italy, another 115 children had Italian-born fathers but mothers native to other countries, and seven children had mothers born in Italy but no father, or fathers born elsewhere. One other person had Italian family origins, but the parental birthplaces were not identified. Consequently, the Italian population included not only 482 adult immigrants but also 278 of their children, a total of 760 men, women, and children, either born in Italy themselves or the child of at least one parent born there.[7]

While they could be found in almost every section of the city, Italians were still largely concentrated in the old Southwark District, which was now the Second, Third, and Fourth Wards of the city, as they had been in the previous census. This area was bounded by Broad Street on the west and the Delaware River on the east, South Street on the north, Ellsworth on the south, until it reached Passyunk Avenue, cutting across, then dipped down to Wharton Street as its lower border. Of 482 individuals born in Italy and living in Philadelphia in 1870, some 308 of them, or nearly 64 percent of all Italians, lived in these three wards (Table 15).

"Little Italy" had not only become more visible during the previous decade; but it was continuing to expand in these wards and in nearby areas, which together held 85 more of the Italian-born. Some 32 Italians lived in the Seventh Ward, just above South Street, and 16 more lived in the Eighth Ward, between Chestnut and Spruce Streets. There were 22 living in the Tenth Ward, bounded by Vine and Arch Streets; 15 more found housing in the Twenty-Sixth Ward, west of Passyunk Avenue. Combined with the three most populated Italian wards, these sections accounted for 393, or nearly 82 percent of all the Italians in the city. The remaining 89 Italian-born residents of the city were distributed among other wards, which ranged from 12 Italians within their limits to none.

The concentration of Italians in South Philadelphia not only reaffirmed an earlier pattern of settlement but also provided a magnet for later arrivals. While the availability of industrial employment and inexpensive housing encouraged the choice in previous years, the emergence of an immigrant colony in these wards was now an additional factor that would attract Italians in later years. But this newer concen-

Table 15. Residential locations of Italians, 1870

Ward	Number	Ward	Number
1	0	15	2
2	156	16	2
3	80	17	2
4	72	18	2
5	4	19	6
6	10	20	12
7	32	21	1
8	16	22	0
9	10	23	1
10	22	24	7
11	5	25	1
12	0	26	15
13	12	27	6
14	5	28	1

Total: 482

SOURCE: *Population Schedule of the Ninth Census of the United States, 1870*, M593, National Archives, Mid-Atlantic Region, Philadelphia.

tration of Italians was not a simple demographic mass without other important social characteristics. The differences among its members in terms of age and sex provided another aspect of its profile (Table 16).

While it has been argued that early Italian immigration to the United States was largely a male phenomenon, it may have become even more true at a later moment of mass immigration. At this point, however, while males were in the majority, women and girls constituted a sub-

Table 16. Distribution of Italians by age and sex, 1870

Age (years)	Males		Females	
0–14	34	(11%)	27	(16%)
15–29	91	(28%)	54	(33%)
30–44	109	(34%)	42	(26%)
45–59	56	(18%)	32	(20%)
60+	27	(8%)	6	(4%)
Unknown	2	(1%)	2	(1%)
Totals	319	(100%)	163	(100%)

SOURCE: *Population Schedules, 1870*.

stantial part of the Italian population. Of 482 Italian-born individuals in the city, 319 of them, about two-thirds, were males; the remaining 163, about one-third, were females. With a two-to-one ratio, males, while clearly in the majority, were far from being the entire population. The excess of adult males could have been tempered somewhat if they had encountered suitable partners among the women of other groups, but many men found themselves without any mates.

The variations in ages of Italians in Philadelphia in 1870 also complicated their lives. Although at first it appears that there was a broad span of young and old, it was actually a young population; almost 75 percent were under 45 years of age. Of 319 males born in Italy, 34, or 11 percent , were younger than 15 years old. Another 91, or 28 percent, were between 15 and 29. Some 109, or 34 percent, were between 30 and 44 years old—the largest single category. A cluster of 56, or 18 percent, were between the ages of 45 and 59. Finally, 27 more, or 8 percent, were age 60 or older. (In two cases, age was not given.) While this may seem to reflect an ordinary distribution, some qualifications are needed. For example, the 34 children under the age of 15 could provide a misleading picture of actual life among the young at this time. With some under the age of 15 already working as street musicians or in other occupations, children in the Italian colony were sometimes found in adult forms of employment at a very early age. Although young in years, they had more in common with older members of their own community than with other children of the more privileged classes in the city.

Regardless of age, males who were engaged in serious employment constituted a large part of the Italian population. The total number of males between the ages of 15 and 59 represented a formidable part of the Italian population. Of the 319 in all, 256 individuals, or 90 percent of the total male population, were within this age span. If males under 15 who were already working were included, the part of the male population that was employed would increase even more. Similarly, men age 60 and over were also likely to still be employed. Because few were either too young or too old to work, male workers dominated the population and already gave it the profile that is associated with the subsequent period of mass migration.

For the 163 Italian-born females, a similar pattern can be discerned, making this too a young population. Some 27 girls, almost 17 percent of the entire female population, were under 15 years of age; another 54 young women, or 33 percent of all females, were between the ages of 15 and 29. Women between 30 and 44 years constituted 42 cases, or 26 percent more of the population. In sum, nearly half of all females were under 30 years old, while more than 75 percent were under 45. Another 32 women, 20 percent of the total, were between the ages of 45 and 59. Only 6 women, 4 percent of the total, were 60 or older. (In two cases, age could not be determined.) Among women, 128 cases, nearly 80 percent, were between 15 and 59 years old. Once again, at least some, and perhaps many, of the younger females were already engaged in the serious work normally associated with adulthood, whether in the labor force or in households. As in the case of the men, women were also a working population; relatively few women, even among the young or the elderly, were not employed when the opportunity was present.

The Italians in Philadelphia in 1870 were more than merely working-age males and females who provided workers to the labor force. Their private lives represented another dimension of adjustment to Philadelphia. Before considering their work experiences any further, it is useful to examine in some detail the families and households they formed in their more personal domain (Table 17).

Although some patterns were widely shared, the differences in family and household types among Italians might have been even more important. As in the previous decade, Italians were still making various adjustments to a new setting in their family and living arrangements. How much of this adaptation was unavoidable and how much was a result of choice remains less clear. The most common pattern, found in 61 cases, was a husband and wife, both natives of Italy, living with children born either in Italy, in the United States, or elsewhere. In 12 other households, both spouses were born in Italy but had no children. In 10 other cases, both spouses were born in Italy, and children were sometimes present, but other adults were also part of a more complex household. In some cases, when an older couple lived alone, there may previously have been children living with them.

The matter of mate selection also reveals some facets of life within the Italian population. Although the precise details of marriages could not be determined, when both spouses were born in Italy, especially if they also had Italian-born children, it is reasonable to conclude that they married before migrating to the United States, and also often had the same or nearby local origins. In the 83 households with both spouses born in Italy, the marriages were almost certainly between

Table 17. Parental nativity and family structure, 1870

Both spouses born in Italy: children	61
Both spouses born in Italy: childless	12
Husband born in Italy; wife elsewhere: children (Pennsylvania, 11; other U.S., 5; Germany, 10; Ireland, 8; England, 4; Spain, 1; France, 1)	40
Wife born in Italy; husband elsewhere: children (Ireland, 1)	1
Either spouse born in Italy; mate elsewhere: childless (Pennsylvania, 3; other U.S., 3; Ireland, 4; England, 1; France, 1; Germany, 1; Switzerland, 1)	14
Father born in Italy; no wife present: children	5
Mother born in Italy; no husband present: children	7
Complex family-based households	
A. Both spouses born in Italy; children or childless; other adults present	10
B. Either spouse born in Italy; children or childless; other adults present; mate born elsewhere (Pennsylvania, 2; Germany, 2; England, 1; Ireland, 1)	6
Males, related or unrelated, living in groups	3
Other situations (living alone, in non-Italian households, or with unrelated others; priests; inmates in institutions; etc.)	54*

SOURCE: *Population Schedules, 1870.*

NOTE: It is necessary to repeat that the census did not identify the relationships of household members at this time, but from sequences of names and ages, reasonably safe inferences can be made about family positions.

* Unlike previous categories that indicate the number of cases, this number refers to the number of individuals found in these situations.

Italians, but an Italian was often likely to have a non-Italian mate. In 40 cases that consisted of a simple household, the husband was Italian-born, his wife was either American-born or a native of a foreign country other than Italy, and the children were born in Italy, the United States, or elsewhere. When an Italian-born husband had a wife from another place, if not another group, she was most likely to be a native of Pennsylvania; but American-born wives also came from Maryland, Massachusetts, New York, and Virginia. If an Italian-born husband had a wife from any other foreign country, it was most likely to be Germany or Ireland, but sometimes she was from England, France, Spain, or Switzerland. One Italian-born wife, in a household that consisted simply of her, her husband, and their children, had a husband who was born in Ireland. Sometimes an Italian father was without a wife but had children; at other times an Italian mother had no husband but had children. When either the husband or the wife was Italian-born but the spouse was not, the likelihood that the couple would be childless was slightly greater than when both partners were natives of Italy.

The organization of these "families" in the 1870 census draws our attention back to the issue of "slave children" as street musicians. Although the newspapers claimed that the returning soldiers had replaced them, Italians would continue to ply this trade and send their children into the streets as musicians until the end of the century. While a household unit headed by a man or woman without a mate but with children may have been a single-parent family, it could also easily have involved the misrepresentation that disguised the situation of slave children and *padrone* master. But the inability of the census enumerator and other authorities to clarify relationships leaves this matter open to speculation.

Living Arrangements

While variations in family structure and mate selection provided devices for making adjustments, other aspects of domestic life also played an important part in the Italian experience. Italians tended to establish rather conventional living arrangements that consisted mainly of families with children in their own households. But Italians usually found themselves in more complicated living arrangements in which families shared households with other adults who were often relatives, such as elderly parents, or siblings of one of the spouses, or even unrelated lodgers. Although a family member sometimes performed domestic service, a few households included one or more unrelated people in this capacity, which indicated that some Italians were prospering and living well in their new surroundings—something their income and property ownership also revealed. In several cases, a married couple, with or without children, formed a subunit of a larger household. In other instances, the household contained only one parent and one or more children and was slightly more often male-headed than female-headed. A number of childless couples formed households of their own or belonged to larger households. While some Italians lodged in hotels or boardinghouses, others lived entirely alone or as groups of unrelated males, as priests in rectories and inmates in institutions for the poor, insane, or ill.

Apart from the variety of households and other domestic groups, the living arrangements of Italians in Philadelphia were complicated by other conditions. While a single family frequently constituted the entire household and the only occupants of a house, other buildings often contained several household units. Frank Megon and his wife, Rose, both born in Italy, lived with their young son in one such dwelling in the Second Ward. In another household of the same building lived the family of Joseph Melanna and his wife, and their five children, all Italian-born. In still another unit, N—— Frajicate, his wife, and their four children, all Italian-born, made their home. In another unit, resided L—— and Anna Nicolas, both Italian-born. In the next unit of the same dwelling, F—— and A—— Campeia lived with their six children, all Italian-born. Finally, A—— Beabeas, a forty-five-year-old male, occupied another part of the same building. At least six separate household units shared the same dwelling. With the relative absence of larger tenement buildings in Philadelphia, the situation in this particular dwelling, and in similar cases, raises our curiosity about the type and exact location of the building in which these households were found.[8]

The relationships of Italians to their neighbors often revealed even broader aspects of their lives in Philadelphia. Many Italian families shared buildings with members of other ethnic groups, particularly the Irish, in areas that eventually became more exclusively Italian enclaves with later immigration but that for the moment remained quite diverse in population. Whether in their dwellings or on the streets, Italians experienced an alternating sequence of interactions with others who were sometimes similar but often quite different from themselves. In addition to other problems related to material survival and well-being, this aspect of their situation presented a more social and psychological challenge to Italians in their adjustment to life in Philadelphia.

The problems Italians encountered in attempting to find a place for themselves in a new society were paralleled and reinforced by the difficulties census enumerators faced in fully recording the presence of culturally different newcomers. The size of the Italian family, and their language, continued to challenge the skills of the census enumerator, whose linguistic competence must have been limited to his native

English and who could list the six Campeia children only by the letters A through F.[9] The communication between the census enumerator and his informants was still unable to transcend the language barrier sufficiently to record the children by their actual names. As in previous years, such failures revealed not only the technical limitations of the census but also the persisting inability of some Americans to recognize and grant a full identity to recent foreign arrivals.

In the complexity of family arrangements, as reported in the 1870 census, however, some dimensions of the Italian community, for that moment as well as for projections for the future, had emerged from earlier shadows. In the Third Ward, the household of Augustus Lagomarsino, a forty-year-old Italian-born macaroni manufacturer with real estate valued at $10,000 and personal wealth of $20,000, lived with his wife, Harriet Lagomarsino, a thirty-nine-year-old native of Bristol, England. Living in their household too was a nephew, Francis Cuneo, thirty-five years old and born in Italy, with real estate valued at $2,000 and personal wealth of $10,000. Felicità, his twenty-five-year-old Swiss-born wife, and a one-year-old son, Augustus, born in Pennsylvania, completed the Cuneo family. The business enterprise was reflected by the household's lodgers, apprentice macaroni manufacturers: Thomas Zacconi, age seventeen and born in England; Augustus Boznano, age twenty and born in Italy; and Dominick Gandolfer, age ten and born in Italy. The household also included three young women working as domestic servants.[10] As we shall see in more detail, Lagomarsino and Cuneo had already transcended the obscurity of the census to positions of visibility, wealth, and leadership within the Italian community.

The frequently transient character of immigrant life also revealed itself in the sequence of birthplace locations for children within the same families. Many families had older children born in Italy but younger ones born elsewhere. The children born to the family of Anthony Fugarre, residing in the Seventh Ward, showed the complicated course that geographical mobility sometimes took. Fugarre, a thirty-seven-year-old fruit vendor (or "fruiterer" as it was called) born in Italy, lived with his wife, Mary, age twenty-nine and also a native of Italy. Their family included Frederic, six years old, born in England; Constantia, three years old, born in Ohio; and John, one month old, born in Pennsylvania. While the places of birth found in most families reflected a more direct path from Italy to Pennsylvania, the Fugarre family showed that Italians sometimes followed a more complex route before arriving at Philadelphia.[11]

While a profile of typical patterns characterized the experiences of most Italians, some atypical families had also reached Philadelphia. In the Eleventh Ward, Sabato Morais, forty-seven years old, lived with his wife Clara, ten years younger, and their seven children. Although the census simply identified him as a "minister (Jewish)," students of Jewish life in Philadelphia will quickly recognize that it is Rabbi Sabato Morais, a native of Leghorn who arrived in 1851 and who as the head of Mikveh Israel Synagogue became a prominent figure in the Jewish community. His election to the clerical roll of the Union League in 1887 reflected his importance not only to the Jewish community but also to the city in general. Morais remained a figure of great influence and stature for nearly half a century until his death in 1897. His son Henry Morais wrote the first study of the Jews in Philadelphia, published in 1894. The Morais family was not typical of ordinary Italian immigrants, but it did reflect a unique facet of that experience, as well as an important chapter of Jewish history in the city.[12]

The more tragic aspects of immigrant life were also sometimes visible in the details of a particular household. August Lenci, a sixty-seven-year-old Italian-born artist, lived in the Twentieth Ward, apparently successful and prosperous. With real estate valued at $3,000 and personal assets of $700, he was head of a household that included his Prussian-born wife, Anna, and their two sons, George, a bookkeeper, and Augustus, a ladies' shoe maker. But another entry listed him as August Senci, a sixty-eight-year-old plaster molder, born in Italy, and an inmate in the Hospital for the Insane.[13]

Patterns of Work and Wealth

These cases are poignant reminders of the difficulties and misfortunes encountered by some individuals and their families, but broader patterns portrayed a more positive picture of the Italians in Philadelphia. The variations in household organization, whether by necessity or by choice, helped Italians deal with their new environment, and the results were reflected in the expansion and redistribution of their occupations in the local economy.

In 1870, Italians in Philadelphia worked in occupations that ranged from laborer and domestic servant to physician and manufacturer (see Table 18). They included the unskilled and the skilled, apprentice and factory owner. Some earned only marginal wages; others had considerable income. They produced goods and provided services, labored with raw materials in heavy industry, sold finished products over store counters, and were employed both in large factories and in small neighborhood shops. But Italians were not found in all industries and levels of employment. With only a few exceptions, they were not likely to be in managerial positions at major firms, or in the professions. These higher opportunities were still in the distant future for most Italians and their families. Among the specific patterns that marked their employment, Italians were found overwhelmingly in two particular areas in the skilled crafts and in small commerce. Of 237 Italians who reported their work in the 1870 census, 51 were occupied in trades related to the production of food, clothing and shoes, and construction. An even greater number of Italians, 110, were employed in selling of various goods, as well as sometimes managing and even owning small businesses.

It may seem odd to classify the shop girl and the store clerk alongside the manufacturer who may be a factory owner, but these broad categories are primarily intended to show the type of work in which Italians were engaged, rather than their level of employment. It is difficult enough to sort out and develop some sense of the ways in which they were employed, but it is probably impossible to know their level of employment. While the census is virtually the only source of information, and provides a relatively crude profile of employment, nevertheless, it gives us some idea of where Italians could be found in their work. Even though much smaller numbers were employed outside of trades and commerce, those categories further revealed the work patterns of Italians. Within the largest category, of the 110 individuals working in some form of commerce, 63, or nearly half, worked at fruit or eating stands or as hucksters and produce dealers. Another 5 were grocers; and 13 more worked as tavernkeepers or at eatinghouses, oyster houses, saloons, or liquor stores. Four other Italians were either macaroni manufacturers or apprentices to them. While the census reported at least 85 Italians as employed in the production and sale of food, the actual number was likely greater. Some of the Italians vaguely identified as "dealers" were probably involved in some aspect of food as an

Table 18. Occupations of Italians, 1870

Tradesmen (baker/butcher/blacksmith/blindmaker/bricklayer/ brickmaker/cabinetmaker/carpenter/compositor/confectioner/ framemaker/iron worker/jeweler/locksmith/machinist/marble maker/miner/piano tuner/seamstress/shoemaker/stonecutter/stone mason/tailor/tanner/teamster/tinsmith/coach factory worker/sugar refinery worker)	51
Artist/sculptor	1
Plaster of paris figure maker/bronze figure maker/plaster or statuary molder	13
Agent/bookkeeper/broker/bronze figure manufacturer/dealer/dry goods/eating saloon, stand or house/fruit stand/grocer/hotel keeper/huckster/iron dealer/liquor dealer or store/ locomotive builder/manufacturer of fancy goods/macaroni manufacturer/merchant/oyster house/produce dealer/keeper of public house/railroad clerk/shoe dealer/shop girl/store clerk/ tavern-keeper/tobacco dealer/related apprentices	110
Musician/organist/dancer/opera singer	16
Mariner/sea captain/waterman	4
Priest, rabbi	4
Laborer	14
Teacher/professor of music/schoolteacher/interpreter	8
Bartender/bootblack/waiter/domestic servant/hotel steward	12
Farmer	1
Physician	1
Miscellaneous (horse jockey/shooting gallery)	2
Total	237

SOURCE: *Population Schedules, 1870.*

industry or commodity. Moreover, when the bakers, butchers, confectioners, bartenders, and waiters who were classified in other general categories are included, it becomes more certain that food-related employment provided much opportunity for Italians at this time.

It is also interesting to anticipate what is known about the employment of Italians in the years not too far ahead. If the Contract Labor Law of 1864, which legalized recruitment of immigrant workers by agents of industry, resulted in laborers being imported from southern and eastern Europe for mines and factories in the United States, there is little indication that Italians in Philadelphia in 1870 were employed in any narrow and concentrated sector. Whether recruitment of contract laborers played an important role or not, there was still no foreshadowing of the considerable employment of Italians as railroad construction and track maintenance laborers of later years.

In contrast, even with the concentration of individuals in food-related areas of work, what can be seen at this point is a far more varied and comprehensive distribution of Italians in the local economy.

While the number of Italians with occupations was only slightly greater than in the previous census, Italian employment in 1870 displayed a different pattern from what it had been ten years earlier (Table 19). In 1860, some 189 Italians gave their occupations; in 1870, only 48 more, or a total of 237 natives of Italy, were listed by work in the census. The changes in the type of employment, however, indicated some significant developments in the economic life of the emerging Italian community. In most categories of employment, there were only slight changes in the percentages of Italians employed, while in some forms of work the actual numbers were too small to warrant any meaningful discussion. In regard to "tradesmen," however, although the numbers showed a substantial increase, from 34 individuals in 1860 to 51 in 1870, the percentage of all Italian workers represented by these figures changed only slightly, from 18 percent to 21 percent. Italians were mainly holding on to their participation in the crafts and trades of the city. In three other areas, however, important changes were evident. For example, the number of individuals who had worked in some manner as plaster figure makers dropped from 27, constituting 14 percent of the employed Italians in 1860, to only 13, or a mere 5 percent of working Italians, ten years later. In a second area of employment, that of musician, which was mainly a euphemism for the organ-grinders of the street, an even greater decline occurred during the decade. In 1860, some 60 Italians, representing 35 percent of the total of all employed, gave their occupations as organist, organ-grinder, organ player, organ man, organ girl, harpist, musician, or the like. By 1870, only 16, amounting to 7 percent of employed Italians, still identified their work in this manner. While nearly half of all employed Italians could be found as either a figure maker and vendor or as a street musician in 1860, that number fell to only 12 percent by 1870.

As the presence of Italians in some occupations was declining, in another area the number of Italians was only beginning to expand. In 1860, only 24 Italians, 12 percent of Italian workers, were employed as "agents"—a quite broad range of occupations, which included a few owners and managers of manufacturing firms but mainly clerks in more modest commercial enterprises, such as retail shops or food vendors. By 1870, there were 110 Italians, 46 percent of Italian work-

Table 19. Occupational change among Italians, 1860–1870

	1860		1870	
	No.	%	No.	%
Tradesmen	34	18%	51	21%
Artists	5	2%	1	<1%
Figure makers	27	14%	13	5%
Agents	24	12%	110	46%
Musicians	60	35%	16	7%
Mariners	2	1%	4	2%
Clergymen	3	1%	4	2%
Laborers	6	3%	14	6%
Teachers	5	2%	8	3%
Personal services	14	7%	12	5%
Peddlers	2	1%	0	—
Farmers	5	2%	1	<1%
Ragmen	2	1%	0	—
Physicians	0	—	1	<1%
Miscellaneous	0	—	2	1%
Totals	189	99%	237	100%

SOURCE: *Population Schedules, 1860 and 1870.*

ers, engaged in such employment. In ten years, the involvement of Italians in this particular area had increased from a relatively modest share to almost half their work force.

Many immigrants undoubtedly still worked and lived in unfavorable conditions, but some Italians in Philadelphia in 1870 fared much better. Their success produced property ownership and personal wealth that put them at a comparable or better level than many other residents of the city. The federal census provided a glimpse of property ownership and wealth among Italians that may also have been somewhat in contrast to conventional wisdom (Table 20). It revealed not only a great range of occupations, but perhaps also a surprising accumulation of wealth and real estate. While not many of them were street musicians or statue vendors any longer, neither were they entirely poor or propertyless.[14]

While property ownership was not extensive among Philadelphia Italians, several owned real estate with a reported value as high as $13,000, as in the case of Peter Galupo. Similarly, personal wealth as high as Lagomarsino's $20,000 was reported. If anything, the actual

Table 20. Real estate and personal wealth, 1870

	Real Estate	Personal Wealth
Anthony Aggue	$3,000	$250
Anthony Alphonso	$2,000	$100
Jacob Arata	$1,000	$100
Louis Bagala	—	$2,500
Ellery Bendel	—	$1,000
Andrew Botto	$5,000	$600
Alfred Cavagnaro	$1,500	$1,000
Paul Cavagnaro	$1,500	$1,000
Thomas Citence	$5,000	$600
Francis (Frank) Cuneo	$2,000	$10,000
Pasquale Dbiasse	$3,000	—
John Fetters	$3,000	—
Peter Galupo	$13,000	$100
Peter Hilyerl	$5,000	$2,000
Benjamin Hirsh	$8,000	$700
Lewis Iennis	$12,000	$500
Augustus Lagomarsino	$10,000	$20,000
August Lenci	$3,000	$700
Andrew Lucreny (Luccarini)	$2,000	—
John Lucreny (Luccarini)	$1,300	$1,300
Francis Malatesta	$10,000	$300
Joseph Malatesta	$8,000	$3,000
Michael Malatesta	$3,300	$700
Louis Mazara	$5,000	$5,000
Stephen Mesano	—	$1,000
Joseph Moore	$1,000	$300
Sabato Morais	—	$2,000
John Mulleney	—	$1,000
Salvatore Musso	$2,000	$100
Lorenzo Nardi	$6,000	$600
Pasquale Piccioni	$3,000	$350
Stephen Ratto	—	$1,500
Joseph Rize	—	$1,500
Agl Rodgers	$8,000	—
Fabio Victri	—	$2,000
William Walker	—	$1,500

SOURCE: *Population Schedules, 1870.*

value of real estate and personal wealth may have been even greater than these individuals and others were willing to indicate to the census enumerator. In any case, as other matters, such as the demographic character of neighborhoods, the wealth of at least some Italians at this time conflicts with popular impression and previous research. The redistribution of Italians in the local economy was producing a new class within the immigrant population with a substantial amount of real estate and personal wealth.

Early Pages from a Family Album

When it encountered problems in the first attempt to enumerate residents of the city in 1870, the Census Bureau was forced to repeat the procedure later in the same year. In a sense, the failed effort and its remedy also provided an unusual opportunity to gauge how well Italians had been absorbed into the general population. One particularly instructive case was a complex household in the Second Ward headed by a fifty-seven-year-old Italian-born woman whose name was listed as "Agl" Rodgers. While it offered a study of almost all the problems faced by Italians in their adjustment to life in Philadelphia, the saga of this family had begun much earlier and far away.[15]

As many other early Italian settlers in Philadelphia, the family had originated in the hill towns above Chiavari on the Ligurian coast, where it had been known not as Rodgers but as Raggio. By the 1850s, Giovanni and Angelina Raggio had migrated to Boston. There, John Rogers, as he was already known, a musician, and his wife, Angelina, residents of Fulton Court in the North End, presented their daughter Catherine for baptism in the parish of St. Stephen in June 1853. Only a year later, in July 1854, with his surname restored to its Italian form, John T. Raggio, a gardener, purchased a three-story brick house on the northeast corner of Federal and Charles Streets that backed onto the Union Burial Ground in South Philadelphia for the sum of $2,400. In April of the following year, Raggio, now a grocer, paid $750 for another three-story house, nearby at 1151 Charles Street (now South Marshall Street).[16]

Although he had enjoyed some prosperity in his new location, John T. Raggio died shortly afterward, probably in early 1857. In a letter of administration filed in February of that year, he left his heirs an estate

City and County of Philadelphia, ss.

Personally came before me, Register of Wills, in and for the said City and County,

_____ *S. R. Wannamaker & John Roger* _____

who upon their solemn oath ~~or affirmation~~ did say, that at the request of the *Administratrix* they did " well and truly, and without prejudice or partiality, value and appraise the Goods and Chattels, Rights and Credits," which were of *John Ragio* _____ deceased, " and in all respects perform their duties as appraisers, to the best of their skill and judgment."

~~Affirmed~~ Sworn to _____ and subscribed this 26th day of Feby _____ 185*7* before me,

S. R. Wannamaker
John Roger
Jos. B. Mollar
Depy **Register.**

Inventory and Appraisement of the Goods and Chattels; Rights and Credits which were of *John Ragio* _____ late of Philadelphia, taken and made in conformity with the above deposition :

1 Rocking Chair	1. 50
1 doz Windsor Chairs.	3. 00
2 pine tables	2. 00
1 Stove	2. 00
1 Mantle Clock	1. 00
2 Mahogany frame glasses	.50
Pots and Pans	1.00
2 Wash Tubs	1. 00
1 Settee	1. 00
3 low post Bed Steads & Beds	10. 00
3 Boxes	1. 00
	$ 23. 00

Amount of goods appraised by the undersigned belonging to *John Rodgers Ragio* Deceased.

$ 23.00

S. R. Wannamaker
John Roger

Letter of Administration of John T. Raggio. In the inventory of his estate, the person who died about 1857 is repeatedly listed as John Ragio, but in the final line the name appears to have been first given as Rodgers before being corrected to Ragio, showing what life in a new country sometimes did to Italian family names. (To confuse matters even more, the second witness to this document was yet another John Roger or Rogers.) (Courtesy of Louis D. Arata Jr.)

consisting mainly of various pieces of furniture and valued at a modest total of $23. The document contained his name spelled both as Ragio and as Rogers, and even at one point had one version written over the other. In the 1860 census, the altered situation of the family was reflected in the listing of Angeline Rodgers, age forty-seven and a native of Genoa, and her three young daughters, Rose, Kate, and Elizabeth, but no other members of the household. Similarly, a local directory listed Angelina Rodgers, as a "gentlewoman," and her residence at the northeast corner of Charles and Federal Streets. Although twenty-one families named Rogers or Rodgers lived in the Second Ward, only two had Italian origins; it was predominantly an Irish neighborhood. In August 1860, the houses, which had changed owners, were sold by Sebastian Ravini (actually Ravani), a shoemaker, to his mother-in-law, Angelina Raggio. At the time of this transaction, the deed indicated that John T. Raggio had died without a will, leaving his widow, Angelina, and six children, identified as Maria Castagneto, John B., Rosa, Catarina, Antonio, and Angelina.

Despite the limiting effects of the war period, by the end of the next decade Angelina Raggio not only endured the loss of her husband but also prospered at the head of the family. In the 1870 census, her occupation was given as "keephouse," and she apparently was quite successful at that, for the value of her real estate was reported as $8,000. The household contained nine other people under her surname: M——, a thirty-one-year-old white female; J.B., a thirty-year-old male; Catherine, twenty-five years old; John, twenty-four years old, an upholsterer (the only other person for whom an occupation was given); and Rosa, fifty years old, all listed as born in Italy; as well as Rose, age twenty-one and born in Massachusetts; Elizabeth, age fifteen; William, age two; and Mary, one month old, the latter three born in Pennsylvania (see Table 21). While their relationships were not specified, M., J.B., and John may have been a daughter and two sons, who had been living elsewhere, perhaps still in Italy where they all were born, during the earlier period of the family in the United States. It was not unusual for immigrant families to endure temporary but sometimes permanent separations of this sort while they sought to establish themselves more securely in their new society, before reuniting members. The household now also included six other males with various last names, ranging in age from fourteen to sixty-five and all born in Italy. Although their occupations were not given, they appear at first as a group of boarders and unrelated to the others, but at least one of them was soon to be recognized as an already familiar member of this household. Finally, if "keephouse" meant that Angelina was proprietor of a boardinghouse it may account for the value of her property, but she was also the owner of the Charles Street properties.

When the second enumeration was carried out, a somewhat different profile of the Rodgers family was compiled. While the first enumeration included place of birth, the second did not, but the second count provided the house number and street name for each residential unit. Although the names were shuffled into a slightly different order, the same family is unmistakably recognized, but with some changes. From the two enumerations, most of the entries can be matched by their names and ages.

The mundane events of everyday existence had certainly occurred within the Rodgers family during the interval between the two enumerations in the summer of 1870. But they must have also observed some of the more special occasions of family life. The family probably celebrated the birthdays of several members, and one major tragedy might have taken place: the death of the infant Mary may have removed her from the later census schedule. Moreover, with one exception the men who could have been temporary lodgers when the census was first taken did not appear in the second enumeration. But the individual

Table 21. The Rogers family in 1870

First Enumeration (with age)	Second Enumeration (with age)	Probable Relationship to Head of House
Rodgers, Agl (57)	Rogers, Jane (58)	Head
Rodgers, M. (31)	Ravani, Ellen (33)	Daughter
Rodgers, J.B. (30)	Rogers, George (30)	Son
Rodgers, Rose (21)	Rogers, Rose (22)	Daughter
Rodgers, Elizb (15)	Rogers, Elizabeth (15)	Daughter
Rodgers, Cath (25)	Rogers, Kate (24)	Daughter
Rodgers, Jno (24)	Rogers, John (24)	Son
Rodgers, Rosa (50)	Rogers, Rose (50)	Unknown
Rodgers, Wm (2)	Rogers, William (3)	Unknown
Rodgers, Mary (1 mo)	(not listed)	Unknown

SOURCE: *Population Schedules, 1870*, M593, 1388:205, 1416:534. Data compiled by Louis D. Arata Jr.

listed as "Sebastama R," a forty-year-old male, in the first enumeration was certainly the same person identified as "Sabastian Ravani" and married to Ellen, who was in turn the former Magdalen Rodgers, found on a different line in the second enumeration. Later events supported by documentary evidence, such as Angelina Raggio's death toward the end of the century, confirmed that Ellen and Magdalen were the same person.

The most interesting dimension of the different profiles of the Raggio family presented by the two enumerations may have involved alterations of a different sort. The slight changes inflicted on the Rodgers family in the manner of listing by the second enumeration suggest a subtle but consistent nudge toward acculturation, even over a brief time of a few weeks. Angelina had been transcribed into Jane; Rosa became Rose; M., for Maddalena, became Ellen; and Cath became Kate. While it might be an exaggeration to argue that the census enumerator acted as a conscious instrument of Americanization, the emendations were symptomatic of the transformation of identity for the Raggio, now Rodgers, family and its members that could immerse them in uncertainty, encourage marginality, and challenge their adjustment to Philadelphia.

The Raggio family embodied many aspects of the situation in which Italian families found themselves in Philadelphia at this moment. They were a part of the Ligurian vanguard that provided the first large component to the Italian population in the city. But before settling here, John T. and Angelina Raggio had briefly tested their fortunes in another city. First as a musician, then as a gardener, and finally as a grocer, John T. Raggio sought to find his occupational and economic niche. Not long after his arrival in Philadelphia, he had accumulated enough wealth to attempt to consolidate the residential position of his family through property ownership. But the family could not avoid the premature tragedy when he died, perhaps only in his mid-fifties.

When Angelina assumed command of her large family after her husband's death, she continued to guide her children in their own pursuit of endeavors that extended from Philadelphia to Atlantic City. The Raggio family, partly obscured by an anglicized name in the 1870 census, which revealed one strategy of acculturation, eventually provided the Italian community in later generations with members who attained positions of wealth and influence. Unfortunately, much of the Raggio family history has been obscured by the passage of time and the obliteration of details, and they were surely not typical of all that marked the larger population of Italians. Enough information remains, however, to preserve them as a valuable prism that illuminates many of the personal attributes and social conditions that defined the Italian experience in Philadelphia in these years.

Unification in Italy and Consolidation in "Little Italy"

For the Raggio family, as well as for the immigrant population as a whole, much more awaited them in the immediate future. Although the number of Italians remained relatively small, the Italian population was about to experience an explosion in growth a decade or two later. Other aspects of group life would also become important in defining its character. This population was now concentrated in the southeastern quadrant of Philadelphia, where the Italians had found their place in the city. In addition, their church and mutual aid society had initiated a more formal group life, enabling the community to approach "institutional completeness." Moreover, several businesses established by fellow immigrants, but now serving the special needs of other Italians, provided a commercial foundation to support group life. And finally, a cadre of individuals had also emerged who would provide leadership for the Italian population in the years ahead. These activities and structures set into place the essential conditions for a more enduring experience. While the volume of immigration diminished in the 1860s, it was also a time of consolidation for what had been previously established. As Italians took advantage of opportunities to improve their lives, they also strengthened the social structure on which mass immigration would be grafted.

At almost the same time that the census was producing a portrait of the population, events in Italy would also mobilize the Italians in Philadelphia. With the taking of Rome in September 1870, the modern nation of Italy was finally completed, but many issues had been left unresolved. The American press continued to describe the problems of political and social order in Italy. With the establishment of a nation, the struggle against foreign powers had ended, but only to be replaced by the difficulties of Italians, particularly in the South, with what was now ostensibly their own government. Widespread dissatisfaction prompted violence against the new regime itself. While Americans first read newspaper accounts of the activities of brigands in Southern Italy, later interpretations described these clashes as a civil war between exploited peasants and an unpopular central government.[17] The result was general ineffectiveness and instability of the national state. At least for a while, the problems of their homeland that drove many Italians elsewhere remained salient issues in their lives in foreign cities, as people in America, whether native-born or foreign-born, were frequently reminded of conflicts and struggles in Europe.

Meanwhile, with the unification of Italy, sympathetic Americans again participated in demonstrations of support. In February 1871, a public meeting in Boston convened to congratulate the Italian people on securing their national unity. On the same night, the American Protestant Association of Buffalo met to endorse the Italian cause. In Philadelphia, news of the political situation in Italy continued to arrive in almost daily dispatches through the winter and spring of 1871. In early June, Italians in the city took to the streets in a public celebration of national unity in their homeland. Led by the Sixth Regiment band of Camden, a large number of participants joined in the procession, carrying the flags of Italy and the United States as well as a handsome banner of the Italian Benevolent Society, as the Società was now identified by its Americanized title. A newspaper account of the event informed readers tersely: "It was the first public demonstration of the resident Italians on the subject of unity, and the day was spent in festivities expressive of their feelings."[18] The parade, which may have been the first demonstration by Italians as a group in the city for any cause, represented a significant indication of the establishment of an Italian community in Philadelphia.

Two months later, at a meeting at Jefferson Hall at Sixth and Christian Streets, the Italian Beneficial Society announced plans to send a delegation to New York City for the celebration of the unification of Italy and the proclamation of Rome as its new capital. In subsequent years, the Società alternated its patriotic activities between Italian and American objectives. When the Società participated, as perhaps the only organization of foreign-born citizens, in the funeral cortege of General George Gordon Meade in 1872, a local newspaper noted: "The Italian Society picturesquely brought up the rear." Similarly, after being proposed by Agostino Lagomarsino three years earlier, and finally organized in 1872, the Columbus Monument Association held a fair in October 1873 that earned $2,000 to erect a statue to honor the explorer. With contributions from various sources, including King Victor Emmanuel II, the project finally culminated with the unveiling in Fairmount Park of the first public monument to Columbus in the United States on October 12, 1876. The massive ceremony, attended by many important local and national figures, including the governor

St. Mary Magdalen de Pazzi was the first Catholic church founded for Italians in the United States. Organized in 1852, the congregation was first housed in a former African American Methodist chapel, before the larger church pictured here was completed in 1891. Father Antonio Isoleri served as pastor from 1870 to his retirement in 1926. (Courtesy Philadelphia Archdiocesan Historical Research Center)

of Pennsylvania and the mayor of Philadelphia, represented a triumphant moment for the officers of the Società as leaders of the Italian community. In subsequent years, the programs of the Società remained emphatically concerned with promoting American citizenship among members.[19]

The Società later demonstrated its political and religious sympathies at a period in which relations between Church and State in Italy were at a low ebb. In early 1878, after the death of King Victor Emmanuel II, and then shortly afterward, when Pope Pius IX died, Società members participated in mourning ceremonies at the church of St. Mary Magdalen de Pazzi, with Father Isoleri officiating on both occasions. With the continuing tensions between Church and State in Rome, the nearly simultaneous manifestation of their identity as Catholics and Italians by members of the Società in Philadelphia would have been almost impossible in Italy itself.[20] The conspicuous presence of the Società was a clear indication that, rather than a formless cluster, the Italians had become a more structured community, although it was not the only instrument in that development. But like the contrasting flags at the first demonstration in 1871, these activities also reflected the odyssey of an immigrant colony that was in transition, moving away from its Italian antecedents and toward a more American future.

Chapter 7

Prosperity and Leadership:
I Primi Prominenti

One objective of the present work has been to document the development of an Italian community in Philadelphia before the beginning of mass immigration, using the 1870 census as a cut-off point in its general history. It has also been to suggest that this early stage of community formation played an important, but often neglected, role in the events of later years. But history is ultimately made by individual actors, and in order to describe the critical part that they played in the emergent community, it is necessary to set these boundaries aside and to look at their lives both well before and long after 1870.

While the American public later engaged in a debate about whether the "new immigration," with its large Italian component, had brought an inferior type of person to the United States, the record of the lives of earlier Italians and their business ventures shows them in a more favorable light. It also reveals that, probably as much as any other Americans, they had acquired the entrepreneurial spirit that swept the nation in the second half of the nineteenth century. And although commercial success was probably modest at best and precarious for most, the entrepreneurs who became business and community leaders had great significance for the Italian experience. Whether they succeeded or suffered dismal failure in their efforts, their lives represented a complicated picture of work and material conditions that served as barometers of commercial and civic developments among their people. When they prevailed and prospered, their accomplishments transcended personal success, and their lives provided the foundations for the subsequent development of their community. For as they pursued their own personal gain, whether they intended to or not, they were also building "Little Italy."

Early Successes and Failures: Statues, Fruit, and Saloons

In the center of the city, in South Philadelphia and other sections, Italians operated viable business enterprises, at least for the time being. In 1850, in the Treaga household of Walnut Ward, headed by an Italian-born figure maker, were several other Italians with the same skill. Three men listed by the census with the surname Lagurane, ranging in age from seventeen to twenty-one, were probably the Luccarini brothers. In 1854, John Luccarini, twenty-four years old, filed a declaration of intention to become a citizen of the United States, forswearing his prior allegiance to the Grand Duke of Tuscany, but this process was not completed for many years. Some years later, John and Andrew Luccarini were in a partnership as statuary molders at 539 Chestnut Street. The original proprietor of the firm had been R. Leuca, John Luccarini's father-in-law, but the Luccarini brothers took over the business about 1868. In 1870, John Luccarini, age forty-two years, lived with his wife, Pauline, a native of Pennsylvania, and their three children in North Philadelphia. Luccarini owned real estate worth about $1,300, and had about $1,000 more in personal property. Andrew, age forty-five, and Joseph, forty-seven, both statuary molders, and Peter, age twelve, all born in Italy, were also members of the household. While it was likely that John, Andrew, and Joseph were brothers, the relationship of Peter remains unclear.[1]

By 1873, in addition to their property on Alder Street and several thousand dollars in other wealth, John and Andrew Luccarini were still operating their business, which had declined somewhat. Although the Luccarini brothers had become slower in meeting their bills, they continued to have good credit and a reputation of being honest, sober, and industrious. Their statuary-molding business remained on Chestnut Street for at least another decade. John also completed his long-delayed naturalization as a citizen in October 1876, listing his address as 1604 Alder Street, with Gustus Lenci, almost certainly the son of Augustus Lenci, as the voucher. The interaction of Lenci, Treaga, and the Luccarini brothers (all statue makers at some time) in matters of work, housing, and citizenship illustrated the support and friendship that Italians provided one another during these years.[2]

By 1883, John Luccarini & Brother, as the firm was then known, remained in operation. John, assisted by his wife, managed the business, which carried good stock, met its expenses, and retained good credit for limited bills. Although he also operated a dry-goods store at 1022 Poplar Street, these enterprises did not continue much longer. By the autumn of 1886, John Luccarini was out of business. Other Italians experienced brief periods of success, but the Luccarini brothers probably prevailed in their commercial ventures longer than most immigrants.[3]

As the distribution of their occupations indicates, Italians were often involved in endeavors that brought them into contact with other Philadelphians. In 1870, fifty-six-year-old Andrew Botto, a fruit seller, owned real estate that he declared to be worth $5,000, plus personal property of $600. He lived in the Tenth Ward with Julia, his fifty-five-year-old Italian-born wife, and their children, Joseph, age thirty-one, also a fruit seller; David, twenty-five, a jockey; and three younger daughters. The first three children had been born in Italy, and the last two were born in Pennsylvania. By 1876, as a fruit merchant on Race Street, Botto was regarded as an industrious and hardworking individual who did a fair amount of business. Although sometimes slow in paying bills, Botto still had good credit for small amounts of debt. Two years later he continued to do a good volume of business, was paying accounts even better than before, and had good credit for moderate amounts. Unfortunately, only three years later, in April 1881, Botto's business career ended with his death at the age of sixty-nine.[4]

Another typical case of the fruit and vegetable vendor was Salvatore Musso, a retail grocer at the corner of Montgomery Avenue and Alder Street, where he had conducted a thriving business in a well-stocked store since about 1866. Musso lived with his wife, Emma, a native of Saxony, and their four young children. In 1870, he reported $2,000 in real estate and another $100 in personal property. With his reputation as an honest and industrious man who paid bills on time, he was able to maintain good credit in business dealings, but he was also described as a person who "always seems to go along at the same gait." These qualities enabled him to persevere despite some difficult moments in his business life. In 1878, at the age of forty-six, Musso applied for American citizenship, and two years later he completed the process, listing his residence as 1783 Alder Street. By the early 1880s, he became slower in paying his bills, and his credit was not as strong as it had previously been. Toward the end of the decade, his son joined him in the business, now known as S. Musso & Son, which provided another example of a commercial venture that had become common among the Italians.[5]

The extension of business interests from one field into another, as in the case of the Luccarini brothers from statuary molding to dry goods, as well as from Philadelphia to other localities, was an important dimension in the lives of some Italian merchants. About 1866, Louis Arata started a fruit business in Philadelphia when he was only twenty-two years old. After nearly twenty years, by 1884, Arata had expanded his business to Atlantic City, New Jersey. In addition to property on South Sixth Street in Philadelphia, he also owned real estate in Atlantic City, altogether worth almost $6,000. About that time, Arata also began manufacturing furniture at a shop on Bainbridge Street in South Philadelphia. He had a generally good reputation as being honest, economical, and quite satisfactory in his business dealings. Despite these attributes, however, his inexperience in the furniture industry left his future somewhat uncertain. In another year, Arata seemed to be struggling in his business affairs, and it was doubtful that he would succeed. Even so, in his wide-ranging commercial ventures and their locations, Arata exemplified the speculative spirit that marked the efforts of some immigrant businessmen.[6]

After some economic success in Philadelphia, a few individuals achieved even more elsewhere. Having arrived at New York in 1856, about ten years later Mark Malatesta operated a saloon at Eighth and Christian Streets in the center of the Italian colony of Philadelphia. By 1873, he owned the property outright, then valued at about $5,000, and his personal worth was estimated at about $6,000–$7,000. Although known as honest, sober, and attentive to his business, by 1879 he had closed his saloon in Philadelphia. In 1880, when he sought naturalization as an American citizen, the Malatesta residence was still in Philadelphia, on May Street, but he soon pursued work and fortune in another location. Although other members of his family remained important for many years in Philadelphia, from this time on Mark Malatesta prosperously operated a resort hotel in Atlantic City.[7]

Other promising younger Italians removed themselves completely from Philadelphia. After an impressive beginning in business, Giovanni Patroni, the Civil War veteran and prominent early figure in the Società di Unione e Fratellanza Italiana, abandoned the local scene. Following military service, Patroni played several strategic roles in the organizational life of the Italians in the city. In addition to his part in the founding of the Società, Patroni apparently conceived the idea of establishing a national alliance among all Italian organizations in the United States. When the first convention of organizations was held in Philadelphia in 1868, Patroni was elected vice-president.[8]

Patroni also became a central figure in an innovative business venture. In 1873, he was employed by the newly formed L. Perkins & Company, brokers in jewelry, real estate, and other merchandise at 325 Walnut Street. Patroni had recently returned from England, where he had purchased jewelry for the company, which intended to distribute its merchandise through the mails. But only two years later, now residing in Beverly, New Jersey, Patroni had evidently withdrawn from any active participation in the affairs of the company, other than merely lending his name to it. In another year, the company had gone out of business and Patroni was no longer a conspicuous part of Italian life in Philadelphia.[9]

While the prospect of money and respect drew individuals into commercial enterprises, the risks remained great and failure was never far away. When it is possible to follow them closely, the difficult and precarious situation of these entrepreneurs becomes more visible. Over a period of years, Nunzio Finelli, believed to have come from Naples to Philadelphia around 1860, experienced a series of alternating achievements and setbacks that reflected a common pattern. The 1860 census listed Nunzio Finella (*sic*) as a twenty-four-year-old cook, born in Italy and lodging in the house of Susan H. Brown in the Second Ward. In another ten years, in 1870, Finelli was a tavernkeeper in West Philadelphia, with a Pennsylvania-born wife, Elizabeth, their four children, and one domestic servant in the household. After serving as a steward at the German Union Club, Finelli opened his saloon in early 1870, but a credit agency, which declared that "this class of men do not possess anything," warned potential suppliers against extending any credit to him and advised that "strictly cash dealings would be the safest in such cases." Despite this limitation on Finelli's ability to raise capital, after only three months in business, dealers in the liquor trade were willing to sell him whatever he needed on a four-month credit term. Finelli, however, generally preferred to make cash transactions and had established a reputation for prompt payments. Although he still lacked capital, Finelli seemed to be doing a large and profitable business that was "making money fast." But with an unfortunate turn in November, he was suddenly out of business. Shortly afterward, Finelli resumed his venture, and three years later he was again described as having done well and as having made some money. Although not known to have owned any property, Finelli was believed to be worth about $5,000 at this point. The potential creditor was now cautioned that Finelli "is thought worthy of fair credit though slow in meeting engagements."[10]

In the years ahead, Finelli's business life continued to oscillate between better and poorer times. In 1874, Finelli was still depicted as a man of fair reputation and average risk for modest amounts of credit. In another year, after having expanded his trade, he was again able to pay his bills and maintain his reputation. By 1876, Finelli had moved his saloon to 1345 Chestnut Street, where he was getting good prices and doing a large trade, but with heavy expenses that slowed his own payments. By the fall of the same year, he was operating at a second location, 43 South Tenth Street. Although both locations attracted a strong volume of patrons, the Chestnut Street saloon had cost a large amount of money and he was in debt. By 1877, with business dropping off, Finelli faced heavy expenses that could only be met slowly. His credit was now more limited, and his estimated worth had fallen to $3,000. In June, a court awarded a judgment of $1,500 against him. In the next few years, his business efforts declined gradually but continuously, until 1884, when Finelli failed entirely. When his son, William, started the business up again, Nunzio Finelli was manager, but it remained on shaky grounds.[11]

Finelli's commercial enterprises were only one side of his life. In addition to operating his saloons, Finelli took an active part in the organizational life of the Italian colony. Although the plan to honor Columbus by erecting a monument was probably initiated by the Società di Unione e Fratellanza Italiana, and Agostino Lagomarsino was generally credited for the idea, all Italians of the city were invited to participate in the project. At a meeting in July 1872, the Columbus Monument Association was organized with Nunzio Finelli as its president. Four years later, in 1876, when the monument was unveiled before an impressive group of dignitaries that included the Italian ambassador to the United States, the governor of Pennsylvania, and the mayor of the city, the final speaker was Finelli. Finelli made the official presentation to the city of Philadelphia on behalf of the Italian citizens. The conspicuous part played by Finelli at perhaps the grandest ceremonial occasion for the local Italian population up to that time indicated his stature in the immigrant community. But the day may have also been the final moment of public importance for Finelli; after the dedication of the Columbus monument, it is difficult to find Finelli again in any similar position of prominence.[12]

When he died at the age of fifty-three in March 1886, the *Public Ledger* identified him in his first-page obituary as a "well-known restaurateur." A few days later a funeral notice indicated ways in which his life had taken a route different from most other Italians. Unlike other Italians, who often had affiliations with Catholic organizations, Finelli was instead a member of the Eastern Star, the Apollo Senate of Sparta, the American Legion of Honor, and the Knights of Birmingham. Similarly, in contrast to a South Philadelphia residence, Finelli lived near Thirty-fourth and Walnut Streets in West Philadelphia. Although he had taken an active part in the affairs of the Italian colony, he had clearly also moved in an orbit far from it.[13]

Paesani and Partnerships

As other Philadelphians did, Italians sometimes formed partnerships that combined business, friendship, and often family ties in their pursuit of economic success. Stephan Ratto and Bartolomeo Picardo provide an illustration of this arrangement. Beginning with a grocery store on Fitzwater Street, Ratto had a personal estate valued at $1,500 by 1870. Along with Mary, his Irish-born wife, and three children, their household included an English-born woman as a domestic servant. They shared the building in which they lived with another family, headed by an English woman, as well as an Italian fruit vendor and his family. Picardo had earlier operated a small bakery on Carpenter Street. In the mid-1870s, Ratto and Picardo started a grocery and liquor store together at 775 South Eighth Street. Although they quickly established a good level of trade among Italians in the neighborhood and proved themselves to be quite industrious and responsible in meeting debts, a credit appraisal characterized the two men as "unpleasant to deal with" and people who "can hardly be called businessmen." Despite this negative view from an observer outside of the colony, Italians were still willing to purchase from them. With the retirement of Ratto in March 1877, the partnership was dissolved. Now characterized as "an industrious man of fair business qualifications," Picardo continued the business alone into the 1880s.[14]

Although begun at nearly the same time, a more enduring and significant enterprise was initiated by Antonio Raggio and Peter Cella. Raggio was born in Cabanne, a village in the province of Genoa, in 1852 and came to the United States at the age of four, entering through the Port of New York in 1856. After working in different trades, including a fruit business at Ninth and Arch Streets, he formed a partnership in the same line with Cella in 1878. But during that year, citizenship was also important for them. About the same time that their new business was launched, they began an effort to become American citizens. On September 16, 1878, Raggio completed the process with his petition for naturalization. One week later, on September 23, at the age of thirty-two and able to sign his name only with an "X," Cella filed his declaration of intention, which was followed by his petition for naturalization two years later. Both men listed their address as 835 Catharine Street, which was virtually at the center of the Italian colony. During five years in business together, Raggio and Cella did a limited volume of retail trade and were able to pay their bills in cash, but they never reached more than a modest level of profit. Described as hardworking and attentive, the two men also were well regarded in terms of their personal character and credit by those with whom they did business. But after about five years together, the partnership was dissolved, and Cella continued the business on his own.[15]

For Raggio, the partnership was merely an early step toward a stronger presence in the Italian colony. After the arrangement with Cella was dissolved, Raggio formed a new partnership with Emmanuel Guano, his brother-in-law, as macaroni manufacturers at 924 South

Seventh Street in 1883. Born in Chiavari in 1852, Guano had migrated to New York City twenty years later. Although both men were regarded as hardworking, Raggio was believed to have provided the capital, while Guano was reputed to have the shrewder mind for their venture. Having taken over a business that had previously been operated without much success, the new owners risked a considerable investment in machinery and property. After purchasing a building for more than $5,000, they immediately mortgaged the property to buy equipment and supplies. Although their own appraisal may have exaggerated the actual value of their business, after only nine months Guano and Raggio were not merely holding their own but doing fairly well.[16]

After five years, Guano and Raggio were characterized as active, attentive, and energetic businessmen who had competently maintained their business and made prompt, regular, and responsible payments to flour suppliers. But a potential disaster was at hand. On a December morning in 1887, a fire destroyed the Guano and Raggio factory, with an estimated loss of $10,000. The two astute partners had, however, covered their investment well with insurance, and within a year, Guano and Raggio were back in business with a restored property reported to have cost more than $8,000 and with machinery, fixtures, and merchandise valued at more than $6,000. With accounts that showed $1,000 owed to them and more than $700 in cash in the bank, but only modest liabilities, the net worth of the Guano and Raggio firm was reported to be more than $15,000. With a factory at 924–930 South Seventh Street, the firm afforded its proprietors affluence and comfort. Guano's home was located in one of the better sections of the city, but he also owned other properties. In addition to his Philadelphia residence, Raggio had a large house in Atlantic City, where he provided accommodations for vacationers during the summer.[17]

Guano and Raggio played more than business roles among Italians; throughout their lives, they participated in many mutual aid and fraternal societies in the immigrant colony. Neither man allowed the passage of years to remove him from these activities. In particular, Raggio continued well into the twentieth century as a leader in such projects. In 1892, when the United Italian Societies celebrated the 400th anniversary of Columbus's discovery of America, the Società di Unione e Fratellanza Italiana led all units in a colorful parade, with Raggio as its marshal. A few years later, when the Società sought improvements to its building, Raggio was a member of the committee. When the Italian cruiser *Ettore Fieramosca* visited the Port of Philadelphia in 1906, Raggio served as a member of the banquet committee. In 1909, when the Verdi Monument Association was formed to commission a statue in honor of the composer, Raggio was again selected for its committee. In 1910, when an effort was made to establish the Society for Italian Emigrants, Raggio contributed financial support and advice in the purchase of a building at Tenth and Bainbridge Streets. With Raggio as treasurer, the organization launched an ambitious program that included a day nursery, a home for emigrants, citizenship classes, and an information bureau. In the next year, Raggio served the newly organized Italian-American Alliance, which helped individuals seeking citizenship, promoted better commercial relations between the United States and Italy, fostered education among the young, and encouraged greater knowledge of Italian art and literature.[18]

In the closing years of the nineteenth century, when another generation of *prominenti,* such as John M. Queroli, Pasquale Del Vecchio, Emmanuel V. H. Nardi, Henry DiBerardino, Eugene V. Allesandroni, and Charles C. A. Baldi, emerged, Raggio represented a major link with the more formative years of the community. He died in August 1933 at the age of eighty and was buried at Holy Cross Cemetery in Yeadon, in a grave adjacent to Guano, his former business associate. The two men, partners in life, remained close to one another even in death.

As these vignettes indicate, the lives of Italians did not follow a single common trajectory. For various reasons, some succeeded and others failed; some found their success in Philadelphia, others found it elsewhere; and some had a continuing influence on the Italian experience, while others had only a momentary impact. The cases that have been already examined illustrate some of these variations. Mark Malatesta left for Atlantic City, where he clearly found some success, but at the same time he deprived Philadelphia of the benefits of his talents. Giovanni Patroni shined brightly but relatively briefly before fading from the scene. And while Nunzio Finelli remained in Philadelphia, persevering through his own struggle for commercial success and achieving even one outstanding public moment, he also played only a temporary role in the affairs of the Italian colony. Rather than sweeping across the landscape of the local economy in a phalanx of uniform experience, Italian entrepreneurs, like the seeds in the biblical parable of the sower, found different results from their aspirations and efforts, and while some put down only transitory and shallow roots, others produced more enduring consequences for their community.

Cut Flowers and Family Dynasties

The emergence of a strongly organized community life among Italians in Philadelphia depended on individuals who could achieve for themselves not only wealth but also prestige and power in their relationships with others. But potential candidates did not always follow a path that brought them to positions of community leadership. Then as now, an individual could pursue a lifestyle that separated him or her almost immediately and entirely from the Italian community. In other cases, talented and distinguished individuals of Italian origin who by their own lives had some impact on life in Philadelphia became "cut flowers."[19] Although these people had significant accomplishments during their own lifetimes, they failed to establish family lines whose members continued to distinguish themselves. The children of Paolo Busti, for example, might have played an important role in the Italian community later in the century, but Busti left no sons or daughters. And if some cases left only "cut flowers," others produced offspring who were hybridized and separated from their Italian antecedents. In such cases, individuals of ability and character were assimilated by their own success into the mainstream of Philadelphia life, with little or no identity as Italians and no role in the immigrant community.

Enrico Francesco Foggini had emigrated from Italy by 1852, the year of his marriage to Lelia Constante in Philadelphia. He left brothers in Italy, including one who was a civil engineer in Milan. After a few years in New Orleans during which he became an American citizen, Foggini had returned to Philadelphia as a teacher of French and Italian by the late 1860s. In 1871, when neither national origin nor religion presented any serious obstacle to membership, he was admitted to the Union League. Foggini died in 1877, but for at least six years his daughter, Maria, continued to operate the language school, whose appointment books list lessons for prominent families. These details of Foggini's life suggest higher class origins in Italy as well as a position of modest stature and prominence beyond the Italian community in Philadelphia. This exceptional case represented one extreme boundary for the experience of Italians at this time.[20]

The Sartori family passed through a similar process, although from their earliest days in the United States their original social position had already separated them from most Italians. By the time Victor A. Sartori died in August 1883, this transition was already quite evident. A lengthy newspaper item identified Victor Sartori as "the son of Giovanni Baptista Sartori, an Italian gentleman of wealth" and as "one of the best known of the old merchants of the city."[21] At the beginning of the twentieth century, members of the Sartori family were listed in the Social Register, were members of the exclusive Rittenhouse Club, were students at Episcopal Academy and the University of Pennsylvania, and were debutantes at the same affairs as the Biddles, the Wisters, the Wetherills, the Cassatts, the Harrisons, and other upper-class families. The early position of G. B. Sartori as a diplomat of the Papal Court suggests that entering upper-class life in Philadelphia did not necessarily mean upward mobility, but perhaps instead a horizontal social relocation. Certainly not "cut flowers," the Sartoris are better described as having been replanted in a different ethnic garden. And once again, we can only speculate on the impact they might have had if their lives had been more contained within the Italian community.[22]

Another type of individual and family had a more enduring impact on the Italian experience in Philadelphia. As in some previous cases, these men also achieved personal wealth and influence, but they differed in at least one important respect, and probably other ways as well. Some who succeeded in their new life in Philadelphia were able to pass on much of their own gains to their children without losing their identity and visibility as Italians. In this way, they transcended their own generation and established power and prominence at the family level. Through the founding of "dynastic" clans, even when they actually lasted only two generations, these families also had far greater significance in shaping the economic and political parameters of the Italian community in Philadelphia. With this shift in individual and family life, their colony acquired a crucial dimension that contributed to its emergence as a community.

The first "dynasty" within the Italian population of Philadelphia was established by the Viti family, which had roots as residents of the city that reach further back than almost any other. Part of the Viti saga has already been presented, but longevity and persistent influence extended its relevance for a later period. The Vitis represented not only one of the more enduring family lines, but also an accumulation of personal wealth, recognition, and influence in the city that rivaled any other among Italians throughout the nineteenth century.

The origins of the Viti family in Philadelphia can be traced to the early nineteenth century. Letters and invoices indicate that Stephen Girard was doing business with Antonio Viti of Volterra, Italy, who shipped merchandise on brigs and schooners, such as the *Free Ocean,* the *Nymph,* the *Ontario,* and the *Water Witch,* from Genoa and Leghorn to the Port of Philadelphia. With Vito Viti as an active member of the firm and probably a brother of Antonio Viti, the Viti brothers were by 1819 identified as merchants in Volterra. Newspaper advertisements many years later declared that the firm of Vito Viti & Sons had been established in Philadelphia in 1815.[23]

Although some accounts also maintain that Vito Viti arrived in Philadelphia as early as 1815, such claims must be regarded with skepticism because they also erroneously identify him as the first Italian immigrant to the city, a point that can be easily rejected.[24] Born in Volterra in 1787, Vito Viti migrated from Lisbon to Alexandria, Virginia, about November 1816, according to his petition for naturalization. In 1817, Girard wrote Viti, now employed by Nicola Fiengo & Company in Baltimore, regarding a shipment on the brig *Water Witch.* When the ship arrived from Genoa at Philadelphia on July 12, 1817, it carried a cargo of cloth, straw hats, alabaster, minerals, watches and jewelry, quicksilver, licorice, cream tarter, shoes and boots, marble blocks and tiles, sweetmeats, fireworks, ice cream molds, writing paper, filberts, and linen. With the ice cream molds consigned to Italian impresario and pleasure-garden proprietor Lawrence Astolfi, the rest of the cargo was intended mainly for Philadelphia businessmen like John Strawbridge and Stephen Girard.[25]

The involvement of Vito Viti in this commerce soon required him to move closer to its final market. Four years later, in December 1820, Viti, by then a resident of Philadelphia, married Martha Redman at Old St. Joseph's Church. The marriage suggests that Viti was already more cosmopolitan in his personal relationships than might have been expected. In addition to his choice of a wife, who almost certainly was not of Italian origin, the witnesses to the ceremony were Anna Corcoran and Bernard Keenan, likely of Irish background. As with other new arrivals at the time, the relative scarcity of Italians in the city encouraged such friendship patterns. But the marriage also indicates that, almost from the start, Viti had pursued a broader ambit of experience and acquaintances.[26]

Viti affirmed his commitment to a new life in an adopted country in June 1823 when he filed a declaration of intention to become an American citizen, stating his occupation simply as "merchant" and his prior allegiance to the Grand Duke of Tuscany. Five years later, in 1828, Viti submitted his petition for naturalization to the Special District Court of the United States, in Philadelphia, with R. Dietz serving as his witness. While he found new friends beyond the small Italian population, he continued throughout his life to play an important role as an intermediary in commercial and political matters between Italy and Philadelphia, as well as between the Italian colony and the rest of the city.[27]

Although he imported a variety of articles, at the core of his business, Viti concentrated on importing marble from Massa-Carrara. In the 1820s, he operated at 206 South Fourth Street, but by the 1840s his address was 151 Pine Street. By 1852, the firm, long endorsed as a good credit risk by one of the largest auction houses in the city, was known as Vito Viti & Sons. In the following year, a credit report stated: "The old *Gent* is said to be very rich and that anything he contracts for will be met in due season." After he became prosperous, Viti pursued his business affairs with the same careful attention he applied at earlier stages, when the firm was still struggling. The credit agency suggested that the long success of the Viti firm could be attributed to the qualities the founder passed on to his sons. After commenting on his strong character, one report concluded that Vito Viti "brings his sons up in the same way."[28]

By 1853, Viti and his two sons, Alonzo and Francis, were regarded as "thorough businessmen" with a large, profitable trade and "first rate" credit. In November 1857, however, Viti withdrew from the firm and his two sons, Alonzo about thirty and Francis about twenty-five, took over the operation. The elder Viti had been grooming them for this moment. While the sons took over formal control of the company, their father remained in the background as an important source of advice and financial support when necessary. Although the sons achieved their own well-deserved reputation as active, prudent, and reliable businessmen, they also knew that their wealthy father would not let them suffer for any shortage of capital. Over the next few years, under its new arrangement, the firm continued to prosper. In 1861, from a location on Fifth Street just above South Street, a well-known and highly respected auction company advertised a fine collection of marble monuments, tombs, and garden vases of Gothic, Grecian, and Roman design that the Viti firm had recently imported from Italy. These sales continued throughout the years of the American Civil War and afterward as a major part of the Viti business. From their location in 1865 on Arch Street, and then, a few years later, back again on Front Street, Viti Brothers continued to receive orders from their local customers and to fill them by importing marble and other products from Europe. Another newspaper advertisement, which succinctly captured the nature of the Viti family business in the late 1860s, declared: "Particular attention given to the special importation of statues of religious subjects, suitable for chapels and churches, and having correspondence with the principal studios in Italy enable us to import on the most reasonable terms."[29]

When Vito Viti retired from business at the age of seventy, it was not only his age but also other interests, such as his service as Consul of the Kingdom of the Two Sicilies, that prompted the action. With his retirement, and while his sons became more prominent in their own business and civic activities, Viti remained a prosperous and important older figure among the Italians of the city. In the 1860 federal census, the seventy-three-year-old importer was listed with real estate worth $100,000 and a personal estate of $25,000. In his household—besides Martha Viti and their sons, Alonzo and Francis—were two African Americans, probably employed as servants to the family.[30]

When Vito Viti died in August 1866, a crowd of mourners attended his funeral at St. Joseph's Church. A newspaper, which described Viti as an Italian resident of Philadelphia for many years, appraised his life: "He was a most extensive dealer in marble statuary . . . and was well rewarded, in the worldly sense. He was honored and respected by a large circle of friends and acquaintances." He also left an estate of $26,000 to his sons, but he had already distributed considerable wealth to them. In his death, there is some expression of his role as an intermediary between his Italian origins and his new country. The executors were his son, Francis A. Viti, and Samuel Castner, whom Viti identified in his will as "my old and valued friend." A codicil to his will listed a house and land on the Piazza del Fornelli in Volterra, left to Vito J. Viti; this is the only indication that another son existed, possibly by a previous marriage, who had remained in Italy during all these years. The same addendum also suggested that there was some lingering issue between the two of them, for Viti forgave and bequeathed to the same son any debts and sums of money that might still have been owed to the father. While the settlement of his estate included further financial obligations to individuals—listed simply as Nardi, for labor and wine; Rondinella, for wine; and Mirabella, for oil and tea—Viti's will also identified additional property in Philadelphia, as well as in St. Louis.[31]

Perhaps the most personal and poignant aspect of Vito Viti's life in these testaments is expressed in his final codicil. While the attempt to reconstruct lives through such documents often produces rather limited portrayals of their subjects, they occasionally provide a glimpse of a once-living human being with personal attitudes and feelings. In this case, a fragment of the emotions that once dwelt in Vito Viti as a husband and father is revealed:

> My said sons having ever proved themselves dutiful and af-
> fectionate to their mother, I urge them to be and remain so
> and without making any direction on the subject I cannot but
> express the hope that they will ever care for her.[32]

For a while after his death, the sons of Vito Viti successfully carried on the family business. From a figure of $50,000–$60,000 in 1865, the estimated worth of the firm reached $75,000–$80,000 in the year 1873. By the 1870s, Viti Brothers had relocated their office to 115 Walnut Street. Like their father, they did not restrict themselves to commercial pursuits. Although Alonzo Viti had been one of the first names drawn in the military draft in 1863, there is no record that he served in the Union forces. But it was Alonzo Viti who displayed the Italian flag in mourning from his residence on Walnut Street after the assassination of President Lincoln in April 1865. At the unification of Italy, when he was asked to serve as the first consular agent of the new nation, his business and other concerns prevented him from accepting the appointment. After the Italian government then nominated him to act as its Honorary Consul for life, Alonzo Viti became more than a ceremonial figure in representing its interests in the city. He played an important role in the attempt to halt the traffic in immigrant children who worked as street musicians in the city.[33] He was also given credit for engaging the sculptor, securing the financial support of King Victor Emmanuel II, and bringing the finished statue of Christopher Columbus from Italy to Philadelphia in 1876. But with the statue widely proclaimed as the first such monument to be unveiled in the United States, the Viti family may have reached the peak of its importance and prominence among the Italians of the city.[34]

In the next decade, the commercial efforts of the Viti brothers did not enjoy the continual growth and success of previous years. In fact, the firm experienced a period of decline, and its ultimate demise was anticipated in 1886. Although it was still buying from sources in Italy with whom it had dealt for many years, and selling these imported objects to a few dealers in Philadelphia, the worth of the company fell to about $25,000, a figure far below what it was previously believed to be. Although they refused to reveal the precise amount of their debts, the Viti brothers claimed to be able to meet them. While still regarded as honorable and straightforward businessmen, their stock was no longer large, their volume of trade was now only moderate, and the competition had become considerable.[35]

To complicate matters, the firm became involved in a series of annoying legal suits in which it alternated between being the plaintiff and the defendant. In 1880, the Viti brothers successfully sued the collector of customs for the Port of Philadelphia to recover excessive duties on imported statues. The verdict of the jury awarded the firm the sum of $242.40 plus one month's interest. In 1888, a damaging judgment was rendered against A. M. Viti for default in payments to a creditor. Some years later, the federal government sued the Viti brothers for $4.80 in a dispute over the value of imported merchandise. Although sometimes involving ridiculously small sums, these actions were not only dissipating the energies and resources of the partners but symptomatic of the declining fortunes of their firm.[36] Despite these difficulties, Alonzo Viti remained an important business and political figure in the Italian colony until his own death in 1902. He left one son, a lawyer; and a daughter, as well as his own brother, Francis, who followed his own business pursuits.

With the death of Alonzo Viti, the final chapter of the older family interests that had lasted about eighty-five years on the local scene reached a conclusion. But with him as its final link, one of the more significant family components, which had endured an unusually long period, in the Italian experience in Philadelphia also came to an end. Vito Viti and his sons were important to the history of the Italian immigrant colony in the city, not only because of their personal success and prominence, but also because they served as conduits for so long in the extension of Italian material culture to the local economy. By their consular service, Vito and Alonzo Viti both also contributed to the diplomatic ties between Italy and the city of Philadelphia. In the conspicuous parts they played in civic life, Vito Viti and his sons were an important influence in the emergence of the Italian colony as a stable and enduring community.

As the Viti saga reached its final stage, other individuals and families emerged among the rapidly growing Italian population of Philadelphia. Although these cases began later than the Viti family, and few if any amassed as much wealth as it had, their influence extended to a later period of the Italian experience in the city. Bartolomeo Alfredo Cavagnaro was another pioneer in the development of the Italian colony, and one of its best known and most esteemed members. Born in 1843 in the village of Monleone in the province of Genoa, he emigrated to the United States in 1859. After earlier efforts at work, Cavagnaro opened a saloon on the corner of Sixth and Lombard Streets that by the 1870s had become popular among Italians as well as others. His establishment faced that of his brother-in-law, Joseph Malatesta. Although he did not reach the level of wealth and power of some of his own relatives and associates, Cavagnaro did achieve moderate success in business, as well as a good reputation. In the early 1870s, Cavagnaro met his financial obligations promptly and earned adequate credit for his business needs; within a few years his income and savings had also improved. By 1880, his material condition, and his personal honesty and worth, made him a safe risk for financial institutions. In another five years, he was a relatively affluent member of the community, with an estimated worth of nearly $9,000, and eventually came to own several buildings in the Italian quarter.[37]

The considerable popularity and respect that Cavagnaro enjoyed enabled him to move to positions in the broader arena of city politics. He had been one of the founders of the Società di Unione e Fratellanza Italiana and its president for many terms, until in later years, when he was also the final survivor of the original members. Active in local politics, Cavagnaro was elected as a school director for the Fifth Ward and served as a member of the executive committee of the Republican Party. He was selected by Count Gerolamo Naselli, the Royal Consul of the Kingdom of Italy, as a delegate to the International Exposition in Milan in 1906. While his personal character made him a likely candidate to become the first Italian elected to the City Councils, Cavagnaro was a modest man who preferred to remain in private business and at a lower level of public life.[38]

When his own years reached their final stage, Cavagnaro had not only succeeded in consolidating his personal wealth and influence, but he had also been able to retain the prominence of his family through another generation. The election to City Councils, which eluded him, was achieved by his only son, Paul Cavagnaro. The younger Cavagnaro also played an influential part in the politics of the Fifth Ward and became the first Italian elected to the Common Council of the city, serving from 1902 to 1904. This transfer of power and prestige from father to son maintained the position of the Cavagnaro family in the Italian community.

Lagomarsino and Cuneo: Feeding and Organizing the Community

Another "dynastic" family closely connected to a formidable part-nership emerged within the Italian colony during this period: the Lagomarsino-Cuneo line. As a result of their early beginnings and long careers, the two principal figures, Agostino Lagomarsino and Frank Cuneo, were rightly regarded as pioneers of Italian business in Philadelphia.

Lagomarsino was born on March 11, 1830, in San Colombano Certenoli, a village near Chiavari, in the province of Genoa. In 1847, he traveled to England, using a passport signed by King Carlo Alberto of Piedmont, a document that Lagomarsino jealously guarded later in life. It was probably during this period that he met Harriet Tucker, a native of Bristol, England, whom he would marry. After working at various jobs for seven years in England, Lagomarsino migrated to

John D. Raggio

John B. Raggio

Joseph Malatesta

Frank Cuneo

Lorenzo Nardi

Agostino Lagomarsino

Leaders of the Italian community. (From *History of the
Società di Unione e Fratellanza Italiana*, 1929)

Canada, where he found work in a frame and mirror shop in 1854. Two years later he moved to Philadelphia and then to Washington, where he managed an Italian boardinghouse for several years. In Philadelphia, however, Lagomarsino finally found his permanent home, as well as great success in subsequent business ventures.[39]

Almost immediately after his return to Philadelphia in 1859, Lagomarsino opened a fruit store and began his rise in the Italian colony. For a while, Lagomarsino (who appeared in the 1860 federal census as Augustus Langestine) and his wife found their lodgings in the Ninth Ward, in the center of the city, in a small hotel operated by Patrick Duffy, an Irish immigrant. From this point on, Lagomarsino prospered in his business affairs, enabling him to begin investing in real estate. In 1864, he purchased property at Eighth and Christian Streets for $1,900, and the following year established a partnership in a large macaroni factory with his nephew, Frank Cuneo, at 801 Christian Street. While others may have initiated earlier efforts, Lagomarsino and Cuneo probably had the first major macaroni factory anywhere in the United States. But they also operated a general market that sold domestic and imported foods, along with wines and liquor, and provided for the special needs of the growing number of Italians in the neighborhood and city. Almost immediately successful after only three years, they had invested about $20,000–$25,000 in real estate and about $8,000 more in machinery. By 1872, Europa Farina Mills Macaroni, as it was called, was deemed a first-rate business.[40]

In his civic leadership and private life, as well as in his business achievements, Lagomarsino enjoyed the fruits of the opportunities Philadelphia offered. In 1867, he was a founder of the Società di Unione e Fratellanza Italiana. In 1870, Agostino and Harriet Lagomarsino lived handsomely at their home in South Philadelphia, with real estate worth $10,000 and another $20,000 in personal wealth. In their large and complex household were several other people, including Agostino's nephew and business partner, Frank Cuneo; Felicità Cuneo, the latter's twenty-five-year-old Swiss-born wife; and their son, Augustus Cuneo, one year old and the namesake of his great-uncle; three apprentice Italians, who worked in the macaroni factory; and three domestic servants.[41]

For both Lagomarsino and Cuneo, success and prosperity in business brought them respect and influence among their fellow Italians. Both men were known to be of excellent character and habits. They were prompt in paying their bills in cash, and they owned other property as well as the mill. Together they were estimated to be worth $30,000–$40,000.

Although the firm continued to flourish, Lagomarsino had other plans. In 1879, he expanded his business interests to a new partnership with two other Italians, Stephen Ratto (already discussed) and Augustus Latour, ship chandlers at 225 South Second Street. By August 1882, when he relinquished his share of his original partnership with Cuneo, it was first believed that Lagomarsino intended to retire in comfort on the money he had already made.[42] But soon afterward, he opened a banking office and continued to play an important role in the immigrant community. Lagomarsino was later regarded as the person responsible for the idea to erect the Columbus monument in Fairmount Park. He also served for fifteen years on the board of directors for the public schools of the city.[43]

Beyond his personal wealth, Lagomarsino's political influence had a significant impact on the Italians of the city. On one level, Lagomarsino played a quiet but important role in the naturalization of Italians as American citizens. In the very early years of Italian life in the city, such individuals as Secondo Bosio emerged as occasional vouchers for naturalization proceedings. Through the 1840s, George Alexander, whose name repeatedly appeared on petitions for naturalization by Italians, was the most conspicuous witness. In the disputed election of 1856, Dominic Coronia was identified in a similar role. In the 1850s also, John B. Rogers (John B. Raggio) served in that capacity for the first time, and continued to do so over the next quarter-century. Other already naturalized Italians performed this function in the years ahead. Before 1880, however, no Italian provided this service more frequently than Agostino Lagomarsino. From 1878 to 1880, he was the voucher on thirty-three occasions for Italians who sought American citizenship. All these cases occurred between late August and early October, making it likely that his motive was actually to recruit registrations for a political party.[44]

Although Italians later became one of the Republican Party's most reliable components, it is not clear when they first aligned themselves with that party in Philadelphia. Lagomarsino's participation in an attempt to resolve the differences among Italian leaders at a series of meetings revealed a complicated picture in the mayoralty election of 1884. In early February, at a gathering of a reported 150 members at Columbus Hall, the Italian Political Club appointed a committee to recommend candidates for municipal offices in the coming elections. Among the members were Lagomarsino and John B. Raggio. At its next meeting a week later, the committee members sharply debated a possible endorsement of the Democratic Party slate led by Incumbent Mayor Samuel G. King. One speaker, who first disagreed with an ordinance of the King administration that had banned the use of firecrackers in the city, a cherished tradition for many Italians at times of public celebration, then introduced an even more important issue. Although King had already broken the race barrier by recruiting the first African American, the mayor had appointed only one Italian to the police force.[45] Claiming that there were 4,000 Italian voters in the city, the same member asserted that Mayor King's police officers "call us dagoes and say that we should be behind bars." At this critical moment of the meeting, the committee offered its endorsement of King. When it met a few days later, however, with Raggio presiding, the Italian Republican Club (as it was now identified in the newspapers) unanimously endorsed challenger William B. Smith and a slate of regular Republican candidates in the Second, Third, Fourth, and Seventh Wards. It also appointed a committee to secure the naturalization of Italian residents in time for the next presidential election.[46]

The mayoralty election of 1884, won by Smith by slightly more than 9,000 votes out of a total of about 150,000 cast, further consolidated Republican control of city government. Despite the difficulty of knowing how Lagomarsino's endorsement of the losing candidate fit into the overall scheme, the election of 1884 may also have been an important moment in local politics for Italians. Although they contributed to the Republican victory in the mayoralty election, Italians did not gain much in return. While some occasionally broke ranks and supported the opposition—perhaps a minority were Democrats all along—Italians generally remained solidly in the Republican camp well into the next century.[47]

Although his apparent political preference had been rejected in the election of 1884, Lagomarsino remained admired by a large segment of the Italian population in Philadelphia. Some sense of the affection and esteem with which Lagomarsino was regarded is indicated by a comment about him in a testimonial volume on the Italian colony: "Lo si considera come padre affettuoso, come maestro, che molto la sua onestà, le sue infinite virtù insegnano" ("He is considered to be an affectionate father and a teacher who by his honesty and many virtues teaches us much").[48]

Lagomarsino died at the age of seventy-six on May 1, 1906, at his home at 758 South Eighth Street, where he had lived for many years. His first wife, Harriet, had died in 1897; his second wife, Rosa, survived him by several years. Even after death, the precision with which he had specified the distribution of his estate revealed his meticulous character in business matters. A frugal and modest man who was not given to self-indulgence, he directed that the expenses for his interment at Holy Cross Cemetery, including religious services, not exceed $500. Yet mindful of the need for spiritual remembrance on the road to salvation, he also provided $100 to each of three churches for Masses for the care of his soul. Two of the churches were St. Mary Magdalen de Pazzi and Our Lady of Good Counsel, the two parishes that served Italians in South Philadelphia; the third church, Santa Maria Certenoli, was in his birthplace, San Colombano Certenoli, in Italy. His final instructions also indicated his concern for the material needs of the three churches. He bequeathed $500 to each of them, "to be used toward the payment of such indebtedness as may be against said churches," and $500 to the girls' orphan asylum of St. Mary Magdalen de Pazzi parish.[49]

Lagomarsino's will also reflected his estimates of the relatives with whom he had shared his life. Having died without any children, Lagomarsino left most of his estate to Rosa, his widow. Although he willed all his real estate to her, the legacy would be reduced to one-third of the net proceeds of the sale of those properties if she married again. He instructed that $1,000 be left to each of his grandnephews, Francis, Frederick, and Alfred, sons of his nephew and former business partner Frank Cuneo; and to each child of his already deceased grandnephew, Augustus, who was another son of Frank Cuneo, to be distributed only after Rosa's death. Lagomarsino further specified that $400 be paid yearly to a niece, Catherine, daughter of his deceased sister, Angela Cuneo. This unusual bequest was to be made from rents of his real estate and to be paid in monthly amounts of $33.33 in satisfaction of any claim that his niece may make against his estate for her services. For the moment, Lagomarsino, left everything else to his wife. But he must have had some special regard for another nephew, David Lagomarsino, whom he appointed to serve with Rosa as co-executor of the will, and who would be the beneficiary of all of the real estate upon her death. In anticipation that the will might be challenged, Lagomarsino also specified that if anyone contested it, any consideration toward that person would be revoked and granted instead to the orphan asylum at St. Mary Magdalen de Pazzi.[50]

The care and shrewdness that had served Lagomarsino in business endeavors during his lifetime obviously operated even in this document that expressed his last wishes on the disposition of his wealth. His commercial sense, however, did not exclusively dictate its preparation. In one special provision, he remembered Rosa, a source of comfort and companionship in his final years, by his wish that she be buried with him at Holy Cross Cemetery in Yeadon. Despite this wish, however, it was not Rosa but Lagomarsino's first wife, Harriet, and his nephew David, that would share the site of their final resting place.[51]

Frank Cuneo, nephew and younger partner of Lagomarsino, was born in San Colombano Certenoli in 1838. When he was only nine years old, Cuneo began working with his uncle in Italy, and did so for the next eight years. At the age of seventeen, Cuneo immigrated to Philadelphia in 1855, but after three years in the city he decided to seek his fortune in California. Upon his return to Philadelphia, Cuneo began a partnership with his uncle in their firm of Lagomarsino & Cuneo, which earned prizes for its pasta at commercial exhibitions at the Franklin Institute in Philadelphia in 1874, at the Centennial Exhibition in Fairmount Park in 1876, and at the International Exposition in Paris in 1878. But the principal responsibility in designing and developing these exhibits may have been carried out by Cuneo's talented wife, Felicità.[52]

After the partnership with Lagomarsino had been dissolved in 1882, the firm continued to grow under Cuneo's direction alone. Basically a good miller, but not well educated or skilled in ownership and management, he found his new partner and help in Felicità, who "was undoubtedly the brains of the business," according to a family member many years later. An intelligent woman who was supposedly fluent in several languages, her assistance enabled Cuneo to develop one of the most successful businesses in the Italian colony, if not in the city itself. With up-to-date equipment, the firm produced pasta that gained a favorable reputation throughout the United States and Europe. Felicità's role in the firm, however, was ended by a devastating accident at the factory, when her hair was caught in a machine and she was seriously injured. Within a few months, Felicità Cuneo died, probably partly as a result of the incident.[53]

Frank Cuneo eventually remarried and resumed his business and social life. While the firm of "Frank Cuneo, Macaroni & Vermicelli Works," in its four-story building at 801–805 Christian Street, the hub of the immigrant colony, continued to prosper, Cuneo also had the only wholesale liquor store operated by an Italian. In 1882, with a confidence bred by success, he refused to make any kind of statement about himself or his business to a credit investigator, adding proudly that he was not seeking any credit and did not intend to in the future. Despite his boast, or perhaps partly because of it, Cuneo was described as "a middle age man of good character and habits" with an estimated

Frank Cuneo's factory and store, located at Eighth and Christian Streets. Cuneo's firm, one of the first major business establishments in the Italian community, not only imported foods sought by immigrant families but also acquainted other Philadelphians with products from Italy. (From *La Colonia Italiana di Filadelfia*, 1929)

FRANK CUNEO,
Maccaroni and Vermicelli Works,
801, 803 and 805 Christian St.

Frank Cuneo logo. The Cuneo-Lagomarsino partnership was often recognized by awards for its products. (Courtesy of Inez Cuneo Bieberman)

personal worth of about $30,000–$40,000. He had also found new partners in his four sons, who had been educated in order to share in the management of the firm with their father.[54]

Like his uncle, Lagomarsino, Cuneo was also a leader in the activities of the Italian colony. Although he had been one of the principal organizers of the Società di Unione e Fratellanza Italiana in the autumn of 1867, Cuneo's name did not appear in the Società's record of activities as consistently in later years. In a quiet manner, however, Cuneo continued to play an important civic role, particularly as treasurer of a fund-raising campaign for improvements to Columbus Hall in the 1890s, which reflected the trust members of his own community had in him.[55] Unfortunately, this high regard was not always enough to protect Cuneo from personal misfortune. In August 1910, attracted to the doorway of his establishment by the sounds of a quarrel between two Italians, Cuneo was struck by a stray bullet that shattered the thumb on his right hand and lodged near his heart. For a while he hovered near death, but eventually he recovered from the freak incident.[56]

During his long lifetime, Frank Cuneo accumulated a formidable personal fortune in his business, but he acquired much more than wealth. His business acumen, political power, and personal character, also earned him a good reputation and respect both among fellow Italians in the colony and among other Philadelphians. In 1892, Cuneo was one of the exceedingly rare Italian names in the *Philadelphia Blue Book,* which, although it was not quite the *Social Register*, meant that Cuneo had at least some prestige in mainstream Philadelphia life.[57]

At one point, Cuneo also had the distinction of being the oldest living member of the Philadelphia Commercial Exchange.[58] A testimonial in the late nineteenth century declared: "Pioneer and representative Philadelphia merchants and manufacturers, like the old landmarks, are yearly becoming scarcer, and it is a pleasure, to run across a business man whose career dates back forty-three years, when Mr. Frank Cuneo established his maccaroni [*sic*] and vermicelli works." Although the time span was somewhat in error and such publications were unquestionably given to hyperbole when describing people who might also have been financial patrons, the characterization still indicated the view of some Philadelphians:

> Mr. Cuneo is by birth an Italian, but by adoption an out-and-out American citizen, a man of unblemished character and loyal to his promises, thorough in business, held in highest esteem by all who know him and have any dealings with him. By square dealing measures and progressive methods, is the motto upon which he has founded his business and gained his success. His sons are Philadelphians by birth, they are gentlemen in the prime of youthful manhood and possessed of unusual business talent, and endowed with those attributes of character which compel success in trade. The honorable policy of the house has made the firm popular throughout financial and commercial circles, where Frank Cuneo's name stands high for mercantile integrity.[59]

When Cuneo died at his home at 830 South Eighth Street early on a spring evening in 1919, at the age of eighty-seven, the Italian community lost another of its early founders and leaders. He left an estate of $102,000, consisting largely of real estate. The inventory of his estate included copper dies for the manufacture of macaroni, a liberty bond, and seven properties, mainly on South Mildred Street, which were sold shortly after his death. Describing him as "one of the most picturesque characters in Philadelphia's Italian colony," a newspaper reported that the gunshot wound he received nine years earlier contributed to his death.[60]

Cuneo made a formidable mark on the Italian colony himself, but he also established a family line that continued to exercise influence within the neighborhood and in the city at large. While his sons eventually took over Cuneo's business interests, in later years their education and interests also led them in other directions. In particular, Frederick Cuneo emerged as probably the most distinguished and important figure in the next generation of the family. Born in September 1872, Frederick attended public schools in the city. After graduating from a business college in 1891, he joined his father's business. In the early twentieth century, Frederick identified himself as a manufacturer, with his business located at 801 Christian Street and his residence still at the family home at 830 South Eighth Street.[61]

While maintaining the family business, Frederick also pursued an active political career. A lifelong Republican, the younger Cuneo took an active part as a leader among the Italians of the Third Ward. As a member of the reform faction led by department store founder John Wanamaker, Cuneo joined in an attempt to defeat machine boss Matthew Quay. After Wanamaker was defeated in the race for the U.S. Senate by Boies Penrose in 1897, Cuneo narrowly lost his own bid for a seat in the state legislature in the following year, in an election that some observers suspected had been decided by questionable practices. Although his supporters urged him to contest the outcome, Cuneo accepted the defeat. He was eventually elected to the Common Council of the city and represented the Third Ward from 1913 to 1915. In later years, Frederick Cuneo served in the Department of Tax Revision and as a real-estate assessor for the city.[62]

A highly favorable biographical sketch while he was still a young man contained a cryptic remark that could have been intended to reveal much more: "He is noted for his social qualities, and his companionship is much sought for."[63] Instead of the serious and responsible demeanor that marked his father, Frederick Cuneo had a more carefree character that ultimately limited his public life. Although she had great affection for him, his own daughter remembered her father as someone whose love of life and good times prevented him from achieving what the family had expected of him.[64]

The great promise that remained unfulfilled in Frederick Cuneo's later years included one distinction that the family perhaps particularly wanted and that also reflected more general changes in the Italian community. In the early twentieth century, although Italians had previously been elected as school directors to represent neighborhoods, no Italian had yet been appointed to the Board of Education. The Cuneo family sought the honor of being first to have a member reach this citywide position. In 1905, a state law that eliminated the election of school directors by wards shifted power to the city's Board of Education, although members of the board were still appointed by judges of the Court of Common Pleas. Because judges were generally nominated by the Republican Party, school board appointments reflected its influence. In 1917, Harry Trainer, a member of the Select Council, led the opposition in the Third Ward against the regular Republican machine. In the contest for power within the party, Cuneo again aligned himself with the wrong faction, as a supporter of Trainer. When William Vare and his brothers won control of the party, any chance for the appointment of Cuneo to the Board of Education was lost. Instead, the Vare machine eventually chose one of its supporters, Charles C. A. Baldi Jr., for the position in 1924. While its members had long ago become prominent, the choice of one of the Baldi family, whose origins were near Salerno, over a member of the Cuneo family, with its Ligurian roots, embodied the succession of Southern Italians over the original Northern founders of the community.[65]

Lorenzo Nardi: From *Figurinaio* to Community-Builder

While most of the principal figures who had emerged during the formative period of the Italian community were of Ligurian origins, what the few Tuscans among them may have lacked in numbers they made up for by the strength of personal character. Among these

Tuscans, Lorenzo L. Nardi played a central role for Philadelphia Italians during these years. Moreover, in the contrast between his life and that of his son, Emmanuel V. H. Nardi, the transition of Italians from their modest material positions when they arrived in Philadelphia to more-affluent, secure, and prestigious lifestyles of later years was clearly illustrated. Born in Decimo in the province of Lucca in 1819, at the age of eighteen Nardi went to France, where he remained for fifteen years. While there, he married Angela Ayrolles, a well-educated young woman from a French family.[66]

In the spring of 1852, Nardi arrived in Philadelphia, where he began his long and productive role in the new community with an important innovation for local industry. For some time the city had been a major center for the manufacture of hats for men and women in a process that relied on wooden forms. Only a few months after his arrival, Nardi introduced plaster hat blocks. After a brief period of collaboration with an American partner, Nardi established his own workshop, where he made hat blocks in plaster, zinc, and iron for the rest of his life.[67]

At the same time, Nardi's business interests followed a diversified if not capricious route. In the 1860 census, as previously noted, Nardi was identified as a forty-two-year-old plaster statue artist from Tuscany living with his family and several other Tuscan *figurinai* in the Twentieth Ward in North Philadelphia. During his early years in the city, records also show that Nardi also attempted to open a china and glass business—although that might be nothing more than a euphemism for the plaster statue vendor. By autumn of 1869, when he established a confectionery business at Eighth and Parrish Streets in North Philadelphia, Nardi owned real estate worth about $5,000 and had modest business capital of no more than $200. He was also known as a steady, honest, and upright man with a first-rate character.[68]

Despite his early accomplishments and reputation, Nardi did not experience consistent success, and he was temporarily out of business by August 1871. By the end of the decade, he returned to manufacturing plaster bonnet blocks at 324 Garden Street. With some personal savings, Nardi also owned property at 33 Parrish Street valued at $4,500. Although he was said to be sometimes slow in meeting payments to creditors, Nardi was nonetheless still esteemed as a man of high character.[69]

Nardi's personal success, and his significance for the Italian community, transcended his business life. At the same time, the matter of becoming an American was a concern for him, and as he pursued that goal, he established the pattern of dual American and Italian identity that would characterize leaders of immigrant communities. In 1866, Nardi filed his first papers to become a citizen of the United States, and two years later, to complete the process, he affixed a shaky signature to his petition for naturalization in the District Court of Philadelphia, with Alfred Cavagnaro as his voucher. With an evident pride in his *Italianità,* Nardi was also now a conspicuous figure in fraternal affairs and in activities that reflected devotion to his country of origin. In addition to being among the founders of the Società di Unione e Fratellanza Italiana in 1867, he was a delegate to the convention of Italian societies held in Philadelphia in the following year; vice-president of the Società for five years and president for one year; vice-president of the committee for the Columbus monument and instrumental in raising funds for that project in the 1870s; and a founder and the first president of the Legione Umberto. Toward the end of his life, he represented the United Italian Societies in the preparation for the Columbian celebration of 1892.[70]

Formidable in his patriarchal appearance, with an elegant beard, Nardi projected a charismatic personality. The strength of his personal character is suggested by an event that was perhaps the high point of his public life. On October 26, 1882, when Pennsylvania observed Festival Day in celebration of the bicentennial of its founding as a colony, the band and membership of the Società participated in a gala parade in Philadelphia. While the first division of marchers was composed of Native Americans, mainly from the Carlisle School for Indians, Italians had been relegated nearly to the end of the parade. The officers of the Società decided to improve the position of its formidable float, whose theme was "Columbus in America." As various units marched down Broad Street toward South Philadelphia, Joseph Malatesta, then president of the Società, and Nardi opened the police line and ordered the Italians into the parade immediately behind the Indians. At this unanticipated disruption, Malatesta and Nardi calmly informed the distracted marshal that although the Indians were in America first, Columbus, certainly next, had to be in the second division of the parade, a position that Società members held throughout the rest of the event.[71]

The values and attitudes toward his Italian origins that Nardi projected in his public role were reflected at a more private level within his family life. Nardi prohibited family members at home from speaking any language other than Italian. Similarly, Nardi and his wife insisted that their children be educated, both in business matters and in music and the arts. After his death, it was noted that the real monument Nardi left was his children's love for Italy. In later years, one of them, Emmanuel V. H. Nardi, became a formidable figure in the Italian community and in the city itself.[72]

Until his death in December 1892, Lorenzo Nardi held a position of prominence, influence, and respect among the Italians of Philadelphia. For nearly thirty years he had been a visible figure in every celebration among them and had played a powerful role in their organizations. Perhaps unable to forget his own early days, Nardi was a generous man who had aided many other Italians, particularly when their colony was so small that a newly arrived immigrant might have difficulty finding someone who could give counsel and assistance.[73]

Nardi's most significant contribution, however, may have been his efforts to build agreement and unity at a time when regionalism still separated Italians from one another. Nardi had risen within a community that had been dominated by leaders with Ligurian origins, but, flooded by newer arrivals from Southern Italy in the late nineteenth century, a more diverse population made organizing the community a more complicated task. Aware of the problems Italians faced in their attempt to achieve cooperation, Nardi was receptive to the need to make room for newcomers. Instead of a parochial regionalism, he saw the desirability, perhaps even the inevitability, of a more nationalistic mode of ethnicity. When he told an audience, "Siete italiani, e non napoletani, genovesi, nè toscani" ("You are Italians, and not Neapolitans, Genoese, or Tuscans"), Nardi accurately anticipated what was already taking place.[74] His observation provided a succinct summary of the transcending of regionalism and the development of a more nationalistic ethnicity that was making *paesani* into Italian Americans and Philadelphians simultaneously. By his leadership, Nardi had served as a catalyst in bringing about this transformation.

Captain Joe: Property and Power

The success of Italians in Philadelphia rested mainly on the accumulation of personal wealth, but it also led to increased political power for them, both within their own community and in the larger city. One could even rise from the family of a street musician to great personal wealth and power. Born in August 1841 in the province of Genoa, Joseph Malatesta came to Philadelphia with his parents at the age of ten. In 1860, the Malatesta family, headed by Francesco, a fifty-five-year-old "organist," lived in the Second Ward. His forty-five-year-old wife, Mary, had already given birth to six children in Italy, including Joseph, their second son.[75]

Joseph Malatesta's life is a "rags to riches" story, although later accounts differ in the details about early stages. At his death many years later, one rendition described his childhood situation: "They were hard-working industrious people, but very poor, and the boy helped to earn the family bread." In this version, Malatesta first worked as a newsboy at a stand at Fifth and Chestnut Streets, the business center of the city, in order to make his contribution to the well-being of his family. Other accounts have him as a fruit vendor, a bootblack, a street musician, and a newsboy on trains between Philadelphia and Baltimore. He may have worked in all these ways at one time or another, and, as he worked, the poor immigrant newsboy may have dreamed that he might someday own a country estate in the same lush countryside through which the trains passed.[76]

From his earnings, the young Malatesta purchased a fruit stand in 1861 at Fifth and Chestnut, the same intersection where he had sold newspapers, and from this point on, his business efforts followed a rapid, upward path. By 1866, at age twenty-five, he operated a grocery and a liquor business. In 1870, he was a tavernkeeper with real estate worth $8,000 and a personal estate amounting to $3,000 more. By 1872, Malatesta was an established importer of wines and liquors at Eighth and Lombard Streets, where he also operated a saloon and hotel.[77]

As his business life developed, Malatesta also appeared to change in his personal character. In 1868, credit investigators described him as an Italian; about thirty-eight years old (which was actually ten years too many); married; in business for about eight years; the owner of some real estate; a hardworking and energetic man who had made money; well spoken of; a man who paid bills promptly; estimated to be worth $6,000–$8,000; and a safe risk for credit and business wants. Through the early 1870s he continued to be described in similar terms. In 1877, although he was still moderately prosperous, there was a newer and less flattering dimension to his personality. People now characterized

Malatesta as unpleasant in business matters, difficult to collect from, and requiring frequent drumming from creditors. It was also reported that some dealers did not care to sell to him at all and that his credit was limited.[78]

From this point on, although the credit reports contained contradictory information, the negative elements gradually became more salient. In 1879, having no barkeeper, Malatesta and his wife attended to the business themselves. He continued to do a fair cash trade in their tavern; he was considered responsible and regular in meeting debts; he was regarded as a fair risk for modest amounts; and he had an estimated worth of about $10,000. But he was also still viewed as a difficult man to deal with and get money from. This profile continued in subsequent years, but other facets became part of Malatesta's personal character and business. He was seen as shrewd; his saloon was patronized principally by Italians; he sometimes disputed accounts in order to give himself more time to pay; and he had the ability to pay at any time—when he chose to do so.[79]

These credit agency profiles reflected the continuing struggle of mainstream Philadelphia to reach a better understanding of its Italian residents. In 1881, although misspelling his first name and declaring that "Guiseppe pronounced Jo-sép-py is Italian for Joseph," who now had a large and handsome saloon that was kept open all hours, the description of its proprietor became even more incongruous. Although he was still regarded as responsible, the credit agency depiction now magnified his less desirable traits. He was seen as unpleasant to deal with, troublesome to collect from, reluctant to pay his bills, and inclined to quibble about amounts. Although he still did a profitable business and his estimated worth was about $10,000, Malatesta's credit with some of the leading financial institutions had become very weak. In the following year, the report revealed further erosion of his credit and reputation. He continued to be slow and troublesome for creditors and was no longer considered a desirable risk. The still quite profitable business was now managed by his wife. The Malatestas were believed to be well able to pay, but again only when they were so disposed. This reluctance also seemed to leave careful parties with little confidence that Malatesta was worth much in readily available assets. Ironically, he was still able to obtain what he needed from sources outside the city. Creditors concluded that he should be handled carefully and given limited amounts of credit.[80]

The inconsistent descriptions of Malatesta's condition continued in later years. It was repeatedly noted, however, that he had invested considerable sums of money in real estate and that even though his creditors found him to be an unpleasant and difficult person, ordinary Italians still regarded him with great favor. The final credit report noted that it was difficult to estimate his worth or character. While the vacillating nature of previous entries made this conclusion understandable, it is clear that Malatesta was a formidable and contentious person.[81]

Despite these problems, Malatesta played an important political role in the immigrant colony. He was the sixth president of the Società di Unione e Fratellanza Italiana for ten years. His leadership of the Società and his personal character were also reflected in the incident involving the disruption of the 1882 Pennsylvania Bicentennial parade. It is impossible to determine whether Malatesta or Nardi had a stronger part in this bold assertion of the interests of Italian participants. Both men were parties to an act that required considerable self-confidence, but also enhanced their reputation and respect among other Italians.[82]

Malatesta's political aspirations were not confined to leadership of immigrant organizations, but aimed at higher objectives that enabled him to emerge as the first broadly visible Italian leader in the larger city. In 1867, he filed his petition for naturalization as a citizen of the United States, with his brother-in-law, Alfred Cavagnaro, as voucher. By the early 1870s, already more than just another new citizen, he was a leader in community affairs. In June 1873, when more than one thousand people, including the mayor of the city, participated in the fourth annual picnic of the Italian Beneficial Society, the success of the event was attributed mainly to Joseph Malatesta, as president. The event began with a parade that moved from Sixth and Christian Streets over a lengthy route, before the marchers boarded public transportation that brought them to the picnic grounds at Wissahickon Park. At the park, young people enjoyed singing, dancing, and games. The program culminated in a grand dinner that included some of the most influential and well-known Italian residents of the city. By his conspicuous involvement in such activities, Malatesta strengthened his influence as a political leader among the Italians.[83]

In the years ahead, Malatesta reaped the rewards for his leadership among the Italians at a higher level of city affairs. For his efforts in gaining support in Italian neighborhoods for William B. Smith in the mayoralty election of 1884, Malatesta was appointed captain of the police patrol service and superintendent of vans. It was generally understood that the mayor had actually created the post solely to give Malatesta an office, and perhaps it was mainly an honorary position. Nevertheless, it represented a new level of attainment for an Italian, and during his tenure in this position he was described as being very popular both inside and outside the Police Department. Further recognition of his political leadership came in the founding of the Joseph Malatesta Republican Club in 1893.[84]

By 1895, having sold the saloon at Eighth and Lombard to his brother, Malatesta and his wife devoted themselves to their farm in Linwood, Delaware County. By the summer of 1899, they had all but retreated to their country home. Malatesta died from pneumonia at the age of fifty-eight in February 1900. An obituary noted: "Not only as a business man, respected by the people of his fatherland and his adopted country alike, but as a politician, Joseph Malatesta was well known. In political circles down town he was long an important factor." A more personal side was also pointed out: "Captain Joe, as he was familiarly called, was well liked by his comrades, in the police department—everywhere he made friends." The account of his death concluded with the observation that he was "well beloved and widely mourned in the Italian colony."[85]

On the day of Malatesta's burial, members of the Italian colony crowded the streets near his residence at 416 South Eighth Street, followed the funeral cortege, and filled the Church of Our Lady of Good Counsel for a Requiem Mass celebrated by three priests. All the Italian beneficial societies participated in the solemn ceremonies. Besides Italians, many prominent Philadelphians joined in the mourning, including former Mayor Smith, whom Malatesta had served, several judges, the assistant district attorney, the postmaster, the current superintendent of police, three police captains, and even a member of the Wanamaker family.[86]

Malatesta's personal character and financial worth, reflected in the ambiguities of the credit profiles, became clearer after his death. His will contained items that revealed a sometimes generous and thoughtful benefactor to faithful friends and favored relatives. The bulk of his estate was left to his widow, Maria, with instructions that his executors invest in a trust for her to last as long as she remained unmarried. He bequeathed his 37-acre Delaware County farm, along with $15,000 in cash and $5,000 more in administration fees, to his nephew Joseph Malatesta. He made bequests of $1,000 to other nephews and nieces, with some restrictions and exclusions, and a legacy of $5,000 to a close friend, Robert von Moschzisker, one of three executors of the estate. Malatesta also provided $4,000 for Elvira Bertolucci, apparently a domestic servant, if she remained with Maria Malatesta at her death.[87]

The several codicils added to the original version suggested a reflective and perhaps capricious person who could reconsider and alter previous decisions. A bequest to Elvira Bertolucci had already been revoked by codicil because she had married the nephew, Joseph Malatesta. A provision distributing the balance of his estate among nephews and nieces had similarly been annulled. The strongest sentiments were contained in Malatesta's rescinding of any inheritance for another branch of his family: "I do not desire that any part of my said estate shall go to the children of said John B. Malatesta under any circumstances." The unequivocal language strongly suggested that relationships within the extended family had not always been harmonious and reflected the contentious character of the writer.[88]

Confused by Malatesta's quarrelsome tendencies and stalling tactics in business dealings, credit appraisers were unable to explain how income from his saloon continued to flow while his credit rating deteriorated, but the will answered the question. With only $9,000 in personal property, Malatesta left real estate worth about $200,000. The tepid comments by credit investigators that he had invested considerably in real estate were weak indicators of the actual extent of his holdings. At the time of his death, Malatesta owned 5 properties on McClellan Street, 10 on South Fairhill, 10 on South Darien, 9 on South Mildred, 1 on Fitzwater, 5 on Lombard, 5 on South Eighth, 1 on Pine, 2 on South Seventh, 3 on Vine, 2 on Wood, 10 in Dilks Court, 3 on Alder, 2 on Christian, 1 on Montrose, 6 in Tisdale Place, and another on the northwest corner of Broad and Race. He had also owned three lots on the east side of Darien Street below Fitzwater that had been sold near the time of his death. He had 220 acres of farmland with improvements at his Linwood estate and a small lot at Cape May, New Jersey. The rents from his properties provided substantial income for their owner. With profit from the saloon and rent from real estate, Malatesta consistently invested in more property, and by the time he died he may have owned more property than any other Italian in the city.[89]

In preparing his will, mindful of the inevitability of death and well aware that he had irritated and offended others, Malatesta had a strong sense that he should protect his own well-being, both spiritually and materially, after his departure from earthly life. Perhaps he was afraid that no one else would do it for him. Malatesta set aside $400 for Masses for the year after his death, but he also directed that between $10,000 and $20,000 be used to build a chapel at Holy Cross Cemetery in Yeadon, and that $2,000 more be invested for income to be used for perpetual maintenance of his tomb. This grand mausoleum remains an impressive monument to Joseph Malatesta: "First Captain of the City Patrols" its inscription still reads.[90]

Personal Success and Community-Building

In the years immediately after the American Civil War, a number of *prominenti*, as later scholars called them, emerged within the Italian immigrant colony in Philadelphia.[91] From modest backgrounds, they began new lives in Philadelphia under difficult conditions, but they were ambitious men who successfully pursued wealth and acquired some prestige and power at the same time. These rewards, however, would not come at the center of Philadelphia life. Despite their own material accomplishments and social ascent, these men were victims of cultural and social marginality in their new city. Their responses were both the cause and the effect of what they were able to do under the conditions provided by the Italian setting of city life. In their thinking and actions, while seeking to become more American, they attempted to hold on to much of their *Italianità*. Whatever efforts they may have made to penetrate the institutions of mainstream Philadelphia, they also founded new organizations through which they created opportunities for themselves to be important, powerful, and recognized by others within a more limited setting. In these achievements, they established their own class system with a new hierarchy and with themselves at its summit.

In the niches that had been created by the lives of these *prominenti*, however, was something more than individual success and self-aggrandizement. Their accomplishments reflected their roles, which fulfilled vital functions in the establishment and maintenance of an immigrant community but also made them the principal instruments of defining and connecting it to the larger society. For example, while Italians were forced to abandon much of their traditional culture, the retention of food products and customs not only eased their adjustment but ultimately provided one of their most visible contributions to American life. Food vendors like Raggio, Lagomarsino, and Cuneo, and restaurateurs such as Cavagnaro, Finelli, and Malatesta, not only met the gastronomic needs of Italians, but helped to initiate the diffusion of their diet to other Americans as well. Similarly, while Italians had to seize the employment opportunities they found in the city, the distinctive skills that they provided in certain areas also consolidated their position in the economy. The stone and marble yards of the Viti family established the presence of Italians in the construction trades, and the furniture factory of John D. Raggio transferred not only the crafts of Chiavari but also the woodworking skills of Italians to the labor market.

Furthermore, while Italians often faced the vicissitudes of a new society alone as individuals, any degree of solidarity offered greater protection and security within its political system. Such community leaders as Lagomarsino, Nardi, Malatesta, and the Raggios mobilized Italians in fraternal and political organizations that sheltered them from exploitation, at least by outsiders, and required candidates for public office to seek their support. In sum, while they were builders of their own community, they were also links between it and the larger social order.

Moreover, while the existence of both Italian and Anglicized surnames implies a certain marginality, it also signifies something else, other than personal acculturation. In the case of John B. Rogers, widely recognized as Giovanni Raggio within the Italian colony, the alternating use of these names reflected his role as a broker between that community and the larger social order. In various activities, particularly in his frequent service as a sponsor, Raggio facilitated the political assimilation of other Italians. But by taking on a dual public identity as both Raggio and Rogers, rather than reflecting a situation of uncertainty and confusion, he made himself simultaneously more salient, and perhaps more convincing, in his efforts to negotiate his leadership in a bicultural setting. By retaining his original surname, Raggio could represent himself to his Italian constituents as an authentic and accessible leader; by assuming an Americanized identity, he could also serve as the solicitor for these Italians before other Philadelphians. At the same time, Raggio was conveying his own experience in the assimilation process, which began at the moment of arrival in America and would inevitably transform Italian immigrants into Italian Americans.

Finally, while it is impossible to recapture all of their "inner life," these fragmentary accounts of their efforts do reveal something of the aspirations and expectations of these men, as well as their implications for later immigration. They believed that it was possible to achieve success and a better life, within the opportunities offered in Philadelphia. Unlike later immigrants who planned to return to their homeland, these men, who intended to stay, were attempting to reconstruct their lives in a new setting. And even if their dreams were often disturbed by harsher realities, by undertaking commercial enterprises in Philadelphia, they were also building a new world within the community that would be called "Little Italy." For them it was an important part of the urban renaissance of the times, by which they contributed to the development of the modern city. But by their commitment to a new life, they were also paving the way for later immigration, which would change the face of America.

These early leaders helped to establish and develop a new community that also represented, as ethnic life often does, another example of the struggle in human affairs between external domination and self-determination. As other subcultures within a larger social order, this new community tested the capacity and provided the means for its members to achieve greater control over their lives. However, at the same time that its internal structure was formed, the struggle for control also shifted to components within that community. It is difficult to assess the degree to which these men were motivated by altruism to serve the group as a whole, or by their own narrower self-interests. But as entrepreneurs, their commercial and civic interests were certainly served by the growing immigrant population, and their efforts in turn built that community.

The end of the earlier era of this community did not diminish the importance of its founders, for what they left for later leaders, such as Charles C. A. Baldi and others, was a firmly rooted community. In pursuing their business interests and helping to establish community institutions, as well as by providing political and civic leadership, these men succeeded in transforming an inchoate immigrant colony into a stable and enduring Italian community. In later years, that community evolved even more into the Italian American presence that continues to characterize the city of Philadelphia today. As a publication commemorating the founding of the Società declared many years later, "the sturdy citizens who founded this Society were pioneers in a movement to place the Italian race on a level with those of native birth and others of foreign extraction who preceded them." If we overlook the antiquated use of the term "race," remembering that Anglo-Saxon Protestant Americans and others held a similarly erroneous sense of the word at the time, the remark is instructive. The Italians of the city had only recently reached a crucial stage in the establishment of their own community. This could not have been achieved simply by the collective mass; it required the personal success and leadership that only outstanding persons could provide. Certainly the public life of individuals and families, such as Raggio, Viti, Cavagnaro, Lagomarsino, Cuneo, Nardi, and Malatesta, exemplified this ideal.

Chapter 8

From Cultural Ideal to Social Reality

Italy, which was my reverie by day, became the torment of my dreams at night.

—Rembrandt Peale, 1831

A straight line might be drawn through Europe from the northwest to the southeast. Above that line the average of immigrants is high. Below that line the average is low. From Greece, Russia, Bulgaria, Turkey, from Southern Italy and from countries of that kind we get immigrants that are a menace.

—*The Public Ledger*, 1903

I do not like to find streets where the name on almost every store is Italian.

—Elizabeth Robins Pennell, 1914

We have already noted that the conventional explanation of Italian immigration and resettlement in the United States is generally presented by a model consisting of three principal elements: (1) a set of conditions that disrupted life and pushed inhabitants from Italy; (2) a tremendous expansion of industry and economic opportunities that pulled them to American locations; and (3) a great revolution in transportation technology that made possible safe, swift, and inexpensive transatlantic passage. This view holds that Italian migration to the United States was insignificant in volume until the 1880s, when it first became a mass movement. It is difficult to disagree with that point, but it also implies that the Italian presence in American cities was not important in any sense before the beginning of large-scale migration. It is not only easier but also necessary to reconsider the latter proposition. It is often asserted, as well, that the formation of Italian communities was abetted by the so-called *padrone* system. This point may similarly require a more complicated examination of the Italian experience in urban America.

The present study offers a different argument. Although the number of arrivals from Italy was relatively small, Italians had already concentrated in their residential locations, developed a network of interpersonal relations, and established institutions such as the family, the boardinghouse, the parish, and the mutual aid society, well before the beginning of mass migration. Moreover, rather than simply cushion the shock of relocation for individuals, these institutions provided the foundation for the immigrant community that emerged in Philadelphia in later years. In this final chapter, we shall summarize the major points of preceding sections, present a few new ones, and integrate these issues.

Although a vast amount of information, for the most part previously ignored, makes it possible to reconstruct a descriptive account of the Italian experience in Philadelphia, a few basic concepts provide an interpretation of that material and enable us to reach a better understanding of this particular case. First, the *images* that Philadelphians formed and held about Italians facilitated or hindered their acceptance as newcomers to the city. Second, the *interactions* of Italians with one another and with other residents greatly affected the way they adjusted to and were integrated into their new setting. Third, the *institutions* Italians established became instruments for achieving their survival as a community. Fourth, the *personal identity* of Italians— that is, their sense of self—brought them together but sometimes also separated them from one another. Each was an important and separate dimension of life in the new setting, but the interplay among them provided structure for the collective experience of immigrant Italians and their families as members of an emerging ethnic group.

Early Images of Italy and Italians

The Italians' discovery of Philadelphia was preceded and even partly precipitated by earlier encounters Philadelphians had with Italy. The founders of the colony, William Penn and Francis Daniel Pastorius, had both been touched by Italy in their early years. Before the arrival of any Italians, Italy had served as a source of scientific, aesthetic, and philosophical ideas for residents of the city. A highly favorable image of Italy provided a positive atmosphere, which allowed Philadelphians to have more direct contact with the material life and culture of Italy. About the same time that Italian musicians and artists first arrived in Philadelphia, the scions of the city's most prestigious and powerful families, motivated by material interests and the pursuit of cultural refinement, followed the reverse route and initiated the Grand Tour to Italy.

In addition to a certain personal growth that visitors achieved in their travels to Italy, they also created new ties between Italy and their own city of Philadelphia. Such individuals as Francis Rawle, Edward and Joseph Shippen, John Allen, and Samuel Powel forged material connections between Italy and Philadelphia; Dr. John Morgan established a similar conduit for scientific and intellectual influence; and Benjamin West and Rembrandt Peale later expanded the links for artistic affairs. From the mid-1750s and many years after, through the Grand Tour, Philadelphians and other Americans visited Italy in search of the "softer arts," by which they would refine themselves. At the same time that they admired and imitated, they also pillaged and imported as much of those arts as they could, to enhance the quality of life to which they would return in Philadelphia. By their appreciation and expropriation of antiquities, high culture, and classical civilization, these privileged adventure-seekers also delivered Italy as a source of idealized standards for the lives of Philadelphians. The favorable attitude toward Italy produced an encouraging climate for Italians who sought an American destination as a venue for their abilities and talents.

Before the Revolutionary War, the overwhelmingly British population, institutions, and cultural character of Philadelphia also shaped the views of inhabitants toward other nations and peoples. During the war, the city was momentarily divided, not only by Tory or patriotic sentiments but also in its reaction to the French. Despite its role in the struggle, Philadelphia afterward remained a center of British sympathies and culture. When the events in Paris in 1789 brought about another revolution, the population of Philadelphia was again split, but now by controversy over the politics of democracy. During the entire period, however, almost all of Philadelphia shared a dislike of Spain and the Spanish. But in contrast to these sentiments, Philadelphia was long united in its approval of Italy and its culture, at least at this early moment.

From Interaction to Institutions

From the colonial period to the early years of the new republic, finding the city not only a hospitable place but also a city of opportunity, a small, enterprising, and colorful contingent of Italians began arriving on the Philadelphia scene. By earlier experience in London, some of these newcomers had already encountered the rewards, as well as a certain receptiveness for what they could offer to the English. Now they could similarly supply the most important overseas city of British America with their arts, learning, and skills. Musicians, singers, composers, and music teachers entertained and edified local audiences. Painters and sculptors created more visual products, while drawing masters instructed students in art. Restaurant and pleasure-garden proprietors fed other appetites of the public. Impresarios produced popular entertainments for theaters and exhibited exotic animals on the streets. Property agents and commodity dealers offered land and material goods. Some Italians played even more dramatic roles for the city and nation. The undercover agent served the espionage needs of the Continental Congress against British military and naval forces. The political polemicist provoked readers with his essays, pamphlets, plays, and translations. And in a unique episode of diplomatic history, the Consul simultaneously represented the interests of the Papal States and the American republic.

As the relatively strict code of conduct that previously governed colonial life was supplanted by more urbane values and the diversity of later arrivals, Italians also contributed to transforming Philadelphia from a previously sedate and sterile colony to a more lively and cosmopolitan city. By their efforts in music, art, and public entertainment, as well as in business and commercial affairs, the small but colorful band of Italians helped to make Philadelphia not only quite different from the "gray Quaker lady" they might have found, but also the cultural center of early American life.

Although their numbers remained small, Italians began to establish themselves as a permanent part of Philadelphia by the early nineteenth century. Previously an aggregate of discrete individuals, they now shared increasing frequent occasions of personal life that ensured a more enduring collective presence. They served as sponsors for the baptism of one another's children; they acted as witnesses for each other in marriages; they testified as vouchers for more recent arrivals in naturalization ceremonies; they comforted one another at the hour of death. By participating in such ceremonies, they were beginning to construct among themselves a network of personal acquaintance and support. Natives of the peninsula that was itself still only a geographical expression were increasingly recognizing their common origins in each other.

These patterns of association and cooperation provided by family and friendship ties constituted an informal foundation upon which more-formal institutions and a more-developed community could be established in later years. Italians were sowing the seeds that eventually led to their own immigrant community. While it remained only partially developed in terms of institutional organization, the Italian colony was about to arrive at a more decisive stage in the immediate future.

Although they reacted with great concern and sometimes overt hostility toward other foreign groups in the early nineteenth century, Philadelphians continued to accept Italians as newcomers. When observers were critical about immigrant groups, and when violence was directed against African Americans and the Irish in the turbulent 1840s, Philadelphians remained tolerant of Italians. In addition to those who distinguished themselves in business and the professions, their sober, industrious, and law-abiding qualities not only won respect and goodwill but also convincingly demonstrated the ability of Italians to govern their own nation and helped to sway public opinion in favor of their more militant compatriots. Italians in Philadelphia, however, maintained a surprisingly low profile in the public demonstrations in support of the struggle for an independent Italy.

As the nineteenth century unfolded, new demographic, ecological, and institutional conditions enabled Italians to establish their own community. With each passing year, the size of the population increased modestly but steadily. The naturalizations that occurred also indicated that Italians were making a permanent commitment as citizens of a new nation. At the same time, the first traces of internal institutions that played an increasingly larger part in the further development of the colony appeared. By the 1840s, the new arrival could find lodging in a boardinghouse operated by another Italian, even if it was also sometimes a place of intragroup hostility and violence. By the 1850s, Italians had grown sufficiently in number to warrant establishing their own parish as Roman Catholics. By the 1860 federal census, Italians for the first time manifested a significant clustering of population in the southeast quarter of the newly expanded city, a precursor of the huge concentration that settled in that area in subsequent years.

While some disappeared from the local scene either by moving elsewhere or by assimilation into American society, other Italians found opportunities in the growth of their own population. Instead of serving a broader public, as they had done in earlier years, Italians more often found one another and turned themselves in a centripetal direction. The earlier hucksters, statue vendors, street musicians, and rag dealers were first supplemented and then supplanted by retail merchants and shopkeepers. To meet the needs of more recent arrivals from their own homeland, they became macaroni manufacturers, grocers, wine importers, and tavernkeepers. Not all their business ventures succeeded; some resulted in bankruptcy and personal failure. In other instances, their efforts produced material success that could be consolidated and passed down within the same family from one generation to the next.

These business enterprises, usually small but sometimes quite formidable, served as a commercial anchor for the emerging Italian neighborhood. By means of the goods and services that they provided, these merchants made their area of the city more suitable for Italian immigrants. The same activities also established a neighborhood economy that generated opportunities for employment and income for the population. The visibility of these shops and stores, both for newcomers from Italy and for other Philadelphians, revealed that this section of the city was indeed the "Italian quarter."

Whether they were unsatisfied with commercial enterprises alone, or whether they saw it as another way to implement their material objectives, successful merchants sought to extend their leadership into the lives of immigrants. In the late 1860s, they founded their first voluntary association, a forerunner of many fraternal, beneficial, political, and religious organizations chartered in later years. By their leadership in these organizations, the *prominenti* converted economic achievements into instruments of political influence and control that granted them prominence and power within the immigrant community but did not extend far into the institutional structures of the city. They remained in positions that were more titular than real, at the top of hierarchies among their own people, with a marginality that was in some sense parallel to the relationship of the immigrant community as a whole to the rest of Philadelphia.

Whether motivated more by personal gain or by the interests of the group, these efforts were mobilizing the immigrant population into a more cohesive community. In founding such formal organizations as a parish and a fraternal society, along with more successful commercial enterprises, the colony was reaching a more mature stage, marked by "institutional completeness," and becoming a visible, cohesive, and politically organized immigrant community.

The roughly 120-year period from the mid-eighteenth century to shortly after the American Civil War was a time of great turbulence and transition for most of western Europe as well as for North America. As events in an older world drove many of its inhabitants to seek better lives and opportunities in a newer land, the fate of Italy became inextricably linked with the growth of such cities as Philadelphia. At some moments the news of the struggle for Italian independence was received in Philadelphia with great public interest and reaction. The Italian residents of the city may have been somewhat delayed in their involvement, but they eventually responded publicly to the military and political events that took place in the peninsula from which they had migrated. With the passing of time, however, these patterns of individual and collective experience also diverged, at least momentarily, from one another. But at the point at which the relationship between experiences in the old country and the new city seemed to have ended, it returned in newer forms, often expressed in ceremonial occasions, and continued to shape the lives of Italians in the city and to sustain their identity as Italians.

The Immigrant Community: The Scaffold for Mass Immigration

By 1870, an Italian community had clearly emerged in Philadelphia, but it was a complex reality. On one level, this community was a physical place. Although Italians were found in various sections of the city, their concentration in the wards of South Philadelphia had become even more visible. On another level, of equal if not greater importance, this community was also a source for a sense of personal identity and social cohesion. Italians now knew where they could find other Italians, and similarly, other Philadelphians knew where they could find Italians. The neighborhood contained such specific institutional features as the boardinghouse, the tavern, the parish, the fraternal society, and various shops and stores, all with a definite Italian character. Such conditions helped an Italian community to become firmly rooted, both as a physical reality and as a social-psychological reference for its own inhabitants, as well as for other residents of the city.

For Philadelphia as a whole, the development of the Italian community was also contributing to the social ecology of the modern city. In addition to the central business district of the downtown area, other hubs of mixed residential, industrial, and commercial character were appearing throughout the city. In some instances, these smaller, outlying districts had been grafted on to the older communities beyond the original limits of the preconsolidation city.

Now, however, these somewhat self-contained communities were becoming the neighborhoods, or "urban villages," of modern America. The Italian case had also attained a peculiar sociological anomaly that tends to mark most ethnic groups in complex societies. With its own internal order and partial autonomy, the Italian community in South Philadelphia formed a distinctive and separate social system in itself. At the same time, as a neighborhood within and dependent on

By the beginning of the twentieth century, this intersection at Eighth and Carpenter was near the heart of "Little Italy." (From *La Colonia Italiana di Filadelfia*, 1929)

the economy, politics, and social life of Philadelphia, it also represented an integral component of a larger, more inclusive city and nation.

The particular character that the Italian community had already assumed by the early 1870s enables us to understand the later stages of immigration much better. Whether for immigration in general or for Italians as a group, many previous studies have examined the case of a specific city. Such studies have needed to identify the conditions that make one case different from another, but they have only partly succeeded. In the late nineteenth century, for example, as a result of a number of factors, New York City became the major place of settlement for Italians arriving in the United States. As the principal port of entry, New York City provided an easy, convenient choice for them as a final destination, and the opportunities for employment reinforced the likelihood that they would remain there. These two principal factors produced a "snowball" effect that led to a massive

A typical scene in the Italian community shows a produce huckster, goats, and some interested observers on a narrow street in South Philadelphia. (Urban Archives, Temple University, Philadelphia)

immigrant population. But New York's experience should not be regarded as typical for urban America, for what happened there did not repeat itself everywhere else.

As a destination for immigrants and as a place to locate and form communities, Philadelphia had its own distinctive patterns of development. Partly because the city never became a major port of arrival for vessels of Mediterranean origins during the steamship era, the choice of Philadelphia as a place to settle was a more complicated process. Italian immigrants coming to Philadelphia generally landed in New York City, then completed their journey by train to their final destination. But why would they make this more difficult choice when New York was more easily reached and certainly attractive as a place of settlement? The generally favorable conditions of life in Philadelphia, as well as the particular opportunities offered by the highly diversified industrial economy, were undoubtedly important

The vendor's cart was more than a vehicle for commercial goods; it also encouraged public gathering. (Multicultural History Society of Ontario)

factors—Philadelphia certainly offered a hospitable material and social climate for newly arrived immigrants. But immigrants from any foreign country must have had additional inducements that accounted for their eventual choice.

The *padrone* system was once a popular explanation for the choices immigrants made regarding destination and the organization of their community life. We can identify specific practices and certain individuals that point to a variation of the *padrone* system in Philadelphia. As early as the disputed election in 1856, for example, attempts were made to mobilize and exploit Italian organ-grinders as voters. Similarly, in a later period, each person who appeared as a frequent witness in naturalization cases either had a remarkably large number of friends among newly arrived immigrants or played some role in the politics of the Italian population. But researchers have become more careful about using the *padrone* system as an explanation; they have found that its influence has been exaggerated, and they call for its qualification, if not rejection, as an explanation. In the case of Philadelphia, what constraints on the *padrone* system might have made it less important for the immigrant experience there than in other places?

If the federal census of 1870 appeared to profile a new community proudly gathered for a collective portrait, it was soon interrupted by the police raids on Catharine Street just three years later. A presence that had begun with composers and performers who had introduced Baroque music to Philadelphia in the previous century had now evolved into street musicians, slave children, and organ-grinders, which challenged the place of all Italians in the city. But in sharp contrast to the case of organ-grinders, who had elicited little sympathy or assistance when they were brought before the magistrate's court to face charges of fraudulent voting in the spring of 1857, the police raids and arrests of the slave children in 1873 produced a different result. With the support of Alonzo Viti and others, when the state assembly passed an act in the following year "to prevent traffic in children" the leadership of the Italian community had successfully asserted itself to protect some part of its population. Despite police action and legislation, however, the specific problem was not quickly resolved, but this public affirmation of collective interests also revealed that there was a firmly established community that could respond to problems that threatened its existence.[1]

While not eradicated by these efforts, the *padrone* system in Philadelphia probably never had the impact on immigrant life that it had in other places. But whatever its role, the *padrone* system alone was certainly not sufficient to explain the growth of Italian immigration to Philadelphia. If the system did not develop in Philadelphia quite the same way that it did elsewhere, was it because a different set of arrangements had developed there? Local bosses did recruit, assist through naturalization proceedings, and enlist Italians as members of political clubs. In return for their political allegiance, Italians were supposedly rewarded with employment opportunities that may have also given them some immunity from further control by the bosses.[2] But before the 1880s, there is little or no indication that the "political boss" had yet fully emerged among Italians; therefore, even the milder version of the *padrone* system is really more appropriate, if at all, for a later period.

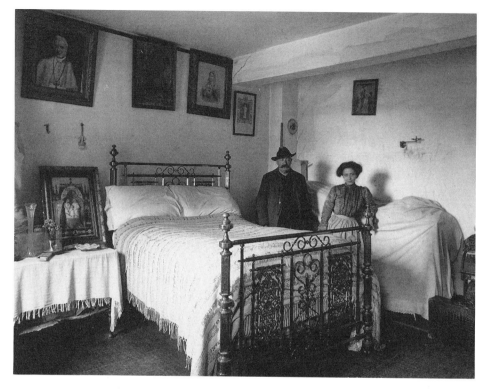

An Italian couple at home in their apartment. This scene captures some of the ambiance of immigrant life. (Philadelphia City Archives)

The Problem of Identity: Italians and Italian Americans

Other forces that generally served the interests of immigrants in the 1870s shaped the Italian experience in Philadelphia. When Massimo d'Azeglio issued his famous admonition about a decade earlier, "We have made Italy, now we must make Italians," he had curiously also identified a problem that faced Italians in America. By the early 1870s, the future of the Italian community in Philadelphia depended on the development of such factors as individual identity and group cohesion. From all indications, the leaders among Italians were able to make their own personal goals as individuals coincide with the interests of

In this "blind alley" in the Italian section, a group of boys make the best of their situation, despite its hardships. (Urban Archives, Temple University, Philadelphia)

the community as a whole. The result of this congruence of individual and collective interests may well have been that d'Azeglio's problem was resolved sooner by Italians in an American city than by their compatriots in the native land.

Lorenzo Nardi's exhortation deserves to be recalled one more time at this point: "Siete italiani, e non napoletani, genovesi, nè toscani" ("You are Italians, and not Neapolitans, Genoese, or Tuscans").[3]

With strength that was sometimes visible, immigrant women and children often faced the ordeal of everyday life together, as in this scene somewhere near Mildred Street or Montrose Street. (Urban Archives, Temple University, Philadelphia)

Grasping the reality of a rapidly growing and changing pattern of immigration, Nardi sought to make himself an instrument of a new type of ethnicity. But what lay ahead for immigrants from Italy was not quite what Nardi had described, for although they might have been becoming more Italian from the first moment that they had arrived in the United States, other influences were making them into Americans. And in response to these challenges, if Lorenzo Nardi had been able to peer far enough into the future, he might have surmised what lay ahead for his audience with the words "Voi siete gia ed i vostri figli saranno nel futuro Italo-Americani" ("You already are, and your children in the future will be, Italian Americans").

The role of men like Nardi may not have been what the great German sociologist Max Weber had in mind when he wrote "Not

Despite the rigors of their lives, etched on some faces, another child in the Italian colony could find a reason to smile. (Urban Archives, Temple University, Philadelphia)

From the doorway of their home in the 700 Block of Clymer Street in South Philadelphia, an Italian mother and her daughter look out on the neighborhood. (PHA/Urban Archives, Temple University, Philadelphia)

By the end of the nineteenth century, the Italian Market on Christian Street in South Philadelphia had become the commercial center of the immigrant community. (PHA/Urban Archives, Temple University, Philadelphia)

ideas, but material and ideal interests, directly govern men's conduct. Yet very frequently the 'world images' that have been created by 'ideas' have like switchmen, determined the tracks along which action has been pushed by the dynamic of interests."[4] But neither ideas nor interests float in the air on their own; they can exist and become determinants of human action only if they are embodied in individuals who influence the lives of others. Perhaps not just "world images," but these leaders themselves, such as Nardi, were actually the switchmen that chose the tracks that the subsequent development of the Italian community would take.

Whatever their faults and limitations—and there must have been some—the motives and actions of these leaders shaped the future for other Italians. Such men as Alfredo Cavagnaro, Frank Cuneo, Agostino Lagomarsino, Joseph Malatesta, and Lorenzo Nardi attained wealth, power, respect, and sometimes even affection from the members of their community. Rather than pursue personal gain through the blatant exploitation of later arrivals, Italian leaders during these years sought to achieve their own success through more legitimate and honorable means. They organized Italians into voluntary associations and other forms of communal institutions; they participated in campaigns to rid the community of abuse and shame; they provided sources of pride and standards of accomplishment for other Italians to emulate; and they served to articulate the Italians as a group to the rest of the city as a larger entity. Through these functions, the personal efforts of these men also built a stable and enduring community for Italians in Philadelphia.

Although the local press continued to identify the *padrone* system in the years ahead, the "institutional completeness" of the Italian community may actually have provided a protective buffer for immigrants in Philadelphia. By the early 1870s, an elaborate internal institutional structure made the Italian community of Philadelphia visible and attractive to prospective immigrants. What the Italian community of Philadelphia had already become by the 1870s is partly the answer to the question of why later immigrants chose that particular destination. The more developed character of the community itself offered advantages and amenities that enhanced the employment and housing opportunities provided by the city at large.

A careful study of subsequent years might reveal, however, that the community was not enough of a refuge to protect later immigrants from exploitation. In another decade or two, when the period of mass immigration had truly begun, the hegemony of these early leaders was challenged. Philadelphia was not immune to efforts by employment agents, bankers, and aspiring "bosses" seeking to mobilize immigrant Italians for their own selfish and corrupt objectives. At that point also, the internal conflicts among leaders and within the Italian community were aired more publicly. But the relative success or failure of later *padrone* leaders followed what had already been accomplished within the Italian community.

And if the subsequent experience of Italians in the United States had remained more consistent with the immigrant community that had been established in Philadelphia by the early 1870s, it would have taken a different course. With a firmly rooted community whose members were achieving some measure of prosperity, respect, and power, the further acculturation and assimilation of Italians might have proceeded more rapidly and smoothly. Instead, a number of other factors emerged that impeded these processes and led in some ways to a deterioration of their position in the city.

Nativism and Newer Immigrants

The decade of the 1870s was a watershed period for Italian immigration to Philadelphia. Earlier generations of Philadelphians, like Rembrandt Peale in his reveries by day and torments at night, dreamed of going to Italy. Later generations of Italians dreamed of going to Philadelphia, and many of them eventually fulfilled that aspiration. From a trickle, within a few years the flow of immigration became a veritable flood. As the origins of Italian immigrants shifted from Italy's northern and central areas to regions of the South and Sicily, newer arrivals, while no longer street musicians or peddlers, were also less educated and less skilled than the artists, musicians, and entrepreneurs of earlier years.

Beyond the extrinsic attributes of literacy, education, and skills, it is virtually impossible to describe the more subjective character traits of Italian immigrants. Personal virtue and moral character have long escaped efforts of objective study, and their measurement perhaps does not belong on any research agenda. Yet, on the eve of a great surge in immigration, the evaluation of the personal character of the foreign-born became a serious issue on the minds of many Philadelphians, and the conclusions reached greatly affected the integration of Italians with their new American society. At first glance, as increasing waves of Italian immigrants arrived in American cities, the perceptions of Italy and her people seem to have undergone a revision, with the earlier romantic and sentimental image being replaced by a deep fear and hostility. Italy was no longer the land of the "softer arts" to be sought by wealthy, privileged Philadelphians, but had become a place from which ignorant and menacing newcomers were arriving in greater numbers each day.

What initially appeared to be a shift in attitude toward Italians, however, was perhaps not new after all, but the emergence of an ideology toward immigration that had been incipient for some time but had been obscured by other concerns. While previous perceptions of Italy had first involved an appreciation of aesthetic culture, then an endorsement of political ideals during the Risorgimento, these interests were focused more on philosophical abstractions than on social realities. The actual experiences of Americans had also been long tempered, whether as travelers in Italy, by restrictions in their contact with ordinary people, or as residents of their own country, by the small number of Italians who had migrated to the United States. Consequently, for a long time the early, highly favorable perception of Italy did not require any attitude toward Italians as a people.

When Italy finally attempted to free itself from foreign domination, Americans, recognizing the reflection of their own recent struggle for independence, could enthusiastically endorse nationalism and the bravery of Italian troops. But while Americans were willing to endorse republicanism, they were not as eager to embrace social democracy. Moreover, when d'Azeglio used the term "demagoguery," he was really concerned that popular democracy might overwhelm aristocratic oligarchy, and the encouragement of mass emigration that he proposed as a solution was precisely what American nativists feared from Europe. Further immigration was likely, as Sidney George Fisher had declared, "to add to the already swollen ranks of radicals and levellers." While they could favor more representative governments in Italy and elsewhere, Americans no longer intended to welcome masses of European immigrants with peasant backgrounds, especially if they had some kind of allegiance to the Pope, but also even if they were his bitter enemies. The support by Americans of republican politics in Italy was about to be replaced by another perception, that Italians were not only a threat to democratic institutions but also generally undesirable in the United States.

As experience with Italians shifted out of the art museums and concert halls to the factories and streets, an ostensibly new attitude came to the surface. While earlier approval of immigration rested on the certainty that the assimilation process would transform newcomers into Americans, large numbers of foreigners with a more resistant culture presented a different situation. When it became more apparent that this was the challenge America would face, the image Americans had of these newcomers also seemed to change. Moreover, Americans of a previous period may also have been less certain about what they themselves were; but by the final decades of the nineteenth century, this uncertainty was being replaced by a stronger sense of their own cultural character, which had great implications for all immigrants from this point on.

The negative attitudes toward more recent arrivals from Italy grew much stronger in the years ahead. Seeing these newcomers more as a liability and a threat, old friends who had once defended immigration shifted judgment and turned against Italians and other elements of the "new immigration" in the closing decades of the nineteenth century.[5] In the 1880s, editorial writers in Philadelphia declared their opposition not to "worthy and industrious people" but to "those undesirable classes whom foreign governments are only too glad to get rid of," and called for immigration restriction.[6] Similarly, the local press criticized education programs that would instruct Italians and others in their native languages, arguing that those who support instruction for the foreign-born in their own languages would soon ask for a movement "to instruct the negroes in African tongues" and asking, "What kind of a nation of tribes would the United States become if such plans were to be carried out?"[7] As reports of violence, crime, exploitation, and pauperism among Italians increased, the "evils of immigration" became a familiar element of headlines and articles, and demands for immigration restriction through federal legislation were frequently presented to the public.[8]

By the next decade, specific events contributed to further erosion of sympathy for the foreign-born that once existed in Philadelphia. Labor violence between immigrants and native-born workers throughout the nation occurred with increasing frequency. In New Orleans, the mob lynching of thirteen Italian workers in 1891 caused the Italian government to react strongly and provoked controversy in the United States. While it condemned the actions of the mob in New Orleans, the *Public Ledger* expressed its new attitude toward immigration by the title of an editorial, "Time to Shut the Gates."[9] In 1893, a writer in the *Philadelphia Inquirer* asked, "Are we becoming a mongrel nation?"[10] By the beginning of the twentieth century, perceptions of Italians had deteriorated even further. Early in 1903, in reporting the mounting problem of the solicitation of immigrant passengers by steamship companies, the *Public Ledger* not only cited the words of an official in New York but tacitly endorsed them as well: "A straight line might be drawn through Europe from the northwest to the southeast.

Above that line the average of immigrants is high. Below that line the average is low. From Greece, Russia, Bulgaria, Turkey, from Southern Italy and from countries of that kind we get immigrants that are a menace."[11]

The mood expressed in the newspapers was shared by prominent individuals, whose voices were also heard. One of the strongest commentaries on the changing character of Philadelphia and its foreign population came from the pen of Elizabeth Robins Pennell, a somewhat successful writer of the period, as well as the wife of Joseph Pennell, a local artist. Even the title of her book, *Our Philadelphia,* suggested a possessive and exclusionary attitude. But for people like the Pennells, the real enemy was change itself, and the immigrant in their midst was a good foil for their fears and insecurities. In her lament on the passing of a cherished age, written from London in 1914, Pennell surveyed the damage done over the past quarter-century to her beloved Philadelphia by the growing intrusion of foreigners. She described herself as "one of those old-fashioned Americans, American by birth with many generations of American forefathers, who are rapidly becoming rare creatures among the hordes of new-fashioned Americans who were anything and everything else no longer than a year or a week or an hour ago."[12]

Pennell noted that although in its earliest days it was the first place distinguished foreigners sought out, but that with the rise of other cities, such as Washington and New York, Philadelphia had lost its attractiveness for foreign visitors. Although her strongest remarks were aimed at Russian Jews, Pennell's comments on Italians are more pertinent here. Raised as a Catholic, Pennell described even the Italian Jesuits at Old St. Joseph's as having "those unpleasant habits of Italian priests that are a shock to the convent-bred American when she first goes to Italy." But the Philadelphia of an earlier time that she so fondly remembered, apart from the Irish and Germans, had only "enough Italians to sell it fruit and black its boots at street corners." What had once made Philadelphia so attractive to Pennell is indicated by her statement that, with only rare exceptions, "the foreigner was seldom seen in Philadelphia streets or in Philadelphia parlours."

Pennell believed that the Centennial celebration in 1876 marked the beginning of significant change for the city. When she left Philadelphia in the early 1890s, Pennell recalled, the Italian "at his fruit-stall was as yet rather the picturesque exception." Her characterization of group life in Philadelphia strikes us as strange today. Pennell's description of the Italians was certainly not an accurate portrayal of the complex community of large numbers of Italians that already existed at the time, so perhaps it was the view of a woman whose family and lifestyle had greatly sheltered her during her younger years from any extensive contact with that reality.[13]

By the time she wrote her book, Pennell was well aware of the extent of the Italian presence in the city, and it bothered her a great deal. While others might be accustomed to this new immigration, Pennell emphatically declared, "To be honest, I did not like it. I do not like to find Philadelphia a foreign town." Again, while she railed against all groups, Pennell singled out the Italians: "I do not like to find streets where the name on almost every store is Italian." It was a bitter diatribe by a bigoted observer whose world, as she once believed it to be, was very visibly changing before her eyes and beyond her control. It probably also expressed the attitudes shared by many other residents that had developed with the growth of the Italian population in the city.[14]

The misperception of the magnitude and significance of Italian immigration and community formation in Philadelphia has continued to the present day. After noting that Italians began to arrive in considerable numbers after 1875, a recent historian adds that by 1900 Italians were not yet ubiquitous in South Philadelphia and that their presence was only then beginning to be noticed. Although lower-class neighbors were prejudiced toward Italians, patricians found them to be "unobtrusive and even charming—an echo of the Italophile and aesthetic inclinations of Anglo-Victorianism."[15] That writer is only partially correct. The numbers of Italians arriving in Philadelphia did increase greatly after 1875, but in the next quarter-century, with their presence as a community well established, patricians and lower-class Philadelphians alike were already displaying their animosity toward Italians.

As for the Italians themselves, the prominence of this unfavorable image was a negative factor that could only make their interaction with other Philadelphians more difficult. Yet it could not erase their intention to go to Philadelphia or their desire to settle there. In the years ahead, the trajectory that describes their experiences in Philadelphia was much like the twisting paths and roads that immigrants had followed as they departed from the villages and towns of their birth. Sometimes this course would suddenly drop, but it would gradually rise at other points—until at the end it opened to a vast new world that might contain disappointment, failure, and sorrow but was also always pregnant with hope, expectation, opportunity, and challenge. And with the passage of time, in Philadelphia and other American destinations, Italy would become a rapidly fading memory that was only occasionally brought to mind by a political event in a far-off land. It would also provide Italians with their own romantic reverie, but now increasingly replaced by the more immediate experiences of a new life in "Little Italy," a reality they themselves had helped to bring into existence.

Abilities, Opportunities, and Images

The experience of Italians in Philadelphia and elsewhere provides a historical lesson that has important implications for group relations in American society today. The acculturation and assimilation of Italians cannot be reduced to the question of whether their personal traits and group culture were more important than the conditions they found in places like Philadelphia, as the present debate on the social mobility of minority groups in American society is inclined to do. The values, aspirations, and skills that early Italians carried with them as a part of their cultural baggage were highly compatible with the material opportunities they found in the expanding economy of urban America in the mid-nineteenth century. At the same time, however, what was also favorable to their situation was the positive manner in which other Americans still regarded Italy as late as the 1870s. But the perception and attitudes of Americans toward Italians were about to become hostile and inhospitable, as the volume of immigration increased and shifted in its sources to the regions of Southern Italy. It is difficult to say whether later arrivals were any less skilled, less capable, less literate, or less suitable for life in the United States—but that became the prevailing opinion, and it changed the course of American history.

When the immigration of Italians to the United States reached its peak between the 1880s and the 1920s, it was not a spontaneously generated occurrence that can be adequately explained by events and conditions found only during those years. The once persuasive contention that "the influx from Italy was barely a trickle, so inconsiderable that a microscope is almost needed to distinguish the Italian resident population in 1850" suffered from the same flaw that most initial attempts to understand anything does. Its authors were essentially right, but they needed to go further. If early Italian migration was only a trickle, it was because it was nearly wiped away by the deluge that followed. Before these pioneers can be dismissed as unimportant, however, another look through the same microscope reveals that their presence was not erased, but left a colorful mark rather than a stain, and that they furrowed and seeded the soil of urban America and constructed a communal niche that would be cultivated by subsequent immigration.

Appendix: Authenticating an Early Presence

If we wish to follow the history of an ethnic group from the earliest period through the later stages of its experience in a particular city, certain issues are immediately apparent. First, in the case of the Italians in Philadelphia, we want to begin by being able to identify the earliest of them to arrive and settle in the city. Second, it is necessary to describe the ways in which these Italians might have affected the character of urban life in these years. Apart from such substantive questions, one fundamental procedural problem must also be addressed. We must determine with some confidence that these individuals actually had Italian origins. Therefore, the reliability of information about them becomes an important concern. When previously published material is cited, it is still necessary to question the data in those sources or to criticize the interpretation of the authors. On the other hand, because the subject of this study has been so neglected, we have provided a large amount of new material, which must also be carefully examined.

The major sources for primary data include the sacramental ledgers of churches, newspaper articles and notices, city directories, manuscript census materials, naturalization records, and wills and letters of administration. When these sources provide definite statements about the origins of individuals, we can regard the material as reliable. But when such information is missing, we must decide whether the nature of the material justifies making any inferences about country of origin. Although the first stage in the early history of Italians in Philadelphia is clouded by such issues, these fragments, however indistinct, are all we have.

The actual number of Italians for the earliest period of their migration, as well as the dates they arrived in Philadelphia, have been difficult to determine. Some early sources provide the names of individuals that are arguably Italian in their origins. One such example can be found in the publication *Pennsylvania Archives*, which includes lists of the names of foreigners who took the oath of allegiance to the province and state of Pennsylvania between the years 1727 and 1775, as well as foreign arrivals between 1786 and 1808. Unfortunately this source does not give geographical origins of the people listed, but the names often encourage certain conclusions. For example, we find the names Patri (1749), Beggari (1753), Martini and Corsini (1753), Alberti (1754), Brogli, Bandelo, and Pilati (1764), Capell (1773), Seroni (1773), and Morauble, Rabane, Domingo, Contono, Cameti, and Poncelli (1774) on the lists of people taking the oath of allegiance. In the later series of foreign arrivals, we find the names Loro, Longenatto, Poggi, Lagni, Massa, and Mulinari (1800), Delmazo, who is identified as being from Turin (1805), and Marete, Ghio, Ghion, and Zenore (1808).

This matter has already been the subject of serious disagreement between previous writers. In his groundbreaking research more than fifty years ago, Howard R. Marraro sought to answer these questions by examining commercial notices published in local newspapers and names listed in city directories. He concluded that Italians had been in Philadelphia as early as the years before the Revolutionary War. According to Marraro, some were merely visitors, pausing there only to give concerts or lectures. But other Italians took up residence in the city, earning their living in a wide range of occupations, as surgeon, composer, music teacher, sculptor, language tutor, dancing master, wine dealer, sausage-maker, brewer, liquor dealer, coffeehouse proprietor, dry-goods merchant, flour merchant, sea captain, or laborer. Quite paradoxically, after providing this impressive list of occupations, Marraro contended that the Italian population of Philadelphia amounted to no more than eight people at the time of the first federal census in 1790. (See Howard R. Marraro, "Italio-Americans in Pennsylvania in the Eighteenth Century," *Pennsylvania History* 7 [July 1940], 159–66.)

It is somewhat anomalous that Marraro presented this total with a reference to the federal census. It suggests that he derived his figure from the census itself. But in view of the previous listing of occupations, if that were the case it is likely that the Italian population of Philadelphia would have been much larger at this time. If they had not been simply overlooked by census enumerators, many Italians who may have lived in Philadelphia between the 1750s and the 1780s had either died or moved to other places by the time of the 1790 census. In some cases, however, the same individual could have passed through a sequence of different occupations, with the proliferation of such job titles producing an exaggerated impression of the actual number of people involved. But it is also important to note that no direct information on ethnic origins was provided by the census until 1850, when a question on place of birth was included for the first time. Therefore, no easily acceptable knowledge about ethnic background is available from the 1790 census. Marraro, therefore, relied on other sources, such as newspaper advertisements and city directories. The commercial notices sometimes indicate that an individual had recently arrived from a foreign place, such as Italy, but the city directories never included any information on origins. For the most part, Marraro used the risky technique of inferring ethnicity from surnames.

Giovanni Schiavo was a contemporary critic of Marraro's work, in terms of its approach and its conclusions. While not an academically trained historian, he was a prodigious researcher and a prolific writer on the Italian American experience. Schiavo argued that Marraro was inept in his attempt to recognize Italian names. Schiavo took a similarly critical position toward a massive project sponsored by the American Council of Learned Societies (ACLS) that sought to determine the ethnic composition of early America. In this project, two historians attempted to analyze the surnames listed in the first federal census in 1790. In contrast to the findings of professional historians, such as Marraro and the ACLS project, that only a few Italians were in America during its early years, Schiavo reached a far different conclusion. By projecting the expected reproduction of population from the handful of early Italian settlers in the colonies, Schiavo vigorously asserted: "At the outbreak of the Revolution there were in the Thirteen Colonies thousands of people whose ancestry could be traced, directly or indirectly, to Italy." Schiavo added that name-changing may have obscured the Italian origins of many other individuals and families. (Giovanni Schiavo, *Four Centuries of Italian American History* [New York: Vigo Press, 1952], 11.)

Ironically, when he turned to the case of Philadelphia in his own research, Schiavo relied on the same type of procedure for which he had severely criticized Marraro—determining ethnicity through the recognition of family names. Apparently, while he considered Marraro lacking in the ability to use this technique, Schiavo was convinced that his own judgment of origins through family names had validity. He used the sacramental records of Old St. Joseph's Church, which had been founded in 1732 as the first church for Roman Catholics in the city, to argue that Italians had been in Philadelphia since before the Revolutionary War. From the 1760s to the 1780s, the baptismal entries include Mignati, Cancemi, Cangemy, Mignio, Orlandy, and Amico among the family names. Similarly, marriage records for Old St. Joseph's during the same period provide the names Polumbo and Morelli, and Schiavo presents these names as examples of Italian families in Philadelphia at this time. Later baptismal records for the same parish in the 1790s also give the family names Botello, Cuneo, and Ghirardini. The baptismal ledgers of Holy Trinity Church, opened primarily for German Catholics in 1789, include the Lammetta family in 1797 and the Molinari family in 1799, with Anna Bossio listed as one of the sponsors in the latter case. Unfortunately, apart from the clues represented by the spelling of the names, these listings generally provide no other information that would unequivocally reveal the Italian backgrounds of these individuals and families. In one notable exception, however, the entry in the records at Old St. Joseph's for the baptism of Anna Maria Orlandino in 1780 includes the phrase "of Paul Orlandino, Genoese." In addition, the Italian origins of the Molinari and Bosio families can be supported by other kinds of documentary materials pertaining to them. But for the most part, these entries still stand alone as indicators of the possible presence of Italians during this early period of Philadelphia history. Despite this problem, religious records may actually represent a scant measure of the size of the Italian population in the city at this time. It is still valuable to be reminded by Schiavo that "few colonial Italians had the opportunity or the desire to observe Catholic practices and that distance and poor means of communication prevented their attending church, except on very special occasions."

Italians may well have been far underenumerated. There may actually have been many more people of Italian birth or descent in Philadelphia and other parts of the American colonies at the outbreak of the Revolutionary War, and in the new nation in the later years of the eighteenth century. But the reliance on family names to identify and count this population remains a difficult problem that is not easily resolved. One major aspect in the attempt to answer this question is the tendency to treat individuals coming from British ports or on British ships as being themselves English. The adoption of Anglo-Saxon surnames, as Schiavo emphatically argued, may have disguised the Italian origins of some emigrant arrivals from England. There is documentary evidence that some Italians living in England adopted English names. If any of these individuals subsequently migrated across the Atlantic, they could only appear in colonial records as British. Italian names were also easily transformed into French names during the eighteenth century, so it is well to remember that some Anglo-Saxon or French names may obscure other origins and that such individuals might sometimes turn out to be Italians when appropriate evidence is available.

A corollary problem, however, is the reverse tendency. Writers who sought to correct the first type of mistake probably too often committed the second error. As previously indicated, determination of the presence of Italians in eighteenth-century Philadelphia has been based largely on inferring ethnic origins from the spelling of family names. The eagerness of an earlier generation of writers to document the argument that Italians were residents of early Philadelphia should not be allowed to obscure the limitations of what has been presented as evidence. Early records for Philadelphia frequently provide names that appear to be Italian but cannot be confirmed as such by these citations alone. For example, the name Maro Saroni appears on a list of foreign arrivals on the ship *Clementina*, which reached Philadelphia from Lisbon, and he later took an oath of allegiance to the colony of Pennsylvania in December 1773. The name Bastia Vene is given as belonging to a person who took an oath of allegiance to the state of Pennsylvania in May 1779. Similarly, the records of Old St. Mary's Church graveyard include the name Angelo Malouici, who was buried there after his death on March 3, 1788, at age fifty-two. Church records also show a Dr. Lorenzo as a member of the same parish in 1790. Dr. Paul Valentine Costari is identified as a member of Old St. Joseph's Church and as a physician who ministered to victims of the yellow fever epidemics of the city in 1793 and 1795. *Pennsylvania Archives* provides the name of John Puglia, listed as a private in the First Company, Third Regiment, of the Militia of the City of Philadelphia in 1794. In the same year, James Philip Puglia served as an interpreter of foreign languages, with Spanish cited in particular, for the Board of Health of the city. The latter Puglia was still serving as a health officer of the Port of Philadelphia fifteen years later. In 1795, a letter of administration to settle the estate of Francis Maggio, who had died without leaving a will, was filed. Joseph Peruani was a local painter and architect whose work was exhibited in 1796. Another artist, identified simply as Bartello, a painter of portraits from which engravings could be made, was employed by T. B. Freeman, also in 1796. Other similar cases can be added to this list of names that appear to be Italian in derivation, but in the absence of further documentation, such names by themselves, however tempting to the social historian, are still names that only appear to be Italian and must remain uncertain in origin. Some of the cases presented in the preceding discussion can be ascertained by using other sources that reveal Italian origins; others must remain only as possibilities.

While it is difficult to ignore these names, it is also not easy to resolve the problems which they present. The use of surnames alone to ascertain ethnic origins is an unsatisfactory procedure. But further documentation and other supportive materials are sometimes available. In newspaper advertisements, for example, it is somewhat fortunate to find in a *Federal Gazette* announcement of the arrival in Philadelphia of Joseph Perovani (who probably was the same person as the previously mentioned Peruani) and Jacint Cocchi that the two men were natives of the Republic of Venice. Similarly, James Philip Puglia is the subject of a rather extensive monograph, but as Santiago F. Puglia, and several of his own publications, which confirm Italy as his birthplace, are still available. In the case of Philadelphia, such family names as Allibone and Latta (both English) and Antelo (Portuguese) have sometimes been treated as Italian—not only purely without justification but also when there is evidence of origins in other countries. And it is not satisfactory to assert that the English names were of Italian origin, without being able to document previous migration from Italy to England. But even when there appears to be independent evidence that an individual was Italian, the researcher must always remain open to some other possibility.

A sufficiently interesting and instructive example of this sort that deserves careful examination is provided by the case of Francis Villato. One official document in the city records gives clear testimony that Villato, in accordance with an act of the state assembly, had become a citizen of the United States by taking an oath of allegiance before Mayor Matthew Clarkson on March 13, 1789. In a duplicate document signed by Clarkson nearly four years later, recording this oath of allegiance, the subject is described as "Francis Villato Merchant Son of Peter Villato of Genoa in Italy Merchant when he was born." If authentic, this document would mean that Villato was one

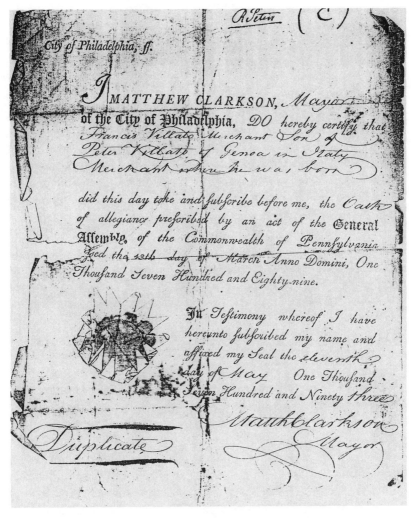

When he declared himself a native of Genoa and swore allegiance to Mayor Matthew Clarkson in 1789, Francis Villato appeared to be one of the first Italians to become an American citizen. At his trial for piracy and treason a few years later, Francisco Billato testified that he had concealed his actual Spanish origins, because he believed that Spaniards were not respected in America. But his testimony also indirectly indicated the high esteem with which Italians were held at this time. (National Archives, Mid-Atlantic Region, Philadelphia)

of the earliest Italian cases in Philadelphia to become a citizen of the United States.

The researcher might ordinarily be satisfied with the validity of the information provided by a source as official as this item. The naturalization of Italian natives and the earliest expression of their political lives in their new community might be also dated from this point onward. Yet the information contained in the document signed by Mayor Clarkson was false. In the criminal case files of the U.S. Circuit Court for the Eastern District of Pennsylvania, there is an instance in 1799 in which an accused individual with the name of Francis Billato is being returned from the West Indies to Philadelphia for trial. In the materials bearing on this case, the names Bilato and Villatot are also provided, along with testimony that the same person also filed a petition for naturalization under the former name, but claimed to be of Spanish origins, in the Court of Common Pleas on April 21, 1797. It becomes apparent that the accused pirate is the same individual as the Francis Villato listed in the earlier document signed by Mayor Clarkson. In his own testimony given in a hearing on the piracy charges, the defendant admits that he is the same person that took the oath of allegiance in 1789 and explains that it was much safer to have been known in Philadelphia at this time as an Italian than as a Spaniard.

This testimony not only clearly indicates the risks that remain even when official documents are available, but also provides some suggestion of the prestige accorded Italy and Italians by the people of Philadelphia during the period. But even when the origin of an individual can be correctly demonstrated, in view of the divided political condition of Italy at this time it is not clear what this information signifies about that person. The reconstructing of immigrant and ethnic history requires more than simple assertions about the origins of individuals accompanied by little more than superficial biographical sketches. At the very least, it involves going beyond the level of names and discrete individuals and reaching some description of the interconnectedness of persons and families with others of similar origins. It should also include some interpretation of the significance of these lives within their new community and society.

Notes

Introduction

1. "1 Italian in 1852; 150,000 Here Now," *Philadelphia Public Ledger,* May 5, 1927, 11.

2. Frederick Jackson Turner, quoted in Edward N. Saveth, *American Historians and European Immigrants,* 2nd ed. (New York: The Free Press, 1964), 149.

3. In the series *L'Emigrazione nelle Americhe dalla Provincia di Genova,* two volumes in particular are important: vol. 1, *Questioni Generali e Introduttive* (Bologna: Patron Editore, 1990), especially for the discussion of Ligurian settlers in American cities, "Un Secolo e Mezzo di Flussi Migratori," by Gaetano Ferro and Adele Maiello, 75–177; and vol. 4, *Questioni di Storia Sociale* (Bologna: Patron Editore, 1992).

4. Elliot Lord, John J. D. Trenor, and Samuel J. Barrows, *The Italian in America* (New York: B. F. Buck & Co., 1905), 2–3.

Chapter 1. First Arrivals

1. U.S. Immigration and Naturalization Service, *Statistical Yearbook of the Immigration and Naturalization Service, 1986* (Washington, D.C.: U.S. Government Printing Office, 1987); U.S. Bureau of the Census, *1990 Census of Population, Detailed Ancestry Groups for States, Supplementary Report,* 1990 CP-S-1-2 (Washington, D.C.: U.S. Government Printing Office, 1992).

2. Spencer M. DiScala, *Italy: From Revolution to Republic, 1700 to the Present* (Boulder, Colo.: Westview Press, 1995), xxii. DiScala offers a lucid, comprehensive, and coherent treatment for the reader who seeks an introduction to the history of modern Italy.

3. It is beyond the scope of the present study to present detailed information on the events of this period of Italian history, but there are a number of excellent recent works that provide a good discussion of the subject. In addition to DiScala's previously cited book, see Harry Hearder, *Italy: A Short History* (Cambridge: Cambridge University Press, 1990); Harry Hearder, *Italy in the Age of the Risorgimento, 1790–1870* (London: Longman, 1983); Giuliano Procacci, *History of the Italian People* (New York: Penguin Books, 1986); Denis Mack Smith, *Italy: A Modern History* (Ann Arbor: University of Michigan, 1969); and Stuart A. Woolf, *A History of Italy, 700–1860* (London: Methuen, 1979).

4. For a description of social conditions in Philadelphia during the period, see Sam Bass Warner Jr., *The Private City: Philadelphia in Three Periods of Its Growth* (Philadelphia: University of Pennsylvania Press, 1968); and the appropriate chapters in Russell F. Weigley, ed., *Philadelphia: A 300-Year History* (New York: W. W. Norton & Co., 1982).

5. Warner, *The Private City,* 5.

6. Richard G. Miller, "The Federal City, 1783–1800," in Weigley, *Philadelphia,* 155–205.

7. Carl and Jessica Bridenbaugh, *Rebels and Gentlemen: Philadelphia in the Age of Franklin* (London: Oxford University Press, 1962), esp. 168–73.

8. William B. Wilcox, ed., *The Papers of Benjamin Franklin* (New Haven: Yale University Press, 1976), 506 n. 7.

9. Rembrandt Peale, *Notes on Italy, Written during a Tour in the Years 1829 and 1830* (Philadelphia: Carey & Lea, 1831), 5, 304.

10. Numerous scholars have examined the experiences of these American visitors as well as the influence of Italy on them. For important earlier studies of these travelers, see Van Wick Brooks, *The Dream of Arcadia: American Writers and Artists in Italy, 1760–1915* (New York: E. P. Dutton & Co., 1958); Paul R. Baker, *The Fortunate Pilgrims: Americans in Italy, 1800–1860* (Cambridge: Harvard University Press, 1964); Giuseppe Prezzolini, *Come gli americani scopririno l'Italia* (1933), 2nd ed. (Bologna: Massimiliano Boni, 1971). Some important more recent treatments of the subject include William L. Vance, *America's Rome:* vol. 1, *Classical Rome;* vol. 2, *Catholic and Contemporary Rome* (New Haven: Yale University Press, 1989); Theodore E. Stebbins Jr. et al., *The Lure of Italy: American Artists and the Italian Experience, 1760–1914* (Boston: Museum of Fine Arts, Boston, in association with Harry N. Abrams, 1992). An important article on the implications of the subject for historical writing is A. William Salomone's "The Nineteenth-Century Discovery of Italy: An Essay in American Cultural History. Prolegomena to a Historiographical Problem," *American Historical Review* 73 (June 1968), 1359–91.

11. See Baker, *The Fortunate Pilgrims,* esp. 80–104.

12. *Pennsylvania Gazette,* January 20, 1757, cited in Giovanni Schiavo, *Four Centuries of Italian American History* (New York: Vigo Press, 1952), 112. A "Large Book of Songs" by Palma, costing five shillings and found in the estate of Cuthbert Ogle at his death in 1755, led Schiavo to conclude that Palma may have arrived even earlier in Philadelphia.

13. Robert A. Gerson, *Music in Philadelphia* (Westport, Conn.: Greenwood Press, 1970). These details begin to reveal the ambiguities and hazards of trying to reconstruct the early history of an immigrant group. After being asserted by one writer, then repeated by others, it becomes nearly axiomatic that Washington attended Palma's second concert in Philadelphia. This particular point, however, is not only vague, but perhaps trivial in content and significance for the Italian experience in the city. But it illustrates the process by which an alleged claim becomes more "factual" with subsequent repetitions. This problem becomes more serious when it involves issues more germane to our central subject matter.

14. Louis C. Madeira, *Annals of Music in Philadelphia and the Musical Fund Society* (Philadelphia: Lippincott, 1896), quoted in Gerson, *Music in Philadelphia,* 1. Gerson points out that the Yearly Meeting of Friends in 1716 warned its members against "going to or being in any way concerned in plays, games, lotteries, music and dancing."

15. For example, see Valentine J. Belfiglio, "Italian Culture in Eighteenth-Century Philadelphia," *Italian Quarterly* 87 (1983): 73–83.

16. Schiavo, *Four Centuries of Italian American History,* 112–13.

17. Ibid., 113, 176.

18. Ibid., 117.

19. For information on Gualdo in Philadelphia, see *Pennsylvania Chronicle,* August 31–September 7, 1767; *Pennsylvania Journal,* September 21, 1769, and November 16 and 30, 1769; cited in Schiavo, *Four Centuries of Italian American History,* 114–15. See also *Pennsylvania Gazette,* April 17, 1768; and *Pennsylvania Journal,* December 15, 1768, and March 2, 1769.

20. *Baker's Biographical Dictionary of Musicians,* 8th ed., rev. Nicolas Slonimsky (New York: Schirmer Books, 1992), 678.

21. See ibid.

22. Matthew Baigell, *A Concise History of American Painting and Sculpture* (New York: Harper & Row, 1984), 19.

23. Richard N. Juliani, "The Ethnic Factor: Backbone of the Commonwealth," *Pennsylvania Heritage*, special tercentenary issue (1981): 19–26.

24. George C. Groce and David H. Wallace, *The New York Historical Society's Dictionary of Artists in America, 1564–1860* (New Haven: Yale University Press, 1957), 507; Alfred C. Prime, *The Arts and Crafts in Philadelphia, Maryland, and South Carolina, 1786–1800* (Topsfield, Mass., 1932); Schiavo, *Four Centuries of Italian American History*, 220.

25. Groce and Wallace, *Dictionary of Artists in America*, 598; Schiavo, *Four Centuries of Italian American History*, 214, 222; Albert T. E. Gardner, *Yankee Stonecutters: The First American School of Sculpture, 1800–1850* (New York: Metropolitan Museum of Art, 1944).

26. Thompson Westcott, *History of Philadelphia*, chap. 417 (unpaginated scrapbook at the American Philosophical Society), originally published in the *Sunday Dispatch*, a local newspaper of the period. All citations to this series refer to the mounted and bound facsimile format available at the APS.

27. Schiavo, *Four Centuries of Italian American History*, 222.

28. Westcott, *History of Philadelphia*, chap. 417. See also J. Thomas Scharf and Thompson Westcott, *History of Philadelphia, 1609–1884*, vol. 2 (Philadelphia: L. H. Everts, 1884), 1045; H. Glenn Brown and Maude O. Brown, *A Directory of the Book Arts and Book Trade in Philadelphia in 1820* (New York: New York Public Library, 1950), 16; and Groce and Wallace, *Dictionary of Artists in America*, 32. These sources, which depend on and borrow from one another, repeatedly identify Bartello as being from Italy.

29. Groce and Wallace, *Dictionary of Artists in America*, 134, 500; Westcott, *History of Philadelphia*, chap. 417.

30. Schiavo, *Four Centuries of Italian American History*, 214.

31. Brown and Brown, *Directory of the Book Arts*, 94; Westcott, *History of Philadelphia*, chap. 417; Schiavo, *Four Centuries of Italian American History*, 214, 219–21. Schiavo provides a highly complimentary assessment of Perovani's work.

32. Westcott, *History of Philadelphia*, chap. 417; Groce and Wallace, *Dictionary of Artists in America*, 117; Schiavo, *Four Centuries of Italian American History*, 215–18; Charles Coleman Sellers, *Benjamin Franklin in Portraiture* (New Haven: Yale University Press, 1962), 204–11; Anna Wells Rutledge, ed., *Cumulative Record of Exhibition Catalogues: Pennsylvania Academy of the Fine Arts, 1807–1870; The Society of Artists, 1800–1814; The Artists' Fund Society, 1835–1845; Memoirs of the American Philosophical Society*, vol. 38 (Philadelphia: APS, 1955), 46.

33. *Pennsylvania Gazette*, August 29, 1765, cited in Schiavo, *Four Centuries of Italian American History*, 108.

34. *Luigi Castiglioni's Viaggio: Travels in the United States of North America, 1785–1787*, trans. and ed. Antonio Pace (Syracuse, N.Y.: Syracuse University Press, 1983). For an earlier examination of the observations of Castiglioni and other Italian visitors to the United States, see "Italian Travellers," chap. 9, in Henry T. Tuckerman, *America and Her Commentators with a Critical Sketch of Travel in the United States* (New York: Charles Scribner, 1868).

35. For material on Giambattista Scandella, see the Scandella Collection, Balch Institute, Philadelphia. See also Antonio Pace, "Giambattista Scandella and His American Friends," *Italica* 42 (1965): 269–84.

36. Miller, "The Federal City," 197.

37. Maldwyn Allen Jones, "Discord and the Growth of American Nationality, 1685–1790," in *American Immigration* (Chicago: University of Chicago Press, 1960), 39–63. Some later research has examined these issues in Pennsylvania in a far more rigorous manner

than previous studies. While this work includes some consideration of German settlers, it focuses more on power struggles involving groups with origins in the British Isles. See Alan W. Tully, "Ethnicity, Religion, and Politics in Early America," *Pennsylvania Magazine of History and Biography* 107 (October 1983), 491–536. Immigrants from places other than Great Britain did have some role, however limited, in the cause for American independence and in the ensuing development of a new nation. As might be expected, Schiavo provided the strongest argument and the most extensive documentation of the contributions of Italians in these affairs. See his chapter "Fighters for American Independence" in *Four Centuries of Italian American History*, 136–42. While it remains easy to criticize aspects of his work, Schiavo's efforts cannot be readily or entirely dismissed. As in other instances, Schiavo left a prodigious body of information that subsequent writers rely on extensively. For example, Glenn Weaver, *The Italian Presence in Colonial Virginia* (New York: Center for Migration Studies, 1988), reexamined and extended Schiavo's seminal assertions on the role of Filippo Mazzei as an influence on Thomas Jefferson and democracy in America in general.

38. *Pennsylvania Archives*, ser. 5, 4:783, also cited in Schiavo, *Four Centuries of Italian American History*, 139.

39. *Pennsylvania Archives*, ser. 6, 5:509.

40. *Papers of Benjamin Franklin*, vol. 24 (New Haven: Yale University Press, 1984), 340–41. See also the discussion of the Ceronio family in Antonio Pace, *Benjamin Franklin and Italy* (Philadelphia: APS, 1958). While Stephen Ceronio was in the West Indies, rather than the desert setting so vividly imagined by his father, his activities provide important clues to some persistent issues in the political history of Philadelphia. The part played by the Willing and Morris firm in the struggle for American independence remains rather ambiguous, and the actions taken by its principal partners were sometimes even more clearly disappointing in the eyes of stronger supporters of the cause. Although both men were delegates to the Continental Congress in the summer of 1776, neither Willing nor Morris voted in favor of the initial motion for separation from England. After it was passed by the Congress, Morris signed the Declaration of Independence, but Willing did not. Similarly, Willing was criticized by more ardent patriots when he remained in Philadelphia to look after business matters during the British occupation of the city in 1777–78. By refusing to swear allegiance to the king, however, Willing never fully joined the ranks of the Loyalists. After the departure of British troops, moreover, while many Philadelphians, including members of the most prominent families, faced charges of treason for having cooperated with the enemy, Willing's decision to remain in the city during the occupation was never challenged. Instead, both Morris and Willing gained positions of the utmost importance for the economy of the new nation. Despite his earlier hesitancy about independence, Morris had become the principal financial supporter of the Continental Congress. In 1781, when Congress began an effort to create a national financial system, Morris was appointed the first superintendent of finance. When Congress established the Bank of North America, although some opposed him, Willing was elected its first president. A decade later, Willing became the first president of the newly chartered Bank of the United States. Morris and Willing may have been guilty of occasional lapses in political judgment, but their immense importance in securing material support for the Continental Congress and its military endeavors eventually brought positions of further responsibility in the economic and financial life of the nation to both of them. See Harry M. Tinkcom, "The Revolutionary City, 1765–1783," in Weigley, *Philadelphia*, 109–54.

41. *Papers of Benjamin Franklin*, 340–41.

42. Pace, *Benjamin Franklin and Italy*, 390.

43. Robert Morris Papers, Levis Collection, Historical Society of Pennsylvania, Philadelphia (HSP), November 9, 1778.

44. Ibid.

45. Ibid.

46. Ibid., December 6, 1778.

47. Stephen Girard Papers, 1784:14, ser. 2, no. 2, APS.

48. Logan Papers, 41: 72–80, HSP.

49. *Marriage Records of Gloria Dei Church, Philadelphia, Pennsylvania, 1750–1863* (Philadelphia, 1879).

50. "A Philadelphia Subscription List of about A.D. 1795," *Records of the American Catholic Historical Society of Philadelphia (ACHS)* 6 (1895): 423–25.

51. Pace, *Benjamin Franklin and Italy,* 75.

52. The principal source for the present discussion is the detailed biography by Merle E. Simmons, *Santiago F. Puglia: An Early Philadelphia Propagandist for Spanish American Independence,* North Carolina Studies in the Romance Languages and Literatures 195 (Chapel Hill: University of North Carolina, 1977). Further information, however, is in Puglia's writings, particularly *The Federal Politician* (Philadelphia: Francis and Robert Bailey, 1795).

53. Puglia, *The Federal Politician,* 61–62.

54. Simmons, *Puglia,* 9–15.

55. Ibid., 15–17. See also John Hill Martin, *Martin's Bench and Bar of Philadelphia* (Philadelphia: Rees Walsh & Co., 1883).

56. Simmons, *Puglia,* 9.

57. Ibid., 17–22.

58. Ibid., 22.

59. Ibid., 26–27.

60. Ibid., 46–49.

61. Puglia, *The Federal Politician,* 153–54.

62. Ibid., xix.

63. He was, of course, joining other thinkers who would express similar objections to the excesses of the republican movement that brought the French Revolution to an end. Edmund Burke had already presented his views in *Reflections on the Revolution in France,* published in 1790, five years before Puglia's book. It would be interesting to know whether Puglia had read Burke's work, as well as the extent to which he might have been influenced by it. Alexis de Tocqueville would offer his indictment of the same events in *The Old Regime and the French Revolution,* published in 1856, more than sixty years after Puglia's book. One wonders whether Tocqueville was familiar with Puglia's writings. While Burke and Tocqueville remain remembered for their views on revolution, Puglia has become obscure.

64. Puglia, *The Federal Politician,* iii–iv.

65. Ibid., 153–54.

66. Ibid.

67. Ibid., 197 n. 19, 281–84.

68. Miller, "The Federal City," 190.

69. Ibid., 193–98.

70. Simmons, *Puglia,* 49–52.

71. Ibid. See also the advertisement that appeared in Puglia's *Forgery Defeated* (Philadelphia, 1822).

72. In the advertisement in *Forgery Defeated* (note 171), the author or the publisher provided information on all these works.

73. See ibid.

74. Simmons, *Puglia,* 68–69.

75. Ibid., 69–71.

76. *Pennsylvania Packet and the General Advertiser,* December 9, 1772. See also Schiavo, *Four Centuries of Italian American History,* 121.

77. *Pennsylvania Packet,* July 14, 1778, and August 23, 1788; Register of Wills, Philadelphia, Letter of Administration, 238 (1793), Anthony Bazaro; Edmund Hogan's *The Prospect of Philadelphia* (Philadelphia: Bailey, 1795–96), 113; Clement Biddle's City Directory for 1791, 134 (hereafter, Biddle's City Directory). Note that the name of the Philadelphia City Directory changes over the years as printers change, but for our purposes we shall consistently refer to each as City Directory.

78. Thompson Westcott, *Names of Persons Who Took the Oath of Allegiance to the State of Pennsylvania between the Years 1777 and 1789* (Philadelphia: John Campbell, 1865), 113.

79. *Luigi Castiglioni's Viaggio,* 213.

80. Hogan, *Prospect of Philadelphia,* 16. See also the map in Abraham Ritter, *Philadelphia and Her Merchants as constituted fifty to seventy years ago* (Philadelphia, 1860); and "A Philadelphia Subscription List of about A.D. 1795," *Records of the ACHS,* 6:4234–25.

81. *Memoirs of Lorenzo DaPonte,* trans. Elizabeth Abbott, ed. and ann. Arthur Livingston (Philadelphia: J. B. Lippincott Co., 1929), 406–9.

82. Register of Wills, Philadelphia, Will Book, 10 (1832), 219, Joseph Mussi.

83. Westcott, *Names of Persons,* 100.

84. Robert Earle Graham, *Inns and Taverns of Colonial Philadelphia,* APS card file, 1950–53.

85. Graham, *Inns and Taverns; MacPherson's Directory for the City and Suburbs of Philadelphia* (hereafter, MacPherson's City Directory) (Philadelphia, 1785), 180; *Pennsylvania Packet,* May 19, 1785, and August 30, 1785.

86. Graham, *Inns and Taverns.*

87. Ibid.

88. Ibid.

89. MacPherson's City Directory for 1791, 100. While there are no known holdings of Pelosi's *Marine List and Price Current,* one should consult *The Brigham Bibliography of American Newspapers,* n.d.; and "Contingent Expenses of the Department of State, 1790–1793," in *Papers of Thomas Jefferson,* vol. 17 (Princeton: Princeton University Press, 1965), 369.

90. Register of Wills, Philadelphia, Letter of Administration, 108 (1793), Vincent M. Pelosi.

91. George R. Prowell, *The History of Camden County, New Jersey* (Philadelphia: L. J. Richards & Co., 1886), 444.

92. Register of Wills, Philadelphia, Letter of Administration, 108 (1793), Vincent M. Pelosi.

93. "Marriages," *Dunlap's American Daily Advertiser,* January 12, 1796; *Notices of Marriages and Deaths in Poulson's American Daily Advertiser, 1791–1799* (Philadelphia: Genealogical Society of Pennsylvania, 1899); Prowell, *History of Camden County,* 444.

94. Placido Dominicus Joseph Marabello, 1796, Petitions for Naturalization, Circuit Court, U.S. District Court for the Eastern District of Pennsylvania, Record Group 21, National Archives, Mid-Atlantic Region, Philadelphia (hereafter, Petitions for Naturalization, RG 21); "Marriage Registers of Holy Trinity Church of Philadelphia, Pennsylvania, A.D. 1791–1799," *Records of the ACHS* 33 (1912): 159.

95. City Directory for 1800, 83; Paxton's City Directory for 1818, 100; "Old Saint Mary's, Philadelphia, Contributors to the Alteration and Improvement of the Church in 1809–10–1," *American Catholic Historical Researches* 13 (1896): 186–92.

96. *Poulson's American Daily Advertiser,* April 28, 1821, 3.

97. Register of Wills, Philadelphia, Will Book, 7 (1821), 67, Placido Domenico Joseph Marabello.

98. In addition to Marabello's will (note 97), see "Legacies and Property of the Corporation of St. Mary's Church," *American Catholic Historical Researches* 11 (1894): 76–80; Martin I. J. Griffin, "Lost Legacies," *American Catholic Historical Researches* 18 (1901): 115–18.

99. Besides his will again, see "Marriage Registers of Holy Trinity Church," 159; City Directory for 1825, 93; *Pennsylvania and New Jersey Marriage and Deaths* (Philadelphia: Genealogical Society of Pennsylvania, n.d.), 82; and "Marble, Elizabeth," *Public Ledger,* December 31, 1838.

100. For general biographical information, see William Chazanoff, *Joseph Ellicott and the Holland Land Company: The Opening of Western New York* (Syracuse, N.Y.: Syracuse University Press, 1970); and Alfonso M. Ressa, *Paolo Busti: A Chapter of American History, 1798–1824* (Philadelphia: National Historical Society of the Order Sons of Italy in America, 1957). See also the letter by Ferdinando Magnani, published in the *Public Ledger,* August 16, 1930, for an earlier source of information used by later biographers. Magnani was an Italian writer and editor who had worked for twenty-five years to obtain recognition of Busti as the founder of Buffalo.

101. Chazanoff, *Ellicott and the Holland Land Company,* 32; 199.

102. Westcott, *History of Philadelphia,* chap. 830.

103. Paul Busti, 1804, Petitions for Naturalization, RG 21.

104. Department of Records, Philadelphia, Deed Book, EF 28, 629–34.

105. See both Chazanoff, *Ellicott and the Holland Land Company,* and Ressa, *Paolo Busti,* for somewhat different views of these matters.

106. *Minutes of the Philadelphia Society for the Promotion of Agriculture,* February 1785–March 1810, 95–98.

107. *Memoirs of the Philadelphia Society for Promoting Agriculture* (PSPA) 2 (1811): 134–36. The recognition that local physiocrats granted to Italian agricultural practices, and their implications for industrial manufacture, is suggested by an anonymous document from the city of Florence also presented before the Society. The document described the cultivation of the wheat "Grano Marzolo," a name derived from the practice of sowing the wheat in the month of March. The straw that grew from this seed was used in the manufacture of "Leghorn hats," straw bonnets that were fashionable in America at the time. See the document titled "On mode of cultivating Florence wheat for Leghorn hats" in the Rare Book Collection, Van Pelt Library, University of Pennsylvania, Philadelphia.

108. *Memoirs of the PSPA* 5:189–91, 203–10, 255–67.

109. Paul Busti, *Daybook or Blockley Farm Journal, 1816–1823,* 5–8, HSP.

110. Ibid., 13.

111. Ibid.

112. Ibid., 29, 35, 38.

113. Ibid., 19, 40.

114. Ibid., 12.

115. Ibid., 40.

116. Department of Records, Philadelphia, County Tax Duplicate, Record Series 1.10, Blockley Township (1822), 254.

117. *Paulson's American Daily,* July 23, 1824, cited in Ressa, *Paolo Busti,* 13.

118. "Old St. Mary's, Philadelphia, Contributors" (see note 95); "Minute Book of St. Mary's Church, 1812–1819," *Records of the ACHS* 42 (1931): 199; *Records of Christ*

Church, Burials 1785–1900, n.d., Genealogical Society of Pennsylvania (GSP) (the GSP collection is held at the Historical Society of Pennsylvania, Philadelphia).

119. Register of Wills, Philadelphia, Will Book, 8 (1824), 87, Paul Busti; within the same file, see also Settlement of Estate (August 25, 1824; November 1, 1825; and December 26, 1826).

120. In 1836, Busti's rural estate in Blockley Township was purchased by the Pennsylvania Hospital. In 1841, the hospital established its Department for the Insane, under the pioneering leadership of Dr. Thomas Kirkbride. Busti's Blockley Retreat had become the site of the Pennsylvania Hospital for Mental and Nervous Diseases. The mansion was maintained for some time as the residence of the physician who served as superintendent of the hospital. In 1844, it became the meeting place for the thirteen physicians who founded what became the American Psychiatric Association. The original building remained standing on the grounds of the hospital until recent years. See Clifford B. Farr, M.D., *Four Papers,* Archives of the Pennsylvania Hospital, n.d.; and Joseph Jackson, *Encyclopedia of Philadelphia,* vol. 2 (Harrisburg: National Historical Association, 1931), 358; and Richard Webster, *Philadelphia Preserved* (Philadelphia: Temple University Press, 1976), 205, 212–13.

121. For the item in the *Federal Gazette,* see Schiavo, *Four Centuries of Italian American History,* 222; for the obituary of the first Mrs. Sartori, see *The True American Commercial Advertiser,* July 9, 1800, in the index of deaths published by Samuel F. Bradford, Philadelphia, held by HSP.

122. On the life and diplomatic career of Giovanni Battista Sartori, see Fanny Morton Peck, "A Roman Consul of the Nineteenth Century," *Historical Records and Studies* 13 (May 1919); Leo F. Stock, "American Consuls to the Papal States, 1797–1870," *Catholic Historical Review* 15 (October 1929), 233–51; Stock, "The Papal Consuls at Philadelphia," *Records of the ACHS* 55 (1944): 178–89; Giovanni Schiavo, *Italian Americans Before the Civil War* (New York: G. P. Putnam's Sons, 1924); Schiavo, *Italian American History,* 2 vols. (New York: Vigo Press, 1947–49); and *The History of Trenton,* anniversary issue (Trenton, N.J., 1929). For the nomination on June 24, 1797, and the confirmation of Sartori two days later, see *Journal of the Executive Proceedings of the Senate* 1 (Washington, D.C., 1828).

123. *A Memoir of the Very Reverend Michael Hurley, D.D., O.S.A. with a Sketch of the History of St. Augustine's Church* (Philadelphia: American Catholic Historical Society, 1886). Hurley was one of two Augustinians who had traveled seventy years earlier to provide religious services at the Sartori estate at Lamberton, before the area had its own church or resident priest.

Although only seventeen years old at the time of her wedding, Henriette had already witnessed some major historical events. After the black uprisings on Santo Domingo, she had been sent to Paris for her safety as well as for an education. With the outbreak of the French Revolution, Henriette fled to the United States with others who shared monarchical sympathies, where she was reunited with her father and brother in Lamberton, New Jersey. See Peck, "Roman Consul," 70–71.

124. Peck, "Roman Consul," 71. These notable refugees included Joseph Bonaparte, once king of Spain; General Jean Victor Moreau, previously one of Napoleon's leading commanders but afterward a bitter rival; and Prince Napoleon Murat, the son of Joachim Murat, king of Naples; and Caroline Bonaparte, Napoleon's sister.

125. Ibid., 67, 74.

126. John Baum, *History of Trenton* (Trenton, N.J., 1871), 237; John J. Cleary, "Trenton in Bygone Days," *Sunday Times-Advertiser,* September 23, 1928.

127. Peck, "Roman Consul," 66–69.

128. "Sacramental Registers—St. Joseph's," *Records of the ACHS* 19 (1908): 326–60; *Records of the ACHS* 19 (1909): 416–54; "Marriage Records—St. Joseph's," *Records of the*

ACHS 20 (1909): 122–92; Department of Records, Philadelphia, Court of Quarter Sessions, Petition for Naturalization, September 23, 1808, Peter Bettini.

129. Peck, "Roman Consul," 74–77.

130. *A Memoir of . . . Hurley,* 212; "Local Affairs—Pleasure Grounds," *Public Ledger,* February 8, 1854, 1.

131. "Obituary: Victor A. Sartori," *Philadelphia Inquirer,* August 31, 1883, 2; "Sudden Death of a Merchant," *Public Ledger,* August 31, 1883, 1.

132. *Pennsylvania Archives,* 2nd ser., vol. 3. See also Westcott, *Names of Persons,* 44, 58–59.

133. Frank George Franklin, *The Legislative History of Naturalization in the United States* (Chicago: University of Chicago Press, 1906); Edward P. Hutchinson, *Legislative History of American Immigration Policy, 1798–1965* (Philadelphia: University of Pennsylvania, 1981).

134. *Pennsylvania Archives,* 2nd ser., 3:67, 76, 78.

135. Department of Records, Philadelphia, Supreme Court of Pennsylvania; Court of Common Pleas, Petitions for Naturalization. See also *Maritime Records, Port of Philadelphia,* sec. 2, Naturalization Records, 1–2, Free Library of Philadelphia.

Chapter 2. The Seeding of Community

1. This discussion is largely based on two sources: Frederic M. Miller, "Philadelphia: Immigrant City," in Gail F. Stern, ed., *Freedom's Doors: Immigrant Ports of Entry to the United States* (Philadelphia: Balch Institute for Ethnic Studies, 1986), 13–24; and Edgar P. Richardson, "The Athens of America, 1800–1825," 208–57, in Russell F. Weigley, ed., *Philadelphia: A 300-Year History* (New York: W. W. Norton & Co., 1982).

2. Richardson, "Athens of America," 208, 239.

3. Matthew Carey, *Reflections on the subject of Emigration from Europe,* 3rd ed. (Philadelphia: Carey & Lea, 1826), iii.

4. Ibid., 25.

5. *Passenger Arrivals at the Port of Philadelphia 1800–1819: The Philadelphia "Baggage Lists,"* Michael H. Tepper, gen. ed. (Baltimore: Genealogical Publishing Co., 1986). The manifest of the *John Burgwin* revealed that the missionary group brought wearing apparel, mechanical tools, Roman habits, and Catholic books for their own use, and bedding for each person. The easily identifiable leader of this group, Father Giovanni Maria Rosati, a native of Milan, would found the Vincentian Mission and Seminary in the Missouri Territory, and later as Joseph Rosati become the first bishop of the Diocese of Saint Louis, Missouri. See Joseph Rosati, C.M., "Recollections of the Establishment of the Congregation of the Mission in the United States of America," trans. and ann. Stafford Poole, C.M., *Vincentian Heritage* 4, no. 2 (1983): 109–39. An index of events pertaining to Rosati's trip and early days in the United States is also available in an invaluable source on early Catholic history, *United States Documents in the Propaganda Fide Archive: A Calendar,* ed. Mathias C. Kieman, O.F.M., and Alexander Wyse, O.F.M. (Washington, D.C.: Academy of American Franciscan History, 1982).

6. *Pennsylvania Archives,* 2nd ser. vol. 17, *Names of Foreigners Who Took the Oath of Allegiance to the Province and State of Pennsylvania, 1727–1775, with the Foreign Arrivals, 1786–1808.*

7. Jacob Mereti, 1815, Declarations of Intention, District Court, U.S. District Court for the Eastern District of Pennsylvania, Record Group 21, Mid-Atlantic Region, Philadelphia (hereafter, Declarations of Intention, RG 21).

8. In the late 1890s, travelers to Sopra la Croce could still find *la Locanda Pittaluga*, an inn identified by a family name that had been conspicuous among Italians in Philadelphia in earlier years. See *Handbook for Travellers*, first part, Northern Italy, 11th remodeled ed. (Leipzig: Karl Baedeker, 1899), 96; *Hand-Book for Travellers in Northern Italy*, 3rd ed. (London: John Murray, 1847). For information on the church itself, as well as on all parishes in Italy, *Elenco Generale delle Parrocchie d'Italia* (Rome, 1924), published by the Vatican to assist priests overseas, is an indispensable source.

9. Unless otherwise noted, the present discussion is based on the record of sacramental ledgers published by the American Catholic Historical Society of Philadelphia. For St. Joseph's, see "Sacramental Registers—St. Joseph's," *Records of the ACHS* 16 (1905): 202–23; 19 (1908): 326–60; 20 (1909): 122–92, 290–341. For Holy Trinity, see "Marriage Registers of Holy Trinity Church of Philadelphia, Pa., A.D. 1791–1799," *Records of the ACHS* 33 (1912); "Marriage Registers of Holy Trinity Church of Philadelphia, Pa., A.D. 1791–1799," ed. with notes by the Rev. Thomas Cooke Middleton, *Records of the ACHS* 24 (1913): 140–61; "Baptismal Registers of Holy Trinity Church of Philadelphia, Pa., A.D. 1790–1795," *Records of the ACHS* 12 (1911): 65–82; "Holy Trinity Baptismal Records— Register Number Two, 1796–1802," ed. the Rev. F. E. Tourscher, O.S.A., *Records of the ACHS* 34 (1923): 151–94; 35 (1924): 159–77; 38 (1927): 168–92. For St. Augustine's, see "Sacramental Registers of Marriages and Baptisms at St. Augustine's, Philadelphia, Pa.," *Records of the ACH,* 13 (1902): 165–210, 497–506. Other useful items include "St. Mary's Graveyard," *Records of the ACHS* 3 (1890–91): 253–94; and Martin I. J. Griffin, "The Rev. Peter Helbron, Second Pastor of Holy Trinity Church, Philadelphia," *Records of the ACHS* 23 (1912): 1–21.

10. *A Memoir of the Very Rev. Michael Hurley, D.D., O.S.A. with a Sketch of the History of St. Augustine's Church* (Philadelphia: American Catholic Historical Society, 1886).

11. *Journal of Common Council,* City of Philadelphia, June 1, 1837, 99; *Public Ledger,* April 4, 1838, 1.

12. *Passenger Arrivals, 1819–1820* (Baltimore: Genealogical Publishing Co., 1967).

13. Register of Wills, Philadelphia, Letter of Administration, 268 (1821), James B. Zanoni.

14. City Directory for 1800, 83; Department of Records, Philadelphia, Court of Quarter Sessions, Petition for Naturalization (September 23, 1808), Anthony Maggi.

15. Register of Wills, Philadelphia, Letter of Administration, 1 (1802), Francis Molinari.

16. George C. Groce and David H. Wallace, *The New York Historical Society's Dictionary of Artists in America, 1564–1860* (New Haven: Yale University Press, 1957), 598. For other sources on Stagi, see Albert T. E. Gardner, *Yankee Stonecutter: The First American School of Sculpture, 1800–1850* (New York: Metropolitan Museum of Art, 1944); Ulrich Thieme and Felix Becker, *Allegemeines Lexikon der bildenden Künstler . . .* (Leipzig, 1907); and Giovanni Schiavo, *Four Centuries of Italian American History* (New York: Vigo Press, 1952), 222.

17. Hogan, *The Prospect of Philadelphia* (1795), 127; City Directory for 1800, 22; City Directory for 1825, 21.

18. "Holy Trinity Baptismal Records . . . ," *Records of the ACHS* 34 (1923): 169; Register of Wills, Philadelphia, Letter of Administration, 1 (1802), Francis Molinari. For the proceedings in which Bosio served as a voucher, see Department of Records, Philadelphia, Court of Quarter Sessions, Petition for Naturalization (June 5, 1804), Dominic Morosi; (September 23, 1808), Antonio Maggi; (May 6, 1826) Giacinto DeAngeli; and Court of Common Pleas, Petition for Naturalization (May 2, 1807), Anthony Poggy; (September 19, 1808), Francis Travella; and (September 21, 1818), Stephano Pichetti.

19. Thompson Westcott, *History of Philadelphia*, chap. 660 (this item is the previously mentioned APS facsimile of the *Sunday Dispatch* series; see chapter 1, note 26). See also the inventory list at the time of Bosio's death, Register of Wills, Philadelphia, Letter of Administration, 376 (1826).

20. J. Thomas Scharf and Thompson Westcott, *History of Philadelphia, 1609–1884* (Philadelphia: L. H. Everts, 1884), 2:878; Westcott, *History of Philadelphia*, chap. 405.

21. Paxton's City Directories for 1813 and 1819; Register of Wills, Philadelphia, Letter of Administration, 376 (1826), Secondo Bosio.

22. Register of Wills, Philadelphia, Letter of Administration, 376 (1826), Secondo Bosio; Burial Records, Board of Health (October 14—December 1826) Collections of the Genealogical Society of Pennsylvania; Poulson's *American Daily Advertiser,* December 21, 1826.

23. *Passenger Arrivals, 1819–1820* (Baltimore: Genealogical Publishing Co., 1967); City Directory for 1925, 41; Members File, APS.

24. All of these names are listed in the *Philadelphia Directory and Stranger's Guide* (1825).

25. Westcott, *History of Philadelphia*, chap. 617. It is surprising to find a period as early as Westcott gave for the appearance of the Italian street musician in the United States. Probably no other writer has assigned a similar date for this aspect of the Italian experience in North America.

26. Ibid., chaps. 668 and 670.

27. Ibid., chap. 671.

28. Ibid., chap. 697.

29. Ibid., chap. 670; Nicholas B. Wainwright, *A Philadelphia Perspective: The Diary of Sidney George Fisher Covering the Years 1834–1871* (Philadelphia: HSP, 1967), 89, 95–96.

30. Westcott, *History of Philadelphia*, chap. 655.

31. Ibid., chap. 668.

32. Ibid., chaps. 666 and 668; H. Glenn Brown and Maude O. Brown, *A Directory of the Book-Arts and Book Trade in Philadelphia in 1820* (New York: New York Public Library, 1950).

33. Schiavo, *Four Centuries of Italian American History,* 176–77. For a more detailed account, see Nicolas Slonimsky in *Baker's Biographical Dictionary of Musicians,* 6th ed. (New York: Schirmer Books, 1978). See also the obituary in the *Public Ledger,* January 10, 1854, where Traetta was erroneously identified as Phil Frajeta.

34. Westcott, *History of Philadelphia*, chap. 672, in which Sega is erroneously identified as James Lega. See also *Memoirs of Lorenzo DaPonte*, trans. Elizabeth Abbott, ed. and ann. Arthur Livingston (Philadelphia: J. B. Lippincott Co., 1929), 420–21, 512. Although published nearly seventy years ago, this book remains an invaluable source on DaPonte's life in general and on his connection to Philadelphia in particular.

35. Westcott, *History of Philadelphia*, chap. 671.

36. *Memoirs of Lorenzo DaPonte*, 368.

37. See Paxton's City Directory for 1819.

38. *Memoirs of Lorenzo DaPonte*, 403–5.

39. Ibid., 406–9.

40. Ibid., 490–91 n. 1. Livingston's biography also describes DaPonte's subsequent experiences in New York City. Through the influence of his friend Clement Moore, DaPonte was appointed Professor of Italian Literature at Columbia College. Instead of a fixed salary, DaPonte was to be compensated directly by the students enrolled in his courses, in the manner of a European docent. After some success in the first year, when no students elected his courses in the following year he attempted to terminate the appointment, but the college

refused to accept his resignation. Although he gave private lessons from his home, DaPonte remained identified as a professor at Columbia until his death in 1838. During his final years, DaPonte also played an active role within the growing cluster of Italians there.

41. Ibid., 490–92 and n. 1.

42. Westcott, *History of Philadelphia,* chaps. 662, 663, and 664.

43. Department of Records, Philadelphia, Mayor's Court, Petition for Naturalization (October 23, 1809), Lawrence Astolfi; Westcott, *History of Philadelphia,* chap. 653; Department of Records, Philadelphia, Petition for Naturalization, Court of Common Pleas (October 27, 1812), Peter Manfridi. Although the actual document for the Manfridi naturalization is missing from the city archives, it appears in a list for the court.

44. *Memoirs of Lorenzo DaPonte,* 368.

45. Westcott, *History of Philadelphia,* chap. 653.

46. Ibid.

47. Ibid., chap. 652.

48. *Memoirs of Lorenzo DaPonte,* 368–69.

49. Westcott, *History of Philadelphia,* chaps. 653–54. Livingston suggested that Astolfi may have returned to his native country; see *Memoirs of Lorenzo DaPonte,* 368 n. 2.

50. Department of Records, Philadelphia, Court of Quarter Sessions, Petition for Naturalization (January 11, 1811), Joseph Diaker; "Sacramental Registers . . . ," *Records of the ACHS* 13 (1902): 503.

51. Westcott, *History of Philadelphia,* chap. 653; City Directory for 1825, 42.

52. Ibid., chap. 655.

53. Ibid., chap. 656.

54. Ibid., chap. 700.

55. Ibid., chap. 802.

56. Ibid., chap. 808.

57. Groce and Wallace, *Dictionary of Artists in America,* 621. See also Anna Wells Rutledge, ed., *Cumulative Record of Exhibition Catalogues: Pennsylvania Academy of the Fine Arts, 1800–1814* (Philadelphia: APS, 1955); and Westcott, *History of Philadelphia,* chap. 587.

58. Groce and Wallace, *Dictionary of Artists in America,* 534; *Journal of Common Council,* City of Philadelphia, May 3, 1838; Rutledge, *Cumulative Record,* 181. See also Thieme and Becker, *Allegemeines Lexikon.*

59. Groce and Wallace, *Dictionary of Artists in America,* 496.

60. Ibid., 440; Westcott, *History of Philadelphia,* chap. 808.

61. *A Memoir of the Very Rev. Michael Hurley, D.D., O.S.A.,* 171; *Population Schedules of the Seventh Census of the United States, 1850,* M432, National Archives, Mid-Atlantic Region, Philadelphia, reel 821, p. 47 (hereafter, *Population Schedules, 1850* with reel and page number separated by a colon, as, e.g., 821:47), National Archives, Mid-Atlantic Region, Philadelphia; *Public Ledger,* August 9, 1853, 2. While the 1850 federal census listed Uberti at the age of forty-five, Groce and Wallace locate him in the 1860 census at the age of fifty-two. See Groce and Wallace, *Dictionary of Artists in America,* 641.

62. Groce and Wallace, *Dictionary of Artists in America,* 602; Westcott, *History of Philadelphia,* chap. 808; City Directories for 1823 and 1840.

63. Westcott, *History of Philadelphia,* chap. 808.

64. Ibid.

65. Groce and Wallace, *Dictionary of Artists in America,* 501; Westcott, *History of Philadelphia,* chap. 809.

66. Groce and Wallace, *Dictionary of Artists in America,* 501; Westcott, *History of Philadelphia,* chap. 804; Schiavo, *Four Centuries of Italian American History,* 227–28. For

a partial list of Persico's works in exhibitions at the Pennsylvania Academy of the Fine Arts, see Rutledge, *Cumulative Record,* 171.

67. Groce and Wallace, *Dictionary of Artists in America,* 501; Westcott, *History of Philadelphia,* chaps. 806, 807, and 679; City Directory for 1825, 110.

68. Groce and Wallace, *Dictionary of Artists in America,* 501.

69. Matthew Baignell, *A Concise History of American Painting and Sculpture* (New York: Harper & Row, 1984), 63–64.

70. Groce and Wallace, *Dictionary of Artists in America,* 8; Westcott, *History of Philadelphia,* chap. 804; Brown and Brown, *Directory of the Book Arts,* 13; Paxton's City Directory for 1813; Kite's City Directory for 1814; Department of Records, Philadelphia, Court of Common Pleas, Petition for Naturalization (September 22, 1810), Pietro Ancora. The date of 1789 in the Works Progress Administration (WPA) Index of Naturalizations for Ancora's declaration of intention is probably wrong, because no other record of that document can be found and there was no federal naturalization procedure available until after the Act of 1790. See also Department of Records, Philadelphia, Board of Health, Death Registers (December 1811), Record Group 37.

71. Groce and Wallace, *Dictionary of Artists in America,* 8; Westcott, *History of Philadelphia,* chaps. 804 and 806; Brown and Brown, *Directory of the Book Arts,* 17; *Mantle Fielding's Dictionary of American Painters, Sculptors, and Engravers,* comp. James F. Carr (New York: James F. Carr, 1965); City Directory for 1825, 11.

72. Westcott, *History of Philadelphia,* chap. 604.

73. See Rutledge, *Cumulative Record,* 15; Groce and Wallace, *Dictionary of Artists in America,* 8.

74. Letter to the Directors of the Pennsylvania Academy of Fine Arts, March 17, 1828, APS, III/3F8-G12. See also a communication from Peter Ancora in *Journal of Common Council,* City of Philadelphia, June 8, 1837, 101 .

75. "St. Mary's Graveyard," *Records of the ACHS* 3 (1890–91): 254; *Public Ledger— Surnames, 1836–1843,* Genealogical Society of Pennsylvania (GSP), n.d.

76. Groce and Wallace, *Dictionary of Artists in America,* 450. See also Agnes Addison Gilchrist, "The Philadelphia Exchange: William Strickland, Architect," in *Historic Philadelphia: From the Founding Until the Early Nineteenth Century,* part 1 of *Transactions of the APS* 43 (1953): 86–95; Nicola Monachesi, 1844, Petition for Naturalization, RG 21. The Hughes letter is described by Martin I. J. Griffin in "History of the Church of Saint John the Evangelist, Philadelphia," *Records of the ACHS* 20 (1909): 350–405. See also *Population Schedules, 1850,* 817:435

77. Gilchrist, "Philadelphia Exchange: William Strickland," 91; Wainwright, *A Philadelphia Perspective,* 44, 76; Wainwright, "The Age of Nicholas Biddle, 1825–1841," in Weigley, *Philadelphia,* 288.

78. Griffin in "History of the Church of Saint John the Evangelist," 363–64; Schiavo, *Four Centuries of Italian American History,* 231.

79. Gilchrist, "Philadelphia Exchange: William Strickland," 91; Nicola Monachesi, "To the building committee of the Philadelphia Exchange," September 4, 1834; reply to Monachesi, September 4, 1834, Claude Unger Collection, HSP.

80. Wainwright, "Age of Nicholas Biddle," 290–91.

81. Gilchrist, "Philadelphia Exchange: William Strickland," 91; "St. Joseph's Church," *The Universe,* December 15, 1866, HSP.

82. "Embellishments of St. Augustine's Church," *Public Ledger,* September 29, 1848, 1.

83. Michael H. Cross, "Catholic Choirs and Choir Music in Philadelphia," *Records of the ACHS* 2 (1886–88): 115–26.

84. *Population Schedules, 1850.*

85. This portrait was reproduced and it appears in *Memoirs of Lorenzo DaPonte* through the courtesy of its owner at that time, identified as Ellery O. Anderson, Esq.

86. Gilchrist, "Philadelphia Exchange: William Strickland," 91.

87. Groce and Wallace, *Dictionary of Artists in America,* 10–11, 240, 338. See also entry under Tardella, January 23, 1831, in *Pennsylvania, New Jersey Marriages and Deaths,* GSP, n.d.

88. Westcott, *History of Philadelphia,* chaps. 417, 794.

89. Ibid., chaps. 417, 808.

90. City Directory for 1800, 151; *Philadelphia Directory and Stringer's Guide* (1825), 74; Brown and Brown, *Directory of the Book Arts,* 60; "Sacramental Registers . . . at St. Augustine's . . . ," *Records of the ACHS* 13 (1902): 359; Rutledge, *Cumulative Record,* 109; Groce and Wallace, *Dictionary of Artists in America,* 338.

91. This account of the Inglesi affair is based on the following sources: Westcott, *History of Philadelphia,* chap. 557; Martin I. J. Griffin, "Life of Bishop Conwell," *Records of the ACHS* 27 (1915): 227–49; 27 (1916): 74–87; 28 (1917): 64–84; Joseph L. J. Kirlin, *Catholicity in Philadelphia* (Philadelphia: John J. McVey, 1909); Francis E. Tourscher, *The Hogan Schism and Trustee Troubles in St. Mary's Church Philadelphia, 1820–1829* (Philadelphia: Peter Reilly Co., 1930); "The Trustees Minute Book at St. Mary's Philadelphia," *Records of the ACHS* 49 (1938): 334–69. It also relies upon the discussion of Inglesi in Philadelphia within the broader context of Catholic history, provided by an indispensable recent study, Dale B. Light's *Rome and the New Republic: Conflict and Community in Philadelphia Catholicism Between the Revolution and the Civil War* (Notre Dame: University of Notre Dame Press, 1996), 172–74, 179–80, 182, 197.

92. For Inglesi's life before Philadelphia, see the excellent summary by Giovanni Pizzorusso in the section on the Archivio della Congregazione de Propaganda Fide, in Giovanni Pizzorusso and Matteo Sanfilippo, "Fonti ecclesiastiche romane per lo studio dell'emigrazione italiana in Nord America, 1642–1922," *Studi Emigrazione* 33 (December 1996): 621 n. 5. I am indebted to Gianfausto Rosoli, Director of the Centro Emigrazione in Rome, for bringing this special issue of its journal to my attention.

93. Griffin, "Life of Bishop Conwell," 248.

94. Angelo Inglesi, *An Address to the Public of Philadelphia: Containing, a Vindication of the Character and Conduct of the Reverend Mr. Inglesi from Charges and Strictures Lately Reported and Published against Him by the Reverend Mr. Harold* (Philadelphia, 1824).

95. Kirlin, *Catholicity in Philadelphia,* 238–39.

96. These figures are derived mainly from the following indexes: for city courts, Court of Common Pleas (1793–1862) and Quarter Sessions Court (1802–60), both available at the Department of Records, Philadelphia; for federal courts, Circuit and District Court of the United States, County of Philadelphia (1812–59), National Archives, Mid-Atlantic Region, Philadelphia; for the Eastern District of the State Supreme Court, *Maritime Records, Port of Philadelphia,* sec. 2, Naturalization Records, vols. 1–2 (1789–1880), Free Library of Philadelphia. The latter item, sometimes referred to as the *WPA Index of Naturalizations,* compiled by the Works Progress Administration, is a comprehensive inventory that includes city, state, and federal courts. The totals are based almost entirely on petitions for naturalization, but they do include some cases in which only a declaration of intention was filed. They also include about ten cases found in the archives of federal courts that do not appear in city records.

97. "Sacramental Registers . . . St. Augustine's," *Records of the ACHS* 13 (1902): 497–506; Department of Records, Philadelphia, Court of Quarter Sessions, Petition for Naturalization (January 11, 1811), Joseph Diacker; City Directory for 1825, 42.

98. City Directory for 1825, 105; "Marriage Registers—St. Joseph's," *Records of the ACHS* 20 (1909): 304; Department of Records, Philadelphia, Court of Common Pleas Petition for Naturalization (October 9, 1828), Joseph A. Oliver. See also marriage of Anthony Pizzini and Catharine Maillot, "Sacramental Registers—St. Joseph's," *Records of the ACHS* 20 (1909): 316; "St. Mary's Graveyard," *Records of the ACHS* 3 (1890–91): 227.

99. *Pennsylvania Archives,* 2nd ser., 78; Schiavo, *Four Centuries of Italian American History,* 156; "Sacramental Registers—St. Joseph's," *Records of the ACHS* 16 (1905): 215. Schiavo notes that the sponsor at the New York baptism was Philip Filicchi, who would become not only a benefactor of Mother Seton's religious efforts but also the first consul general of the United States at Leghorn in 1795.

100. "Baptismal Records of Holy Trinity Church," *Records of the ACHS* 22 (1911): 65–83; and 38 (1927): 168–92; "Holy Trinity Baptismal Records, Register Number Two, 1796–1802," ed. Rev. F. E. Tourscher, O.S.A., *Records of the ACHS* 34 (1923): 151–94; "Sacramental Records—St. Joseph's," *Records of the ACHS* 19 (1909): 326–60, 416–454; 20 (1909): 122–92; "Sacramental Records . . . St. Augustine's," *Records of the ACHS* 13 (1902): 165–210, 497–506; *Memoir of the Very Rev. Michael Hurley* (1886).

101. Register of Wills, Philadelphia, Letter of Administration, 182 (1807), Pieter Purkett, alias Pietro Pachette; and Wills, 197 (1847), Andrew Pichetti. For similar information on Molinari, Mussi, and Busti, see the preceding chapter.

102. See the entries in Rutledge, *Cumulative Record,* for Monachesi, Riboni, and Persico.

103. Register of Wills, Philadelphia, Wills, 576 (1868), Giacinto DeAngeli.

104. Westcott, *History of Philadelphia,* chap. 598.

105. Ibid., chap. 664.

Chapter 3. The City as Incubator

1. "Died of His Wounds," *Public Ledger,* August 1, 1843.

2. For a general discussion of Philadelphia in this period, see Nicholas B. Wainwright, "The Age of Nicholas Biddle, 1825–1841," in Russell F. Weigley, ed., *Philadelphia: A 300-Year History* (New York: W. W. Norton & Co., 1982), 258–306; Elizabeth M. Geffen, "Industrial Development and Social Crisis, 1841–1854," in the same volume, 307–62; and Sam Bass Warner Jr., *The Private City* (Philadelphia: University of Pennsylvania Press, 1968).

3. Richard Saul Wurman and John Andrew Gallery, *Man-Made Philadelphia: A Guide to Its Physical and Cultural Environment* (Cambridge, Mass.: MIT Press, 1972).

4. Ibid., 66; Wainwright, "Age of Nicholas Biddle," 280–81; Geffen, "Industrial Development and Social Crisis," 309.

5. Warner, *The Private City,* 127; Geffen, "Industrial Development and Social Crisis," 309.

6. Frederic M. Miller, "Philadelphia: Immigrant City," in Gail Stern, ed., *Freedom's Doors: Immigrant Ports of Entry to the United States* (Philadelphia: Balch Institute for Ethnic Studies, 1986), 13–24; W. J. Bromwell, *History of Immigration* (New York: Redfield, 1856), 13–18, 21–125.

7. Elliot R. Barkan, "New York City: Immigrant Depot, Immigrant City," in Stern, *Freedom's Doors,* 1–12; Miller, "Philadelphia: Immigrant City," 15; *Philadelphia as It Is* (Philadelphia: Lindsay & Blakiston, 1852), 19.

8. "Deaths at Sea," *Public Ledger,* November 21, 1853, 2; "The Plague Ships," *Public Ledger,* December 6, 1853, 1.

9. "Deaths at Sea," *Public Ledger,* November 21, 1853, 2; untitled editorial, *Public Ledger,* November 28, 1856, 2.

10. "Things in New York," *Public Ledger,* February 13, 1854, 1.

11. "Shameful Imposition on Emigrants in New York," *Public Ledger,* December 12, 1853, 1; "Treatment of Emigrants in New York," *Public Ledger,* December 29, 1853, 1; "Immigrants Defrauded," *Public Ledger,* January 11, 1854, 1.

12. "Frauds upon Emigrants," *Public Ledger,* February 24, 1848, 2; "New Society," *Public Ledger,* March 10, 1848, 2; "The Emigrants' Friend Society," *Public Ledger,* April 6, 1848, 2; "Emigrants," *Public Ledger,* April 6, 1848, 2; "The Emigration Frauds," *Public Ledger,* December 16, 1853, 1; "The Emigrant Society's Boarding House," *Public Ledger,* November 3, 1853, 1.

13. Miller, "Philadelphia: Immigrant City," 14; Geffen, "Industrial Development and Social Crisis," 309.

14. "Departure of the Osceola," *Public Ledger,* January 17, 1849, 3. In addition to the foreign-born who passed through on their way west, many Philadelphia natives were joining in the same migration. For an account of this aspect of westward movement, see "The California Emigrants," *Public Ledger,* January 16, 1849, 2.

15. Geffen, "Industrial Development and Social Crisis," 309; *Statistics of the United States in 1860: The Eighth Census* (Washington, D.C., 1866), lvii.

16. Geffen, "Industrial Development and Social Crisis," 326–27.

17. *Philadelphia as It Is,* 20.

18. Geffen, "Industrial Development and Social Crisis," 307.

19. Ibid., 335–39.

20. *Philadelphia as It Is,* 15–16.

21. Geffen, "Industrial Development and Social Crisis," 309–15; Warner, *The Private City,* 49–62.

22. Geffen, "Industrial Development and Social Crisis," 322–23; *Philadelphia as It Is,* 19.

23. Russell F. Weigley, "The Border City in Civil War," in Weigley, *Philadelphia,* 379–81.

24. *Philadelphia as It Is,* 15.

25. Geffen, "Industrial Development and Social Crisis," 309–10, 315.

26. *Philadelphia as It Is,* 17.

27. Weigley, *Philadelphia,* 375.

28. Warner, *The Private City,* 59.

29. Geffen, "Industrial Development and Social Crisis," 315; Weigley, *Philadelphia,* 373; and Warner, *The Private City,* 52–53.

30. *Philadelphia as It Is,* 18.

31. Geffen, "Industrial Development and Social Crisis," 335–36.

32. Ibid., 317–18.

33. *Philadelphia as It Is,* 17.

34. Geffen, "Industrial Development and Social Crisis," 327–39, 348–50; Warner, *The Private City,* 64–66; 79–98.

35. Geffen, "Industrial Development and Social Crisis," 309, 318, 352–53; Warner, *The Private City,* 139.

36. "Christmas Rioting," *Public Ledger,* December 27, 1848, 2.

37. Geffen, "Industrial Development and Social Crisis," 350–56.

38. Ibid., 346–48; Weigley, *Philadelphia,* 368, 371–72. For more extensive examinations of the fire companies and the gangs, see Bruce Laurie, "Fire Companies and Gangs in Southwark," 71–87, in Allen F. Davis and Mark H. Haller, eds., *The Peoples of Philadelphia:*

A History of Ethnic Groups and Lower-Class Life, 1790–1940; and David R. Johnson, "Crime Patterns in Philadelphia, 1840–1870," 89–110, in the same volume.

39. Warner, *The Private City,* 123–37; Wainwright, "The Age of Nicholas Biddle," 295–96.

40. Geffen, "Industrial Development and Social Crisis," 353–54; Warner, *The Private City,* 140–43.

41. Warner, *The Private City,* 143–51.

42. "Done Up in Short Metre," *Public Ledger,* January 15, 1848, 3.

43. Geffen, "Industrial Development and Social Crisis," 359–60; Warner, *The Private City,* 94–95; Weigley, *Philadelphia,* 368–70; Howard O. Sprogle, *The Philadelphia Police* (Philadelphia, 1887), 102. Although somewhat dated, Sprogle remains an important source on the early history of the police force.

44. *Philadelphia Merchant: The Diary of Thomas Cope, 1800–1851,* ed. with introduction and appendixes by Eliz Cope Harrison (South Bend, Ind.: Gateway Editions, 1978), 409–10.

45. Ibid., 437.

46. Ibid., 441.

47. Ibid., 446, 449.

48. Ibid., 457.

49. Nicholas B. Wainwright, ed., *A Philadelphia Perspective: The Diary of Sidney George Fisher Covering the Years 1834–1871* (Philadelphia: HSP, 1967), 177.

50. Ibid., 195.

51. *Journal of Select Council,* City of Philadelphia, March 26, 1846, 75; *Journal of Common Council,* City of Philadelphia, March 26, 1846, 87; "Sanitary Agents," *Public Ledger,* December 18, 1848, 2.

52. *Report of the Committee on Police, Journal of Common Council,* Appendix 13, City of Philadelphia, June 14, 1855, 41–57.

53. Ibid., 43–44.

54. Mayor's Annual Message, May 16, 1855, R. T. Conrad, Mayor, *Journal of Select Council,* City of Philadelphia (1955), 2, app. 8, 15–16.

55. Warner, *The Private City,* 91–98; Weigley, *Philadelphia,* 371–72.

56. Geffen, "Industrial Development and Social Crisis," 349–50.

57. Weigley, *Philadelphia,* 383–94.

58. Ibid., 396–411.

59. Ibid., 411–16.

60. Warner, *The Private City,* 61–62, 99–123.

61. A consul is primarily a commercial official who attends to mercantile interests and the welfare of citizens of a nation in a foreign location.

62. Westcott, *History of Philadelphia* (see chapter 1, note 26), chap. 704.

63. Giovanni Schiavo, *Four Centuries of Italian American History* (New York: Vigo Press, 1952), 149. According to Schiavo, this item is a manuscript in the Library of Congress.

64. Ibid., 150.

65. Gaetano Ferro and Adele Maiello, "Un Secolo e Mezzo di Flussi Migratori," *L'Emigrazione nelle Americhe dalla Provincia di Genova, 1, Questioni Generali e Introduttive* (Bologna: Patron Editore, 1990), 105.

66. National Archives, Department of State files, Cicognani to John Quincy Adams (December 31, 1824), cited in Leo F. Stock, "The Papal Consuls of Philadelphia," *Records of the ACHS 55* (1944): 180.

67. In ibid., 181.

68. *Register of Vessels from Foreign Ports, 1825–1848,* National Archives, Mid-Atlantic Region, Philadelphia.

69. "Sacramental Registers—St. Joseph's," *Records of the ACHS* 20 (1909): 304.

70. Jasper Ridley, *Garibaldi* (New York: Viking Press, 1974), 3.

71. John Parris, *The Lion of Caprera* (New York: David McKay Co., 1962), 13–14; David Larg, *Giuseppe Garibaldi* (Port Washington, N.Y.: Kennikat Press, 1970), 8–9; George Macaulay Trevelyan, *Garibaldi's Defense of the Roman Republic* (London: Longmans, Green & Co., 1912), 9–15.

72. Register of Wills, Philadelphia, Letter of Administration, 337 (1835), Angelo Garibaldi.

73. In the early twentieth century the stone was reported to be at a marbleyard near Holy Cross Cemetery in Yeadon, Pennsylvania. By 1933 it was in the museum of the American Catholic Historical Society of Philadelphia. Today, it seems to have disappeared entirely. See Martin I. J. Griffin, "History of the Church of St. John the Evangelist, Philadelphia," *Records of the ACHS* 20 (1909): 380–81; William J. Lallou, "The Vaults in St. John's Graveyard," *Records of the ACHS* 13 (1912): 212–48; "List of Historic Treasures in the Museum of the American Catholic Historical Society," *Records of the ACHS* 44 (June 1933): 97–117.

74. Ridley, *Garibaldi,* 3; Parris, *Lion of Caprera,* 118.

75. Giovanni Battista Vitalba, 1825, Petitions for Naturalization, RG 21.

76. S. Eugene Scalia, "Federico Confalonieri in America," *Italy America Monthly,* March 15, 1934, 10–13, and April 15, 1934, 12–15; Joseph Rossi, *The Image of America in Mazzini's Writings* (Madison: University of Wisconsin Press, 1954), 13.

77. "Albinola is now at Philadelphia in the position of clerk to the attorney, Mr. Castillia, in the well-known business of the estate of Mussi." This letter, dated July 24, 1837, to Borsieri, also a lawyer, in Princeton, New Jersey, appears in *Carteggio del Conte F. Confalonieri* (Milano: Società per la storia del Risorgimento Italiano, 1913), 733. The *fuorusciti* who found their way to Boston have been discussed by S. Eugene Scalia, "Figures of the Risorgimento in America: Ignazio Batolo, alias Pietro Bachi and Pietro D'Alessandro," *Italica* 42, no. 4 (1965): 311–57.

78. This information comes from a newspaper clipping of an article originally published more than sixty years ago, provided by the late Professor S. Eugene Scalia, formerly Professor of Italian at Brooklyn College. See Kenneth McKenzie, "McKenzie Presents Letter Written by an Italian Exile in Princeton," *Princeton Herald,* January 19, 1934.

79. Dennis Mack Smith, *Mazzini* (New Haven: Yale University Press, 1994).

80. Rossi, *Image of America,* 19.

81. Ibid., 24–25.

82. "Italian Without a Master," *Public Ledger,* February 22, 1848, 2. For a typical example of the frequent reviews of the highly popular productions of Italian opera at this time, see "The Opera," *Public Ledger,* October 16, 1848, 1. While the performances themselves were widely enjoyed by the public, the newspaper reviews could be critical.

83. Harry Hearder, *Italy: A Short History* (Cambridge: Cambridge University Press, 1990), 171–72; Howard R. Marraro, *American Opinion on the Unification of Italy, 1846–1861* (New York: Columbia University Press, 1932), 4–14; "Notices—Italy—Public Meeting," *Public Ledger,* January 6, 1848, 1; "Testimonial of Respect to Pope Pius IX," *Public Ledger,* January 7, 1848, 3.

84. "The Mass Meeting of Germans," *Public Ledger,* April 10, 1848, 2; "The Great Mass Meeting," *Public Ledger,* April 19, 1848, 2; "Liberty for Europe—Immense Demonstration," *Public Ledger,* April 25, 1848, 2; "Mr. Hecker and the Germans," *Public Ledger,* October 12, 1848, 2. The Philadelphia meeting was originally scheduled for April 20, but wet grounds postponed it until April 24.

85. "Stability of Republicanism in France and Its Effects in Europe," *Public Ledger,* May 17, 1848, 2. The proposal by the *Public Ledger* expressed an American sense of republicanism, but it was also congruent with, and possibly even derived from, the views of Vincenzo Gioberti, the exiled Turinese priest and patriot who had argued in his 1843 book, *Il Primato Morale e Civile degli Italiani* (The Civil and Moral Primacy of the Italians), that an independent and unified confederation of princes could be formed with the Pope as its president.

86. "A Word for Italy," *Public Ledger,* June 30, 1849, 1.

87. "Statistics of Cholera," *Public Ledger,* July 9, 1849, 2.

88. "Meeting of French Citizens," *Public Ledger,* July 10, 1849, 2.

89. "Heavy Penalty," *Public Ledger,* July 2, 1841, 2.

90. "Died of His Wounds," *Public Ledger,* August 1, 1843, 2.

91. "Brutality," *Public Ledger,* September 19, 1848, 2.

92. "Declaration of War by Southwark Against the World," *Public Ledger,* May 13, 1848, 2.

93. *Hand-Book for Travellers in Northern Italy . . . ,* 3rd ed. (London: John Murray, 1847), 89.

Chapter 4. Shaping a New Life: Census, Parish, and Courtroom

1. The discussion in this section is based on documents in *Despatches from the United States Ministers to the Italian States, 1832–1906,* reel 6, National Archives, Mid-Atlantic Region.

2. Nathaniel Niles to N. M. Moro, February 18, 1850, in ibid.

3. Nathaniel Niles to John M. Clayton, February 24, 1850, in ibid.

4. Ibid.

5. Ibid.

6. Ibid., Enclosure B. D'Azeglio had written: "L'Europe en est arrivée à ce point qu'il n'est plus possible de s'aveugler sur les consequences de la position actuelle et qu'il indispensable de prendre un part."

7. See Salvatore Saladino, "Parliamentary Politics in the Liberal Era, 1861 to 1914," 29; and Denis Mack Smith, "Regionalism," 135–36, both in Edward R. Tannenbaum and Emiliana P. Noether, eds., *Modern Italy: A Topical History Since 1861* (New York: New York University Press, 1974).

8. The woman listed after the man's name in these cases is never clearly identified as his wife. Similarly, neither are the relationships of other individuals in the household unit specified. It was not until the tenth census of the United States, in 1880, that the actual relationship of each person to the head of the family or the household was given. In the absence of the clear specification of relationships, it is necessary to make inferences from the information provided about each individual in attempting to reconstruct family and household units. The first name given can generally be assumed to have been the head of the household. When the next line gives a first name, with a blank line drawn in place of a surname, if the age and sex are appropriate, it is feasible to assume that the second individual is the spouse of the first. If a similar format gives much younger ages, it is logical to assume that these are children of the latter. But there are numerous anomalies, and each unit must be carefully considered.

9. See George C. Groce and David H. Wallace, *The New York Historical Society's Dictionary of Artists in America, 1564–1860* (New Haven: Yale University Press, 1957), 635, provided first names as Santonio and Genoz; they also made these inferences about family relationships. See also *Population Schedules, 1850,* M432, 813:431.

10. Ibid., 814:48.

11. Ibid., 821:305.

12. City Directory for 1825, 31; Groce and Wallace, *Dictionary of Artists in America,* 128, 161; "Married . . . ," *Public Ledger,* June 25, 1853, 2. Groce and Wallace probably relied on the manuscript census for their information, but they appear to have read the same entries quite differently than we have at points.

13. *Population Schedules, 1850,* 821:186; St. Mary's Church, Baptismal Register, January 19, 1840. Zanona was probably an erroneous recording of Zanone, a family name that first appeared among the arrivals from Santa Maria di Prato.

14. This newspaper item was found as a clipping inserted into the death register in the rectory of St. Mary Magdalen de Pazzi Parish. The newspaper in which it was published was not identified. The item accompanied the entry in the register for Emanuel Vernazzano.

15. Department of Records, Philadelphia, Court of Common Pleas, Petition for Naturalization (October 8, 1844), Joseph Mereto; State Tax Assessor's *Ledger,* Middle Ward (1840); McElroy's City Directory for 1842, 181; and for 1843; City Directory for 1847.

16. *Population Schedules, 1850,* 814:81, Ninth Ward, 63; *Population Schedules of the Eighth Census of the United States, 1860,* M653, National Archives, Mid-Atlantic Region, Philadelphia, 1159:63 (hereafter, *Population Schedules, 1860*); City Directory for 1875, 1053; Register of Wills, Philadelphia, Letter of Administration (1881), 494, Joseph R. Mereto.

17. *Population Schedules, 1850,* 813:287; Herman LeRoy Collins, *Philadelphia: A Story of Progress* (New York: Lewis Historical Publishing Co., 1941), 4:468.

18. *Population Schedules, 1850,* Byberry (809:230), Kit (809:294), Kiddice (51:96). It is unfortunately not feasible to include females as easily in this discussion, because of the possibility that their names had been changed by marriage. These cases, nevertheless, show the need to find more valid techniques than relying on any attempt to recognize the origins of individuals and families through surnames.

19. "State of Italy," *Public Ledger,* March 24, 1853, 1.

20. "The Independence of Italy," *Public Ledger,* November 9, 1853, 2.

21. "Austrian Rule in Italy," *Public Ledger,* January 20, 1859, 2. By the spring and summer of 1859, articles of this sort were appearing nearly every day in city newspapers.

22. "The Sardinian Line of Steamships," *Public Ledger,* June 4, 1853, 2.

23. Ibid.; "By the Pilot Line," *Public Ledger,* November 2, 1853, 2.

24. "Varieties," *Public Ledger,* June 6, 1853, 1.

25. "New Catholic Church," *Public Ledger,* June 18, 1853, 1; "Things in New York," *Public Ledger,* June 25, 1853, 1. For a much later consideration of the Bedini visit, see "Gaetano Bedini," *Historical Researches and Studies, United States Catholic Historical Society* 23 (1933): 87–170.

26. Two early editions of his lectures are the principal sources of information on Gavazzi. See *Father Gavazzi's Lectures in New York . . . , the Life of Father Gavazzi, corrected and authorized by himself, together with reports of his addresses in Italian . . . ,* trans. and rev. J. DeMarguerettes (New York: Dewitt & Davenport, 1853); and *The Lectures of Father Gavazzi as delivered in New York . . . the Life of Gavazzi by G. B. Nicolini* (New York: M. W. Dodd, 1854). See also the 1933 article, "Gaetano Bedini" (previously cited in note 25), 99–108. A new scholarly study of Bedini's life and ideas is long overdue.

27. "The Canadian Riots—Account by Gavazzi of the Attack upon Him," *Public Ledger,* June 13, 1853, 1; "The Gavazzi Riot," *Public Ledger,* June 13, 1853, 2. In a few

days, the disturbances in Montreal died away. After he returned to Italy, Gavazzi served as a chaplain with the troops of Giuseppe Garibaldi and, after the struggle for independence ended, founded the evangelical Free Christian Church in Rome.

28. For an excellent examination of Bedini's visit to the United States and its implications for American Catholicism, see Dale B. Light's *Rome and the New Republic: Conflict and Community in Philadelphia Catholicism Between the Revolution and the Civil War* (Notre Dame: University of Notre Dame Press, 1996), 322–24, 329.

29. "Gaetano Bedini," 87–170. For contemporary accounts, see "Great Excitement in Cincinnati—The Pope's Nuncio Mobbed by 500 Germans—Conflict with the Police—Sixty Persons Arrested—Nine Persons Shot—One Dead," *Public Ledger,* December 28, 1853, 3. For the West Virginia episode, see "Bedini at Wheeling," *Public Ledger,* January 12, 1854, 1.

30. "Bedini at Wheeling," *Public Ledger,* January 12, 1854, 1.

31. "Things in New York," *Public Ledger,* January 21, 1854, 3. Subsequent articles in the same month provided details on these developments.

32. The public in Philadelphia was informed almost daily of these events. See the regular feature "Things in New York," in the *Public Ledger,* January 30—February 2 and 3–4, 1854.

33. For a note on the Neumann letter to Bedini, see "Gaetano Bedini." For a description of the Philadelphia protest, see "Notices—Bedini and the Senate," *Public Ledger,* February 11, 1854, 1; and "Local Affairs—The Anti-Bedini Demonstration," *Public Ledger,* February 13, 1854, 1.

34. "Meeting in Favor of Hungarian Independence," *Public Ledger,* July 13, 1859, 2.

35. This number was given in an article on Bishop Neumann's efforts on behalf of Italians in the city, published in a German-language Catholic newspaper, *Katholische Kirchen-Zeitung,* October 14, 1852, cited many years later by the Rev. John F. Byrne, "The Redemptorists in America," *Records of the ACHS* 43 (1932): 48.

36. John Nepomucene Neumann, Pastoral Letter to the Reverend Clergy, October 2, 1859, HSP, Wg 699, vol. 2.

37. J. Thomas Scharf and Thompson Westcott, *History of Philadelphia, 1609–1884* (Philadelphia: L. H. Everts & Co., 1884), 2:1384. The article on Catholicism in the city was written by Martin I. J. Griffin.

38. Robert F. Foerster, *The Italian Emigration of Our Times* (Cambridge: Harvard University Press, 1924), 330.

39. "Church for the Italians," *Catholic Herald,* October 21, 1852, 2.

40. "New Catholic Church," *Public Ledger,* June 18, 1853, 1. Further information on the history of the parish is in the well-detailed commemorative publication entitled *Souvenir and Bouquet* (Philadelphia, 1911).

41. In later years, the growth of Italian population in the area, especially from Southern Italy, required the founding of another national parish, Our Lady of Good Counsel, located even closer to St. Paul's. Within a few more years, St. Paul's itself would become, "de facto," an Italian parish by the ethnic composition of its membership.

42. *Hand-Book for Travellers in Northern Italy* (London: John Murray, 1847), 111–12; *Italy: Handbook for Travellers* (Leipzig: Karl Baedeker, 1899), 96.

43. Foerster, *Italian Emigration of Our Times,* 5. Migration from the province of Genoa has been extensively examined in its demographic, economic, political, and other social aspects in a series of excellent monographs under the general title *Geografia e organizzazione dello sviluppo territoriale,* under the auspices of the Istituto di Studi Economici, Università degli Studi di Genova, Facoltà di Scienze Politiche. The most relevant section of this series is "Viaggi e viaggiatori," in which four volumes in particular are indispensable to the student of emigration from the region. The first three volumes, all edited by Gaetano Ferro and titled *L'emigrazione nelle Americhe dalla Provincia di Genova,* are subtitled as follows: vol. 1, *Questioni generali e introduttive;* vol. 2, *La parte occidentale della provincia e il capoluogo;*

and vol. 3, *La parte orientale della provincia;* and the last volume, vol. 4, is edited by Adele Maiello, and subtitled *Questioni di storia sociale* (Bologna: Patron Editore, 1990–92).

44. For a discussion of this immigration by an Italian scholar, see Maria Elisabetta Bianchi Tonizzi, "Il Movimento dell' Emigrazione nel Porto di Genova dalla Metà dell' Ottocento agli Anni Trenta del Nostro Secolo," in Maiello, 21–42.

45. *Hand-Book for Travellers in Northern Italy,* 90.

46. Ibid., 101.

47. Cited in Howard Marraro, "Italians in New York in the Eighteen Fifties," *New York History* 30 (1949): 198.

48. Robert Ernst, *Immigrant Life in New York City, 1825–1863* (New York: King's Crown Press, Columbia University, 1949).

49. Giovanni Schiavo, *Four Centuries of Italian American History* (New York: Vigo Press, 1952), 271.

50. Ernst, *Immigrant Life,* 123–29.

51. "Things in New York," *Public Ledger,* January 21, 1859, 2.

52. "New York Italians," *Public Ledger,* May 9, 1859, 2.

53. Ernst, *Immigrant Life,* 240–41 n. 79.

54. Joseph Rossi, *The Image of America in Mazzini's Writings* (Madison: University of Wisconsin Press, 1954), 13.

55. Ibid., 108–10; "Notices," *Public Ledger,* March 14, 1859, 1; "Madame Mario," *Public Ledger,* March 15, 1859, 1.

56. "Local Affairs—Police Affairs," *Public Ledger,* November 21, 1853, 2.

57. The details of this incident are based on *Report of the Proceedings of the Case of the Contested Election for District Attorney* (Philadelphia: G. T. Stockdale, 1857).

58. Ibid., 129.

59. Ibid., 378–79.

60. Department of Records, Philadelphia, Court of Common Pleas, Petition for Naturalization (October 6, 1854), Dominick Carone (Caroni). See also similar documents for John Baptiste Lagamessina, John Smith, and Joseph Bijon, all in the same court on the same date.

61. Department of Records, Philadelphia, Court of Common Pleas, Petitions for Naturalization (October 9, 1854), Joseph Rippert, John Canned, and James R. Dido; and Court of Common Pleas, Petitions for Naturalization (April 25, 1855), Joseph Reppetto, John Cinelli (Cirelli), Jacob Bigginio, and Lewis Miller.

62. John Repetto and Gaetano Bernero, September 28, 1855; Agostino Ratto, Nicholas Canssa, and Power Cohanuo, October 4, 1856; Jerome Reppetto, October 6, 1856; and Beagio Fagausi (Fogosse), October 8, 1856, Petitions for Naturalization, RG 21.

63. "Hand Organs," *Public Ledger,* May 10, 1859, 1; Robert A. Gerson, *Music in Philadelphia* (Westport, Conn.: Greenwood Press, 1970), 79. Since her debut, not quite at the age of eight at the Musical Fund Society Hall in 1852, Patti had already performed as a concert singer for several years.

64. "Along Shore—Arrivals and Departures—Emigration," *Public Ledger,* June 27, 1859, 1.

Chapter 5. Family, Faith, and Fraternity

1. Alfred LeGoyt, *L'emigration Europeene: Son importance, ses causes, ses effets* (Paris, 1861). Extract translated and quoted by Edith Abbott, *Historical Aspects of the Immigration Problem: Select Documents* (Chicago: University of Chicago Press, 1926), 151.

2. "Letter from Europe," *Public Ledger,* January 3, 1860, 3; January 4, 1860, 3; and January 6, 1860, 1; "The Pope and Congress," *Public Ledger,* January 11, 1860, 2.

3. Untitled editorial, *Public Ledger,* March 16, 1860, 2. These articles appeared in the *Public Ledger* almost every day and can be located easily by the interested reader.

4. "Things in New York," *Public Ledger,* May 29, 1860, 3.

5. Ibid., May 25, 1860, 3.

6. Edwin Fenton, *Immigrants and Union: A Case Study, Italians and American Labor, 1870–1920* (New York: Arno Press, 1975), 38–39.

7. "Garibaldi's Triumphs and His Dangers," *Public Ledger,* July 26, 1860, 2; "Position of Garibaldi," *Public Ledger,* August 4, 1860, 2; and "Local Affairs—Hamburg Park," *Public Ledger,* October 17, 1860, 1.

8. "Garibaldi's Retirement," *Public Ledger,* December 15, 1860, 2.

9. "Local Affairs—Arrival of a Foreign War Vessel," *Public Ledger,* May 21, 1863, 1; "Local Affairs—Entertainment on Board the San Giovanni," *Public Ledger,* June 8, 1863, 1.

10. "Local Affairs—Arrival of an Italian Frigate," *Public Ledger,* October 4, 1864, 1; "Local Affairs—The Italian Frigate Principe Umberto Which Lies in the Delaware," *Public Ledger,* October 6, 1864, 1; "Local Affairs—The Italian Frigate," *Public Ledger,* October 13, 1864, 1; "Local Affairs—Sailed," *Public Ledger,* October 20, 1864, 1.

11. Untitled editorial, *Public Ledger,* October 10, 1867, 2.

12. "Civilization and Liberty," *Public Ledger,* October 18, 1867, 2.

13. Untitled editorial, *Public Ledger,* December 24, 1867, 2.

14. *Population Schedules of the Eighth Census of the United States, 1860,* M653, National Archives, Mid-Atlantic Region, Philadelphia (hereafter, *Population Schedules, 1860).* It is unclear why the census reported a total of 585,529 for the city when the combined reported figure for the American-born and foreign-born is 543,344, unless the difference is represented by residents whose nativity was not known. Other scholars give the population of the city as 565,529 in 1860 (Warner, *The Private City,* 51; Weigley, *Philadelphia,* 363). The foreign-born who settled in Philadelphia were part of a growing movement of immigration. But in contrast to immigrants who took up residence in Philadelphia at this time, many more were merely passing through the city on their way elsewhere. In 1859, the Pennsylvania Railroad Company carried 14,359 immigrant arrivals farther inland, mostly to final destinations west of Pittsburgh; many of them settled in Kansas and Iowa. Although 7,620 had first landed in New York City, already the major port of arrival for newcomers to the United States, they used the Pennsylvania route to reach their ultimate destinations. See "Local Affairs—Emigrant Travel," *Public Ledger,* January 24, 1860, 1.

The volume of individuals and baggage being served by the Pennsylvania system was steadily growing. In the following year, of the 103,621 people who landed in New York, 14,000 were reported as heading for some part of Pennsylvania. In the spring of 1860, disembarking at the ports of New York and Philadelphia, the large numbers of German and Irish immigrants in particular had increased the volume of passengers on the Pennsylvania Railroad to about 1,000 per week. The Germans were heading to Kansas, Missouri, Iowa, Illinois, and other states to purchase farmland. The Irish were destined for the cities between Philadelphia and Chicago. The Pennsylvania Railroad Company reported a yearly average of 9,353 immigrants passing through Philadelphia for destinations in the west during the previous four years. Another 10,696 had passed each year through New York. The company also estimated that about 9,690 had sought to make Philadelphia and places south of the city (a somewhat odd and puzzling classification) their destination. See "Things in New York—Varieties," *Public Ledger,* January 19, 1861, 4; "Emigrants for the West," *Public Ledger,* May 23, 1860, 1; "Local Affairs—Board of Trade," *Public Ledger,* June 28, 1860, 2.

Although still a major port of entry in 1860, Philadelphia was soon overwhelmed by the shift in preference of new arrivals for New York City. The aggregate annual number of immigrant arrivals for all destinations during the previous four years was given as a steady 25,000. In contrast, the figures for New York were described as fluctuating greatly. Despite the imposition of a fifty-cent tax on arrivals at the Quarantine Station, as well as another levy at the same cost imposed by the Guardians of the Poor, it was argued, many immigrants preferred to make their way through Philadelphia rather than through New York. The same day this information was made public, however, an apparently contradictory report showed that more than 47,000 arrivals had already reached New York so far in 1860, a number well above the 39,000 total for the same interval of the previous year. The Pennsylvania Railroad Company continued to release reports showing steady growth in the numbers of new arrivals who opted to use its lines, including many who had originally landed in New York City, to make their way to final destinations farther inland. See "Local Affairs—Board of Trade," *Public Ledger,* June 28, 1860, 2; "Things in New York," *Public Ledger,* June 28, 1860, 3.

15. "Local Affairs—Emigrant Travel," *Public Ledger,* April 2, 1861, 1; "Few Emigrants from Great Britain," *Public Ledger,* April 6, 1861, 1; "Local Affairs—Emigrants," *Public Ledger,* May 18, 1861, 1; "Local Affairs—Arrival of Emigrants at the Port," *Public Ledger,* July 29, 1861, 1; "Local Affairs—Falling Off," *Public Ledger,* November 25, 1861, 1; "Missing Vessels," *Public Ledger,* May 11, 1863, 1.

16. "Local Affairs—Tax on Emigrants," *Public Ledger,* January 30, 1860, 1; "Tax on Emigrants" *Public Ledger,* January 30, 1860, 2; untitled article, *Public Ledger,* February 18, 1860, 2.

17. Maldwyn Allen Jones, *American Immigration* (Chicago: University of Chicago Press, 1960), 183–87; Philip Taylor, *The Distant Magnet* (New York: Harper Torchbooks, 1972), 145–66; "The Lost Steamship Hungarian," *Public Ledger,* February 23, 1860, 2; and "Local Affairs—The Steamship Line for Europe," *Public Ledger,* March 24, 1863, 1.

18. "Steam Traffic Across the Atlantic," *Public Ledger,* August 9, 1866, 2.

19. "Immigration," *Public Ledger,* June 25, 1869, 2; untitled editorial, *Public Ledger,* May 14, 1868, 2.

20. "The Working People," *Public Ledger,* December 27, 1867, 2.

21. Dorothy Gondos Beers, "The Centennial City, 1865–1876," in Russell F. Weigley, ed., *Philadelphia: A 300-Year History* (New York: W. W. Norton & Co., 1982), 422.

22. Untitled editorial, *Public Ledger,* May 14, 1868, 2; "The Army of Immigrants," *Public Ledger,* November 16, 1869, 2.

23. "American Character," *Public Ledger,* July 22, 1869, 2.

24. "German Immigrants," *Public Ledger,* December 2, 1869, 2.

25. "Progress of Races," *Public Ledger,* August 10, 1866, 2.

26. Ibid.

27. Russell F. Weigley, "The Border City in Civil War, 1854–1865," in Weigley, *Philadelphia,* 366.

28. Beers, "Centennial City," 427–29.

29. "The Growth of Philadelphia," *Public Ledger,* January 14, 1868, 3; untitled editorial, *Public Ledger,* July 20, 1867, 2; "Philadelphia Industry," *Public Ledger,* August 30, 1867, 2.

30. "Local Affairs—The Sanitary Conditions of Certain Streets of the City," *Public Ledger,* August 16, 1861, 1; "Cellar Tenements," *Public Ledger,* September 9, 1861, 1; "Local Affairs—A Great Nuisance," *Public Ledger,* November 26, 1862, 4; Weigley, *Philadelphia,* 373.

31. "Local Affairs—Improvements in Southern Philadelphia," *Public Ledger,* November 20, 1862, 1; "Houses Finished," *Public Ledger,* November 28, 1864, 1.

32. Ibid.

33. Walter F. Willcox, ed., *International Migrations* (New York: National Bureau of Economic Research, 1929), 1:378. Before 1854, however, no distinction was made between individuals who intended to remain and become citizens, and people who were merely travelers, visitors, or passengers in transit through this country. See *Population Schedules, 1860,* lii.

34. For the reported figures on the state of Pennsylvania and the city of Philadelphia, see *Population Schedules, 1860,* xxxii. The smaller figure was derived from a direct examination of the census manuscripts.

35. Ibid., xxxii.

36. For an excellent recent discussion of these issues, see Paola A. Sensi Isolani, "Italian Image Makers in France, England, and the United States," and John Zucchi, "New Yorkers and Italian Child Street Musicians in the 1870s," both of which appeared in *Italian Americans Celebrate Life: The Arts and Popular Culture,* ed. Paola A. Sensi Isolani and Anthony Julian Tamburri, Selected Essays from the 22nd Annual Conference of the American Italian Historical Association (New York: American Italian Historical Association, 1990).

37. In contrast, of the 221 Italians who arrived at the Port of Philadelphia in 1874, some 177, or 80 percent of the total, were males. For six other places of origin, the percentage of males ranged from 51 percent to 60 percent of the total. See Commonwealth of Pennsylvania, *Second Annual Report of the Bureau of Statistics of Pennsylvania, for the years 1873–1874* (Harrisburg: B. F. Moyers, 1875).

38. *Population Schedules, 1860,* 1152:82.

39. Ibid., 1152:268, 622.

40. Ibid., 1155:129.

41. Ibid., 1171:106.

42. Ibid., 1155:227 (Viti), and 1158:325 (Parelli).

43. Robert A. Gerson, *Music in Philadelphia* (Westport, Conn.: Greenwood Press, 1970), 68–80, 122; untitled, *Public Ledger,* February 29, 1860, 2; "Local Affairs," *Public Ledger,* November 16, 1861, 1; "Local Affairs—Funeral of Signor Perelli," *Public Ledger,* March 5, 1867, 1.

44. "DeAmarelli," *Public Ledger,* November 29, 1853, 1; "Local Affairs—Re-elected," *Public Ledger,* November 11, 1863, 1; Schiavo, *Four Centuries of Italian American History,* 266.

45. "Local Affairs—Sale of Italian Marble Monuments," *Public Ledger,* September 12, 1861, 1.

46. "Local Affairs—Foreign Fruit," *Public Ledger,* February 28, 1861, 1; "Local Affairs—Another Cargo of Foreign Fruit," *Public Ledger,* March 4, 1861, 1; "Foreign Arrival," *Public Ledger,* April 25, 1861, 1.

47. "Foreign Fruit," *Public Ledger,* May 22, 1865, 1.

48. "Lowlife in the City," *Public Ledger,* July 21, 1869, 1; "Local Affairs—Sending Paupers from New York to This City," *Public Ledger,* September 14, 1860, 1.

49. "Violent Assault upon a Child, by an Alleged Thief," *Public Ledger,* May 12, 1861, 1; "Coroner's Inquest—Alleged Homicide," *Public Ledger,* October 25, 1864, 1; "Stabbing Affray," *Public Ledger,* June 4, 1870, 1; "Local Affairs—Police Intelligence," *Public Ledger,* November 19, 1866, 1.

50. "Court of Quarter Sessions—A Curious Case," *Public Ledger,* September 20, 1861, 4; "Quarter Sessions—Judge Ludlow," *Public Ledger,* September 21, 1861, 4; "Local

Affairs—Quarter Sessions," *Public Ledger*, September 23, 1861, 1; "Local Affairs—A Boarder Carrying Off the Household Goods," *Public Ledger*, November 3, 1862, 1; "Theft of Diamond Rings," *Public Ledger*, February 20, 1864, 1; "Theft of Jewelry," *Public Ledger*, February 24, 1864, 1; "Theft of Diamond Rings," *Public Ledger*, February 25, 1864, 1; "More of Jewelry Identified," *Public Ledger*, February 27, 1864, 1; "Local Affairs—Counterfeit Postal Currency," *Public Ledger*, October 14, 1864, 1.

51. "Local Affairs—Attempted Suicide," *Public Ledger*, February 22, 1862, 1; "Local Affairs—Drowned," *Public Ledger*, July 1, 1870, 1; "Local Affairs—Accidents," *Public Ledger*, July 10, 1871, 1; "Violent Assault upon a Child, by an Alleged Thief," *Public Ledger*, May 12, 1861, 1; "Coroner's Inquest—Alleged Homicide," *Public Ledger*, October 25, 1864, 1; "Local Affairs—Police Intelligence," *Public Ledger*, November 19, 1866, 1; "Stabbing Affray," *Public Ledger*, June 4, 1870, 1; "Local Affairs—Stabbing Affray," *Public Ledger*, July 1, 1871, 1.

52. "Local Affairs—About a Child," *Public Ledger*, April 15, 1867, 1. A more sensational case in 1873 led to arrests of 152 men, women, and children, supposedly members of a street-musician system. Despite the initial furor, however, all charges were eventually dropped. The Contract Labor Law of 1864 permitted agents of American industries to recruit foreign workers in their native countries. Although once regarded as a major factor in American immigration before being declared illegal by the Foran Act of 1885, more recent research has concluded that the importance of such practices may have been greatly exaggerated. While the extent of its impact remains a subject of considerable disagreement, most scholars concur that the system had some influence on mass migration from Italy to the United States. In particular, federal law and community action against these activities encouraged subtle variations that were conducted mainly within the law and within Italian colonies. In time, the *padrone* system increased in scope, from inducing immigration in the first place to providing services to newcomers in their adjustment to American life. These systems of influence and control lingered in the Italian communities of American cities well into the twentieth century.

53. For a discussion of how the war affected immigrants in general in the United States, see Maldwyn Allen Jones, *American Immigration* (Chicago: University of Chicago Press, 1960), 169–76. A brief treatment of the involvement of Italians in particular is provided by Luciano J. Iorizzo and Salvatore Mondello, *The Italian Americans* (Boston: Twayne Publishers, 1980), 47–48. As usual, Giovanni Schiavo provides a detailed record of the participation and achievements of Italians in both the Union and the Confederate armed forces; see his *Four Centuries of Italian American History*, 317–25.

54. He might have been the same individual who was said to have fled Italy "after a revolution" in which he presumably had some involvement. A biographical note once identified Robert Downing Taylor, a prominent Philadelphian, as the grandson of Nina Grennello Taylor, daughter of Francesco Grenello, a Genoese "who fled Italy after a revolution." See Herman LeRoy Collins, *Philadelphia: A Story of Progress* (New York: Lewis Historical Publishing Co., 1941), 4:3. An earlier Francis Granello, a confectioner and grocer, first at 251 North Second Street, then at Front and Pine Streets, had died in 1845. See *O'Brien's Commercial Intelligencer, City and County Merchants* (Philadelphia, 1840), 30; McElroy's City Directory for 1842, 101; for 1846, 135; and Register of Wills, Philadelphia, Index of Wills and Administration Records, file 8, Book P, 308 (1845), Francis Granello.

55. "Local Affairs—Military Affairs," *Public Ledger*, August 15, 1861, 1; "Local Affairs—Military—Independent Zouaves," *Public Ledger*, August 29, 1861, 1.

56. "Local Affairs—Meeting for the Purpose of Raising an Irish Regiment," *Public Ledger*, August 30, 1861, 3; "Local Affairs—Military Affairs," *Public Ledger*, August 31,

1861, 1; "Local Affairs—Military Affairs," *Public Ledger,* September 14, 1861, 1; "Local Affairs—Military Affairs," *Public Ledger,* September 17, 1861, 1.

57. "The Draft Commences—The Fourteenth Ward First—Who Drew the Prizes," *Public Ledger,* July 16, 1863, 1; "The Draft in the Twentieth Ward," *Public Ledger,* July 21, 1863, 1; "The Draft in the First District," *Public Ledger,* July 28, 1863, 1; "The Draft for the 5th Ward," *Public Ledger,* July 30, 1863, 1; "The Draft in the Eighth Ward," *Public Ledger,* August 3, 1863, 1; "The Draft," *Public Ledger,* February 28, 1865, 1. The problem of accurately determining ethnicity from names reoccurs at this point. These names appear to be Italian, but that conclusion cannot be verified in all cases. On the other hand, there may have been others with anglicized spellings that are easily overlooked. Given the number of young Italian males reported in the census at the time, perhaps not as many as expected appear in the draft lists. Moreover, aliens could be exempted from military service if they were documented as citizens of another nation by a foreign consulate. But we do not know how many of them actually entered the military service of the United States during the war.

58. None of these men was an American citizen when he entered military service, but in later years each became naturalized in Philadelphia. Department of Records, Philadelphia, Court of Common Pleas, Petitions for Naturalization (September 3, 1874), Justice Buttinghausen; (September 28, 1866), Samuel Bright; (August 9, 1869), John Patroni; (September 24, 1878), Joseph Barsuglia; Court of Quarter Sessions (September 27, 1866), Ignazio Allegretti; (September 20, 1870), Carlo Capelli; and United States District Court (October 8, 1866), Baldo Muzzarelli. Their residences at the time they entered military service are not known. By submitting a petition for naturalization, each man, we can presume, was a resident of Philadelphia, at least temporarily. In some cases, an address that confirms the residence at this time was given. When he was naturalized, Buttinghausen's address was 3404 North Eleventh Street; Patroni lived at 746 South Fourth Street; Barsuglia lived at 523 Columbia Avenue; and Capelli lived at 902 South Eighth Street, an adjacent address to his voucher, John B. Rogers, who probably was John B. Raggio.

59. "Local Affairs—The National Mourning—Philadelphia in Crepe," *Public Ledger,* April 18, 1865, 1.

60. "Naturalization," *Public Ledger,* September 21, 1869, 1.

61. These figures were compiled from the indexes of records of the various courts, either from materials of the Philadelphia Department of Records or from the National Archives, Mid-Atlantic Region.

62. "Death of a Catholic Clergyman," *Public Ledger,* March 9, 1866, 1; "Funeral of a Catholic Clergyman," *Public Ledger,* March 12, 1866, 1.

63. "Bequests," *Public Ledger,* March 12, 1866, 1. The executor of Mariani's estate was City Recorder James Eneu, who had also served as one of the executors of Joseph Marabello's estate in 1821. Eneu later married Marabello's widow, Jane, in 1827. By 1853, Joseph Eneu, who was either the same person as James or a son of James, was serving as an alderman. The Eneus possibly represent figures of relatively long linkage between the earliest days of Italian settlement in Southwark and the establishment and expansion of their later community in the same area, by then a part of South Philadelphia. It would be useful to know more about them.

64. "Religious News," *Public Ledger,* May 26, 1866, 1; *Souvenir and Bouquet* (Philadelphia, 1911), 22; "The New St. Mary Magdalen De-Pazzi's Church," *The Catholic Standard,* June 20, 1891, cited in *Souvenir and Bouquet,* 37. With the appointment of Isoleri in October 1870, this scholarly and dynamic priest, a native of Villanova d'Albenga in the region of Liguria, began a remarkable tenure not only as the pastor of St. Mary Magdalen de Pazzi, but as one of the most important and powerful figures in the Italian community until his death

more than sixty years later, in 1932. Under his leadership, the parish resolved its problems and became an even more dominant institution for Italians than it had previously been.

65. Sam Bass Warner Jr., *The Private City: Philadelphia in Three Periods of Its Growth* (Philadelphia: University of Pennsylvania Press, 1968), 61–62. While Warner's analysis has focused on the special case of Philadelphia, a more ambitious attempt to develop a similar argument is in Gunther Barth, *City People: The Rise of Modern City Culture in Nineteenth-Century America* (New York: Oxford University Press, 1980). Barth presents municipal parks, metropolitan newspapers, department stores, baseball parks, and vaudeville houses as the principal mechanisms by which city residents of the late nineteeth century reconstructed personal identity and group cohesion.

66. "Local Affairs—Philadelphia Emigrant Union," *Public Ledger,* February 8, 1861, 1; "Local Affairs—Haytian Emigration," *Public Ledger,* October 3, 1861, 1; "Encouragement to Emigrate," *Public Ledger,* April 21, 1863, 1; "Local Affairs—Hebrew Relief Association," *Public Ledger,* February 12, 1861, 1; "Local Affairs—Benevolent and Charitable Institutions," *Public Ledger,* July 18, 1866, 1; "The Fenian Demonstrations," *Public Ledger,* January 9, 1868, 1.

67. *History of the Società di Unione e Fratellanza Italiana,* souvenir program, 62nd Anniversary Banquet (Philadelphia, 1929), n.p. Among the many sources for information on Avezzana's political life, see Howard R. Marraro, *American Opinion on the Unification of Italy, 1846–1861* (New York: Columbia University Press, 1932); Joseph Rossi, *The Image of America in Mazzini's Writings* (Madison: University of Wisconsin Press, 1954); Alexander DeConde, *Half Bitter, Half Sweet: An Excursion into Italian-American History* (New York: Charles Scribner's Sons, 1971); Luciano J. Iorizzo and Salvatore Mondello, *The Italian Americans* (Boston: Twayne Publishers, 1980); and Deanna Paoli Gumina, *The Italians of San Francisco 1850–1930* (New York: Center for Migration Studies, 1978).

68. *History of the Società di Unione e Fratellanza Italiana.*

69. Ibid.

70. "The Italians," *Public Ledger,* March 24, 1868, 1. See also the original charter for the Società in Department of Records, Philadelphia, Miscellaneous, JTO1:589; and *History of the Società di Unione e Fratellanza Italiana.*

71. "The Italians," *Public Ledger,* March 24, 1868, 1; *History of the Società di Unione e Fratellanza Italiana.*

72. "Italian Benefit Societies," *Public Ledger,* July 15, 1868, 1; "Convention of Italians," *Public Ledger,* July 20, 1868, 1; *History of the Società di Unione e Fratellanza Italiana.*

73. "Italian Convention," *Public Ledger,* July 22, 1868, 1.

74. Ibid., "Semi-Annual Sessions of K of P of Pennsylvania," *Public Ledger,* July 31, 1869, 1.

Chapter 6. The 1870 Census: A Community Portrait

1. Robert F. Foerster, *The Italian Emigration of Our Times* (Cambridge: Harvard University Press, 1924), 323.

2. "Local Affairs—Street Music," *Public Ledger,* July 20, 1866, 1.

3. Dorothy Gondos Beers, "The Centennial City, 1865–1876," in Russell F. Weigley, ed., *Philadelphia: A 300-Year History* (New York: W. W. Norton & Co., 1982), 422.

4. Lorin Blodgett, "The Census of Industrial Employment, Wages and Social Condition in Philadelphia, in 1870," in Commonwealth of Pennsylvania, *First Annual Report of the Bureau of Statistics of Labor and Agriculture, for the Years 1872–1873* (Harrisburg, Pa., 1874), 419.

5. Ibid., 417–39.

6. Commonwealth of Pennsylvania, *First Annual Report of the Bureau of Statistics of Labor and Agriculture, 1872–1873,* 26–27.

7. *Population Schedule of the Ninth Census of the United States, 1870,* M593, National Archives, Mid-Atlantic Region, Philadelphia (hereafter, *Population Schedules, 1870*). The discussion that follows is based on the tabulation and analysis of data from this source. There are, however, some problems. First, the published figure for the number of Italians differs from the total generated by a direct count of cases in the census manuscript pages. Because of errors, moreover, the federal census of 1870 actually counted the population of Philadelphia twice, but the recount probably did not significantly change the enumeration of the city's Italian population. The first enumeration is therefore acceptable to use to examine the number and the social characteristics of Italians in Philadelphia at the beginning of the 1870s. The later publication of an index to the manuscript census—that is, to the actual ledger pages on which the original entries for each household were recorded—further facilitates the use of these materials. See "Phila 1870, U.S. Census, Index, Series M593" (Precision Indexing, Bountiful, Utah). The index lists in alphabetical order the names of all households. It also includes anyone in a household with a different surname, regardless of age; any male age fifty or older; any female age seventy or older; any color or race change (when the surname stays the same); and all individuals living in institutions, such as an orphanage. After the surname for each listing, the index also provides age, sex, race, place of birth, and the ward and district of residence. This information might be sufficient in itself for certain purposes, but in order to reconstruct a clear profile of the Italian population in the city at the time, it was necessary to take the procedure a step further. The index therefore also provides roll and page numbers for the microfilm copies of the original ledger entries, where the information was first recorded by the census enumerator on the streets of Philadelphia in 1870. The index was used in this manner as a reference device to identify Italians, but it led to a direct examination of the actual census manuscript entries in each case. This procedure provides a relatively comprehensive way to reconstruct the Italian population at that time. It is probably not exhaustive, because, for example, it does not catch the Italian-born woman under age seventy and married to someone born elsewhere who was the head of this household. It could be argued that such cases may have been few, but that can be known only after an inspection of the entire manuscript census line by line. With this limitation in mind, we can still say that the procedure does provide a nearly complete picture of the Italian population.

Several other problems should be noted. Because of the techniques used in compiling the index to the census, the number of cases involving children with mothers born in Italy, but with no father or fathers born elsewhere, could be underreported. In addition, some individuals who were Italian-born or children of an Italian-born parent might not in any meaningful sense be truly an "Italian," however further defined. A careful inspection of individual entries can reveal this possibility, but such cases are rare. On the other hand, if we consider the possibility of the married women whose Italian origins slipped through the net of the census indexing, the underenumerated cases may balance out the "false" entries. These problems will never be entirely resolved, but they should not represent a factor numerically large enough to alter the profile of the population to any serious degree.

8. *Population Schedules, 1870,* M593, 1388:289–90.

9. Ibid., 1388:290. It is unfortunate that the listing procedure did not include actual addresses. That protocol was not introduced until the next decennial census.

10. Ibid., 1389:533.

11. Ibid., 1392:231.

12. Ibid., 1396:142; "Rabbi Morais," *Public Ledger,* March 20, 1891, 3; "Four

Decades," *Public Ledger,* March 31, 1891, 7; "Rabbi Morais Dead," *Public Ledger,* November 12, 1897, 2.

13. *Population Schedules, 1870,* 1407:662, 1411:419.

14. Certain procedural problems with this information must be considered before examining its substance. Some people listed as born in Italy may not have actually been Italians. In the absence of any reliable answer to that question, it is necessary to follow the only available consistent rule and use place of birth.

All these are individuals who were born in Italy, and the recording of the names was in the handwriting of the census enumerator, which at times is almost illegible and very difficult to decipher. The names are provided here as near to the way they appear on the manuscripts as possible. Some names appear to have been anglicized. In addition, some people who reported smaller amounts of wealth or real estate are omitted from the table. There are probably other limitations to these data that resulted from the interaction between Italians and the enumerators as officials of the government. The information given depended on what any individual was willing to tell the enumerator, and for many the manuscripts give no answer. From other sources it can be surmised, for example, that Nunzio Finelli, a tavernkeeper, had as much property and wealth as some other individuals who gave that information, but nothing was reported for him. Even people who responded to these questions may have deliberately understated the value of their personal property and wealth. Some probably did not want to reveal their true financial worth to the stranger asking the questions. It is likely that the numbers give a lower level of the actual wealth among Italians at this time. As a result of such problems, the listing cannot be regarded with complete confidence, but the information provides another view of the material condition of Italians at the time.

15. *Population Schedules, 1870,* 1388:205. For the detailed information on this case, I am deeply indebted to Louis D. Arata Jr., a descendant of the Raggio and Arata families, who has generously shared the fruits of his extensive labors and illuminating ideas on these pioneers of Italian settlement in Philadelphia.

16. There were actually at least two men named John Raggio, both of Genovese origins, living in South Philadelphia at this time. In addition to John T. Raggio, who was dead by early 1857, the other was John B. Raggio, listed in the federal census of 1860 as John Rodgers, a fifty-three-year-old innkeeper. Although his birthplace was given as Pennsylvania by means of ditto marks under the preceding entry of an unrelated person, Rodger's wife, Mary, and two children were listed as natives of Genoa, making it likely that he too was born in Italy. It was probably this John Raggio who served as the only member with an Italian name on the building committee for St. Mary Magdalen de Pazzi Church in the late 1850s. The second baptism performed at the church was that of Luisa Maria Magdalene Raggio, daughter of Giovanni Raggio and Mary Devoto, in 1854.

17. "Troubles in Italy," *Public Ledger,* April 21, 1870, 2; "Brigandage in Italy," *Public Ledger,* May 2, 1870, 2.

18. "The Latest News," *Public Ledger,* February 24, 1871, 1; "Local Affairs—Italian Unity," *Public Ledger,* June 6, 1871, 1.

19. "Local Affairs—Italian Patriotism," *Public Ledger,* August 21, 1871, 1; "Monument to Columbus," *Public Ledger,* August 4, 1873, 3; "Fair of the Columbus Monument Association," *Public Ledger,* September 30, 1873, 2; "The Italian Celebration—Columbus Monument," *Public Ledger,* July 6, 1875, 1; "Local Affairs—Unveiling of the Columbus Monument," *Public Ledger,* October 13, 1876, 1; *History of the Società di Unione e Fratellanza Italiana,* souvenir program, 62nd Anniversary Banquet (Philadelphia, 1929), n.p.

20. "The Italians and Their Late King," *Public Ledger,* February 11, 1878, 1; "Funeral Services for the Pope at the Italian Church," *Public Ledger,* February 11, 1878, 1; "Requiem

Mass Yesterday at the Italian Church to Commemorate the Death of Pius IX," *Public Ledger,* February 19, 1878, 1.

Chapter 7. Prosperity and Leadership: *I Primi Prominenti*

1. Because of changes in the listing of names, it is difficult but nonetheless sometimes possible to trace by linkage techniques these lives and careers. Despite the difficulties, this is absolutely necessary for reconstructing the evolution of Italian life in Philadelphia. For the sequence of sources on the Luccarini brothers, see *Population Schedules, 1850,* reel 813:431, entry for Treaga household. See also Department of Records, Philadelphia, Court of Common Pleas, Petition for Naturalization (October 5, 1876), John Luccarini (October 5, 1876), "Pennsylvania," vol. 145:137, 421, R. G. Dun & Co. Collection, Baker Library, Harvard University Graduate School of Business Administration (hereafter, Dun Collection); and *Population Schedules, 1870,* 1407:531; entry for John Lucreny.

2. Department of Records, Philadelphia, Court of Common Pleas, Petition for Naturalization (October 5, 1876), John Luccarini; and "Pennsylvania," vol. 145:137, 421, Dun Collection.

3. "Pennsylvania," vol. 145:137, 421, Dun Collection.

4. *Population Schedules, 1870,* 1395:349; "Pennsylvania," vol. 145:596, Dun Collection.

5. *Population Schedules, 1870,* 1407:651; "Pennsylvania," vol. 145:229, 483, Dun Collection; Department of Records, Philadelphia, Court of Common Pleas, Petition for Naturalization (September 30, 1880), Salvadore Musso.

6. "Pennsylvania," vol. 16:245, Dun Collection.

7. Department of Records, Philadelphia, Court of Common Pleas, Petition for Naturalization (August 30, 1880), Mark Malatesta; Pennsylvania, vol. 140, 151, Dun Collection.

8. *History of the Società di Unione e Fratellanza Italiana,* souvenir program, 62nd Anniversary Banquet (Philadelphia, 1929), n.p.

9. Pennsylvania, vol. 155, Dun Collection.

10. *Population Schedules, 1860,* 1152:283; *Population Schedules, 1870,* 1445:15; "Pennsylvania," vol. 148:128, 469, Dun Collection.

11. "Pennsylvania," vol. 148:128, 469, Dun Collection.

12. *History of the Società di Unione e Fratellanza Italiana.*

13. "The Latest News," *Public Ledger,* March 19, 1886, 1; death notices, *Public Ledger,* March 20, 1886, 2.

14. *Population Schedules, 1870,* 1389:542; "Pennsylvania," vol. 145:303, Dun Collection.

15. *La Colonia Italiana di Filadelfia* (Philadelphia, 1906), n.p.; "Pennsylvania," vol. 151:32; vol. 160:15, Dun Collection; Department of Records, Philadelphia, Court of Quarter Sessions, Petition for Naturalization (September 16, 1878), Antonio Raggio; and Court of Common Pleas, Petition for Naturalization (September 30, 1880), Peter Cella.

16. "Pennsylvania," vol. 160:15, Dun Collection; *La Colonia Italiana.*

17. Ibid.

18. *History of the Società di Unione e Fratellanza Italiana.*

19. This concept is borrowed from the influential studies of upper-class life in Philadelphia by E. Digby Baltzell; see especially *Puritan Boston and Quaker Philadelphia* (New York: The Free Press, 1979), 30.

20. Papers of Henrico Francisco Foggini and his daughter, Maria, HSP; Maxwell Whiteman, *Gentlemen in Crisis: The First Century of the Union League of Philadelphia, 1862–1962* (Philadelphia: Union League, 1975), 160–63, 484.

21. "Obituary: Victor A. Sartori," *Philadelphia Inquirer*, August 31, 1883, 5.

22. The Sartoris provided a rich and complex saga of family experience right up to the present time. For a glimpse of their lives in the early twentieth century, see the *Social Register—Philadelphia* 20 (1906), as well as the regular "society" features of the local press: "Personal and Social," *Public Ledger,* December 24, 1903, 7; "Society: The Debutantes," *Public Ledger,* December 27, 1903, 10; "The Benedicks' Ball," *Public Ledger,* December 30, 1903, 7. For more academic matters, see "Honors for Young Students," *Public Ledger,* December 24, 1903, 2; and University of Pennsylvania, *Directory and Club Book,* 1908–9.

23. Stephen Girard Papers, APS. This rich collection contains numerous letters, bills of exchange, invoices, shipment orders, and other documents on the commerce between the Viti firm and Stephen Girard between 1817 and 1825. See also the advertisement for Viti Brothers in *The Catholic Standard,* May 30, 1868, 5.

24. *La Colonia Italiana.* See the section entitled "I primi italiani emigrati in Philadelphia," which begins: "Vito Viti fu il primo italiano, per quanto si può sapere, che giungesse in Philadelphia. Toscano di nascita, venne qui nell'anno 1815" ("Vito Viti was the first Italian, as far as anyone knows, that reached Philadelphia. Tuscan by birth, he came here in the year 1815"). This may have been all that was known at the time, but we know much more about early Italian arrivals now.

25. Vito Viti, February 27, 1828, Petitions for Naturalization, RG 21; Stephen Girard Papers, APS; and *Passenger Arrivals at the Port of Philadelphia, 1800–1819: The Philadelphia "Baggage Lists,"* Michael H. Tepper, gen. ed. (Baltimore: Genealogical Publishing Co., 1986).

26. "Sacramental Register—St. Joseph's," *Records of the ACHS* 20 (1909): 168. Bernard Keenan was ordained a priest two days later and eventually became a "venerable missionary of Eastern Pennsylvania."

27. Vito Viti, February 27, 1828, Petitions for Naturalization, RG 21.

28. *Philadelphia Directory and Stringer's Guide* (1825), 144; McElroy's City Directory for 1845, 369; "Pennsylvania," vol. 131:246, Dun Collection.

29. "Pennsylvania," vol. 131:246; vol. 137, 543, 573, 576, 904, Dun Collection; "Local Affairs—Sale of Italian Marble," *Public Ledger,* September 12, 1861, 1; "Local Affairs—Sale of Italian Marble Monuments," *Public Ledger,* June 20, 1862, 1; "Viti Brothers" (advertisement), *The Catholic Standard,* May 30, 1868, 5.

30. *Population Schedules, 1870,* 1155:227.

31. "Funeral of a Prominent Catholic," *The Catholic Standard,* August 18, 1866, 5; Register of Wills, Philadelphia, Wills, 466 (1866), Vito Viti. See also the codicil attached later to the same document.

32. The remark is contained in the previously cited codicil to the original will.

33. Throughout the summer of 1873, public concern mounted over the use of Italian "slave children" as street musicians by *padroni* masters. In September the mayor ordered a series of police raids in South Philadelphia that produced the arrest of 152 men, women, and children, but all charges were later dismissed. For the extensive coverage of these events by local newspapers, see "A Raid on Padrones," *Inquirer,* September 16, 1873, 7; and "Remarkable Police Operation," *Public Ledger,* September 16, 1873, 1. In response to the situation, in May 1874 the General Assembly of Pennsylvania passed an act to prevent traffic in children "for the purpose of singing, playing on musical instruments, begging . . . in the streets, roads and other highways of this commonwealth"; *Constitution of the Commonwealth; Also Laws of the General Assembly of Said Commonwealth, Passed at the*

Session of 1874 . . . (Harrisburg, Pa., 1874), 179–80. According to one scholar, Alonzo M. Viti was responsible for promoting the bill in the Pennsylvania legislature; see John Zucchi, "New Yorkers and Italian Child Street Musicians in the 1870s," 128, in *Italian Americans Celebrate Life: The Arts and Popular Culture*, ed. Paola A. Sensi Isolani and Anthony Julian Tamburri (New York: American Italian Historical Association, 1990). Despite these efforts, Italian children were still being arrested for playing musical instruments on city streets twenty years later. See "Music Hath Charms," *Inquirer*, April 6, 1893, 6.

34. See the discussion of the Viti family in the section entitled "I primi Italiani emigrati in Philadelphia" in *La Colonia Italiana*. See also *History of the Società di Unione e Fratellanza Italiana*.

35. "Pennsylvania," vol. 137:904, Dun Collection.

36. Special Verdict, Circuit Court of the United States for the Eastern District of Pennsylvania, *Alonzo M. Viti and Francis Viti, trading as Viti Brothers, v. Alexander P. Tutton, Collector of the Port of Philadelphia*, no. 55, April Sessions, 1880; "Pennsylvania," vol. 137:904, Dun Collection; U.S. District Court, Eastern District of Pennsylvania, *United States v. Alonzo M. Viti and Francis A. Viti, trading as Viti Brothers*, no.4, November Sessions, 1891.

37. *La Colonia Italiana*; "Pennsylvania," vol. 152:240, Dun Collection.

38. Ibid., A. Frangini, *Italiani in Filadelfia* (Philadelphia, 1907), 52–53; *History of the Società di Unione e Fratellanza Italiana*.

39. *La Colonia Italiana*.

40. *Population Schedules, 1860*, 1159:197, Augustus Langestine; "Pennsylvania," vol. 147:171, Dun Collection; personal correspondence from Mrs. Inez Cuneo Bieberman, September 14, 1981. Mrs. Bieberman was a granddaughter of Frank Cuneo.

41. *Population Schedules, 1870*, 1389:533, Agostino Lagomarsino (also Frank Cuneo).

42. "Pennsylvania," vol. 147:171, Dun Collection.

43. *History of the Società di Unione e Fratellanza Italiana*; *La Colonia Italiana*.

44. This information was compiled from the indexes of local courts in which naturalization proceedings took place.

45. On the recruitment of the first African American as a member of the police force, see Nathaniel Burt and Wallace E. Davies, "The Iron Age, 1876–1905," in Russell F. Weigley, ed., *Philadelphia: A 300-Year History* (New York: W. W. Norton & Co., 1982), 493. For the early hiring of Italians as police, the authoritative work is Howard O. Sprogle, *The Philadelphia Police: Past and Present* (Philadelphia, 1887). Joseph Ratto, a native of Italy, was probably the first Italian member of the police force in Philadelphia. He was appointed by Mayor William S. Stokley in February 1879, resigned in August 1879, and reappointed by Mayor Smith in January 1887. John Sbarbaro, a native of Brooklyn, was appointed a police officer in April 1883. He was probably the Italian policeman mentioned at this meeting. Smith later appointed at least two other Italian-born officers to the department, one in April 1884 identified by Sprogle as James Malatesta, and one in February 1885 identified as Antoine Cappelli. Although he mentions the appointments of James and Joseph Malatesta in the same year, Sprogle treats them as two different individuals. He says that James Malatesta was born in Italy on August 8, 1852. The appointments reported in the police sections of the Mayor's Annual Message and Reports of the City Departments also list the two men as different persons, with James Malatesta appointed as a patrolman in District 3 in 1884, and Joseph Malatesta as a sergeant of Patrol 17 in 1887.

46. "Italian Political Club," *Public Ledger*, February 4, 1884, 1; "Italian Political Club," *Public Ledger*, February 11, 1884, 1; and "Italian Republican Club," *Public Ledger*, February 16, 1884, 4. For a more detailed report on the second meeting, see "Italians Tell Their Grievance," *Philadelphia Press*, February 11, 1884.

47. The study of Italians in local politics begins with work of Hugo V. Maiale, *The Italian Vote in Philadelphia Between 1928 and 1946* (Philadelphia: University of Pennsylvania Press, 1950). In referring to the election of 1928, Maiale contended: "It was in the election of that year that the Italians dared to shift their allegiance from the Republicans to the Democrats for the first time in Philadelphia political history" (iii). In addition to Maiale, more-recent studies on Italians in local politics by John Shover, Sandra Featherman, and Stefano Luconi are important; see Sources and Resources at the end of this book.

48. *La Colonia Italiana.*

49. "Deaths of a Day: Augustino Lagomarsino," *Public Ledger,* May 3, 1906, 9; "Lagomarsino," *Inquirer,* May 3, 1906, 7; Register of Wills, Philadelphia, Will Book, 227 (1906), 973, Augustus Lagomarsino. See also Inventory Book, 45 (1906), 329; and Account Book, 247 (1906), 133.

50. Register of Wills, Philadelphia, Will Book, 227 (1906), 973, Augustus Lagomarsino.

51. Ibid.

52. *La Colonia Italiana;* Bieberman correspondence, September 14, 1981; *Southwark, Moyamensing, Weccacoe, Passyunk, Dock Ward for Two Hundred and Seventy Years* (Philadelphia: Quaker City Publishing Co., 1892), 119. Mrs. Bieberman also believed that a relationship to General William Tecumseh Sherman through marriage had enabled her grandfather to operate a commissary behind Union lines during the Civil War.

53. Bieberman correspondence, September 14, 1981.

54. *Southwark, Moyamensing . . . ,* 119; George W. Englehardt, *Philadelphia, Pa.: The Book of Its Bourse and Co-operating Public Bodies* (Philadelphia, 1898–99), 227; "Pennsylvania," vol. 152:387, Dun Collection.

55. *History of the Società di Unione e Fratellanza Italiana.*

56. "Victim and Scene of Shooting," *Philadelphia Evening Telegraph,* August 3, 1910, 1.

57. *The Philadelphia Blue Book, 1891–1892* (Philadelphia, 1892), which was not nearly as exclusive as the *Social Register.* Other Italians listed in the *Blue Book* included members of the Finelli, Muzzarelli, Nardi, Passano, Rondinella, Sartori, and Viti families.

58. Sam Hudson, *Philadelphia and Its Public Men* (Philadelphia, 1909), 168.

59. *Southwark, Moyamensing . . . ,* 119.

60. Register of Wills, Philadelphia, Letter of Administration, 1512 (1919), Frank Cuneo; "Frank Cuneo," *Public Ledger,* April 23, 1919, 9; Bieberman correspondence, February 24, 1983. The value of his estate was provided by his granddaughter, Inez Cuneo Bieberman. The letter of administration listed personal property and real estate that was to be sold and amounted to about $40,000, but it did not include what the family kept, such as the house at 830 South Eighth Street that became the residence of his son, Frederick.

61. Hudson, *Philadelphia and Its Public Men,* 168.

62. Ibid. This information is also derived from several volumes of *Manual of the City Councils of Philadelphia.*

63. Hudson, *Philadelphia and Its Public Men,* 168.

64. This characterization was provided by his daughter, Inez Cuneo Bieberman, in an interview, September 24, 1981.

65. For a discussion of the school reforms of 1905, see Sam Bass Warner Jr., *The Private City* (Philadelphia: University of Pennsylvania Press, 1968), 218. The details of the Cuneo failure to attain this position were provided by Inez Cuneo Bieberman. It is beyond the scope of the present study to examine Baldi's life and career. He was, however, the most dominant leader in the Italian community from the late nineteenth century through the early decades of the next century. His selection as a member of the school board reflects the final transition of the Italian population and its leadership during this period when the earlier colony of Ligurians and Tuscans was overcome by a huge number of immigrants from Southern Italy and

Sicily. The emergence of Baldi was reaffirmed by the internal politics of the Republican Party. The choice of Baldi, an immigrant from Castelnuovo Cilento in the province of Salerno, over Cuneo, a second-generation descendant of Ligurian origins, symbolized the changes within the Italian community. That transition deserves careful consideration in another study.

66. *La Colonia Italiana*. On Lorenzo L. Nardi, see both the primary entry for Emanuele V. H. Nardi and the briefer sketch, within the section "I primi italiani emigrati in Philadelphia."

67. Ibid., "I primi italiani emigrati in Philadelphia."

68. *Population Schedules, 1860*, 1171:106; "Pennsylvania," vol. 150:286, Dun Collection.

69. Ibid.

70. *La Colonia Italiana*.

71. *History of the Società di Unione e Fratellanza Italiana*.

72. *La Colonia Italiana*.

73. Ibid.

74. Ibid.

75. *Population Schedules, 1860*, 1152:270.

76. "Joseph Malatesta Has Passed Away," *Inquirer*, February 27, 1900, 3; *La Colonia Italiana*; Sprogle, *The Philadelphia Police: Past and Present*, 388–91.

77. "Joseph Malatesta Has Passed Away," *Inquirer*, February 27, 1900, 3; Sprogle, *The Philadelphia Police: Past and Present*, 388–91; *Population Schedules, 1870*, 1390:279; *La Colonia Italiana*.

78. "Pennsylvania," vol. 145:70, Dun Collection.

79. Ibid.

80. Ibid., 155, 412.

81. Ibid., 412.

82. *History of the Società di Unione e Fratellanza Italiana*.

83. Joseph Malatesta (September 28, 1867), Petitions for Naturalization, RG 21; "In the Woods: The Italians Celebrate Yesterday by a Grand Pic-Nic," *Public Ledger*, June 10, 1873, 2.

84. Sprogle, *The Philadelphia Police: Past and Present*, 388–91; "Joseph Malatesta," *Public Ledger*, February 27, 1900, 2; "Joseph Malatesta Has Passed Away," *Inquirer*, February 27, 1900, 3; Department of Records, Philadelphia, Charter Books, 19, 375.

85. "Joseph Malatesta," *Public Ledger*, February 27, 1900, 2; "Joseph Malatesta Has Passed Away," *Inquirer*, February 27, 1900, 3.

86. "Italian Leader Buried," *Public Ledger*, March 4, 1900, 2.

87. Register of Wills, Philadelphia (1900), 366, Will Book 216, 104; Inventory Book, 32 (1900), 284; Account Book, 177 (1900), 541.

88. See sources cited in note 87.

89. See sources cited in note 87.

90. See sources cited in note 87.

91. The lives of other individuals, such as John B. Raggio, John D. Raggio, Stephen Ratto, Stephen Cuneo, Francesco Romano, Giuseppe Mazza, Antonio Raffetto, and Michele Lastrico, could be also used as illustrations, but the object of this book is not to compile a comprehensive inventory of the achievements of every Italian in Philadelphia at the time. The availability of materials influenced which individuals were focused on, and the intent is to concentrate on people who were well established in economic and political activities and to bring the argument only to the federal census of 1870, the eve of mass immigration. But history does not come conveniently packaged. In cases such as the Viti family, the Philadelphia episode began much earlier than for others. Some cases have continued to

recent years in order to make the main point. Complete biographies and a social history of the later period would exceed the focus and purposes of the present work.

Chapter 8. From Cultural Ideal to Social Reality

1. For efforts against the *padrone* system, see "Italian Slave Cases," *Inquirer*, July 28, 1873, 4; "The Italian Slave Children," *Inquirer*, August 29, 1873, 4; "The Farce of Inhumanity," *Inquirer*, September 16, 1873, 4; "Philadelphia and Suburbs: A Raid on Padrones," *Inquirer*, September 16, 1873, 7; "Local Affairs—Remarkable Police Operation," *Public Ledger*, September 16, 1873, 1. A decade later, a spirited but short-lived campaign led by Dr. Domenico A. Pignatelli sought the elimination of such practices again. See "Local Affairs—Denouncing an Anonymous Letter Writer—Concerning Italian Laborers," *Public Ledger*, May 1, 1884, 1; and the articles in *L'Eco d'Italia*, April 21, 1883; May 22, 1883; April 4, 1884; and April 20, 1883, cited in Edwin Fenton, *Immigrants and Unions, A Case Study: Italians and American Labor, 1870–1920* (New York: Arno Press, 1975), 99–100. In an article titled "Italians in the Labor Movement," *Pennsylvania History* 26 (1959), Fenton identified Pignatelli as an Italian American physician. Pignatelli, a native of Naples who operated a pharmacy at Eighth and Fitzwater Streets in South Philadelphia, was licensed for the practice of medicine by the state, although he lacked a physician's degree. See Department of Records, Philadelphia, *Medical Register, Philadelphia County*, 1:353.

2. This argument was first proposed a century ago in a seminal essay by John Koren, *The Padrone System and Padrone Banks*, Bulletin of the Department of Labor, no. 9 (Washington, D.C.: March 1897). It was subsequently repeated by Joan Younger Dickinson, "Aspects of Italian Immigration to Philadelphia," *Pennsylvania Magazine of History and Biography* 90 (October 1966): 445–65. Koren argued that a principal reason for the relatively successful resistance against the *padrone* system in Philadelphia was that Italian immigrants were quickly recruited as members of political clubs. Koren identified the Società Operaia di Mutuo Soccorso as an organization that Italians joined in order to find work in streetcleaning. Dickinson correctly pointed out that the Philadelphia politicians who controlled these organizations were both like and unlike the *padroni* of New York. The charter records in the city archives ironically show that the Società Italiana di Mutuo Soccorso e Beneficenza, founded in January 1887 and probably the same organization Koren had identified, included Dr. D. A. Pignatelli among its officers.

3. *La Colonia Italiana di Filadelfia* (Filadelfia: 1906), n.p.

4. Max Weber, "The Social Psychology of the World Religions," in *From Max Weber: Essays in Sociology*, ed. H. H. Gerth and C. Wright Mills (New York: Oxford University Press, 1958), 280.

5. Although it has a different regional focus, the most detailed study of this inversion of thought remains Barbara Miller Solomon, *Ancestors and Immigrants: A Changing New England Tradition* (Chicago: University of Chicago Press, 1956). Other relevant works include Glenn C. Altschuler, *Race, Ethnicity, and Class in American Social Thought, 1865–1919* (Arlington Heights, Ill.: Harlan Davidson, 1982), and Alan M. Kraut, *The Huddled Masses: The Immigrant in American Society, 1880–1921* (Arlington Heights, Ill.: Harlan Davidson, 1982).

6. "Immigration Restriction," *Inquirer*, January 23, 1888, 4.

7. Untitled editorial, *Inquirer*, April 5, 1888, 4.

8. "Restrict Immigration," *Inquirer*, July 19, 1888, 2; "Foreign Immigration," *Inquirer*, July 31, 1888, 1; "Stop Pauper Immigration at Once," *Inquirer*, July 31, 1888, 4.

Items on the investigation into pauper immigration and other abuses continued throughout July and August 1888.

9. "Time to Shut the Gates," *Public Ledger,* April 4, 1891, 4.

10. Henry Gannett, "Are We Becoming . . . A Mongrel Nation," *Inquirer,* January 8, 1893, 16.

11. "Immigrants Gaining Entrance by Deceit," *Public Ledger,* January 4, 1903, 4.

12. Elizabeth Robins Pennell, *Our Philadelphia* (Philadelphia: J. B. Lippincott, 1914), 35.

13. Ibid., 191, 225–26, 468–72.

14. Ibid., 472.

15. John Lukacs, *Philadelphia: Patricians and Philistines, 1900–1950* (New York: Farrar, Straus & Giroux, 1981), 26.

Sources and Resources:
A Bibliographic Essay

Thirty years ago, except for a few scholars whose interests were largely limited to colonial history or to upper-class life, Philadelphia was almost totally ignored as a subject of research on urban life in the United States. Beginning in the late 1960s and continuing to the present time, a remarkable eruption of studies by historians and sociologists reversed this situation, and the city has become of great interest to researchers. Despite this turn of events, the social character of Philadelphia, as it developed through the years, is still too frequently described from a relatively narrow perspective. In particular, the ethnic dimension of Philadelphia history, as well as the experience of specific groups, such as the Italians, remains to be adequately examined.

A brief review of previous research indicates the extent to which these studies have been concerned with immigration and ethnic group life. In *The Private City* (Philadelphia, 1968), Sam Bass Warner Jr. provoked considerable interest in the social history of Philadelphia but provided only limited consideration of the ethnic diversity within the city. In *The Peoples of Philadelphia* (Philadelphia, 1973), edited by Allen F. Davis and Mark H. Haller, partly in response to Warner's earlier analysis, with a few notable exceptions the contributors focused more on the class structure of the city than upon its ethnic groups. In *Working People of Philadelphia, 1800–1850* (Philadelphia, 1980), Bruce Laurie almost entirely omitted any discussion of ethnicity and emphatically argued that immigration had far less influence on social cleavages than did the development of capitalism and the previous working experiences of the population. Although E. Digby Baltzell, probably the most prolific sociological commentator on group life in Philadelphia, did include a brief discussion of the Irish in his *Puritan Boston and Quaker Philadelphia* (New York, 1979), he concentrated almost exclusively on the role of members of the Society of Friends in the history of the city. The general work, *Philadelphia: A 300-Year History* (New York, 1982), edited by Russell F. Weigley, took little note of the great ethnic diversity that has always been an important feature of the city's population and its basic institutions.

Some scholars have taken a more pluralistic perspective and have put immigration and ethnicity at the center of their work. Although concerned mainly with the Polish experience, in *Immigrant Destinations* (Philadelphia, 1978), Caroline Golab made an important contribution to the understanding of Philadelphia history. The most consistently developed focus on a specific ethnic group is found in the works on the Irish in Philadelphia by the late Dennis Clark. Beginning with *The Irish in Philadelphia: Ten Generations of Urban Experience* (Philadelphia, 1973), Clark demonstrated the continuity of Irish life in the city. In *The Irish Relations: Trials of an Immigrant Tradition* (Rutherford, N.J., 1982), he explored the adjustment of the Irish in their work life, the role of nationalism in the immigrant community, and Irish interaction with other ethnic groups. In *Erin's Heirs: Irish Bonds of Community* (Lexington, Ky., 1991), Clark explained how the Irish were able to maintain themselves as a community over many years in Philadelphia. In these books, Clark argued that ethnic history is most effectively studied by concentrating on a single group within the context provided by a particular city. A similar perspective is evident in the volume of essays edited by Murray Friedman, *Jewish Life in Philadelphia, 1830–1940* (Philadelphia, 1983). The Philadelphia Social History Project represented an ambitious effort to examine a wider range of immigrant and ethnic life, which is well reflected in the anthology *Philadelphia: Work, Space, Family, and Group Experience in the Nineteenth Century* (New York, 1981), edited by Theodore Hershberg. And although focused in another direction, the entries in an encyclopedic work, *Invisible Philadelphia: Community Through Voluntary Organizations* (Philadelphia, 1995), edited by Jean Barth Toll and Mildred S. Gillam, provide a basic introduction to immigrant and ethnic groups.

Going beyond Philadelphia, after an earlier period in which acculturation and assimilation were presented as inevitable processes, historians and social scientists have renewed their interest in ethnicity. The study of the Italian American experience, in particular, enjoyed a recent period of strong growth, which includes an important debate about whether Italian Americans are in the "twilight of ethnicity." Research by many scholars has contributed to a more complete documentation and more complex interpretation of the social and cultural history of the United States, and to a better understanding of Italian Americans. It has also strengthened the intellectual and scientific character of Italian American studies through the revision and even rejection of earlier, less sophisticated accounts of previous writers. Some representative works of this genre include Humbert Nelli's *The Italians in Chicago, 1880–1930: A Study in Ethnic Mobility* (New York, 1970); Richard Gambino's *Blood of My Blood: The Dilemma of the Italian Americans* (Garden City, N.Y., 1974); Virginia Yans McLaughlin's *Family and Community: Italian Immigrants in Buffalo, 1880–1930* (Ithaca, N.Y., 1977); Luciano J. Iorizzo and Salvatore Mondello's *The Italian Americans,* revised edition (Boston, 1980); James A. Crispino's *Assimilation of Ethnic Groups: The Italian Case* (New York, 1980); Donald Tricarico's *Italians of Greenwich Village: The Social Structure and Transformation of an Ethnic Community* (New York, 1984); Donna Gabaccia's *From Sicily to Elizabeth Street: Housing and Social Change Among Italian Immigrants, 1880–1930* (Albany, 1984); Michael LaSorte's *La Merica: Images of Italian Greenhorn Experience* (Philadelphia, 1985); Robert Anthony Orsi's *Madonna of 115th Street: Faith and Community in Italian Harlem, 1880–1950* (New Haven, 1985); and Richard D. Alba's *Italian Americans: Into the Twilight of Ethnicity* (Englewood Cliffs, N.J., 1985). These titles represent only a partial list of the many works on Italian

Americans that have been published in the last two or three decades. The purpose here is not to provide an exhaustive listing or an extensive analysis, but simply to document the renewed interest in the subject.

Critical appraisals of the current generation of Italian American studies are readily available. The interested reader can consult George Pozzetta's "Immigrants and Ethnics: The State of Italian American Historiography," *Journal of American Ethnic History*, Fall 1989, whose author was a distinguished contributor to such research. Similarly, several conferences sponsored by the Center for Migration Studies have produced critical examinations of the field of Italian American studies, which include *Perspectives in Italian Immigration and Ethnicity*, edited by S. M. Tomasi (New York, 1977); *Italian Americans: New Perspectives in Italian Immigration and Ethnicity*, edited by Lydio F. Tomasi (New York, 1985); and *The Columbus People: Perspectives in Italian Immigration to the Americas and Australia*, edited by Lydio F. Tomasi, Piero Gastaldo, and Thomas Row (New York, 1994). In addition, it is important to mention the *Annual Proceedings of the American Italian Historical Association*. Since 1966, this interdisciplinary society of scholars has published a series of thirty volumes of papers from its conferences that provide an important source of information and analysis of all aspects of the Italian American experience.

In the vast and still rapidly growing body of work on Italians in the United States, although it has embraced a wide range of topics, relatively little research has given serious attention to the period before the Civil War. Published studies include broad social histories of the Italians in the United States as well as more focused examinations of such issues as the immigrant colonies of particular American cities; the organization and functions of religious institutions; the measurement of social mobility and assimilation in later generations; and the transformation of urban communities. But these studies reflect a strong tendency to be concerned with the Italian American experience from the 1880s to the present, and share the implicit premise that little significance can be attached to earlier periods of Italian life in the United States. While social historians have tended to begin in the middle of the story, sociologists have examined the end of the experience.

While some writers have examined earlier Italian migration and settlement, the limitations of these efforts have become increasingly apparent. The most important examples still are the prolific endeavors of Giovanni Schiavo, as represented by his *Italians in America Before the Civil War* (New York, 1924) and *Four Centuries of Italian American History* (New York, 1952). As writers on other ethnic groups of his era, however, Schiavo treated his subject mainly as a panegyric celebration of the accomplishments of heroic individuals in support of the claim that their contributions to American life had not yet been sufficiently recognized. Although it is now fashionable for a generation of revisionist "new historians" in Italian-American studies to indict Schiavo's work as hagiographic, his pioneering efforts produced an extensive body of information. Despite his filiopietism, Schiavo remains an invaluable reference, and even his present-day critics are forced to consult his encyclopedic work. Schiavo himself was well aware of the limited but heuristic nature of his contribution. With characteristic candor, he began one work by describing it as primarily a sourcebook or an outline to serve only as a guide for subsequent writers.

While not as general in scope as Schiavo, Howard R. Marraro showed the much greater analytical sophistication of an academic historian. One major work, *American Opinion on the Unification of Italy, 1846–1861* (New York, 1932), while not concerned with immigration, had important implications for the study of Italians in the United States. In his essays, such as "Italo-Americans in Pennsylvania in the Eighteenth Century," *Pennsylvania History*, July 1940; "Italians in Eighteenth-Century New York," *New York History*, July 1940; "Italians in New York During the First Half of the Nineteenth Century," *New York History*, July 1945; and "Italians in New York in the Eighteen Fifties," *New York History*, April–July 1949, Marraro focused on Italians in specific locations from the colonial period to the Civil War. By examining announcements and notices in local newspapers, he provided clear documentation of the Italian presence during an early period, but his intention was only to show that Italians were among the population of these cities.

While commendable for providing a foundation, the endeavors of Schiavo and Marraro now deserve to be expanded and revised. Schiavo anticipated this when he explicitly indicated that he did not intend to deal with the social implications of Italian immigration, a task that he regarded as more germane to sociology than to history. Although recent scholars would certainly dismiss this sharp separation by Schiavo of the tasks of the sociologist from those of the historian, they might be even more critical of his concern with relatively prominent individuals rather than the everyday lives of more ordinary men and women.

Despite their reservations about Schiavo's approach, few scholars have made anything more than perfunctory efforts to consider the earlier years in the study of the Italian experience in America. The "revisionists" of recent years have tended, somewhat out of necessity but also as a matter of choice, to concentrate on the period of mass immigration—that is, after the 1870s. On one hand, the relative scarcity of systematic data for previous years forced scholars to define the time frame of their research as the 1880s and later. But because of the emergence of immigration as a social problem in American cities, many scholars also consciously decided that the later period was more important.

The implications of this emphasis were important. Whether the subject was immigration in general or a specific group, an earlier time of a smaller volume and lesser visibility of the ethnic population could be overlooked, but not without some risk. Although it was in some cases the period of community origins, this stage of development has often been lost. For the Italians, with only a few exceptions, this phase has not been adequately treated as an important aspect of their experience in the United States. In *The American Italians:*

Their History and Culture (Belmont, Calif., 1972), Andrew F. Rolle includes some information on explorers, travelers, missionaries, and others before the period of mass immigration. Deanna Paoli Gumina perhaps provides the most systematic effort to include early settlers in *The Italians of San Francisco, 1850–1930* (New York, 1978), her analysis of the development of the Italian community in one city, which also has the unusual distinction of being published in a simultaneous English and Italian edition. It is difficult to believe, however, that San Francisco is the only city in which Italians settled before the beginning of mass migration that deserves serious attention.

Another notable exception to the tendency to neglect this stage of Italian life in North America can be found in Glenn Weaver's *Italian Presence in Colonial Virginia* (New York, 1988). In his opening page, Weaver cites the observation of early migration as "barely a trickle," but mainly to develop his own argument to the contrary. While he has made an important effort to redress the neglected presence of Italians in early Virginia history, and despite his disclaimer at the outset, it is flawed by his use of surnames as *sufficient* evidence of Italian origins for the subjects of his study. But it is also limited by his failure to relate the lives of these individuals in a more systematic manner to the culture and social structure of the larger community and the region. This particular case also has limited relevance, because it focuses on a geographical area that did not receive large numbers of arrivals from Italy during a later period.

Most writers of Italian American history, however, do not go even as far as Weaver in his attempt to reexamine the early period, but remain content to ignore the early years altogether or to fall back on Schiavo and Marraro. Instead of using them as points of departure, they have remained dependent on Schiavo and Marraro as sources and have failed to generate new primary data for this period. The result is still too often an episodic, superficial, and almost anecdotal treatment of these years, rather than more systematic analysis.

Beginning with early reports and studies, the Italians of Philadelphia have made occasional appearances in more broadly focused works in treatments that range from a few sentences to longer sections of more inclusive chapters. Some important examples include *The Slums of Great Cities* (1894), the seventh special report of the U.S. Commissioner of Labor; John Koren's "Padrone System and Padrone Banks," *Bulletin of the United States Department of Labor* 9 (1897); Emily Dinwiddie's *Housing Conditions in Philadelphia* (1904), a report of the Octavia Hill Housing Association; Philip M. Rose's *Italians in America* (New York, 1922), a study by a Protestant missionary pastor to immigrant Italians; Robert M. Foerster's *Italian Emigration of Our Times* (Cambridge, Massachusetts, 1924), a classic, comprehensive, and still useful work; Edwin Fenton's *Immigrants and Unions, A Case Study: Italians and American Unions, 1870–1920* (1957), originally a doctoral dissertation at Harvard University, also reprinted in the immigration series of the Arno Press (New York, 1975). Because the principal interests of these items were other issues, although frequently relevant, they provide limited information on the Italian experience in Philadelphia.

A few writers have focused directly on the Italians in Philadelphia. Sister Agnes Gertrude Spielman, a member of the Franciscan community that served the parish of St. Mary Magdalen de Pazzi, chose *Italian Immigration into Philadelphia, 1880–1924* (1946) as the topic of her master's thesis in the history department at Villanova University, which was also published in installments in *The Records of the American Catholic Historical Society of Philadelphia* 58 (1947) and remains an invaluable introduction to the subject. Not long afterward, Hugo V. Maiale completed a more specialized doctoral dissertation, *The Italian Vote in Philadelphia Between 1928 and 1946*, in political science at the University of Pennsylvania, which was published by the press of the same institution (Philadelphia, 1950), with the author's name anglicized as Hugo V. Mailey. Joan Younger Dickinson's "Aspects on Italian Immigration to Philadelphia," based mainly on previously published sources, appeared in the *Pennsylvania Magazine of History and Biography* 90 (October 1966): 445–65.

With the renewal of ethnic self-consciousness in the late 1960s, a surge of interest in the Italians in Philadelphia also occurred with doctoral dissertations by graduate students at local universities. At the University of Pennsylvania, Richard N. Juliani's *Social Organization of Immigration: The Italians in Philadelphia* (1971), also reprinted by the Arno Press (New York, 1980), described migration patterns and traced the origins and development of the Italian community from the 1850s to the present; and Rosara L. Passero's "Ethnicity in the Men's Ready-Made Clothing Industry, 1880–1950: The Italian Experience in Philadelphia" (1978) focused on work experiences in one industry. At Temple University, Richard A. Varbero's *Urbanization and Acculturation: Philadelphia's South Italians, 1918–1932* (1975) examined economic and political adjustment in a particular era. Similarly, at the master's degree level, Bianca Arcangeli's thesis, "The Italians in Philadelphia, 1880–1920: Their Origins and Geographical and Occupational Distribution" (1975), at the University of Pennsylvania, contributed new information on Italians in the city. Except for Arcangeli, a native Italian, these researchers were second- and third-generation Italian Americans whose scholarly efforts also expressed their own ethnic identity and heritage.

Varbero's later work on religious, educational, and political aspects of immigrant life is in "Philadelphia's South Italians in the 1920s," in the previously cited Davis and Haller's *Peoples of Philadelphia*, and his "Workers in City and Country: The South Italian Experience in Philadelphia, 1900–1950," in *Italian Americans: The Search for a Usable Past*, edited by Juliani and Philip V. Cannistraro (Staten Island, N.Y., 1989). Articles with a general focus by Juliani have included "The Origin and Development of the Italian Community in Philadelphia," in *The Ethnic Experience in Philadelphia*, edited by John E. Bodnar (Lewisburg, Pa., 1973); "The Italian Community of Philadelphia," in *Little Italies in North America*, edited by Robert F. Harney and J. Vincenza Scarpaci (Toronto, 1981); and "Immigrants in Philadelphia: The World of 1886," in *Italian Americans: The Search for a Usable Past*, edited by Juliani and Cannistraro (1989). Among several more narrowly focused articles, the internal meaning of immigration was explored by Juliani in "American Voices, Italian Accents: The Perception of Social Conditions and Personal Motives by Immigrants," *Italian Americana* 1 (1974). Although not exclusively concerned with Philadelphia, a similar approach is found in Michael LaSorte's *La Merica* (Philadelphia, 1985).

In addition to Maiale and Varbero, several other scholars have also focused specifically on political aspects of the Italian experience in Philadelphia. John L. Shover produced several important essays, including "Ethnicity and Religion in Philadelphia Politics, 1924–1940," *American Quarterly* 25 (1973), and "The Emergence of a Two-Party System in Republican Philadelphia, 1924–1936," *Journal of American History* 60 (1974). Similarly, Sandra Featherman's "Italian American Voting in Local Elections: The Philadelphia Case," which appeared in *Italian Americans: The Search for a Usable Past*, edited by Richard N. Juliani and Philip Cannistraro (New York, 1989), is also valuable. The most recent researcher, Stefano Luconi, after obtaining a *dottorato di ricerca* at the University of Rome, has also become the most prolific contributor on political organization and voting patterns among Italians in the City of Philadelphia and Commonwealth of Pennsylvania. His publications include "The Political Dimension of Multicultural Society: Italian Americans and Ethnically Balanced Tickets in Philadelphia during the New Deal," in *Italian Americans in a Multicultural Society*, edited by Jerome Krase and Judith N. DeSena (New York, 1994); " 'Mobsters' at the Polls: The Mafia Stereotype of the Media and Italian American Voters in Philadelphia in the Early 1950s," in *Through the Looking Glass: Italian and Italian American Images in the Media*, edited by Mary Jo Bona and Anthony Julian Tamburri (Staten Island, N.Y., 1994); and "Machine Politics and the Consolidation of the Roosevelt Majority: The Case of the Italian Americans in Pittsburgh and Philadelphia," *Journal of American Ethnic History* 15 (1996).

Among students and scholars in Italy who have become interested in the Italian American experience, in addition to Luconi, several others have focused on the Philadelphia case, beginning with Ellen Ginzburg Migliorino's article "Il Proletariato Italiano di Filadelfia all'inizio del secolo," in *Studi Emigrazione* 41 (March 1976). Since then, at various levels of university training, Italian students have pursued similar concerns. Marina Fida, for example, completed her *corso di laurea* at the University of Genoa with a thesis on Italian immigration to Philadelphia.

The total output of previous studies remains relatively meager, however, when viewed against the data on Italians in Philadelphia. The researcher may begin with the *Morton Allen Directory of European Steamship Arrivals, 1890–1930*, an indispensable inventory of ship arrivals by port of entry that also quickly reveals that departures from Genoa and Naples were far more likely to have had New York, rather than Philadelphia, as their destination. After using this source, the researcher may find valuable material on the immigrant population by turning to passenger lists that were required since

1821 from all ships arriving at American ports. A choice must be made between using the massive record series for Castle Garden and Ellis Island, which provides the final destination of each passenger in later years, or the more limited records of direct arrivals to Philadelphia, which represent a much smaller sample of all immigrants to the latter city. (An examination of passenger lists also reveals that many ship arrivals at Philadelphia were not recorded in the *Morton Allen Directory*.)

Microfilm records of passenger arrivals at the Port of Philadelphia for the years 1800–1921 are available at the Mid-Atlantic Region office of the National Archives, located in Philadelphia. Although the lists for earlier years give only the name, age, sex, occupation, and citizenship, these items were steadily increased until thirty-three columns of information were provided for each passenger by the early 1900s. These materials can generate an invaluable profile for any immigrant population at the point of arrival in Philadelphia. The National Immigration Archives Project of Temple University at the Balch Institute is converting these records to a computerized system that will make retrieval and analysis possible.

When the focus shifts to their experience after their arrival, John Maneval, in his report *An Ethnic History of South Philadelphia, 1870–1980*, prepared for the Balch Institute for Ethnic Studies (Philadelphia, 1991), provides very basic information on the residential distribution of Italians in the neighborhoods in which they settled in the largest numbers. Other important sources of demographic and social materials are the original manuscripts (that is, the *Population Schedules*) of the U.S. Census Bureau. The published census reports provide already aggregated information for large units such as cities and states, and for smaller units such as wards and tracts, but the *manuscripts* are the original ledger pages the enumerator filled out as he went from household to household. These pages enable us to reconstruct a profile of age, sex, occupation, household structure, and living arrangements and to delineate residential distribution and neighborhood formation at the time of the census. Manuscript census materials are available on microfilm at the library of the University of Pennsylvania; at the Free Library of Philadelphia; and at the regional branch of the National Archives.

This information can be amplified by the vital statistics data for births, deaths, and marriages that are held by the City Archives of the Records Department of the City of Philadelphia. Because they are not arranged according to ethnicity, however, these records may be more helpful in conjunction with other research strategies. Also, because considerable effort would be required to convert them into systematic data, the researcher may find them to be a more useful source of biographical material on particular individuals.

City directories, published at irregular intervals from colonial times to the 1930s, and containing alphabetical listings of household heads with their addresses and occupations, are convenient tools for year-to-year biographical linkages for specific people. They are also probably best used as a supplement to more systematic sources when the research focuses on an entire group.

Although the directories in the City Archives must now be used in microfilm format, they are still available in bound volumes at various college, university and public libraries and at the Historical Society of Pennsylvania.

Naturalization records in the City Archives, mainly for city and county courts, and at the Pennsylvania Historical and Museum Commission and the National Archives regional branch, for state and federal courts respectively, provide an excellent source of data on Italians who became American citizens. Extending as far back as the 1790s, these documents vary in what they contain. The researcher can often find information on date of birth; town and region of birth; previous allegiance; date and port of departure; date and port of arrival; ship of passage; occupation; address of residence; and names of witnesses. This material not only contributes to a fuller description of the Italian population in the city but can also be useful in analyzing such issues as the process of Americanization or the structure of friendship patterns among immigrants. The researcher who intends to use declarations of intention and petitions for naturalization can begin with the convenient Index of Naturalizations compiled by the Works Projects Administration (WPA), which is available at The Free Library of Philadelphia under the title *Maritime Records—Port of Philadelphia,* or at the Historical Society of Pennsylvania. A careful comparison of the WPA Index with the naturalization records at the City Archives reveals many discrepancies. Instead of relying on the WPA Index, researchers will find more accurate and certainly more detailed information in the actual documents of the city, state, and federal archives.

The general conditions that affected the adjustment of Italians in Philadelphia can be explored by seeking out relevant information in the *Mayor's Annual Message,* which includes the reports of all city departments. Available at the Library of the University of Pennsylvania and at the City Archives, the reports of the Departments of Public Safety; Charities and Corrections; and Health (later consolidated as Public Health and Charities); and the Board of Education are especially informative. Although examining these volumes requires patience and care, the results are worthwhile, for they frequently contain material on the problems of the foreign-born, particularly in their relationship to city agencies. The Minutes of Select and Common Councils, however, do not provide sufficient information on immigrant groups to warrant much attention.

The publications of the Pennsylvania Department of Labor and Industry contain valuable data on working conditions among immigrant groups. In its *Annual Report* as well as the *Monthly Bulletin,* especially in the early twentieth century, the department frequently gathered valuable information on housing conditions, employment, ethnic succession, industrial safety, child labor, and other issues.

Several other state agencies published regular reports that include useful information on the development of community structure among Italians in Philadelphia. From 1904 on, annual reports of the auditor general present tax receipts from private bankers and brokers that also provide a measure of their volume of business. For about twenty years, the auditor general's report also provided financial data on regular banks, trust companies, and savings and loan associations that served the Italian community. For a comparable period, the *Annual Report* of the commissioner of banking included detailed information on similar institutions, giving the names of officers and directors, the dates of incorporation, locations, and total resources. For building and loan associations, these reports give the number and total amount of real estate loans, the number of shares and shareholders, and the number of homes built or purchased for each year. By the 1920s, the *Report of the Insurance Commission* included data on mutual aid societies among Italians. Taken altogether, these records reveal the shift from a reliance on private bankers, who basically provided financial services to a transient population of workers, to more conventional banking institutions, which facilitated home ownership and community stability.

Tax records and property deeds, available in the City Archives, offer another source on the material growth of the Italian population of the city. By using them to examine the accumulation of wealth and property, they reveal patterns of economic stratification within the community. The credit ledgers of R. G. Dun & Company, the predecessor of Dun & Bradstreet, in the Baker Library of the Graduate School of Business at Harvard University, contain assessments of financial worth and viability and of general character for entrepreneurs within the immigrant community.

The upward mobility and development of professions among Italians are reflected in various occupational registers in the City Archives collections. For a limited period of years, which varies in each case, separate volumes contain listings of physicians, osteopaths, dentists, and midwives. The medical, osteopath, and dental registers give place of birth, current residence, year and institution of professional degrees, and date of state licensing. They also indicate that some individuals were permitted to practice their professions without any recorded medical degree, perhaps because they had been performing in these capacities before the passage of the medical registration law of 1881. We also find a graduate of the Women's Medical College of Pennsylvania in 1899, who was probably the first Italian female physician in Philadelphia. The *Midwife Register*, a single volume for the period 1920–1934, lists thirty-six women born in Italy and another three with Italian surnames, among 133 midwives in the city. These records give clues of the medical care available to Italians, and also allow us to examine the emergence of medical practitioners within their own community.

Wills and letters of administration represent another measure of material attainment by indicating personal wealth and property at the time of death. Beyond the inventory of an estate, these documents, which first appear in the late eighteenth century for Italians in Philadelphia, sometimes present unique personal glimpses of the individual. The instruction that Vito Viti left to his sons in 1866 provides a most poignant example: "Having ever proved themselves dutiful and affectionate to their mother I urge them to be and remain so and without making directions on the subject I cannot but express the hope that they will ever care for her."

While the organizational life of Italian immigrants and their descendants in Philadelphia also remains to be more fully explored, one attempt can be found in Juliani's essay "Italian Organizations in Philadelphia," in the previously cited *Invisible Philadelphia: Community Through Voluntary Organizations.* Many sources for further study, however, are readily available. Religious life can be reconstructed through the records of the churches. While Episcopal and Presbyterian agencies, which also served the needs of and attracted Italians to their congregations, left some records, the Archives of the Roman Catholic Archdiocese of Philadelphia contain more extensive materials on the religious experience of Italians. Before the time the first Italian parish was founded in 1853, it is necessary to locate relevant entries from the records of earlier parishes, which served all types of Catholics. In later years, the nationality parishes compiled not only a massive record of births, marriages, and deaths, but also a record of the diffusion of Italians into newer neighborhoods. In some cases, information on regional origins, occupations and arrival in Philadelphia, as well as changes in internal group identity and solidarity, can be gleaned from these sources. The techniques of historical demography have been applied to this data by Juliani to study the early development of this community; see "Church Records as Social Data: The Italians of Philadelphia in the Nineteenth Century," *Records of the American Catholic Historical Society of Philadelphia* 85 (1974). Parish histories, usually prepared on the occasion of anniversary celebrations of the founding of a parish or a jubilee of the ordination of its pastor to the priesthood, often include much valuable information. More systematic annual reports, which include a brief census of each parish, were also required from each pastor. The archdiocesan press, which frequently reported on activities and events involving Italians, is especially useful as a source on the founding of parishes and schools, on conflicts with other denominations over proselytization, on the Catholic settlement house movement, and on the attitude and policy of the bishops toward Italians. Juliani has also used the *Consultors' Minutes,* the records of advisers to the archbishop, in matters of improvements and expansion programs, to explore the relationship of Italian parishes and pastors to the hierarchy; see "The Parish as an Urban Institution: Italian Catholics in Philadelphia," *Records of the American Catholic Historical Society of Philadelphia* 96 (1985). A great number of materials that provide a continuous record of Italian Catholics and their organized religious experience are available in the collections of the Philadelphia Archdiocesan Historical Research Center. Finally, any discussion of sources on Italian Catholics must include the vast body of materials in various Church agencies in Rome. The interested researcher should begin, however, with the extraordinarily useful inventory by Giovanni Pizzorusso and Matteo Sanfilippo, "Fonti ecclesiastiche romane per lo studio dell'emigrazione italiana in Nord America, 1642–1922," in *Studi Emigrazione* 33 (December 1996): 549–733.

The *Miscellaneous* and *Charter Books* of the City Archives offer information on voluntary associations among Italians. For the first case, the Società di Unione e Fratellanza Italiana, chartered on March 2, 1868, the charter includes the articles of organization; the names, addresses, and occupations of officers; and its objectives. Although some years passed before similar groups were founded, mutual aid societies, political clubs, labor organizations, and religious sodalities were rapidly proliferating by the 1880s and 1890s. As did the parishes, secular bodies also celebrated anniversaries by publishing histories that contained extensive material not only on the organization but also on the community in general, such as the document published by the Società di Unione e Fratellanza Italiana for its banquet in 1929. Although they must be used with care because they may present a highly favorable point of view of their subject, such documents are invaluable sources from inside of the community. From the beginning of such activities until the recent past, the records of several hundred voluntary associations that were eventually established might have provided an important means of understanding community organization among Italians in Philadelphia. Unfortunately, most of this material was discarded or destroyed long ago.

The organizational life of the Italian community, however, not only was a matter of internal institutions formed by its own members, but also included external agencies that sought to meet the needs of immigrants and their families. Although it is customary to identify the beginning of the settlement house movement with Toynbee House in London in 1884, the House of Industry was founded in Philadelphia in 1847. After first serving Irish families, by the late nineteenth century it also had many Italian, as well as East European, clients. Several other settlement houses that provided activities and services for Italians included the College Settlement, the Starr Centre, St. Martha's House, Reed Street Settlement, and Germantown Settlement. The Protestant origins and character of these institutions encouraged Roman Catholics to establish the Madonna House and La Nunziata House in the early twentieth century. Although records for Catholic agencies may have been destroyed or are still unavailable, the Urban Archives at Temple University is a rich repository of materials consisting mainly of monthly and annual reports for the other settlements. These records reveal that the philosophies and policies that defined the settlement house movement in Philadelphia were often in sharp contrast to the tolerant pluralism associated with Jane Addams at Hull House in Chicago or Lillian Wald at Green Street in New York.

The newspapers of the city are another important source on immigration and immigrant life. By the late nineteenth century, seven major daily newspapers competed with each other for readers in Philadelphia. The press regularly reported events in the Italian community, along with local, national, and foreign news that affected immigrants in the city. By comparing the treatment of Italians in different newspapers, one can see how Italians and members of other groups were viewed. Microfilms of newspapers are readily available in libraries and research centers in the city, but the holdings of The Free

Library and The Library Company of Philadelphia are the most extensive. Special collections, such as the Campbell Collection at the Historical Society of Pennsylvania, contain items that are occasionally relevant. The American Philosophical Society (APS) also holds five volumes of newspaper clippings from a series of articles on local history by Thompson Westcott that originally appeared in the *Sunday Dispatch* in the 1870s and 1880s.

In addition to mainstream newspapers, the foreign-language press offered another important view of immigrant life. Although one Italian was already publishing a price current for the English-speaking public in the late eighteenth century, newspapers for Italian readers in their native language did not appear for another half-century. *L'Eco d'Italia*, published in New York City, included news about "la colonia di Filadelfia" on an intermittent basis. Unfortunately, few issues of *L'Eco d'Italia* have survived to the present; the most extensive holdings are found in the New York Public Library. About twenty-five Italian newspapers were published, some on a daily basis, others weekly, at one time or another in Philadelphia, although how many provided news on the local community remains unclear. These papers reflected a wide range of interests and ideologies—humor, radicalism, organized labor, Catholicism, and local Republican politics. The few papers that do remain are on microfilm at the Balch Institute and at Paley Library of Temple University, principally *L'Opinione*, published by the Baldi family from 1905 to 1935 before it was absorbed by Generoso Pope's *Il Progresso Italo Americano*, a national paper from New York City.

Newspapers also published special items, such as *La Colonia Italiana di Filadelfia*, an album of biographical, organizational, and institutional sketches, prepared by *L'Opinione* for the Milan Exposition of 1906. The success of such projects may have been the inspiration for similar efforts that followed: *Italiani in Filadelfia*, a special issue, published also by *L'Opinione* as a New Year's Day bonus, for local readers in 1907. As in the case of commemorative programs of organizational celebrations, these materials must be used with great caution because they reflect efforts to define communal life by members who were also attempting to establish positions for themselves within the community. But rather than diminish its value, this aspect of the politics of publication may open up another dimension in understanding the development of an ethnic community.

Many Italians had successful careers and achieved prominence in their own community, but so far none appears to have left an extensive personal manuscript collection. Busti's *Blockley Farm Daybook*, held by the Historical Society of Pennsylvania (HSP), perhaps represents the most outstanding single item of this sort. Prominent Philadelphians, such as Benjamin Franklin and Stephen Girard, left materials, now in the manuscript collections of the American Philosophical Society, that are related to Italians in the city and should not be overlooked.

Although the data are sometimes flawed and their interpretation became part of the national debate over immigration, the information gathered in special reports by governmental agencies remains useful. At the federal level, the Select Committee of the House of Representatives, known also as the Ford Committee, provided an important early report on the illegal importation of contract laborers (1888). Subsequently, the nineteen volumes of the *Report of the Industrial Commission* (1900–1902), and especially the massive forty-one volumes of the *Report of the Immigration Commission* (1911), the controversial Dillingham Commission Report, generated enduring sources of information on immigrants in American life. While some of the states prepared similar reports, except for what has been previously noted in regard to banking, industry, and labor, Pennsylvania did not publish as much. Private agencies, however, left special reports bearing on Italians in Philadelphia. In addition to the Dinwiddie report mentioned earlier, similar studies on housing conditions and public health were conducted by the Henry Phipps Institute, which was especially concerned with the problem of tuberculosis in the early 1900s, and by the International Institute in the 1930s. These reports are readily accessible at the Urban Archives of Temple University.

As a part of its Ethnic Survey of Philadelphia, the Works Projects Administration also collected field notes, interviews, and case histories from 1938 to 1941, as well as some draft chapters, on the Italians of Philadelphia. Based on nearly 37,000 cases from the files of the DiBerardino firm, these materials, which provide information on the recruitment of laborers and the operations of immigrant banking, are available both in the library of the Pennsylvania State Historical and Museum Commission and at the Balch Institute for Ethnic Studies.

At the time of mass immigration, Italy also viewed this movement of its people with great concern. Among many documents of the Italian government, *Il Bollettino dell'Emigrazione*, in 345 issues and more than 36,000 pages from 1902 through 1907, included various items, such as periodic reports by Italian consuls, related to the Italian colony in Philadelphia. Although it is probably the best source of an official Italian perspective on the local immigrant community, no library or research center in Philadelphia currently holds *Il Bolletino*. For the researcher who is interested in diplomatic and consular relations, another invaluable source, the *Diplomatic Dispatches from United States Ministers to the Italian States, 1832–1906*, is readily available from the National Archives Mid-Atlantic Region office.

While the present condition, along with the future of the population and various communities of Philadelphia's Italians, has frequently attracted the attention of newspaper writers, social scientists have paid less attention to these subjects. As a result of recent conferences at the University of Pisa in March 1993 and May 1995, two articles by Richard N. Juliani have appeared: "Images, Interactions, and Institutions: The Emergence of an Italian Community in Philadelphia," in Mario Aldo Toscano, ed., *Origins and Transitions: Toward Plural Citizenship* (Los Angeles and Naples: Ipermedium, 1996), and "Social Change and the Ethnic Community: The Italians in Philadelphia," in Mario Aldo Toscano, ed., *Dialettica Locale-Globale: continuita e contraddizioni del mondo* (Los Angeles and Naples: Ipermedium, 1997). In tracing this experience to the present debate over the "twilight of ethnicity," both articles redefine the problem as the "twilight of community," in general, among the remnants of the mass immigration and in the old neighborhoods of settlement among Italians in American cities.

These sources for the study of Italian immigration and Italian American life in Philadelphia present many challenges to the scholar. The basic problem is not the scarcity of relevant materials but how to select from these vast resources and how to synthesize raw and disparate pieces into a coherent picture of the patterns of community life. While some records can be used in research on other topics, any attempt to examine the Italian experience, whether for a limited or more extended period, must include biographical materials on individuals; information on groups, organizations, institutions, and neighborhoods; and macro-level data on the population as a whole and on its relationship to the larger city. But in addition to the contention that this effort would fill an important gap in the history of Philadelphia, the major argument of this brief essay is that the resources for this endeavor are abundant and available.

Index